Palgrave Macmillan Studies in Banking and Financial Institutions

Series Editor: **Professor Philip Molyneux**

The Palgrave Macmillan Studies in Banking and Financial Institutions are international in orientation and include studies of banking within particular countries or regions, and studies of particular themes such as Corporate Banking, Risk Management, Mergers and Acquisitions, etc. The books' focus is on research and practice, and they include up-to-date and innovative studies on contemporary topics in banking that will have global impact and influence.

Titles include:

Steffen E. Andersen
THE EVOLUTION OF NORDIC FINANCE

Seth Apati
THE NIGERIAN BANKING SECTOR REFORMS
Power and Politics

Vittorio Boscia, Alessandro Carretta and Paola Schwizer
COOPERATIVE BANKING IN EUROPE
Case Studies

Roberto Bottiglia, Elisabetta Gualandri and Gian Nereo Mazzocco (*editors*)
CONSOLIDATION IN THE EUROPEAN FINANCIAL INDUSTRY

Dimitris N. Chorafas
CAPITALISM WITHOUT CAPITAL

Dimitris N. Chorafas
SOVEREIGN DEBT CRISIS
The New Normal and the Newly Poor

Dimitris N. Chorafas
FINANCIAL BOOM AND GLOOM
The Credit and Banking Crisis of 2007–2009 and Beyond

Violaine Cousin
BANKING IN CHINA

Vincenzo D'Apice and Giovanni Ferri
FINANCIAL INSTABILITY
Toolkit for Interpreting Boom and Bust Cycles

Peter Falush and Robert L. Carter OBE
THE BRITISH INSURANCE INDUSTRY SINCE 1900
The Era of Transformation

Franco Fiordelisi
MERGERS AND ACQUISITIONS IN EUROPEAN BANKING

Franco Fiordelisi, Philip Molyneux and Daniele Previati (*editors*)
NEW ISSUES IN FINANCIAL AND CREDIT MARKETS

Franco Fiordelisi, Philip Molyneux and Daniele Previati (*editors*)
NEW ISSUES IN FINANCIAL INSTITUTIONS MANAGEMENT

Kim Hawtrey
AFFORDABLE HOUSING FINANCE

Jill M. Hendrickson
REGULATION AND INSTABILITY IN U.S. COMMERCIAL BANKING
A History of Crises

Otto Hieronymi (*editor*)
GLOBALIZATION AND THE REFORM OF THE INTERNATIONAL BANKING AND MONETARY SYSTEM

Sven Janssen
BRITISH AND GERMAN BANKING STRATEGIES

Alexandros-Andreas Kyrtsis (*editor*)
FINANCIAL MARKETS AND ORGANIZATIONAL TECHNOLOGIES
System Architectures, Practices and Risks in the Era of Deregulation

Caterina Lucarelli and Gianni Brighetti (*editors*)
RISK TOLERANCE IN FINANCIAL DECISION MAKING

Roman Matousek (*editor*)
MONEY, BANKING AND FINANCIAL MARKETS IN CENTRAL AND EASTERN EUROPE
20 Years of Transition

Philip Molyneux (*editor*)
BANK PERFORMANCE, RISK AND FIRM FINANCING

Philip Molyneux (*editor*)
BANK STRATEGY, GOVERNANCE AND RATINGS

Imad A. Moosa
THE MYTH OF TOO BIG TO FAIL

Simon Mouatt and Carl Adams (*editors*)
CORPORATE AND SOCIAL TRANSFORMATION OF MONEY AND BANKING
Breaking the Serfdom

Anders Ögren (*editor*)
THE SWEDISH FINANCIAL REVOLUTION

Özlem Olgu
EUROPEAN BANKING
Enlargement, Structural Changes and Recent Developments

Ramkishen S. Rajan
EMERGING ASIA
Essays on Crises, Capital Flows, FDI and Exchange Rate

Yasushi Suzuki
JAPAN'S FINANCIAL SLUMP
Collapse of the Monitoring System under Institutional and Transition Failures

Ruth Wandhöfer
EU PAYMENTS INTEGRATION
The Tale of SEPA, PSD and Other Milestones Along the Road

The full list of titles is available on the website:
www.palgrave.com/finance/sbfi.asp

Palgrave Macmillan Studies in Banking and Financial Institutions
Series Standing Order ISBN 978-1-4039-4872-4

You can receive future titles in this series as they are published by placing a standing order. Please contact your bookseller or, in case of difficulty, write to us at the address below with your name and address, the title of the series and the ISBN quoted above.

Customer Servics Department, Macmillan Distribution Ltd., Houndmills, Basingstoke, Hampshire RG21 6Xs, England

---

Bank Performance, Risk and Firm Financing

Edited by

Philip Molyneux
Professor of Banking and Finance, Bangor Business School, Bangor University, UK

palgrave
macmillan

First published 2011 by
PALGRAVE MACMILLAN

Palgrave Macmillan in the UK is an imprint of Macmillan Publishers Limited, registered in England, company number 785998, of Houndmills, Basingstoke, Hampshire RG21 6XS.

Palgrave Macmillan in the US is a division of St Martin's Press LLC, 175 Fifth Avenue, New York, NY 10010.

Palgrave Macmillan is the global academic imprint of the above companies and has companies and representatives throughout the world.

Palgrave® and Macmillan® are registered trademarks in the United States, the United Kingdom, Europe and other countries.

ISBN: 978–0–230–31335–4 hardback

This book is printed on paper suitable for recycling and made from fully managed and sustained forest sources. Logging, pulping and manufacturing processes are expected to conform to the environmental regulations of the country of origin.

A catalogue record for this book is available from the British Library.

Library of Congress Cataloging-in-Publication Data

Bank performance, risk and firm financing / edited By Philip Molyneux.
p. cm.
Includes bibliographical references and index.
ISBN 978–0–230–31335–4 (alk. paper)
1. Banks and banking. 2. Banks and banking – Risk management.
3. Bank management. 4. Financial institutions – Management. I. Molyneux, Philip.

HG1601.B147 2011
332.1068′1—dc22 201101206

10 9 8 7 6 5 4 3 2 1
20 19 18 17 16 15 14 13 12 11

Printed and bound in Great Britain by
CPI Antony Rowe, Chippenham and Eastbourne

Contents

Tables and Figures

Tables

Figures

Contributors

Mario Anolli is Full Professor in Banking at Università Cattolica del Sacro Cuore, Italy, where he is Dean of the School in Banking and Finance. He has written widely in the area of financial institutions and financial markets. His research interests include risk management, investment management, regulation of financial markets, and financial analysts.

Elena Beccalli is Full Professor in Banking at Università Cattolica del Sacro Cuore, Italy and Visiting Fellow in Accounting at the London School of Economics, UK. She is the author of books and articles in international journals in the area of economics of financial institutions. Research interests include stochastic efficiency measurement, technology and performance, mergers and acquisitions, and analyst forecasts.

Luciana Canovi is Lecturer in Finance at the 'Marco Biagi' Faculty of Economics at the University of Modena and Reggio Emilia, Italy, where she teaches Corporate Finance. Her main research interests are finance for SMEs, the real option approach to investment valuation and the life cycle of the firm and financial constraints. Her research papers have been published by Italian academic journals. She is a member of CEFIN – Centre for Studies in Banking and Finance.

Santiago Carbó-Valverde is Full Professor of Economics at the University of Granada, Spain. He was Head of the Department of Economics during 2004–6 and Dean of the School of Economics and Business during 2006–8 at the University of Granada, Spain. He is the Head of Financial Studies of the Spanish Savings Bank Foundation (FUNCAS). He has also been a Consultant at the Federal Reserve Bank of Chicago since 2008. He has acted as consultant for a variety of public institutions, including the European Central Bank, the European Commission, the Spanish Ministry of Science and Innovation, the Spanish Ministry of Labour, Institute of European Finance, Caja de Ahorros de Granada and various leading economic consulting companies. Recent publications include those in the *Review of Finance, Journal of Money, Credit and Banking, Journal of International Money and Finance, Journal of Banking and Finance, Journal of Financial Services Research, Annals of Regional Science, Regional Studies* and *Journal of Economics and Business*.

Georgios E. Chortareas is Associate Professor at the Department of Economics, University of Athens. Before joining the University of Athens, he was a Reader in Finance at the University of Essex and a research economist at the Bank of England. He received his PhD from the University of Connecticut (1999) and has been a postdoctoral fellow at Harvard University and visiting scholar at various universities (e.g. Columbia University) and policy institutions (e.g. Federal Reserve Bank of New York, European Central Bank). He is a member of the Money Macro and Finance Research Group Committee, a board member of the European Public Choice Society, and president of the European Economics and Finance Society. He also serves as a member of the Council of Economic Advisers of the Greek Ministry of Finance. His recent research appears in a number of journals, including *Public Choice, The Economic Journal, Oxford Bulletin of Economics and Statistics, Journal of Banking and Finance, Economics Letters* and *Review of International Economics*.

Andi Duqi is a PhD student in Banking and Finance at the Department of Management, University of Bologna, Italy. His interests include the study of R&D effects on market stock prices and returns, R&D financing and financial constraints of innovative projects.

Francisco Rodríguez Fernández is Associate Professor of Economics at the University of Granada, Spain. He is senior researcher at the Financial Studies Department of the Spanish Savings Bank Foundation (FUNCAS). He has published over 80 articles on banking and finance, industrial organization and economic development in journals such as *Review of Finance, Journal of Money, Credit and Banking, Journal of Banking and Finance, Regional Studies, Journal of Economics and Business, European Urban and Regional Studies* and *Journal of International Financial Markets, Institutions and Money*. He has been (and in some cases still is) consultant for several public and private institutions, in particular financial institutions. He has been a visiting researcher at institutions such as the European Central Bank, the Federal Reserve Bank of Chicago and Bangor University, Wales.

Claudia Girardone is Reader in Finance at the Essex Business School, University of Essex. Her research focus is on modelling bank efficiency and productivity and competition issues in European banking. She has co-authored a textbook entitled *Introduction to Banking* (2006) and has published widely in international peer-reviewed journals with articles on bank performance, integration and market power. Her most recent publications appear in *Review of Development Economics, Economics*

Letters, *Journal of Business, Finance and Accounting* and *European Journal of Finance*.

Elisabetta Gualandri is Full Professor in Banking and Finance and co-director of the MA Course in Corporate Finance and Management Control at the 'Marco Biagi' Faculty of Economics of the University of Modena and Reggio Emilia, Italy, where she is a member of the governing board of CEFIN – Centre for Studies in Banking and Finance. Recent research topics include regulatory guidelines and supervisory architecture in the EU, capital adequacy and the New Basel Accord, and the financing of innovative SMEs and public intervention programmes. She has participated in Italian and international conferences on these subjects, with a large number of published papers. She recently edited two books for Palgrave Macmillan: *Bridging the Equity Gap for Innovative SMEs* and *Consolidation in the European Financial Industry*. She was appointed as an auditor of Banca d'Italia in 2007.

Juan Fernández de Guevara is Assistant Professor at the Universitat de València, where he graduated in Economics in 1995 and received his PhD with special honours in 2005. From 1997 to 2008 he was a member of the technical staff at the Instituto Valenciano de Investigaciones Económicas (Ivie). Currently he is also a regular collaborator at Ivie. His research interests are financial economics, banking and social capital. He has jointly published more than six books and several articles in Spanish and international journals such as *Journal of Banking and Finance*, *Regional Studies*, *Journal of International Money and Finance*, *The Manchester School*, *Revista de Economía Aplicada* and *Revista de Economía Financiera*, among others. He has collaborated in more than 20 research projects for firms and institutions. He has also been associate researcher of several projects of the Spanish National R+D+I Plan.

David Humphrey is F.W. Smith Eminent Scholar in Banking at Florida State University, Visiting Fellow at the Payment Cards Center at the Federal Reserve Bank of Philadelphia, and previously Visiting Research Professor, University of Wales, Bangor. He received his PhD in Economics from the University of California, Berkeley and earlier worked at the Federal Reserve Board and Federal Reserve Bank of Richmond for 16 years, dealing with banking, systemic risk and payment system issues. His current research remains focused on these topics.

Mario La Torre is Full Professor in Banking and Finance and Director of the MA course in Film Art Management at the University of Rome 'La Sapienza'. He has been a member of the Board of Directors of Cinecittà

Holding and Consultant for the Ministry of Cultural Affairs. He is one of the lawmakers of the Italian Tax Credit Law for the film industry. He is currently a member of the Board of the Italian National Committee for Microcredit. His main publications include *Securitisation and Banks* (1995); *Postbank in Italy* (1996); *Mergers & Acquisition in Banking* (1997); *Film Financing* (2006); *Microfinance* (2006); and 'Banks in the Microfinance Market', in Molyneux, P. and Vallelado, E. (eds), *Frontiers of Banks in a Global Economy* (2008). Recent articles include 'Modern Microfinance: the Role of Banks' and 'Ethical Finance and Microfinance'.

Ted Lindblom is Professor in the Department of Business Administration at the School of Business, Economics and Law, Gothenburg University, Sweden. His current research mainly concerns corporate finance, with particular focus on corporate governance, capital budgeting and financial structure decisions. He has also studied pricing strategies in decreasing cost industries and deregulation reforms in industries like electricity, banking and retailing. In the banking sector he has for more than 20 years been studying the pricing of payments services and market structural changes, mainly in retail banking. He has authored and co-authored several articles and books regarding these issues.

Fabiomassimo Mango is Lecturer in Banking and Finance at 'La Sapienza' University in Rome, Italy. He previously obtained a PhD from the same university in Banking and Finance. He has published studies on various dimensions of banking including *Sistema bancario e sviluppo economico locale – una verifica empirica* (December 2007) and *La Banca del Territorio: 'Costruzioni' teoriche e verifica empirica nel SLL di Civitavecchia*.

Joaquín Maudos is Professor of Economic Analysis at the University of Valencia, Italy. His specialized fields are banking and regional economics. He was visiting researcher during 1995–6 at the Florida State University Finance Department and during 2008–9 at the University of Bangor, UK, and he has acted as consultant to the European Commission. He has jointly published 8 books and over 50 articles in specialized journals, both Spanish (*Investigaciones Económicas, Moneda y Crédito, Revista Española de Economía* and *Revista de Economía Aplicada*, among others) and international (*Annals of Regional Science, Applied Economics, Applied Financial Economics, Economics Letters, Entrepreneurship and Regional Development, International Journal of Transport Economics, Journal of Comparative Economics, Regional Studies, Review of Income and Wealth and Transportation Research, Journal of Banking and Finance, Journal of Financial Services Research* and *Journal of International Money and Finance*, etc.). He is a member of the Editorial Board of the *European Review of Economics and Finance* and *Economics Research International*, and principal researcher of several competitive projects (Spanish Ministry of Education and Science, BBVA Foundation), as well as projects for enterprises and public institutions.

Ewa Miklaszewska is Professor of Finance and Banking at Cracow Economic University, Poland and Associate Professor of Economics in the Department of Management and Public Communication at Jagiellonian University, Poland. She has held several visiting positions in Polish and foreign universities and Polish regulatory bodies. She specializes in strategic developments in the global banking industry.

Katarzyna Mikolajczyk is Assistant Professor of Finance at Cracow Economic University, Poland. She has published many articles on the outcomes of privatization programmes in transition countries and on the impact of structural changes in the banking industry (including M&As) on bank efficiency.

Philip Molyneux is Professor in Banking and Finance and Head of Bangor Business School at the University of Bangor, UK. He has published widely in the banking and financial services area, including articles in *European Economic Review, Journal of Banking and Finance, Journal of Money, Credit and Banking, Economics Letters* and *Economica*. Between 2002 and 2005 he acted as a member of the ECON Financial Services expert panel for the European Parliament. His most recent co-authored texts are *Thirty Years of Islamic Banking* (2005), *Introduction to Banking* (2006) and *Introduction to Global Financial Markets* (2010). He recently (2010) co-edited (with Berger and Wilson) *The Oxford Handbook of Banking*.

Pierluigi Morelli works at the Research Department of the Italian Banks Association (ABI). He graduated in Statistics and Economics at the University of Rome 'La Sapienza' in 1988. From 1988 to 2010 he has worked at the Centro Europa Ricerche (CER). As Research Director of the CER Monetary and Banking sector, he was responsible for the econometric models of the Italian economy, of the banking sector and of pension expenditure. He has published numerous articles on monetary economics, banking and insurance.

Ottorino Morresi has been Assistant Professor of Finance at the University of Roma Tre since 2009. He holds a PhD in Corporate Finance from the University of Trieste. He won a scholarship for a research period as post-doctoral student at the Cass Business School, UK in 2008. He has written on Corporate Finance, Corporate Governance and Capital Market issues. The outcome of his research is published in national and international academic peer-reviewed journals such as *Research in International Business and Finance, Rivista di Politica Economica, Finanza Marketing e Produzione* and *Corporate Ownership and Control*. His research mainly focuses on issues such as Capital Structure, M&As, Ownership and Board Structure, Managerial Compensation, Share Prices and News Announcements. He is referee of the *Journal of Management and Governance*. He teaches Corporate Finance, Small Business Finance, and Financial Analysis.

Magnus Olsson is a Researcher at the School of Business, Economics and Law, Goteborg University. His research interests are mainly in banking and finance. Olsson is also the CEO of a Swedish savings bank and is involved with economic and legal issues at the Swedish Savings Banks Association.

Alberto Pezzi is Assistant Professor of Business Management at the University of Roma Tre since 2004. He holds a PhD in Banking and Finance from the University of Rome 'Tor Vergata'. The outcomes of his research are published in national and international academic peer-reviewed journals. His research interests are in Corporate Strategy, Corporate Finance, and Information Management. He teaches the courses of Strategic Management and Business Planning.

Gert Sandahl is Senior Lecturer at the Department of Business Administration at the School of Business, Economics and Law, Gothenburg University, Sweden. His current areas of research are capital budgeting and capital budgeting practices, financial decision-making and corporate governance (board composition and remuneration systems). He has also been working with real estate issues related to housing area development and facility maintenance.

Elena Seghezza is Lecturer in Economics at Genoa University, Italy. She previously worked as an economist at the Department of Economic Affairs of the Italian Government and at the Organization for Economic Cooperation and Development (OECD). She has a PhD in International Economics from the Graduate Institute of International Studies, Geneva, and an MSc in Economics and Econometrics from Southampton University. She has published several articles on political economy, interest groups, inflation and international trade.

Stefan Sjögren is Associate Professor/Lecturer at the Department of Business Administration at the School of Business, Economics and Law,

Gothenburg University, Sweden. He obtained his doctorate at Gothenburg University in 1996. His research interests involve a broad range of corporate finance issues, including capital budgeting, valuation, deregulation and efficiency measures. He is currently working with projects concerning determinants for capital structure in larger Swedish companies, foreign exchange risk management, deregulation and alliances in the airline industry, and valuation of and markets for ideas.

Giuseppe Torluccio is Professor of Financial Intermediation at the School of Economics at the University of Bologna, Italy. His research interests are focused on banking, corporate financial structure, R&D financing, ICT in financial industry and asset management.

Alexia Ventouri is a Lecturer in Financial Studies in the Department of Business and Management at Sussex University, where she teaches banking and financial markets. Her research focus is in the areas of bank performance, business cycles and regulation. Her publications appear in internationally recognised journals such as *Journal of Business, Finance and Accounting* and *Applied Financial Economics*.

Valeria Venturelli is Associate Professor in Banking and Finance at the 'Marco Biagi' Faculty of Economics of the University of Modena and Reggio Emilia, Italy, where she teaches Financial Markets and Institutions at both undergraduate and graduate level. Her main research interests are the economics of banking and other financial institutions, regulation of the asset management industry in the EU, finance for SMEs, valuation methods and the cost of capital. She is the author of several articles in leading academic journals. She recently edited a book for Palgrave Macmillan: *Bridging the Equity Gap for Innovative SMEs*. She is a member of CEFIN – Centre for Studies in Banking and Finance.

Magnus Willesson is currently teaching at the Linnaeus School of Business and Economics, Linnaeus University, in Växjö, Sweden, and obtained his PhD from the School of Business Economics and Law, University of Gothenburg, Sweden. His research interest encompasses a broad spectrum of questions related to the governance of banks. His recent focus is on risk management, especially operational risks, in banks. This research has resulted in international publications on the effects of regulation on banks' risk management. Other publications in international academic journals address the effects of the transition from paper-based to electronic payments to banks and how banks should price their payment services.

Introduction

Philip Molyneux

This text comprises a selection of chapters that focus on dimensions of bank performance, risk and firm financing. These chapters were originally presented as papers at the European Association of University Teachers of Banking and Finance Conference (otherwise known as the Wolpertinger Conference) held at Bangor University, Wales, in September 2010.

Chapter 1 by Joaquín Maudos and Juan Fernández de Guevara (both from the University of Valencia) examines the relationship between bank size, market power and financial stability in Europe, North America and Japan between 2001 and 2008. The chapter reviews the competition–fragility and competition–stability hypotheses and presents results that suggest an inverted U-shaped relationship between the size of banks and market power. The chapter also illustrates that an increase in market power leads to greater stability, which lends support to the more traditional view that an excess of competition in banking markets can be prejudicial for financial stability. The results also indicate that, although size negatively affects financial stability, the relationship is not linear, so that beyond a threshold (corresponding to a very big bank) increases in size decrease the probability of bankruptcy.

Risk-taking in banking has been the focus of many recent studies, especially since the 2008 credit crisis. In Chapter 2 Mario Anolli and Elena Beccalli (both from the Università Cattolica del Sacro Cuore) explore the ability of financial analysts to perceive the risk taken by (listed) banks, and investigate whether this ability deteriorated during the financial crisis. Using a sample of 36,343 analyst forecasts issued for 411 banks over the period 2003–9, their findings indicate that analysts are subject to forecast errors, and that these errors are not constant over time but tend to grow during phases of market tension. The higher risk of banks during the crisis is neither immediately expected nor quickly built into analyst forecasts. In contrast, during the crisis, the dispersion in the forecast errors increases markedly and there is an increase in the correlation between forecast errors and risk. Excluding explanations based either on a poor systematic ability of the entire community of financial analysts to predict risk or on a distortion of their incentives (expectations management), these findings can be interpreted as indicative of a still insufficient ability of accounting data to provide adequate and timely estimates of the risk faced by issuers in the banking industry. These findings, the authors argue, further emphasize the importance of strengthening the disclosure requirements of banks.

Chapter 3 by Ewa Miklaszewska and Katarzyna Mikolajczyk (both from the Cracow University of Economics) focuses on the performance and governance of foreign banks operating in Central and Eastern Europe (CEE). The authors examine two periods, post-EU accession and 2007–9, when economies in the region faced near collapse due to the credit crisis. Empirical evidence supports the market-seeking hypothesis, namely, that the opportunity to earn relatively higher profits in fast-growing transition countries was a crucial element explaining the massive inflow of foreign banks to the main CEE countries. On analysing the importance of the mode of foreign bank entry (retail-based model with partial foreign control, or a wholly foreign-controlled limited subsidiary model), the results are less clear. Wholly foreign-controlled banks appeared to be the least risky, while banks with foreign majority control appeared less profitable and more risky. Foreign banks with US owners appeared to be the most profitable, although banks owned by Belgian, Dutch and German parents were the least risky. US-owned banks were also the most efficient. Overall, the chapter concludes that both owners' home country governance models and host country macroeconomic and institutional characteristics are important factors in explaining bank performance.

Chapter 4 by Ted Lindblom (University of Gothenburg), Magnus Olsson (University of Gothenburg) and Magnus Willesson (Linnæus University) examines the impact of the financial crisis on the profitability and risk-taking of Swedish banks. At the beginning of the crisis many banks experienced liquidity problems due to a mismatch in their funding of loans. These banks had for a number of years been financing an increasing long-term (mortgage) lending with short-term borrowing on the market. The financial crisis radically changed the risk premiums on both money and capital markets, and banks' refinancing on these markets became extremely expensive and more or less impossible to accomplish. Even though Swedish banks seem to comply well with the new Basel accord, three of the four largest commercial banks issued new equity in connection with the crisis in order to strengthen their capacity to absorb anticipated credit losses, primarily on the Baltic markets, in a 'worst case scenario'. Overall, the analysis of the profitability and risk-taking of Swedish banks during the financial crisis shows that the banks did in general perform well domestically. If it had not been not for credit losses due, it appears, to over-aggressive lending by commercial banks, first of all in the Baltic States, the average profitability of the banks would have been only marginally affected by the crisis, given the stability measures assumed by the government and the central bank. In that respect this crisis is different from the one in the early 1990s.

Mario La Torre and Fabiomassimo Mango (both from the University of Rome 'La Sapienza') examine the rating of securitized assets in Chapter 5. The analysis aims to examine the promptness of ABS security downgrades in the context of the recent financial crisis, using a European sample of securitization programmes of residential mortgages. More specifically, the chapter evaluates whether variations in macroeconomic variables are incorporated promptly into ratings and whether this determines a downgrading lag, producing what has been defined as a 'secondary derivative effect' on the stability of the financial system. Results of the descriptive analysis indicate, in the first place, the presence of a 'primary effect', or, rather, highlight the fact that ABS contributed to the systemic crisis due to a significant number of downgrades. Regression estimates also suggest that in the pre-crisis period rating agencies tended to delay downgrading.

Chapter 6 by Santiago Carbó-Valverde (University of Granada), David Humphrey (Florida State University) and Francisco Rodríguez Fernández (University of Granada) presents a novel model of banking sector competition based on revenue frontier estimations. Measuring banking competition, the authors note, using the HHI, Lerner Index, or H-statistic can give conflicting results. Borrowing from frontier analysis, the chapter presents an alternative approach and applies it to Spain during 1992–2005. Controlling for differences in asset composition, productivity, scale economies, risk, and business cycle influences, they find no differences in competition between commercial and savings banks or between large and small institutions, but conclude that competition weakened after 2000. This appears related to strong loan demand, whereby real loan–deposit rate spreads rose and fees may have not fallen as fast as scale economies were realized.

Chapter 7 by Georgios E. Chortareas (University of Athens), Claudia Girardone (University of Essex) and Alexia Ventouri (University of Essex) considers the relationship between bank regulation, supervision and performance for a sample of European Union countries in the early new millennium. The approach taken compares the efficiency scores of banks operating in New Member States (NMSs) and selected countries from the 'old' EU15 bloc. The main results show that there is a strong link between various forms of banking regulation and supervision and bank performance and efficiency. In particular, strengthened regulatory practices from Basel 2 relating to Pillars I and II appear to be associated with lower inefficiencies, whereas more demanding regulation on Pillar III decreases the efficient operation of banks.

Chapter 8 by Pierluigi Morelli (Centro Europa Ricerche, Rome) and Elena Seghezza (University of Genoa) evaluates the governance and performance features of Italian popular (cooperative) banks. The ownership of these banks is extremely fragmented, similar to public companies. However, the principle of 'one head, one vote' shields popular banks from takeovers. Competition and other forces encourage managers to pursue profitable and efficient strategies stemming from the informal commitment of banks to guarantee a predetermined rate of return on shares, namely, stability of dividend payouts. The authors present a theoretical model with empirical support showing that the informal commitment constrains managers to achieve levels of profits at least sufficient to pay the expected dividends. In this way they are discouraged from any form of short-term behaviour and expense preferencing.

The remaining chapters in this text focus on dimensions of firm financing and value creation. Chapter 9 by Luciana Canovi, Elisabetta Gualandri and Valeria Venturelli (all at the University of Modena and Reggio Emilia and CEFIN – Centro Studi Banca e Finanza) looks at the availability of equity financing for new, innovative Italian firms. In particular, the chapter examines the financing of small and medium enterprises (SMEs) in the Modena. The main aim is to analyse the means by which start-ups are financed, especially in the form of equity, and attempt to identify any financial constraints, in particular in the form of an equity gap, which restrict the growth and development for this kind of firm. The main finding that emerges is that investors need to combine their financial contribution with the supply of managerial inputs. The analysis of the sources of finance used by firms appears to point to a preference for managing investment processes internally or with bank partners. The entry of new partners into the company's ownership structure is more likely to solve problems relating to a lack of expertise than to be a strategy for obtaining new financial resources.

Chapter 10 by Andi Duqi (University of Bologna) and Giuseppe Torluccio (University of Bologna) investigates the relationship between research and development (R&D) expenditures and the market value of European listed companies that implemented R&D during the years 2001–7. According to the theory of efficient financial markets, investors should correctly value tangible and intangible firm assets, and these valuations should therefore be reflected in the market value of any company. Overall, the authors find a strong positive and significant influence of R&D expenditure on firm market value. Nevertheless, the relevance of this effect differs among countries. In addition, younger and smaller firms that operate in high-tech markets are able to spend more efficiently on R&D – the effects of R&D investment on firm market value in these types of companies is stronger compared with older and low-tech sectors. Various robustness checks confirm the evidence that R&D expenditure has a significant and positive impact on the stock prices of European companies.

Another interesting dimension, covered in Chapter 11 by Ottorino Morresi and Alberto Pezzi (both at the University of Roma TRE), relates to the internationalization strategy of medium-sized Italian companies and the impact on firm value. Using survey evidence on the value creation of different equity entry modes, the analysis focuses on a sample of 140 announcements of international investments performed by all Italian medium-sized firms listed on the Italian Stock Market between 1986 and 2006. Using an event study methodology, the authors find a positive and significant market reaction to announcements of internationalization strategies. The results are largely affected by the abnormal return of high-equity entry modes carried out in advanced economies. Low-equity entry modes do not show any significant market reaction, and neither do the international operations performed in emerging countries. We also find that the relative size of the deal, firm age, country risk, and the evolution of information disclosure regulations are important in explaining the outcomes.

Finally, Chapter 12 by Ted Lindblom, Gert Sandahl and Stefan Sjögren (all at the University of Gothenburg) examines an age-old issue in corporate finance: capital structure and the pecking order puzzle. This chapter tests the explanatory power of the pecking order theory on the financial decisions of large Swedish firms. It also explores how these decisions relate to the trade-off theory in its static and extended forms. The results are compared with findings in the US and in the

UK. Most empirical studies of financial structure decisions find evidence supporting both the static trade-off theory and the pecking order theory. The survey evidence presented in this chapter also indicates decision-making in accordance with both theories in the same firm. An explanation that has been put forward is that under certain conditions a trade-off is prevalent, when a manager makes a capital structure decision, and under others a pecking order approach is more relevant. Even if this may sound reasonable, the explanation is not fully convincing, as the notion of an optimal capital structure is not relevant in a pecking order setting. One interesting result the authors find is that managers who set targets are unlikely to deviate from a pecking order scheme.

1
Bank Size, Market Power and Financial Stability

Joaquín Maudos and Juan Fernández de Guevara

1.1 Introduction

The financial crisis in which the world has been living since the summer of 2007 has shown the importance of the financial sector for the proper functioning of economies. For the European countries the financial crisis has signified a reduction in the volume of credit granted, decreased activity in international markets and an increase of risk and instability. Financial entities have seen how they have had to change their way of operating, adapting to a situation in which difficulties exist in obtaining finance in international markets, both in volumes and in terms of interest rates, and in which the levels of risk are substantially higher. Moreover, financial entities' degree of risk aversion has increased considerably, which has translated into a hardening of credit conditions.

The experience of these two years of crisis shows that its intensity has been different depending on which countries are analysed. Thus, countries like the United States, the United Kingdom, France and Germany have needed the recapitalization of part of the financial sector (see European Central Bank, 2010). However, in other countries, such as Italy or Spain (except in the cases of the savings banks of Caja Castilla La Mancha and CajaSur), though government support has taken the form of guarantees for the issue of debt and the acquisition of financial assets, the public recapitalization of financial entities has not been necessary, at least up to mid-2010.

In the current context of economic and financial crisis, it is of special interest to analyse the importance of size, given its habitual connection with systemic risk. In the recent discussions of the G-20, the Financial Stability Board and the Bank for International Settlements (BIS), among others, specific proposals are aimed at preventing the possible systemic risk of the biggest banks, with higher requirements in terms of capital or restructuring plans in the event of failure (with the so-called living wills). Though our *a priori* is that this connection is imprecise (since what makes a bank systemic is not so much its size as the complexity of its operations and the products with which it works, and the difficulty of controlling the risks assumed and of its management as a whole), the importance of size (with such important implications in terms of *too big to fail*) may have consequences for banks' market power. The objective of this paper is to determine these consequences.

It is also of interest to analyse the relationship between the intensity of competition and financial stability, since economic theory does not offer us unequivocal results. Thus, on the one hand, the most traditional hypothesis postulates that, since competition reduces a bank's market value, a problem of moral hazard will arise, giving the bank incentives to take more risks in order to increase its returns, which will cause greater financial instability. On the other hand, an alternative hypothesis postulates a positive relationship between competition and financial stability: if a bank has market power it will be able to set a higher loan interest rate, leading to an increase in more risky projects. Furthermore, on the (questionable) assumption that a more concentrated banking market permits the biggest banks to exercise more market power, these banks enjoy an insurance due to the fact that they are too big to fall, so it may induce them to take more risks. Consequently, since it is theoretically possible to postulate both a negative and a positive relationship between market power and financial stability, it is necessary to offer empirical evidence.

In order to analyse the relationship between size, market power and financial stability, in the study we estimate indicators at bank level for a large number of countries and years. Specifically, market power is proxied by means of the Lerner index, while financial stability is measured by the so-called Z-score (which is an inverse measurement of banking risk or probability of failure). The Lerner index has the advantage over other indicators of competition of proxying market power at firm level, and not at country level (like market concentration or Panzar and Rosse's *H* statistic).

As well as this introduction, the paper is structured in five sections. Section 2 reviews the most recent literature on the relationship existing between size, market power and financial stability, paying special attention to the importance of size in explaining both variables. Section 3 describes the empirical approach to the measurement of the variables and Section 4 presents the sample used. In Section 5 the results of the estimation of the determinants of market power and financial stability are presented and analysed. The article closes with Section 6, dedicated to the conclusions of the study.

1.2 Size, market power and financial stability

1.2.1 Size and market power

Although, as pointed out by Bikker et al. (2007), from a theoretical point of view the models which result in a positive relationship between size and market power predominate, the empirical evidence does not seem to bear out this theoretical result.

The oligopolistic version of the Monti–Klein model of banking competition among a number N of banks shows that, in equilibrium, the Lerner index of market power depends negatively on the number of competitors and on the demand elasticity, so that market power is maximum in monopoly and decreases as the number of competitors increases. Therefore, if the number of competitors is reduced, as a consequence, for example, of mergers resulting in bigger banks, the model predicts a positive relationship between size (and market concentration) and market power.

The model of Courvosier and Gropp (2002) also predicts a positive relationship between size and market power for setting higher margins. Though this relationship is not immediately apparent in the study by Courvosier and Gropp, the demonstration is more immediate in the adaptation of that model made in Fernández de Guevara et al. (2005), where the Lerner index depends positively on the average size of each bank. The result obtained in the latter study shows a non-linear relationship between market power and size, so that market power increases up to a certain size, and decreases from then onwards. It is important to mention that the positive effect of size is compatible with the fact that market share (in the national market) is not relevant when explaining market power, so what is relevant is not that a bank is 'big' in its own country (i.e. has a high domestic market share), but that it is big at the international level.

Although market concentration is a variable distinct from size, both variables are closely related insofar as a market is more concentrated if the market share of one or a few banks is very large. And, in this context, a possible positive correlation between concentration and market power may be due to two completely different reasons. First, as indicated by the structure–conduct–performance paradigm, if a small number of big banks predominate in the market (high concentration), it is easier to adopt collusive agreements, market power and profitability (extraordinary profits) being consequently greater. But, second, an alternative interpretation is as follows: if a bank is efficient, it will gain market share and concentration will increase as a consequence. Therefore, the positive relationship between concentration and profitability would be, not a consequence of market power, but due to greater efficiency. Furthermore, the more 'contestable' a market (i.e. the lower the barriers to entry), a small number of competitors (high concentration) will not necessarily imply greater market power, so market concentration is not a good indicator of competition.

As pointed out by Bikker et al. (2007), there may be several explanations for big banks having greater market power. First, the authors note the better position of a big bank to be able to reach collusive agreements with others. Second, the reputational effect associated with size may be utilized in the form of extraordinary profits. Third, a big bank has the ability to create new products, permitting it to enjoy, at least initially, monopoly rents. Fourth, a big bank may operate with different products and in different markets, where on occasions only a small number of big entities offer wholesale products, in which they exercise market power. In any case, these are possible explanations that must be tested in the empirical investigation.

Finally, the famous principle of *too big to fail* is usually invoked to indicate the possible market power associated with size. The fact that size, *per se*, is a guarantee that a bank with problems will never be allowed to 'fall' may affect business behaviour due to a problem of moral hazard. If a big bank knows that it will never be allowed to fail, it may take advantage of this circumstance to offer lower interest rates on liabilities and carry out riskier operations, since that bank's clientele will feel more secure.

On the empirical side, there is no conclusive evidence regarding the effect of size on market power. When we review the most recent studies, in some the size affects market power positively, while in others just the opposite occurs.

On the basis of the estimation of Panzar and Rosse's *H* statistic (one of the indicators most frequently used to measure the intensity of competition), Bikker and Haaf (2002) find that competition increases with size. Using the same indicator of competition, De Bandt and Davis (2000) show that in some countries the smallest banks enjoy more market power, competition therefore increasing with size.

Fernández de Guevara et al. (2005) obtain a positive effect of size on market power (proxied by the Lerner index), though the relationship is not linear but quadratic. Therefore, for the specific case of the European banking system, their results show that there exists a size beyond which market power diminishes, so that for very small banks, or very big ones, market power is reduced.

Using the same methodological approach, Fernández de Guevara and Maudos (2007) show that, in the case of Spanish banks, the effect of size on market power is negative, though the relationship is not linear. Consequently, small and big banks enjoy greater market power, while competition is greater for intermediate sizes. In the case of the small banks, the authors justify the result by alluding to the local presence of these banks, which usually have a dense network of branches that acts as a barrier to entry. In the case of the big banks, they allude to a position of market domination.

Bikker et al. (2007) estimate Panzar and Rosse's *H* statistic by quartiles of size using a broad sample of banks from 101 countries. Their results indicate that big banks possess more market power in practically all the countries analysed, contradicting earlier studies which affirm that competition increases with size.

1.2.2 Market power and financial stability

As has been remarked in the Introduction, there are basically two alternative points of view regarding the relationship between market power and financial stability. The more traditional point of view gives arguments to propose that an excess of banking competition can lead to financial instability for various reasons. In a situation of competition, narrow banking margins cause banks to have to assume riskier projects in order to increase their profits, which ends up increasing the banks' fragility. This thesis is supported by the empirical evidence of Keeley (1990), in which, for the specific case of the United States, the increase in competition that took place during the 1980s increased the number of banks with problems. In the same line, other studies (e.g. Hellman et al., 2000) offer evidence that, after processes of deregulation and liberalization of the financial sectors, the increase in competition diminishes profitability, which induces riskier behaviours.

A second justification of the negative effect of competition on financial stability is through the franchise value (market value) of a bank. If competition increases, profits fall, which provokes a decrease in the value of the franchise. In this case, the bank has incentives to undertake more risky activities, to capture less capital, and so on, thus increasing financial instability.

The alternative view, which associates greater market power with less financial stability, utilizes as argument the effect that a higher interest rate (associated with market power) has on the investment projects that reach the bank (see Boyd and De Nicolo, 2005). When the cost of financing is high, borrowers take on riskier projects with a greater probability of failure. In that case, banks' bad debt rates will be higher, increasing the probability of bank failures.

The existing empirical evidence on the effect of market power on financial stability is not conclusive. Thus, focusing on the studies published in recent years, the evidence from Boyd et al. (2006) is favourable to the existence of a positive relationship between competition (market power) and financial stability (banking risk). In the same line, the study by Schaeck et al. (2009) also shows that stability is greater in the most competitive banking systems, given the lower probability of a financial crisis occurring (proxied by an indicator of systemic risk). Finally, the most recent study by Uhde and Heimeshoff (2009), using aggregate data for the banking sectors of the EU-25, obtains a negative impact of market concentration (proxy for market power) on financial stability.

On the other hand, Berger et al. (2009) show that a growth of market power leads to greater financial stability, which implies offering evidence favourable to the traditional view that an excess of banking competition may be prejudicial to financial stability. In the first case, the evidence refers to 23 developed countries, while in the second study the sample of banks used covers 60 countries in the period 1999–2005.

In the specific case of Spanish banks, Jiménez et al. (2010) analyse the relationship between market power and banking risk, using the Lerner index as an indicator of market power. The results referring to the period 1988–2003 show a negative relationship between market power and banking risk, the latter being proxied by the bad debt rate. The authors find partial evidence of the existence of a non-linear relationship between market power and financial stability.

1.3 Empirical approach and statistical sources

The analysis of the determinants of market power combines information at firm level and at country level. In the first case, we use the data on the balance sheet and the profit and loss account of banks offered by the BankScope database. In the second case, the information is taken from databases of international bodies such as the International Monetary Fund (IMF), European Central Bank (ECB), etc.

1.3.1 The Lerner index and its determinants

The analysis of the relationship, on the one hand, between market power and size and, on the other, between market power and financial stability is based on the estimation of two econometric regressions whose dependent variables are market power and financial stability, respectively.

In the first case, the model proposed by Courvoisier and Gropp (2002) and its extensions by Fernández de Guevara and Maudos (2007) are taken as reference. From this model, it is possible to derive an indicator of market power and its explanatory factors. Specifically, the model assumes that banks can exercise market power when setting the interest rate on their loans and that the demand for loans from bank *'k'* depends on the size of the market and the interest rate on loans offered by the bank compared with its competitors.

From the first order conditions of the problem of profit maximization we obtain an expression of the Lerner index, among whose determinants are the following: the probability of failure, the bank size, the number of competitors, the elasticity of demand for loans of type *k* compared with the interest rate differentials of the competitors, the elasticity of total demand for loans in relation to the average interest rate, and the level of interest rates.

The empirical approach of these explanatory variables of market power is as follows:

a) The number of competing banks is usually proxied by the degree of market concentration, in our case the Herfindahl–Hirschmann index (*HHI*), defined as the sum of the squares of the market shares. This index of concentration solves some of the problems that arise with other absolute indicators of concentration, such as the market share of the biggest firms (CR3, CR5, etc.). The information for the HHI index is taken directly from the European Central Bank. For those countries for which the European Central Bank does not offer information, the index has been calculated directly from the information given by BankScope.
b) The size of each bank (*Total Assets*) is proxied by total assets (in logs). In order to be able to capture the possible non-linear influence of size, an additional quadratic term is introduced.
c) Elasticity of total demand is proxied, following Courvoisier and Gropp (2002) and Fernández de Guevara et al. (2005), by the value of the stock market capitalization as a percentage of GDP (*stock market capitalization /GDP*). It is to be expected that the greater the relative

importance of the financial markets in relation to the weight of the banks (financial structure of the country), the greater will be the elasticity of demand. In other words, the *a priori* is that the lower a country's dependence on banking finance (higher value of stock market capitalization), the lower will be the influence of bank market power. The information is taken from the World Bank's *World Development Indicators* database.

d) The probability of failure is proxied by the ratio of provisions for insolvencies to loans (*provisions/loans*), given the lack of available information on each bank's rate of bad debt.

Although the above variables are those which appear explicitly in the theoretical model as determinants of market power, it is customary to introduce ad hoc other possible determinants, among them:

e) *Market share.* Though it could initially be thought that the effect of size has already been captured by introducing total assets, there may exist an additional influence of a bank's market share in its national market. The thesis to be tested is whether size *per se* is what confers market power on a bank or whether, on the contrary, it is the market share that determines greater power. It is possible for a bank to be small in the international context but to have a high market share in its national market, so it is of interest to test which indicator of size (absolute or relative) is relevant for explaining market power. The variable is constructed on the basis of BankScope data. Similarly to the case of size, we also introduce a quadratic term.
f) *Banking specialization.* The evidence from other studies shows different levels of competition (and integration) in different banking markets (e.g. wholesale vs. retail). Even at product level, some reports (Fundación de Estudios Financieros, 2009; European Central Bank, 2010) show that both the levels and the evolution of relative banking margins (Lerner indices) differ between products, being higher in some liability products (such as current accounts) and lower in products such as term deposits, loans to firms, and so on. Therefore, in estimating the determinants of market power we control for the effect of specialization. In particular, the importance of retail activity is proxied by the weight of loans in total assets (*loans / total assets*).
g) *Efficiency* in management is also a determinant of market power that has been analysed in other studies. Some test the influence of market power on efficiency, in order to test the so-called quiet life hypothesis. But in our case the direction of causality is just the opposite, as

we want to analyse whether efficiency in management ends up being passed on to the client in the form of lower margins or whether the bank takes advantage of that efficiency to raise its profitability.

h) Finally, in the empirical applications that include different banking sectors at international level, it is usual to introduce control variables specific to each country, such as the economic cycle (*GDP growth*), the *inflation rate* and per capita GDP (*GDP/Population*). Both variables are obtained from the World Bank's *World Development Indicators*.

With respect to the dependent variable, the Lerner index is used as an indicator of market power, measuring a bank's power to set rates above marginal cost. For total banking activity, the index is constructed as follows:[1]

$$P_A = (P_A - MC_A) / P_A \qquad (1)$$

where P_A is the mean price of banking output and MC_A its marginal cost. The usual proxy (Fernández de Guevara et al., 2007; Berger et al., 2009; Carbó et al., 2009; Turk Ariss, 2010, among others) is to use total assets as an indicator of activity banking, estimating their average price as a quotient between total income and total assets.

The marginal costs of each bank are calculated from the estimation of a translogarithmic costs function, where the total costs (operating and financial) depend on the price of inputs and on total assets. Unlike other studies, in our case we estimate a frontier costs function[2] for the whole sample, as we want to analyse the effect of efficiency on market power. For the indicator of efficiency to be comparable between banks of different countries, it is necessary to estimate a common frontier for the whole sample, which requires controlling in the estimation for the possible influence of environmental variables. Otherwise, the efficiencies estimated at bank level would be biased, as they would attribute to a firm inefficient behaviour when the firm is located in a country with an environment requiring it to bear greater costs. Specifically, the environmental variables used are:

- Income per capita, calculated as the quotient between the GDP at constant prices and the population. It is usually used as a control variable, since it can affect factors related to the demand and the supply of banking products. It is also usually used as proxy for a country's institutional development. Source: *World Development Indicators* of the World Bank.

- Density of population (inhabitants per km^2). Since in countries with lower population density the banks usually have a larger branch network in order to be able to serve a more geographically scattered population, operating costs are higher. Therefore, unless this environmental variable is included, the banks located in countries with low population density will erroneously appear to be more inefficient. The information is obtained from the World Bank's *World Development Indicators*.
- Branch Network Density (population per branch). A higher network density brings with it higher operating costs, which may negatively affect efficiency. The information on the branch network is obtained from the European Central Bank and from the Central Banks of different countries.
- GDP growth rate. The variable is introduced to capture the influence of the economic cycle.
- In addition, the estimation of the costs function includes a dummy variable for each country that captures the influence of other determinants of the costs specific to each banking sector (e.g. differences in regulation).

1.3.2 The measurement of financial stability

One of the most widely used indicators of financial stability is the *Z*-score, which measures the distance from a situation of insolvency (failure). Specifically, this indicator is constructed as follows:

$$Z = \frac{ROA + K / A}{\sigma_{ROA}} \tag{2}$$

where *ROA* is the return on assets, *K* equity, *A* assets and σ the standard deviation of *ROA* in the period of time analysed. Observe that the Z-score increases with profitability and solvency (proxied by *K/A*) and decreases as the volatility of the return increases. In this way, by combining information on profitability, solvency and risk, it is a proxy for the probability of failure. The higher the value of the Z-score, the lower is the probability of failure and, therefore, the greater the financial stability.[3]

Since the elements making up the construction of the Z-score are available at bank level, the indicator of financial stability is constructed at firm level. Specifically, we have available an indicator by bank and year, since, although the denominator of the expression is constant in the time period analysed, the numerator varies every year. We thus have available panel data, and can furthermore analyse the effect of market power (for which data by bank and year are also available) on financial stability.

Regarding the determinants of financial stability, as well as market power and size (which are the centre of attention), the review of the empirical studies published shows that this may depend on: a) the portfolio composition, proxied by the weight of loans in total assets; b) variables specific to each country, such as GDP per capita (indicator of institutional/economic development), the GDP growth rate and the inflation rate. To the extent that the economic cycle affects the components of the Z-score (such as *ROA*), they may affect financial stability.

1.4 Sample used and descriptive statistics

The sample used includes banks, savings banks and credit cooperatives in the period 2001–8. The criteria for filtering of the sample are as follows: a) the observations corresponding to the extreme values of the distribution of each variable have been eliminated, considering as extremes those situated outside the interval defined by the mean and 2.5 times the standard deviation of the variable; b) since to construct the Z-score we need information on the standard deviation of the profitability of each of the financial entities over the course of time, we have eliminated those entities for which information is not available for at least five consecutive years; c) we eliminated the observations for which no information was available on some of the variables necessary for estimating the Lerner index and its determinants. With these criteria, the sample contains a total of 30,471 bank-observations (27,470 when the growth of the entity's total assets is included as regressor).

The countries analysed include most of the European Union, plus the United States, Canada and Japan. More specifically, the list of countries analysed is as follows: Austria, Belgium, Canada, Cyprus, Czech Republic, Denmark, Finland, France, Germany, Greece, Ireland, Italy, Japan, Latvia, Lithuania, Luxembourg, Holland, Norway, Poland, Slovakia, Slovenia, Spain, Sweden, Switzerland, the United Kingdom and the United States. Some other countries have been removed from the sample for one or more of the reasons commented on in the previous paragraph.

Table 1.1 contains the main descriptive statistics of the variables used: mean, standard deviation, coefficient of variation and 25th, 50th and 75th percentiles of the distribution. The mean values by countries offered in Table 1.2 show a wide range of variation and inequalities for the two variables of interest for the study: the Lerner index and the Z-score. In the first case, and taking as reference the last year available (2008), the difference between the country with the greatest market power (Bulgaria, with a Lerner index of 0.49) and the one with the least (the United Kingdom, 0.12) is 1 to 4, showing the wide range of variation. In general, it is not possible to appreciate a defined temporal behaviour for all the countries, as countries where market power increased from 2001 to 2008 coexist with countries where it decreased.

In the case of the Z-score, the differences are sharper, with a maximum value in 2008 (Switzerland, 67) 13 times the minimum value (5 in Belgium). Though the effects of the crisis that started in summer 2007 are felt much more strongly in 2009 (a year for which we do not yet have available information at bank level in the database used), already in 2008 a fall in the Z-score value can be appreciated in a fair number of countries, almost certainly as a consequence of the reduction in the levels of profitability. The fall is especially steep in Ireland, Japan, Finland and the United Kingdom.

Table 1.1 Descriptive statistics of the sample used. 2001–8 averages

	Mean	Standard deviation	Coefficient of variation	Percentile 25	Median	Percentile 75
Lerner Index	0.26	0.11	0.44	0.19	0.24	0.31
Z-score	23.33	33.11	1.42	17.98	31.01	48.57
Log(Total Assets)	18.31	2.06	0.11	12.50	13.43	14.65
Efficiency	0.90	0.06	0.06	0.88	0.91	0.93
Market share	0.06	0.09	1.58	0.00	0.00	0.00
HHI	0.05	0.05	1.13	0.02	0.02	0.04
GDP growth	0.02	0.01	0.66	0.01	0.02	0.03
Log(GDP population)	14.85	1.28	0.09	14.29	14.75	15.12
Loan loss provisions / Total assets	0.01	0.02	2.86	0.00	0.00	0.01
Loans total assets	0.49	0.19	0.38	0.53	0.64	0.74
Market capitalization / GDP	0.93	0.48	0.51	0.44	0.57	1.10
Inflation rate	0.02	0.01	0.59	0.01	0.02	0.03

Source: BankScope, Banco Mundial, FMI, BCE and authors' own work.

Table 1.2 Market power and financial stability. Average values

	Lerner Index				Z-score			
	2001	2006	2007	2008	2001	2006	2007	2008
Austria	0.18	0.19	0.17	0.21	26.58	37.50	38.56	38.66
Belgium	0.15	0.19	0.15	0.16	16.04	7.68	7.29	5.01
Canada	0.23	0.23	0.21	0.22	35.37	24.98	24.04	26.20
Cyprus	0.24	0.42	0.27	–	6.22	9.01	10.75	–
Czech Republic	0.19	0.33	0.31	0.32	16.74	24.51	21.08	20.33
Denmark	0.23	0.26	0.22	0.25	18.64	15.88	13.81	10.33
Finland	0.28	0.31	0.26	0.27	27.65	11.79	9.32	5.60
France	0.23	0.21	0.19	0.22	18.55	22.27	15.76	13.97
Germany	0.11	0.18	0.18	0.13	33.60	29.31	28.33	45.40
Greece	0.26	0.31	0.27	0.20	22.61	22.85	21.33	16.10
Ireland	0.14	0.20	0.18	0.13	14.66	11.61	11.12	5.78
Italy	0.29	0.28	0.23	0.18	23.14	25.45	26.96	26.11
Japan	0.31	0.31	0.28	0.26	16.29	26.53	25.36	13.13
Latvia	0.34	0.38	0.33	0.26	17.71	15.78	17.92	15.93
Lithuania	0.07	0.35	0.36	0.30	4.41	14.17	15.09	10.43
Luxembourg	0.18	0.19	0.15	0.19	20.99	25.91	18.91	22.36
Netherlands	0.21	0.25	0.30	0.27	49.40	57.11	13.39	23.56
Norway	0.19	0.25	0.19	–	24.73	21.82	23.21	–
Poland	–	0.29	0.33	0.33	–	20.48	22.08	19.44
Portugal	0.23	0.24	0.20	0.16	28.99	29.04	28.01	23.04
Slovakia	0.20	0.34	0.34	0.38	28.20	27.70	27.85	26.03
Slovenia	0.22	0.25	0.27	0.23	29.06	19.03	18.61	18.47
Spain	0.28	0.28	0.27	0.22	44.14	41.70	34.18	32.75
Sweden	0.25	0.23	0.22	0.27	9.21	9.68	9.07	8.04
Switzerland	0.28	0.32	0.29	0.27	23.47	70.00	72.28	67.14
United Kingdom	0.12	0.11	0.12	0.10	34.95	26.89	27.13	22.20
United States	0.31	0.29	0.28	0.30	20.76	20.29	20.31	18.41
Total	0.24	0.25	0.23	0.24	24.23	25.17	23.62	22.37

Source: authors' own work.

1.5 Results

Tables 1.3 and 1.4 present the results of estimating different models in which the dependent variables are, respectively, the indicator of market power and the Z-score of financial stability. In both cases, given the panel structure of the sample available, the estimation includes fixed effects[4] as well as time effects.

As for the results relating to the determinants of the Lerner index, Column 1 of Table 1.3 gives the results of the 'base' estimation in which market power is explained by size, efficiency, market concentration,

Table 1.3 Market power determinants. Dependent variable: Lerner index

	1	2	3	4
Log(Total Assets)	0.000	0.055**	0.075**	0.081**
	(0.002)	(0.010)	(0.011)	(0.011)
Log(Total Assets)^2		−0.002**	−0.003**	−0.003**
		(0.000)	(0.000)	(0.000)
Credit growth			0.010**	0.010**
			(0.003)	(0.003)
Efficiency	0.234**	0.232**	0.226**	0.226**
	(0.010)	(0.010)	(0.011)	(0.011)
HHI	0.121**	0.123**	0.184**	0.188**
	(0.037)	(0.037)	(0.040)	(0.040)
Market share				0.341*
				(0.147)
Market share^2				−0.261
				(0.265)
GDP growth	1.320**	1.311**	1.387**	1.388**
	(0.039)	(0.039)	(0.042)	(0.042)
Log (GDP/Population)	−0.242**	−0.232**	−0.185**	−0.182**
	(0.016)	(0.016)	(0.018)	(0.018)
Loan loss provisions / Loans	0.369**	0.372**	0.413**	0.413**
	(0.026)	(0.026)	(0.030)	(0.030)
Loans / Total assets	0.086**	0.083**	0.091**	0.091**
	(0.006)	(0.006)	(0.006)	(0.006)
Market capitalization / GDP	0.001	0.000	0.002	0.001
	(0.002)	(0.002)	(0.003)	(0.003)
Inflation rate	−0.636**	−0.646**	−0.698**	−0.714**
	(0.062)	(0.062)	(0.066)	(0.066)
Observations	30,471	30,471	27,470	27,470
R^2	0.21	0.21	0.23	0.23
Sum squared residuals	51.83	51.77	44.68	44.66
F	434.83	411.56	373.14	336.54
Log likelihood	53,913	53,931	49,220	49,226

Note: *p<0.05, **p<0.01. All estimations include fixed and time effects.

Source: authors' own work.

Table 1.4 Determinants of financial stability. Dependent variable: Z-score

	1	2	3	4	5
Lerner	16.887***		20.668***	19.968***	19.944***
	(1.232)		(3.638)	(3.628)	(3.628)
$Lerner^2$			–6.788	–7.388	–7.326
			(6.609)	(6.567)	(6.569)
HHI		–19.354***			
		(7.031)			
Log(Total Assets)	–5.848***	–5.862***	–17.708***	–16.655***	–16.979***
	(0.335)	(0.336)	(2.023)	(2.105)	(2.140)
$Log(Total Assets)^2$			0.425***	0.386***	0.400***
			(0.071)	(0.074)	(0.076)
Credit growth				–1.457***	–1.454***
				(0.505)	(0.505)
Market share					–27.377
					(27.681)
Market $share^2$					52.818
					(50.265)
Loans / Total assets	0.226	1.581	0.823	1.303	1.288
	(1.127)	(1.126)	(1.130)	(1.158)	(1.158)
GDP growth	50.828***	70.489***	53.761***	57.785***	57.809***
	(7.933)	(7.832)	(8.014)	(8.058)	(8.059)
Log (GDP/ Population)	–5.056*	–8.548***	–7.114**	–1.906	–1.953
	(3.063)	(3.063)	(3.080)	(3.223)	(3.227)
Inflation rate	26.549**	13.800	28.747**	29.957**	30.301**
	(12.434)	(12.485)	(12.434)	(12.385)	(12.415)
Observations	31,194	31,194	31,194	28,128	28,128
R^2	0.04	0.03	0.04	0.04	0.04
Sum of squared residuals	2,250,053	2,265,323	2,246,959	1,713,889	1,713,808
F	73.22	58.95	65.98	57.61	51.27
Log likelihood	–110,994	–111,099	–110,972	–97,711	–97,711

Note: *p<0.10, **p<0.05, ***p<0.01. All estimations include fixed and time effects.

Source: authors' own work.

GDP growth rate, per capita income, the provisions ratio (as percentage of loans), specialization (relative importance of loans in total assets), stock market capitalization (as percentage of GDP) and inflation.

In general, the explanatory variables are shown to be significant (from a statistical point of view) when explaining the differences in market power between banks. Although in this 'base' estimation size is not relevant in explaining the Lerner index, the variable is indeed significant when its square is introduced in addition, showing the existence of a non-linear relationship in concordance with the results obtained in Fernández de Guevara et al. (2005) and Fernández de Guevara and Maudos (2007). Thus, although a bank's market power grows as its size increases, there exists a maximum beyond which the power diminishes.[5] Specifically, from Estimation 4, which includes all the explanatory variables, we deduce that, for entities of a size of less than 422 million Euros (12.95 in logarithms) in total assets, market power increases with size. However, beyond this volume of business, the relationship is negative. Although a balance sheet of 422 million Euros corresponds to a small-sized entity, in the sample there are a considerable percentage of banks below this size, since this inflection point is situated above the 25th percentile of assets value, as shown in Table 1.1. Specifically, of the 27,470 observations making up the sample used in the estimation of Column 4, 10,007 banks (36 per cent) have total assets below the inflection point. In our sample, a majority of the entities with total assets below the inflection point are credit cooperatives, especially German (Genossenschaftsektor, Kreditgenossenchaft) and Italian (Banche di Credito Cooperative).

When valuing the influence of total assets on market power, therefore, we can establish two distinct regimes. First, for rather more than one-third of the sample, those smallest in size, there is a positive relationship, such that the market power grows as the size of the institution increases. These entities are characterized by having a substantial local presence and operating in small banking markets. Possibly, their market power rests on the existence of barriers to entry into these local markets. However, once the size threshold described above has been crossed, increases in size imply reduction of market power.

In relation to efficiency, the results show that the most efficient banks enjoy greater market power, given the positive sign of the parameter estimated. This result may indicate that the better-managed banks use this advantage in costs as a barrier to entry, thus enjoying monopoly rents. Therefore, the most efficient banks do not appear to pass on their cost advantages to clients by applying lower margins, but use them to create extraordinary profits. Similar results are obtained in Fernández de Guevara et al. (2005) for a sample of European countries and Fernández de Guevara and Maudos (2007) in the case of Spanish banks.

One variable deserving special attention is the effect of concentration when explaining market power. The positive and statistically significant sign accompanying the variable HHI (Herfindahl–Hirschmann index) shows that in more concentrated markets it is easier to attain monopoly rents, in harmony with the most traditional hypothesis. Nevertheless, it is important to note that market concentration is not necessarily a good indicator of banking competition, since the latter depends on many more factors (existence of barriers to entry, institutional characteristics of the country, presence of public banks, market share of foreign banks, etc.). Also, economic theory itself teaches that it is possible for rivalry to be intense (resulting in perfect competition) in highly concentrated markets (e.g. the so-called Bertrand paradox).[6]

Both the proxy variable for specialization (loans/assets) and the indicator of risk (provisions/loans) affect market power positively and significantly. In the first case, the results indicate that the banks more specialized in the traditional retail intermediation business enjoy greater market power, a result that may be due to the lower degree of integration at international level in these retail markets than in wholesale activities (investment banking, inter-bank, etc.). And, in turn, this lower integration may be due to the existence of many kinds of barriers to entry (such as the lower integration of the infrastructures underlying these markets, natural differences like the language, barriers induced by economic policy in the form of differences in taxation, etc.).

In the case of risk, the results show that the riskiest banks must apply a risk premium, which is reflected in a higher margin and, therefore, in a higher value of the Lerner index. Nevertheless, a higher value of the index should not necessarily be interpreted as greater market power, since strictly the Lerner index should be corrected by the influence of the level of risk, something that it is not possible to do for lack of available information at firm level.[7]

With respect to the macroeconomic control variables, the results indicate that market power is: a) greater in boom times (higher GDP growth rates); b) lower when the rate of inflation is higher; and c) lower in more developed countries, with higher levels of per capita income. On the other hand, the variable *stock market capitalization / GDP* (which attempts to proxy the elasticity of the demand for loans) presents a non-significant coefficient.

In Column 3 the growth in the size of each bank is introduced additionally as a variable explaining market power. The *a priori* that in times of rapid growth the entities that grow most can gain market power is confirmed by the results, without affecting the rest of the results commented on above.

As remarked above, the effect of size on market power is compatible with a possible differential effect of market share, since, in the international context, the absolute size of a bank is one thing and its relative size (within its country) is quite a different thing. There may be banks that are small on a worldwide scale but are very big in their own countries, and perhaps for this reason enjoy market power.

When, additionally, the market share and its square are introduced into the estimation (Column 4), the variable has a positive and statistically significant effect, and the relationship is linear. Furthermore, the significance and positive sign of the size variable are maintained, which shows the importance of having both a large absolute size internationally and a high market share at national level. Therefore, a small bank can have market power if it has a significant market share in its country.

To determine which of the variables has greatest explanatory capacity from the economic point of view, Table 1.5 contains the estimated

Table 1.5 Elasticities of the variation of market power and Z-score

	Lerner index	Z-Score
Log(Total Assets)	4.367	–5.700
Log(Total Assets)^2	–2.345	1.836
Credit growth	0.003	–0.002
Efficiency	0.803	Not included
Lerner	Not included	0.127
Lerner^2	Not included	
HHI	0.033	Not included
Market share	0.005	Not included
Market share^2		Not included
GDP growth	0.095	0.025
Log (GDP / Population)	–10.419	
Loan loss provisions / Loans	0.011	
Loans / Total assets	0.223	
Market capitalization / GDP	0.005	Not included
Inflation rate	–0.056	0.015

Source: authors' own work.

elasticities of market power and of the Z-score calculated from the coefficients and (unweighted) mean values of the sample to variations in each of the determinants. The blank cells correspond to elasticities that have not been calculated as the corresponding coefficient was not statistically significant. The first column shows that the country's level of development (proxied by per capita GDP) is the variable with greatest impact on the Lerner index: a growth of 1 per cent in per capita GDP (in logarithms) generates a reduction of 10 per cent in the Lerner index. The variable with the second greatest influence on market power is size and its square, with elasticities of 4.3 per cent and –2.3 per cent, respectively. Efficiency also stands out for its elasticity in relation to market power. Thus, an increase of 1 per cent in efficiency generates a growth of 0.8 per cent in market power. The elasticities of the rest of the variables are notably lower.

In order to analyse in greater detail the importance of each of the explanatory variables, it is necessary to take into account the sample range of variation of each one of them. With this objective, we calculated what the variation of the Lerner index would be if it were calculated starting from an observation situated at the value of the 25th percentile of each of the independent variables and increasing up to the value defined by the 75th percentile. Taking into account this variation in the independent variable and the coefficient estimated in Column 4 of Table 1.3, we find that the greatest effect on market power is generated by size, since the growth from the 25th percentile to the 75th percentile would signify an 83 per cent growth of market power. At the same time, although the elasticity of per capita GDP was the highest, if its sample range of variation is taken into account the impact on the Lerner index is less than the effect of size, representing a fall of 73 per cent in market power in relation to the level of the 25th percentile. The impact of the variations of the rest of the variables are notably lower, only the case of GDP growth standing out. Specifically, the growth of GDP from the value of the 25th percentile to that of the 75th percentile implies a growth of market power of 12 per cent from the value of the 25th percentile.

Once the determinants of market power have been analysed, Table 1.4 shows the results corresponding to the Z-score of financial stability and its explanatory variables. It should be remembered that a higher value of the index comes from a higher profitability, from greater capitalization or from lower volatility in profits, so that higher values of the index imply more financial stability (less probability of failure).

In the first column of Table 1.4 the Lerner index is used as indicator of market power, while in Column 2 market concentration (HHI) is used alternatively. In the first case, the parameter is positive and statistically significant, providing evidence in favour of the 'competition–instability' hypothesis that, since banking competition reduces the value of the firm, the banks have incentives to take more risks. In Regressions 3–5, the square of the Lerner index is also included in order to capture the possible non-linear effect of the variable, and a non-significant coefficient is obtained. In this sense, the results do not agree with Berger et al. (2009) and Turk Ariss (2010) who obtain a quadratic relationship.

If, instead of the Lerner index, we use the HHI index as the indicator of competition (as is usual in other studies), the results are inverted: increases in concentration lead to a lowering of financial stability. This result, which is just the opposite of that obtained in terms of the Lerner index, shows the limitations of using market concentration indicators as proxies for competition. The result agrees with that obtained for the Spanish case by Jiménez et al. (2010), who obtain a negative relationship between the Lerner index and the credit risk. However, when they use measurements of market concentration, the results change depending on the indicator used (CR5 – five-firm concentration ratio, HHI or number of banks).

The results also indicate that size affects financial stability, with a non-linear effect. It is verified that the effect of the size of the entity is U-shaped, being initially negative up to a certain inflection point, beyond which it starts to have a positive effect. If we take Equation 4 as reference, we find that this inflection point occurs for a type of bank with a really high balance sheet, 2.3 billion Euros. Therefore, the stability of financial entities is greater in small banks and decreases as their size increases. However, for very big entities the Z-score increases.

In Column 5 of Table 1.4 we introduce the market share and its square, attempting to capture the differential effect of the relative size of a market in relation to its national market. As can be observed, neither coefficient, of the market share or of its square, is statistically significant.

With respect to the macroeconomic variables, the economic cycle affects stability positively. It has to be taken into account that banking profitability is an increasing function of GDP (high rates of growth of banking activity), which increases the Z-score. In the case of the inflation rate, its effect is also positive, which may be due to the fact that, in general, banking margins are higher with high rates of inflation.[8]

Just as above we calculated the economic impact associated with a variation of the variables of market power, in the second column of Table 1.5 we have calculated the elasticities of the Z-score to changes in each of the explanatory variables. The highest elasticity is found to correspond to the size of the entities, both in levels and squared. Next after this variable is the Lerner index (in level, not the square, since its coefficient is not statistically significant). The same conclusion is obtained if we calculate the range of variation of the Z-score when each of the explanatory variables changes from a value equivalent to the observation situated at the 25th percentile to another at the 75th percentile. Taking into account the coefficients estimated, it can be calculated that the increase in size by a value equivalent to the inter-quartile range generates a reduction of 190 per cent of the Z-score in relation to the value of the 25th percentile. The Lerner index also substantially affects the indicator of the stability of the financial entity, as an increase in market power equivalent to the inter-quartile range generates an increase in the Z-score (and therefore of financial stability) of 12 per cent.

1.6 Conclusions

In recent years, the principal banking sectors of the world have been subjected to the pressure of competition in an ever more globalized world where the barriers to integration are lower. This reduction of the barriers to competition, though it may be beneficial for firms and consumers to the extent that it implies a reduction in the cost of financing, may negatively affect financial stability.

Economic theory does not offer a unique vision of the effect of market power on financial stability; there exist, broadly, two alternative hypotheses. On the one hand, the most traditional thesis affirms that market power can have beneficial effects on financial stability, as the extraordinary profits associated with the lack of competition increase the value of the bank, thus reducing the incentives to invest in more risky activities. On the other hand, the alternative competition–stability hypothesis postulates that, if competition ensures lower loan interest rates, this causes riskier projects to be ruled out, thus increasing financial stability.

In the current context of economic and financial crisis, the supposed benefits associated with the processes of deregulation have been called into question, given the consequences that more deregulated banking activity (above all in the United States) has had for the intensity of competition and, through it, for financial stability. The absence of restrictions on banking activity and the perverse incentives to gain size have increased competitive rivalry in the banking markets, which has ended up negatively affecting financial stability.

In this context, our study contributes evidence for a broad panel of banks of various countries (EU-25, Canada, Japan and the United States) in the period 2001–8. For this, we construct an indicator of market power and another of financial stability at bank level. Specifically, market power is proxied by the Lerner index and financial stability by the so-called Z-score.

The results show that as banking competition increases, so does financial instability, so a certain level of market power can in the long term be beneficial. According to this result, the deregulation process of recent years and the measures implemented to increase competition may have negatively affected financial stability. Therefore, the results shown here posit a dilemma that society has to resolve. On the one hand, strictly from the point of view of economic efficiency, financial markets have to be as competitive as possible to prevent the losses of welfare associated with situations of imperfect competition (Maudos and Fernández de Guevara, 2007) and for the financial sector to make its full contribution to economic growth (Maudos and Fernández de Guevara, 2007; Fernández de Guevara and Maudos, 2009). On the other hand, an excess of competition may affect the stability of the financial sector. The objective of the economic authority should therefore be to design a system of incentives that can achieve an adequate level of competition in the financial sector without generating problems of stability.

The study also analyses the effect of size on market power. The results show a positive effect, although the relationship is not linear, since beyond a certain size threshold market power decreases. Therefore, very big banks are not necessarily a danger in terms of market power, since in fact the maximum value of market power is reached at an intermediate size (specifically, for an asset value of 422 million Euros, corresponding to an entity of small size in the sample used).

Another result of interest is the effect of size on financial stability, a question of concern in the current context of financial crisis. After the events occurring since the start of the present crisis in summer 2007, several authors have highlighted the role played by the big banks which has aggravated the crisis, generating systemic risk. The maximum tensions in the financial markets that occurred after the failure of Lehman Brothers demonstrate the importance of the big banks in generating financial instability. In this context, our results show that, although size negatively affects financial stability, the relationship is not linear, so that beyond a certain threshold (corresponding to a very big bank, specifically, 2.3 billion Euros) growth in size diminishes the probability of failure.

One of the conclusions to be drawn from the results obtained is that the possible risk associated with big banks and the implications deriving therefrom (such as the thesis that they are too big to allow them to fail) do not come from their higher probability of failure, since financial instability diminishes beyond a very high asset value. A very different matter is that, if it is a big bank that fails, this can create systemic risk. In other words, there is no reason why big banks should have a higher level of risk (probability of failure), but if, unfortunately, it is a very big bank that fails, this creates systemic risk, so this may require special regulation, given the greater negative external effects of the failure of a big bank.

Acknowledgements

The authors are grateful for the financial support of the Spanish savings banks foundation (Funcas). The results were obtained within the context of research projects SEC2007–60320 and ECO2010–17333 of the Ministerio de Educación y Ciencia-FEDER and project PROMETEO/2009/066 of the Generalitat Valenciana.

Notes

A previous version of this chapter was published in Spanish in *Perspectivas del Sistema Financiero* (FUNCAS).

1. See Fernández de Guevara et al. (2007).
2. For this we use the stochastic frontier approach proposed by Aigner et al. (1977) and Meeusen and van den Broeck (1977). This approach modifies the standard costs function by assuming that inefficiency forms part of the error term of the regression. Therefore, the error term has two components. The first is symmetrical and captures the random term, while the second is an asymmetric component that measures inefficiency in relation to the frontier.
3. See a description in Boyd and Graham (1986).
4. The Hausman test indicates that this specification is preferable to that of random effects.
5. The result is similar to that obtained in Fernández de Guevara et al. (2005) for an international sample. On the other hand, for the specific case of Spanish banks, the result is the opposite: as size increases, market power decreases, with a non-linear relationship.
6. See European Central Bank (2010).
7. Jiménez et al. (2010) analyse the relationship between market power and banking risk by estimating Lerner indices corrected by the influence of risk. For this purpose, they use confidential information only available to

researchers of the Bank of Spain. They also estimate Lerner indices separately for various banking products using information (also confidential) on rates of interest on new operations.

8. Huybens and Smith (1999) show that inflation artificially increases banking margins and therefore profitability. Demirgüç-Kunt et al. (2004) also comment that inflation and the economic cycle can affect banking margins. Indeed, they find that inflation has a positive effect on financial margins. See also Carbó et al. (2009).

References

Aigner, A., Lovell, C.A.K. and Schmidt, P. (1977) 'Formulation and estimation of stochastics frontier production function models', *Journal of Econometrics*, 86, 21–37.

Berger, A., Klapper, L. and Turk Ariss, R. (2009) 'Bank competition and financial stability', *Journal of Financial Services Research*, 35(2), 99–118.

Bikker, J.A. and Haaf, K. (2002) 'Competition, concentration and their relationship: an empirical analysis of the banking industry', *Journal of Banking and Finance*, 26, 2191–14.

Bikkert, J.A., Spierdijk, L. and Finnie, P. (2007) 'The impact of bank size on market power', manuscript.

Boyd, J.H. and Grahan, S.L. (1986) 'Risk, regulation and bank holding company expansion into nonbanking', *Federal Reserve Bank of Minneapolis Quarterly Review*, 10, 2–17.

Boyd, J.H., and G. De Nicolò (2005) 'The Theory of Bank Risk Taking and Competition Revisited,' *Journal of Finance*, 60, 1329–43.

Boyd, J.H., De Nicolo, G. and Jalal, A. (2006) 'Bank risk taking and competition revisited; new theory and evidence', *Working Paper WP/06/297*, IMF.

Carbó, S., Humphrey, D., Maudos, J. and Molyneux, P. (2009) 'Cross-country comparisons of competition and pricing power in European Banking', *Journal of International Money and Finance*, 28, 115–34.

Carbó, S., Rodriguez, F. and Udell, G. (2009) 'Bank market power and SME financing constraints', *Review of Finance* 13, 309–40.

Courvosier, S. and Gropp, R. (2002) 'Bank concentration and retail interest rates', *Journal of Banking and Finance*, 26, 2155–89.

De Bandt, O. and Davis, E.P. (2000) 'Competition, contestability and market structure in European banking sectors on the eve of EMU', *Journal of Banking and Finance*, 24, 1045–2066.

Dermirgüç-Kunt, A., Laeven, L., and Levine, R. (2004) 'Regulation, market structure, institutions and the cost of financial intermediation', *Journal of Money, Credit and Banking*, 36, 592–622.

European Central Bank (2010) *Financial integration in Europe*, April.

Fernández de Guevara, J. and Maudos, J. (2007) 'Explanatory variables of marker power in the banking system', *Manchester School*, 75, 275–96.

Fernández de Guevara, J. and Maudos, J. (2009) 'Regional financial development and bank competition: effects on firms' growth', *Regional Studies*, 43, 211–28.

Fernández de Guevara, J., Maudos, J. and Pérez, F. (2005) 'Market power in European banking', *Journal of Financial Services Research*, 27, 109–37.

Fernández de Guevara, J., Maudos, J. and Pérez, F. (2007) 'Integration and competition in the European financial markets', *Journal of International Money and Finance*, 26, 26–45.

Fundación de Estudios Financieros (2009) *La reforma de los mercados financieros europeos* (Madrid).

Hellmann, T.F., Murdock, K. and Stiglitz, J. (2000) 'Liberatization, moral hazard in banking and prudential regulation: are capital requirements enough?', *American Economic Review*, 90, 147–65.

Huybens, E. and Smith, B. (1999) 'Inflation, Financial Markets, and Long-run Real Activity', *Journal of Monetary Economics*, 43, 283–315.

Jiménez, G., López, J.A. and Saurina, J. (2010) 'How does competition impact bank risk-taking?' *Working Paper*, Bank of Spain, 1005.

Keeley, M. (1990) 'Deposit insurance, risk and market power in banking', *American Economic Review*, December, 1183–200.

Maudos, J. and Fernández de Guevara, J. (2007) 'The cost of market power in the European banking sectors: social welfare loss vs. inefficiency cost', *Journal of Banking and Finance*, 31, 2103–25.

Meeusen, W. and van den Broeck, J. (1977) 'Efficiency estimation from Cobb-Douglas production function with composed error', *International Economic Review*, 18, 435–44.

Schaeck, K., Cihak, M. and Wolfe, S. (2009) 'Are competitive banking systems more stable?', *Journal of Money, Credit and Banking*, 41, 711–34.

Turk Ariss, R (2010) 'On the implications of market power in banking: Evidence from developing countries,' *Journal of Banking and Finance*, 34, 765–75.

Uhde, A. and Heimeshoff, U. (2009) 'Consolidation in banking and financial stability in Europe: empirical evidence', *Journal of Banking and Finance*, 33, 1299–311.

2
Bank Risk and Analysts' Forecasts

Mario Anolli and Elena Beccalli

2.1 Introduction

The financial crisis has highlighted, *inter alia*, that the financial community as a whole suffered from important limitations and distortions in the perception of risk faced by banks. The distortion materialized in a marked underestimation of risk by the major players in the system: top management, board of directors, rating agencies, regulatory and supervisory authorities, and so on.

Agents subject to regulation tend to adapt their behaviour to minimize its impact; regulatory and supervisory authorities can react to this behaviour by adapting the rules. However, regulatory and supervisory authorities have difficulties in keeping up with players (by generating new rules always fully adapted to current situations), because players have strong financial incentives to minimize the cost of regulation by exploiting the areas of action allowed by the regulation itself. Market discipline, at least ideally, consists of dynamic and highly motivated entrepreneurs, seeking to minimize the cost of regulation to maximize the return on their investment, in the guise of investors, who wish, acting in a competitive market, to maximize the return on their investment per unit of risk taken. In this context, avoiding regulation (gaming the system) would cease to be profitable because it could be immediately identified, and punished, by investors watching the actual risk-taking rather than the formal observance of the rules.

The ability of outsiders to perceive the risk faced by a bank is essential for the functioning of so-called market discipline. In an ideal situation, market discipline sanctions banks that take risk considered to be excessive by increasing the cost of unsecured funding (equity) and subordinated debt (wholesale deposits and bonds) and by lowering the levels of their activity. Market discipline tends, therefore, to moderate the consequences of moral hazard that leads banks to assume the maximum risk (in order to maximize profitability) given the cost of funding. The correction to the banks' incentives realized through market discipline, which makes risk-taking progressively more expensive, would align the incentives with those of society overall, given the known general implications of banking activity. The logic of the *third pillar* of Basel regulation, which promotes transparency in risk communication, does indeed have the objective of strengthening market discipline. According to the third consultative package of Basel 2,[1] 'The purpose of Pillar 3 – market discipline is to complement the minimum capital requirements (Pillar 1) and the supervisory review process (Pillar 2)' by developing 'a set of disclosure requirements which will allow market participants to assess key pieces of information on the scope of application, capital, risk exposures, risk assessment processes, and hence the capital adequacy of the [financial intermediaries]'.

However, market discipline does not seem to have prevented banks from taking excessive amounts of risk in the period preceding the financial crisis that began in summer 2007, by taking insufficient levels of capital resources in respect of the risk taken and by operating with excessive levels of leverage. Clearly, the market was misinformed, or did not react adequately to the available information.

Financial analysts, as a key component of the financial community, should show distinctive ability to perceive the risk taken by (listed) banks. One might indeed expect that analysts, being professionals highly specialized in the study of the financial and economic characteristics of listed companies, are the agents in the best position both to estimate the risk faced by the issuers of securities for which they provide investment recommendations and to perceive, in advance of the rest of the financial community, the variation in risks taken by the issuer (in the case of interest a financial institution) whose securities they closely and thoroughly follow. A good ability to estimate the risk of an issuer should also translate into a ready ability to predict changes in the issuer's profitability.

This chapter aims to explore the accuracy in the perception of risk by financial analysts and whether this ability has shown changes (in the direction of an improvement or a deterioration) in concurrence with the financial crisis.

The chapter is organized as follows. Section 2.2 presents the motivations for this study in light of the literature on analysts' forecasts. Following on, Section 2.3 considers the methodological issues concerning the measurement of analysts' forecast errors and bank risk, and Section 2.4 illustrates the sample and data. Section 2.5 describes the empirical results, and Section 2.6 provides robustness tests. Finally Section 2.7 concludes.

2.2 Literature review

The investigation of the bias and rationality of financial analysts has a long tradition, partly because the forecasts of the key financial parameters (including earnings) made by analysts are collected and stored in specialized databases (such as I/B/E/S, Value Line, Zacks and First Call) and the back-testing of the accuracy of those forecasts has great economic importance and is relatively simple.

The empirical evidence on the accuracy of analysts' forecasts shows that earnings forecasts tend to be biased. For the 1980s and 1990s analysts showed an excessive optimism, and the positive bias in the forecasts could be foreseen on the basis of the available information (see Kothari, 2001). Nevertheless, since the year 2000 there has been a shift towards pessimism (perhaps excessive) in the United States (Heflin *et al.*, 2003; Kadan *et al.*, 2009). This shift is explained by the legislative changes, which on the one hand introduce a limitation in the interrelationships between investment units and research units in investment banks, and on the other hand restrict the flow of private information from management to analysts. Contextually, there is evidence of a shift from optimism to pessimism within the same year (i.e. a reduction of analysts' optimism as the date of the annual earnings announcement approaches).[2] In the investigation of the phenomenon the methodological issues should not be neglected; Gu and Wu (2003) in particular suggest that analysts, in their attempt to minimize the average forecast errors in absolute terms, maximize their utility function by producing an estimate of the median earnings forecast. This results in a rational and expected pessimism in periods of expansion, and vice versa in bad times.

The extensive banking literature on bank risk employs risk measures based on both accounting data and market data. The accounting-based proxies most commonly used are: the number of non-performing loans (Jiménez *et al.*, 2007), the indexes on the degree of bank insolvency, such as the Z-score (Boyd, 1993; Konishi *et al.*, 2004) and the median standard deviation of the rate of return on equity (Boyd, 1993). The market-based proxies relate to systematic risk, bank-specific risk, market risk and interest rate risk (Demsetz and Strahan, 1997; Saunders *et al.*, 1990). Although the construction of proxies based on accounting data is affected by accounting conventions and policies, which may differ between banks and which are not uniform across countries, their use is widespread in the literature.

Despite an extensive literature on both the bias in analysts' forecasts and the measurement of banks' risk based on public (accounting and market) data, less attention has been paid to the role of analysts as a 'bridge' between the market data and their dissemination and interpretation for the evaluation of risk. As far as we are aware, this is the first study to link the two streams of the literature, by investigating the ability of financial analysts to perceive the risk taken by banks and to incorporate this risk into their forecasts.

2.3 Methodology

The methodology is based first on the estimation of analysts' forecast errors and bank risk (derived from relevant accounting data), and then on the investigation of the relationship between these two measures. Our study specifies this relationship both over the overall period under investigation (January 2003 – June 2007) and in two sub-periods around the crisis that began in summer 2007 (pre-crisis: January 2003 – June 2007; acute crisis: July 2007 – March 2009). According to Bank for International Settlements (2010), it has been decided that the acute crisis period ended in March 2009.

2.3.1 Accuracy of analysts' forecasts

The first step requires the estimation of a measure of the accuracy of analysts' forecasts. We first take into consideration earnings, because they are clearly the item on which the financial community focuses most of its attention. Although earnings are subject to accounting conventions, they are the ultimate synthesis of company 'health'. Earnings forecast accuracy is defined as the difference between actual earnings and analysts' earnings forecasts.

In the study, the measure of accuracy is defined as the forecast error of each analyst y for each bank j in each period t (FE_EPS_{yjt}), measured as follows:[3]

$$FE\_EPS_{yjt} = \frac{EPS_{jt} - FEPS_{yjt}}{P_{jt}} \tag{1}$$

where: EPS_{jt} = actual current earnings per share for each bank j for forecast period t;
$FEPS_{yjt}$ = current earnings forecast of each individual analyst y for each bank j for each forecast period t;
P_{jt} = last available stock price for each bank j for period t.

Specifically, we employ two measures of the forecast error according to the type of earnings forecasts used:

a. Mean forecast error, where the forecast EPS is the mean consensus forecast calculated as the mean value of all individual forecasts available from the day of the previous annual earnings announcement till the day of the present annual earnings announcement (as done in Lang and Lundholm, 1993);
b. Last announced forecast error, where the forecast EPS is the last announced consensus forecast calculated from all individual forecasts available from the day of the previous annual earnings announcement till the day of the present annual earnings announcement. When there is more than one forecast released by an analyst during this period, the most recent forecast before the earnings announcement is used in the calculation of the last announced consensus EPS (as used in Simpson, 2010).

2.3.2 Bank risk

In addition to earnings, analysts are also involved in the estimation of bank risk. For the purposes of this study, among the various risk measures used in the literature,[4] we decided to employ a measure of risk based on accounting data, named the Z-Score (Boyd, 1993). This risk measure is a statistic indicating the probability of bankruptcy, and is calculated as follows:

$$Z-score_{jt} = \left\{ \sum_{q=1}^{4} \left[2\pi_{jq} / (A_{jq} + A_{jq-1}) \right] / n + \sum_{q=1}^{4} \left[(E_{jq} + E_{jq-1}) / (A_{jq} + A_{jq-1}) / n \right] \right\} / s_{ROA\,jt} \quad (2)$$

where: π_{jq} = net accounting income after taxes for bank j in each quarter q of year t;
A_{jq} = total assets from the balance sheet for bank j in each quarter q of year t;
E_{jq} = total equity from the balance sheet for bank j in each quarter q of year t;
n = number of sample quarters;

S_{ROAjt} = estimated standard deviation of ROA_j (where $ROA_j = \frac{\pi_j}{A_j}$) for bank j in year t, which is computed as the standard deviation of r over the four quarters q in each year t.

Given that bank risk is a complex and critical variable in our analysis, as a robustness test we also use an alternative measure, namely the standard deviation of the rate of return on assets (ROA) for each bank j, computed as the standard deviation of ROA over the four quarters q in each year t–1.

While higher values of Z-score imply lower risk, higher values of *ROA-Stdev* imply higher risk.

2.3.3 Bank risk and accuracy in analysts' forecasts

It is expected that analysts are able to forecast, in addition to earnings, any change in risk assumed by the banks; this ability would be particularly useful in view of major discontinuities such as those represented by the financial crisis. To test this ability, a preliminary investigation relates to the correlation between forecast errors and the risk indicator (Z-score).

To further examine the relationship between forecast error and bank risk, and to adequately consider the variety of factors that influence the forecast error,[5] we estimate the following regression:

$$\begin{aligned} FE\_EPS_{yjt} &= \alpha_0 + \alpha_1 Risk_{jt-1} + \alpha_2 LEV_{jt-1} + \alpha_3 EPS_{jt-1} \\ &+ \alpha_4 Market\_size_{jt-1} + \alpha_5 B/P_{jt-1} + \alpha_6 Growth_{jt-1} \\ &+ \alpha_7 Past\_return_{jt-1} + \alpha_8 FE\_EPS_{yjt-1} + \alpha_9 Volatility_{jt} + e_{jt} \end{aligned} \quad (3)$$

where: Z-score_{jt-1} = risk measure of the previous year for bank j;

LEV_{jt-1} = leverage (mean value of equity over total assets) of the previous year for bank j;

EPS_{jt-1} = actual current earnings of the previous year for bank j;

$Market\_size_{jt-1}$ = natural logarithm of market value (number of shares outstanding at the end of year t–1 times stock price at the end of year t–1) for bank j;

B/P_{jt-1} = book-to-price ratio of the previous year for bank j, calculated as the last available book price per share at the end of year t–1 and the stock price at the end of year t–1;

$Growth_{jt-1}$ = growth in total assets for bank j, calculated as the difference between $Assets_{t-2}$ and $Assets_{t-1}$, divided by $Assets_{t-2}$;

$Past\_return_{jt-1}$ = past stock raw return for bank j cumulated over a window starting one year before the end of year t–1;

FE_EPS_{yjt-1} = past analysts' forecast error;

$Volatility_{jt-1}$ = past stock volatility for bank *j*, computed as the annualized standard deviation of log over weekly price changes for bank *j*; it measures the range of variation over year *t*.

The inclusion of the control variables is motivated by prior evidence on factors that affect the properties of analysts' forecasts. As there are no studies, as far as we are aware, on the factors that affect the properties of analysts' forecasts specifically in banking, our paper also extends the banking literature in this respect. Frankel and Lee (1998) show that analysts tend to overreact to past growth and book-to price ratio. We thus include book-to-price and asset growth that are observable to the analyst at the time of making the forecast. Abarbanell (1991) shows that analysts do not fully reflect the information in price movements prior to their forecasts; therefore we include past raw return. Kormendi and Lipe (1987) document the persistence of earnings; we therefore include earnings per share of the previous year. Simpson (2010) controls for scale effects; accordingly, we include the market capitalization of each bank at the end of the previous year. Similarly, although no previous studies have analysed the impact of leverage on analysts' forecast errors, we include leverage for two reasons: on the one hand, the banking literature suggests its extreme relevance in the definition of the structural characteristics of banks and its strong pro-cyclicality, and on the other hand new banking regulations (Basel 3) foresee its disclosure from 2015.

All regressions are estimated with pooled cross-sectional time-series data. The standard errors of the coefficient estimates are adjusted for panel-level heteroscedasticity (White's t-statistics) and non-independence of time-series observations (clustering by analyst). As an alternative to the clustering-by-analyst approach, we also estimate the regressions with fixed-analyst effects. Year-indicator variables are included in all regressions to control for fixed-time effects.

2.4 Sample

The sample comprises European listed banks composing the Stoxx600 Banks index over the period January 2003 – March 2009. The construction of the sample required a complex aggregation between different sources: I/B/E/S detail for data on individual analyst forecasts; Datastream for market data on bank stocks (daily closing price, number of outstanding shares) and on the Stoxx600 Bank index (composition in each year, price index); and Compustat Global Financial for quarterly financial statements of the European banks in the sample (i.e. banks composing the Stoxx660 Bank index over the period January 2003 – March 2009).

The sample (Table 2.1) consists of 411 banks in 18 European countries over the period January 2003 – March 2009. Because of the composition of the index, the banking systems with a higher incidence are those of Italy, Spain and the UK.

With regard to analysts' forecasts on the banks under investigation (Table 2.2), the sample consists of 942 analysts over the period, for a total of 36,343 forecasts issued. The average number of forecasts per analyst in each year over the sample period is 38.58, and the average number of forecasts on a given bank in each year is 88.43.

Table 2.1 Number of banks in the sample (by country and year)

Year	2003	2004	2005	2006	2007	2008	2009 (Q1)	Panel
Country								
Austria	1	1	2	2	2	2		10
Belgium	3	3	3	3	4	4	1	21
Denmark	1	2	3	3	3	3		15
Finland	1	1	1	1	1	1		6
France	5	4	3	4	4	4		24
Germany	4	5	5	5	5	4	1	29
Greece	5	5	6	6	6	6		34
Iceland				3	3			6
Ireland	2	3	4	4	3	3	1	20
Italy	13	15	16	14	10	10	1	79
Luxembourg	1	1	1	1	1	1		6
Netherlands	1	1	1	1	1			5
Norway	1	1	1	1	1	1		6
Portugal	3	3	3	3	3	3		18
Spain	3	3	4	5	6	7		28
Sweden	4	4	4	4	4	4		24
Switzerland	3	3	3	4	4	4		21
United Kingdom	11	10	10	10	10	7	1	59
Panel	62	65	70	74	71	64	5	411

Note: The Table shows the number of banks under observation in each year and country over the period 2003–9 (Q1). A bank is included in the sample when it is in the Stoxx600 Bank index in a given year. Data on the index composition are obtained from Datastream.

Table 2.2 Number of analysts' earnings forecasts (by year)

Year	Total number of forecasts	Number of analysts	Number of revisions per analyst	Average number of revisions per bank
2003	5,288	423	12.50	85.29
2004	4,607	381	12.09	70.88
2005	6,985	402	17.38	99.79
2006	5,655	394	14.35	76.42
2007	6,030	422	14.29	84.93
2008	7,508	417	18.00	117.31
2009 (Q1)	270	66	4.09	54.00
Panel	36,343	942	38.58	88.43

Note: Descriptive statistics for each year (2003–9) on (1) total number of earnings forecasts, which occur when there is a change in the value of two consecutive earnings forecasts produced by a given individual analyst, (2) total number of analysts issuing revisions, (3) total number of revisions per analysts and (4) number of revisions per bank. Individual analysts' forecasts are obtained from I/B/E/S. Over the period 2003–9, the total number of revisions is 36,343 and the total number of analysts issuing revisions is 942.

2.5 Empirical results

We first analyse descriptive statistics for analysts' forecast error, bank risk and control variables over the entire period and in each of the two sub-periods (pre-crisis and during the crisis (Tables 2.3 and 2.4). The empirical findings reveal that both the mean forecast error and the last announced forecast error are negative over the entire period, equal respectively to −0.4932 and −0.0240 (Table 2.3). Even more interestingly for our purposes, we find very different results before and during the crisis (Table 2.4). Before the crisis the mean forecast error is positive (and equal to 0.0053); this implies a systematic and modest pessimism by analysts. In contrast, the forecast error becomes very negative (and equal to −1.0065) during the crisis period, thereby indicating a heavy underestimation by analysts of the effects of the crisis on the earnings of banks (alternatively, this result could represent a manifestation of the crisis itself by a decrease in the earnings of banks).

We now turn our attention to bank risk (Table 2.4). The Z-score (a proxy for risk based on accounting measures) showed a significant decrease during the crisis, from an average value of 76.45 to 52.46. Given the measurement procedure for the Z-score (as explained in Equation 2), higher Z-score values suggest lower risk in accounting

Table 2.3 Descriptive statistics of mean and last announced forecast errors (by year)

Mean forecast error					Last announced forecast error				
Year	Mean	Standard dev.	Max	Min	Year	Mean	Standard dev.	Max	Min
2003	0.2726	3.3795	42.6655	−6.9566	2003	0.3198	4.1188	48.9910	−6.9566
2004	−0.1031	1.1859	5.4136	−28.6162	2004	−0.0696	1.1708	7.3882	−28.6162
2005	0.0066	0.1789	1.6867	−1.5080	2005	0.0137	0.1812	2.0921	−1.4846
2006	0.0645	0.2226	2.2249	−0.3915	2006	0.0520	0.2002	2.2371	−0.7592
2007	−0.0767	0.6299	3.5437	−5.9125	2007	−0.0426	0.5984	3.5437	−5.9125
2008	−1.8215	13.0398	54.2227	−176.1159	2008	−0.3945	13.3510	278.3117	176.9680
2009	−1.5080	0.7867	0.4888	−3.2135	2009	−0.9590	1.1590	1.9404	−3.2135
Panel	−0.4932	6.7463	54.2227	−176.1159	Panel	−0.0240	5.7363	278.3117	−176.968

Note: The table shows descriptive statistics for analysts' forecast errors in each year and over the entire period. In the mean forecast error, the forecast EPS is the mean consensus forecast calculated as the mean value of all individual forecasts available from the day of the previous annual earnings announcement till the day of the present annual earnings announcement. In the last announced forecast error, the forecast EPS is the last announced consensus forecast calculated from all individual forecasts available from the day of the previous annual earnings announcement till the day of the present annual earnings announcement. When more than one forecast is released by an analyst during this period, the most recent forecast before the earnings announcement is used in the calculation of the last announced consensus EPS.

Table 2.4 Descriptive statistics of analysts' forecast error, bank risk and control variables

	No. observations	Mean	Standard dev.	Max	Min
Analysts' forecast variables					
Mean forecast error	6,248	–0.4932	6.7463	54.22	–176.1159
Mean forecast error pre-crisis	3,160	0.0053	0.0632	0.2452	–3.4178
Mean forecast error during the crisis	3,078	–1.0065	9.5853	54.2227	–176.1158
Bank risk metric					
Z-score	6,176	130.4982	363.4183	3,684.52	–1569.49
Z-score pre-crisis	6,252	76.4468	200.3349	2,580.62	0.00
Z-score during the crisis	6,252	52.4651	313.9433	3,684.52	–1,569.49
Control variables					
EPS	6,100	7.8820	17.9273	127.1270	–2.2142
Market_size	6,316	23.5254	1.3967	27.20	19.61
B/P	6,216	1,216.3568	2,195.3389	16,438.84	3.09
Growth	6,228	0.1752	0.26117	1.9600	–0.89
Past return	6,316	–0.1019	0.5781	9.1700	–0.95

Note: The table shows descriptive statistics for analysts' forecast errors, bank risk and control variables over the entire period and in each of the two sub-periods (pre-crisis and during the crisis). Z-score is a bank risk measure based on accounting data. EPS is the actual current earnings per share of a bank. Market_size is the natural logarithm of market value (number of shares outstanding at the end of year t–1 times stock price at the end of year t–1) of a bank. B/P is the book-to-price ratio for a bank, calculated as the last available book price per share at the end of year t–1 and the stock price at the end of year t–1. Growth is the growth in total assets for a bank, calculated as the difference between Assetst–2 and Assetst–1, divided by Assetst–2. Past return is the past stock raw return for a bank cumulated over a window starting one year before the end of year t–1.

terms. This suggests a lower risk before the crisis. Instead the Z-score value decreases during the crisis, showing an increase in risk.

Preliminary evidence on the relationship between analysts' forecast errors and bank risk is provided by the comparison of their respective standard deviations (Table 2.4). During the crisis the standard deviation of the risk measure doubles, whereas the standard deviation of mean forecast error increases by a factor approximately equal to 150 (from 0.06 to 9.58). This finding seems particularly interesting, because if the analysts lose accuracy during the crisis (as could be demonstrated by an increase in the dispersion of their forecasts), they could contribute

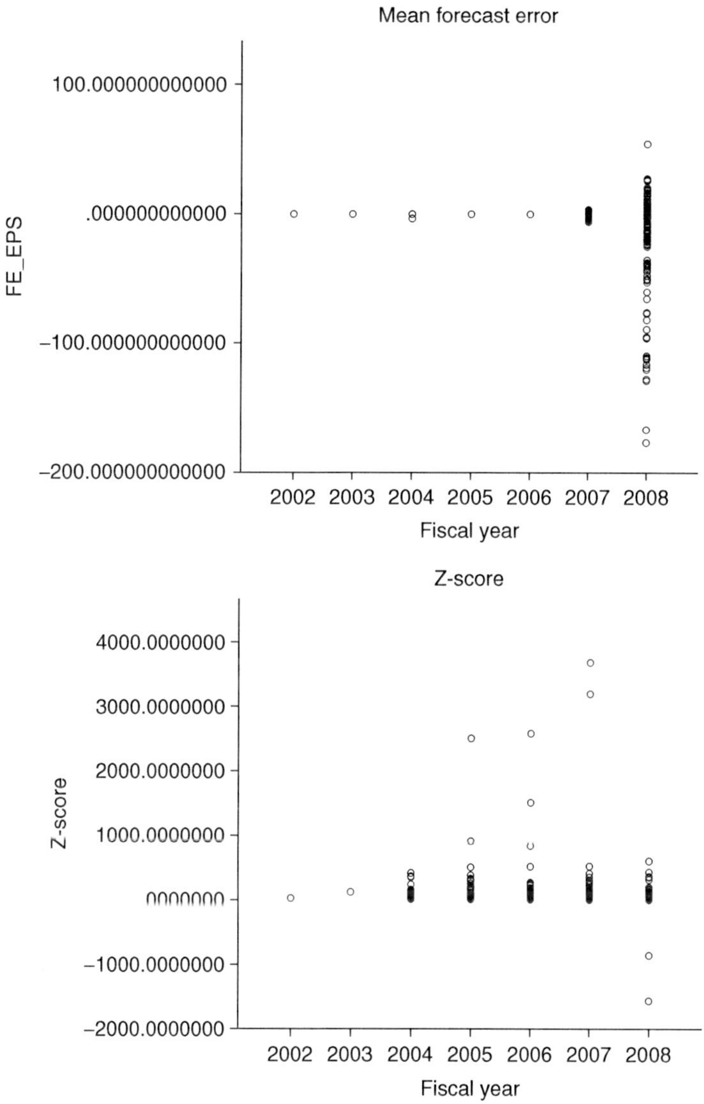

Figure 2.1 Dispersion of mean forecast error and Z-score over the entire period
Source: authors' own estimates

Table 2.5 Correlation analysis

Pearson Spearman	FE_EPS	FE_EPS pre-crisis	FE_EPS acute crisis	Z-score	Z-score pre-crisis	Z-score acute crisis	Beta	Beta pre-crisis	Beta acute crisis	EPS	Market size	B/P	Growth	Past return	Volatility
|FE_EPS|		1.000***	1.000***	−0.207***	−0.089***	−0.276***	0.162***	−0.293***	0.374***	0.257***	−0.184***	0.186***	−0.174***	−0.392***	0.237***
|FE_EPS pre crisis|	1.000***		–	−0.089***	−0.089***	–	0.044**	0.044**		0.078***	0.092***	0.174***	−0.121***	0.070***	.144***
|FE_EPS acute crisis|	1.000***	–		−0.276***	–	−0.276***	0.258***	–	0.258***	0.363***	−0.320***	0.208***	−0.189***	−0.559***	0.138**
Z-score	−0.523***	0.069***	−0.585***		0.241***	0.310***	−0.333***	−0.013	−0.163***	0.078***	0.023	−0.207***	0.174***	0.040***	−0.102**
Z-score pre-crisis	0.069**	0.069***	–	1.000***		–	−0.348***	−0.348***	–	−0.192***	−0.106***	−0.360***	0.157***	−0.110***	−0.136***
Z-score acute crisis	−0.585***	–	−0.585***	1.000***	–		−0.321***	–	−0.321***	0.013	0.090***	−0.108***	0.168***	0.040**	−0.044**
Beta	−0.045***	−0.035**	−0.060***	0.039***	−0.119***	0.111***		0.217***	0.322***	−0.123***	−0.104***	0.263***	−0.168***	−0.035***	0.294***
Beta pre-crisis	0.063***	−0.035**	–	−0.054***	−0.119***	–	0.324***		−0.850***	−0.292***	0.160***	0.0.51***	−0.18***	0.713***	−0.240***
Beta acute crisis	−0.094***	–	−0.060***	0.075***	–	0.111***	0.365***	−0.762***		0.226***	−0.197***	0.089***	−0.070***	−0.706***	0.382***
EPS	−0.241***	0.134***	−0.235***	0.132***	−0.023	0.152***	−0.011	−0.264***	0.250***		0.236***	−0.176***	0.153***	−0.220***	0.083**
Market size	0.066***	0.009	0.075***	−0.107***	−0.169***	−0.080***	−0.078***	0.142***	−0.190***	−0.093***		0.393***	0.073***	0.377***	−0.288**
B/P	−0.302***	0.026	−.322***	−.026*	−.102***	−0.005	0.116***	−.067***	0.144***	0.101***	0.185***		−0.090***	0.052***	−0.089**
Growth	−0.002	0.000	−0.008	0.033**	−0.045**	0.055***	−0.079***	0.005	−0.060***	0.132***	0.048***	0.074***		0.045***	−0.185*
Past return	0.095***	−0.297***	0.146***	−0.037**	0.067***	−0.040**	0.051***	0.551***	−0.508***	−0.301***	0.293***	−0.079***	0.031**		−0.386**
Volatility	−0.041***	−0.018	−0.036**	−0.056***	−0.053**	−0.091***	0.294***	−0.091***	0.291***	0.048**	−0.273***	−0.056***	−0.184**	−0.184***	

Note: Pearson (Spearman) correlation coefficients are presented for mean forecast errors (above for the absolute value of mean forecast errors) the diagonal. * indicates correlation coefficient significant at 10%, ** significant at 5%, and *** significant at the 1% level. Variable definitions are presented in Table 2.4.

to boosting the market perception rather than contributing to a correct interpretation by the market of the issuers' prospects.

Analysing the pattern over time of the two variables of interest (Figure 2.1) confirms a significant increase in the dispersion of the mean forecast error during the crisis, together with a marked trend towards a negative error (i.e. forecasts lower than actual EPS values). With regard to risk, the effect of the crisis is a clear move of the Z-score value towards the lower end side, confirming an increase in the risk level in banking.

To further investigate the relationship between analyst accuracy and bank risk, we estimate the correlation between the bank risk metrics and the mean forecast error, both in absolute terms and in relative terms for the forecast error (Table 2.5). In absolute terms, the correlation indicates a positive relation with bank risk both before and during the crisis, with the only exception being market risk pre-crisis.[6] There is a positive correlation between risk and the ability to predict earnings, and this correlation is particularly pronounced during the crisis. In relative terms, used to infer the presence of optimism vs. pessimism in analysts' forecasts, the correlation pre-crisis is positive (0.069 for the Z-score and 0.063 for beta, all significant at 99 per cent), whereas the same correlation becomes negative during the crisis (respectively equal to −0.585 and −0.094, all significant at 99 per cent). For accounting-based risk, this suggests that lower risk is associated with higher positive forecast errors before the crisis, whereas higher risk is associated with higher negative forecast errors during the crisis. For market-based risk, on the other hand, this suggests that higher risk is associated with higher positive forecast errors before the crisis, whereas lower risk is associated with higher negative forecast errors during the crisis. The unexpected pre-crisis Z-score result requires further analysis, as it would suggest that, in the presence of lower risk, forecast errors increase; in other words, bank risk is a factor that has an effect on forecast errors opposite to that expected in the pre-crisis period.

Scatter plots are then used to get a graphical representation of the relationship between bank risk and mean forecast errors in relative terms, both pre-crisis and during the crisis (Figure 2.2). Before the crisis, mean forecast errors tend to be above zero (i.e. actual EPS values higher than analyst forecasts and thus pessimism by analysts), whereas during the crisis mean forecast errors tend to be lower than zero (i.e. underestimation by analysts of the effects of the crisis). Moreover, the positive pre-crisis forecast errors are positively associated with the Z-score, which means that lower risk is found together with higher pessimism. On the other hand, during the crisis, analysts' perception of risk is as

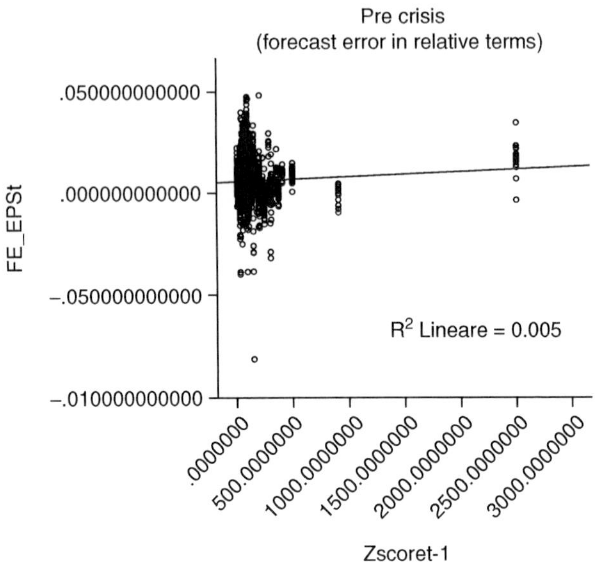

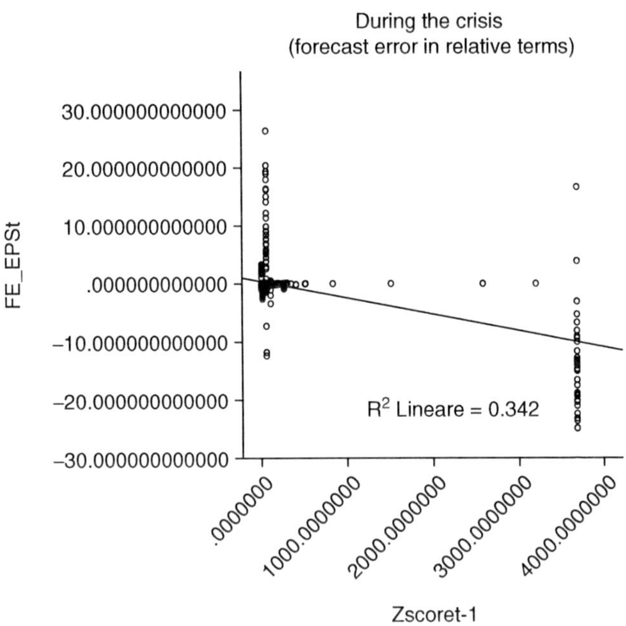

Figure 2.2 Continued

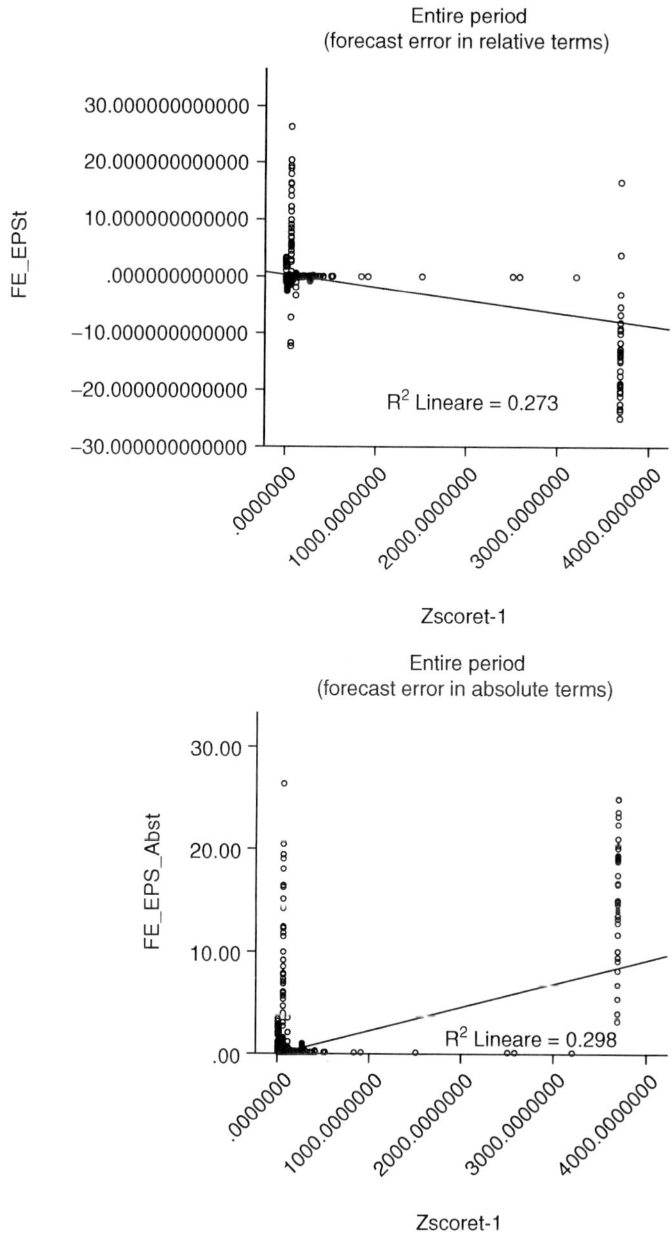

Figure 2.2 Forecast error and bank risk

Source: authors' own estimates

expected: higher risk, higher forecast errors. The surprising results of the correlation analysis are confirmed.

To better investigate the above preliminary evidence, we perform a regression of analysts' forecast errors on Z-score and control variables, by using the analyst-cluster regressions previously outlined in Equation 3. The regression for the entire period is first estimated (Table 2.6, Panel A). The main outcome here is that the coefficient of the Z-score is negative (and statistically significant at 1 per cent), suggesting that a higher Z-score (meaning a lower risk) determines lower forecast errors (i.e., forecast errors are lower in the presence of lower bank risk). Moreover, multicollinearity diagnostic statistics (variance inflation factor, VIF)[7] confirm that no multicollinearity problem affects the variables assumed to be determinants of the analysts' forecast error. Finally, the explanatory power of the model is high (R^2 equals 39.34 per cent).

The estimated coefficients on the control variables indicate the following (Table 2.6, Panel A): the association between prior earnings and analyst forecast bias is positive and in line with the findings of Abarbanell and Bernard (1992) and Mendenhall (1991) on analysts' under-reaction to previous earnings information. The coefficient on market size is negative and significant at 1 per cent, which implies that analysts are more optimistic in their forecasts for bigger banks. The coefficient of the B/P ratio is positive and statistically significant, which implies that analysts are more biased in their forecasts for value stocks (stocks with higher fundamentals in comparison to their market prices) than for glamour stocks. The coefficient on past forecast error (FE_EPS_{t-1}) is negatively related to the current forecast error, implying that analysts' bias does not persist over time. This is not in line with prior research, and it is likely due to the emergence of the crisis during the sample period. The coefficient on asset growth is positive, suggesting that high (low) past growth is positively associated with excessive optimism (pessimism). This is consistent with the evidence from Frankel and Lee (1998). The positive and statistically significant coefficient on past return indicates that analysts under-react to prior stock price performance and predict systematically lower earnings than the actual realizations. This is consistent with the evidence from Abarbanell (1991) that analysts discount previous price change information in their forecasts. Finally, the negative and statistically coefficient on market volatility is unexpected, suggesting that analysts are more biased in the presence of lower levels of market uncertainty at the time when the forecast is made.

In order to identify the existence of any effect of the crisis on the relationship between analysts' forecast error and bank risk, the overall

Table 2.6 Regression of forecast error on bank risk (Z-score) and control variables (entire period)

	Panel A: Entire period (analyst cluster)				Panel B: Pre-crisis (analyst cluster)				Panel C: Acute crisis (analyst cluster)			
	β	Dev.St.	t	VIF	β	Dev. St.	t	VIF	β	Dev. St.	t	VIF
Z-score$_{t-1}$	−0.0028***	0.0001	-41.71	1.08	0.0001	0.0001	0.38	1.08	−0.0033***	0.0004	−8.12	1.10
Leverage $_{t-1}$	−0.8122	1.3329	−0.61	1.14	0.0059	0.0151	0.39	1.12	−6.0563*	3.2548	−1.86	1.25
EPS $_{t-1}$	0.0253***	0.0029	8.68	1.26	0.0006***	0.0001	12.37	1.72	0.0302**	0.0131	2.31	1.26
Market_size $_{t-1}$	−0.1360***	0.0225	−6.04	1.48	−0.0006*	0.0003	−1.82	1.89	−0.2215***	0.0563	−3.94	1.69
B/P $_{t-1}$	0.0001*	0.0001	1.64	1.33	−0.0001	0.0001	−0.23	1.44	0.0001	0.0001	1.35	1.29
Mean forecast error$_{t-1}$	−1.2401***	0.2861	−4.33	1.05	(dropped)				−0.9245	2.2559	−0.41	1.06
Growth $_{t-1}$	0.8869***	0.1416	6.26	1.20	0.0135***	0.0025	5.31	1.09	1.1945***	0.3616	3.30	1.28
Past return $_{t-1}$	0.2978***	0.0941	3.16	2.47	0.0125***	0.0015	8.37	1.04	0.6917***	0.1804	3.83	2.87
Volatility$_{t-1}$	−0.1845**	0.0872	−2.12	2.55	−0.0289***	0.0060	−4.83	1.16	−0.0663	0.0567	−1.17	2.50
(Constant)	3.4272***	0.5501	6.23		0.0190**	0.0087	2.18		5.7858***	1.3822	4.19	
Number of observations	2,919				1,245				1,674			
Number of clusters (analyst)	472				300				350			
R^2	0.3934				0.1730				0.4645			

Note: The table presents results from Equation 3, where risk is an accounting-based measure proxied by Z-score. The equation is estimated with observations pooled across time and analysts. The regression is estimated by using the analyst-cluster model (i.e. the standard errors of the coefficient estimates are adjusted for panel-level heteroscedasticity and non-independence of time-series observations). The equation is estimated both for the pre-crisis period (January 2003 – June 2007) and for the period during the crisis (July 2007 – March 2009). Year-indicator variables are included to control for fixed-time effects. The regression is estimated by using the analyst-cluster model (i.e. the standard errors of the coefficient estimates are adjusted for panel-level heteroscedasticity and non-independence of time-series observations). *indicates a regression coefficient significant at 10%; ** significant at 5%; *** significant at the 1% level. Variable definitions are presented in Table 2.4.

Table 2.7 Regression of forecast error on bank risk (ROA-STDEV) and control variables (pre-crisis and during the crisis)

	Panel A: Pre-crisis			**Panel B: During the crisis**		
	β	**Dev.St.**	**t**	**β**	**Dev.St.**	**t**
(Constant)	5.1411***	1.0144	5.07	150.2768	139.3775	1.08
ROA-Stdev$_{t-1}$	0.2591	0.3689	−0.70	192.2424***	43.8640	4.38
EPS $_{t-1}$	0.0006***	0.0001	13.64	−0.0031	.0136	0.23
Market_size $_{t-1}$	−0.0006*	0.0003	1.79	0.0171	0.0384	0.44
B/P $_{t-1}$	0.0001**	0.0001	2.31	−0.0001	0.0001	−0.27
Mean forecast error$_{t-1}$	–			−2.1146	2.6987	0.78
Growth $_{t-1}$	0.0112 ***	0.0025	4.38	1.0266***	0.3249	3.16
Past return $_{t-1}$	0.0123***	0.0018	6.87	0.2706**	0.1329	2.04
Number of observations	1,264			1,674		
Number of clusters (analyst)	302			350		
Adj-R_2	0.1584			0.0350		

Note: The table presents results from Equation 3, where risk is proxied by ROA-Stdev instead of Z-score. The equation is estimated with observations pooled across time and analysts. The equation is estimated both for the pre-crisis period (January 2003 – June2007) and for the period during the crisis (July 2007 – March 2009). Year-indicator variables are included to control for fixed-time effects. The regression is estimated by using the analyst-cluster model (i.e. the standard errors of the coefficient estimates are adjusted for panel-level heteroscedasticity and non-independence of time-series observations). * indicates a regression coefficient significant at 10%; ** significant at 5%; *** significant at the 1% level. Variable definitions are presented in Table 2.4.

period is split into the pre-crisis period (January 2003 – June 2007) and the acute crisis period (July 2007 – March 2009). As shown in Table 2.6 (Panels B and C), we first observe that the number of observations in the crisis period is higher than the number of observations in the pre-crisis period (1,674 vs. 1,245): this suggests that, even if the crisis period is shorter (seven quarters only) than the pre-crisis period, analysts have been much more active and issued more forecasts than in the entire pre-crisis period. An interesting result emerges regarding the bank risk: the coefficient of the Z-score is not statistically significant in the pre-crisis period, whereas it becomes negative and statistically significant at the 1 per cent level during the crisis. This indicates that bank risk does not affect analysts' forecast errors in the pre-crisis period, so that bank risk is not among the factors that affect the properties of analysts' forecasts. During the crisis, on the other hand, bank risk positively affects analysts' forecast errors, which means that a higher bank risk determines higher analysts' forecast errors. Moreover, the coefficients of the control variables remain the same as for the entire period previously discussed, with one exception only (leverage). Whereas before the crisis leverage did not impact on analysts' forecast errors, it becomes relevant and statistically significant during the crisis: the higher the leverage of the bank, the higher the bias in the analysts' forecasts. Finally, the explanatory power of the model is higher in the crisis period than in the pre-crisis period (R^2 equal respectively to 46.45 per cent and 17.30 per cent).

2.6 Robustness tests

As a first robustness test, we use an alternative accounting-based risk measure, which is the standard deviation of ROA over the four quarters in each year *t–1* (Table 2.7). By splitting the overall sample into the pre-crisis period and the acute crisis period, we find confirmation of the results based on the Z-score: the coefficient of *ROA-Stdev* is not statistically significant in the pre-crisis period, whereas it becomes positive and statistically significant at the 1 per cent level during the crisis. This confirms that bank risk does not affect analysts' forecast errors in the pre-crisis period; however, it does positively affect analysts' forecast errors during the crisis. It is also interesting to note that the explanatory power of the model is lower than that observed when using the Z-score, suggesting that this more sophisticated risk measure is better able to proxy for bank risk (especially during the crisis).

2.7 Conclusions and policy implications

The ability of the market to monitor and regulate risk-taking by banks is a crucial factor for prudential regulation in banking. Several factors, such as financial innovation and internationalization, enable supervisory authorities to rely also on market signals (logic of the Basel third pillar); moreover, an efficient market would be able, if properly informed, to provide automatic adjustments to the risk assumed by banks. For the market to be able to act in such a manner, the market itself must be able to efficiently assess the conditions (especially in terms of risk) of banks and to put in place 'disciplinary actions' in the case of excessive risk-taking by banks.

The present study attempts to answer two research questions:

- whether the market, in its 'information frontier' made by the financial analysts, can properly assess the risk assumed by banks;

- whether the market reacts quickly enough to break up the marked discontinuity determined by a financial crisis.

Empirical preliminary results indicate that:

- analysts are subject to forecast errors, and these errors are not constant over time but tend to grow during phases of market tension;
- the higher risk of banks during the crisis is neither immediately expected by analysts nor quickly built into their forecasts. In contrast, during the crisis, the dispersion in the forecast errors rises markedly and there is an increase in the correlation between forecast errors and risk (i.e., when the risk faced by banks increases, the analysts' forecast error increases too).

Obviously, the ability of the market to estimate and correct bank risk-taking depends on many factors, such as the design of corporate governance specific to each bank and common to the banking industry in which the bank operates (compare, e.g. Italy and the UK). It is obvious here that the governance structure can act either to amplify or to mitigate the effects of information arriving from the market: the presence and extent of implicit or explicit guarantees provided by the government (e.g. too big to fail); the different attitudes of governments (in time and space) tend to 'pollute' the pure market data; the dissemination of additional (and sometimes instrumental) information other than the information originating from the market, such as the information released by the rating agencies. All these factors may influence the outcome of our estimates, and, we suggest, should be the object of future research in the area.

Our findings enable us to state that, in times of crisis, analysts are not able to correctly predict accounting-based measures of bank risk. Excluding explanations based either on a poor systematic ability of the entire community of financial analysts to predict risk or on a distortion of their incentives (expectations management), the results can be interpreted as indicative of an as yet insufficient ability of accounting and market data to provide adequate and timely estimates of the risk faced by issuers in the banking industry. This further emphasizes the importance of pursuing a higher effectiveness in implementing the instructions of the third pillar of Basel 2 (i.e. strengthening the disclosure requirements of banks).

Notes

1. See, among others, Basel Committee on Banking Supervision (2003).
2. The shift in bias within the year is, in turn, explained by two phenomena: expectation management and earnings management (Matsumoto, 2002). In banking, earnings management is conducted by using mainly the loan loss provision at the end of the year.
3. The measure is considered both in relative terms, taking into account the sign (for construction of the indicator, negative and positive values indicate optimism and pessimism respectively), and in absolute terms to capture the magnitude of the error.
4. Other measures of the risk faced by the bank, estimated on the basis of accounting data, could be identified in the median standard deviation of the rate of return on equity (Boyd, 1993) and the number of non-performing loans (Jimenez *et al.*, 2007). Market-based measures are the classical standard deviation of the stock returns, its decomposition into systematic risk (beta) and idiosyncratic risk (Saunders *et al.*, 1990; Demsetz, 1997; Konishi *et al.*, 2004[Query: Konishi and Yasuda in references; please check and amend as necessary]). Another market-based measure of risk is the yield spread, calculated as the difference between the yield on a particular bank bond and a government security of a comparable maturity from the bank's home country (Choi *et al.*, 2010).
5. Among these the literature has already suggested including the book-to-price of the previous year, size, growth in revenues, return and earnings per share of the previous year, and autoregressive values of the error itself.
6. It also interesting to note that the value of the correlation for the Z-score over the entire period of analysis is equal to –0.207 (significant at 99 per cent): the few months of the crisis thus contribute to making the negative correlation much more pronounced.
7. Since, for each independent variable, tolerance = $1 - R^2$, low values indicate high multivariate correlation. The variance inflation factor is 1/tolerance, it is always ≥ 1 and it is equal to the number of times the variance of the corresponding parameter estimate is increased due to multicollinearity compared with its value if there were no multicollinearity. There is no formal cut-off value to use with VIF for determining presence of multicollinearity. Values of VIF exceeding 10 are often regarded as indicating multicollinearity, but in weaker models, which is often the case in logistic regression, values above 2.5 may be a cause for concern.

References

Abarbanell, J.S. (1991) 'Do analysts' earnings forecasts incorporate information in prior stock price changes?', *Journal of Accounting and Economics*, 14(2), 147–65.

Abarbanell, J.S. and Bernard, V.L. (1992) 'Tests of analysts' overreaction/underreaction to earnings information as an explanation for anomalous stock price behavior', *Journal of Finance*, 47(3), 1181–207.

Bank for International Settlements (2010) *80th Annual Report*, June, Basel.
Basel Committee on Banking Supervision (2003), Basel II: The New Basel Capital Accord – Third Consultative Paper (Bank for International Settlements: Basel).
Boyd, J.H. (1993) 'Bank holding company mergers with non-bank financial firms: Effects on the risk of failure', *Journal of Banking and Finance*, 17, 43–63.
Choi, S., Francis, B.B. and Hasan, I. (2010) 'Cross-Border Bank M&As and Risk: Evidence from the Bond Market', *Journal of Money, Credit and Banking*, 42(4), 615–45.
Demsetz, R.S. and Strahan, P.E. (1997) 'Diversification, size, and risk at bank holding companies', *Journal of Money, Credit and Banking*, 29(3), 300–13.
Frankel, R. and Lee, C. (1998) 'Accounting valuation. Market expectation and cross-sectional stock returns', *Journal of Accounting and Economics*, 25, 283–319.
Gu, Z. and Wu, J. (2003) 'Earnings skewness and analyst forecast bias', *Journal of Accounting and Economics*, 35(1), 5–29.
Heflin, F., Subramanyam, K.R. and Zhang, Y. (2003) 'Regulation FD and the Financial Information Environment: Early Evidence', *The Accounting Review*, 78, 1–37.
Jiménez, G., Lopez, J.A. and Saurina, J. (2007) 'How Does Competition Impact Bank Risk-Taking?', *Working paper 2007-23, Federal Reserve Bank of San Francisco*.
Kadan, O., Madureira, L., Wang, R. and Zach, T. (2009) 'Conflicts of Interest and Stock Recommendations: The Effects of the Global Settlement and Related Regulations', *Review of Financial Studies*, 22, 4189–217.
Konishi, M. and Yasuda, Y. (2004) 'Factors affecting bank risk taking: Evidence from Japan', *Journal of Banking and Finance*, 28, 215–32.
Kormendi, R. and Lipe, R.C. (1987) 'Earnings innovations, earnings persistence, and stock returns', *Journal of Business*, 60(3), 323–45.
Kothari, S.P. (2001) 'Capital market research in accounting', *Journal of Accounting and Economics*, 31, 105–231.
Lang, M.H. and Lundholm, R.J. (1993) 'Corporate disclosure policy and analyst behavior', *The Accounting Review*, 71(4), 467–92.
Matsumoto, D.A. (2002) 'Management's incentives to avoid negative earnings surprises', *The Accounting Review*, 77, 483–514.
Mendenhall, R.R. (1991) 'Evidence on the possible underweighting of earnings related information', *Journal of Accounting Research*, 29(1), 170–79.
Saunders, A., Strock, E. and Travlos, N.G. (1990) 'Ownership structure, deregulation, and bank risk taking', *Journal of Finance*, 45(2), 643–54.
Simpson, A. (2010) 'Analysts' Use of Non-financial Information Disclosures', *Contemporary Accounting Research*, 27, 249–288.

3
Foreign Banks in Central Eastern Europe: Impact of Foreign Governance on Bank Performance

Ewa Miklaszewska and Katarzyna Mikolajczyk

3.1 Introduction

This research belongs to a vast body of literature analysing the impact of foreign capital on the bank performance of Eastern European countries. This topic has attracted considerable attention in the past, with most studies in the literature stressing the positive consequences of foreign capital for bank efficiency and overall market competitiveness. Our aim, however, is to look beyond short-term impact on profitability and instead carry out research into a broader question, namely: has foreign capital brought more fundamental, long-term changes to Eastern European banking markets through its use of different strategies, business models and corporate governance principles, imported from the home countries of foreign owners? A related question is whether the type of entry matters, as foreign banks differ in the way they entered the so-called emerging markets, opting either for a model of limited presence in many countries (wholly controlled subsidiary model) or for a strong retail presence in selected countries (majority shareholder model). The former's advantage over competitors is its decisiveness and technological superiority: ability to act quickly and build strategy around transfer of technology and managerial skills across borders. The latter's strong points are local flexibility, better customer relationship and longer time frame for strategic decisions.

Thus, the main research questions posed in this chapter are: which characteristics are more important for successful bank performance in Eastern Europe (bank home country corporate governance and business model or host country macroeconomic and institutional characteristics);

and which business model works better in EE banking (broad retail-based with partial foreign control, or limited subsidiary wholly foreign owned). The analysed period consists of two phases: the post-EU accession period of dynamic economic growth and the period of global economic and financial collapse of 2007–9. This raises a further question about how foreign-owned banks performed in Eastern Europe, not only during a boom period, but also in times of global financial collapse.

This chapter concentrates on a large and relatively homogeneous group of Central Eastern European Countries, CEE-5, characterized by a similar stage of institutional development, macroeconomic potential and financial reform. When analysing CEE banks, the chapter uses a database of the 96 largest retail/universal banks operating in CEE-5, of which 56 were wholly foreign-owned, 15 majority foreign-owned, 15 privately owned and 10 state-owned domestic banks. Of the foreign banks, 17 came from Austria, 14 from Belgium and the Netherlands (together), nine each from Germany, France and Italy, eight from the US and five from other countries (Table 3.A1 in the Appendix). The data came from the Banscope database, supplemented by other sources.

The chapter is organized into seven sections. Section 3.2 contains a review of the literature, Section 3.3 characterizes the analysed group of countries, Section 3.4 contains a description of the sample and research methodology, and Sections 3.5 and 3.6 present the empirical results of regressions and DEA models. The final section presents the conclusions.

3.2 Corporate governance and bank business model: literature review

The financial literature pays a great deal of attention to the question of bank performance, whose assessment, historically, was frequently based on isolated profitability indicators. However, the 2007–9 global financial crisis negatively verified bank assessment methods, particularly those which concentrated on isolated variables, such as short-term profitability (Bikker and Bos, 2008). The crisis highlighted certain fundamental problems underlying the operations of large, global banks, such as the over-dependence on risky strategies and wrong business models of large banks, accompanied by the pursuit by central banks of loose monetary policies, ignoring asset price inflation in the pre-crisis period. As Allen *et al.* (2009a) have pointed out, banks remained susceptible to panics and runs in spite of an increase in bank complexity and innovations in the transfer of credit risk over the last two decades. The difference – as the recent crisis has made clear – is that the last run involved the drying up of liquidity in the short-term inter-bank markets (a wholesale run) instead of, or in addition to, depositor withdrawals (a retail run). Thus the financial crisis has highlighted the importance of selecting a sound business model, based on the bank's own depository base, as part of strategy selection.

Despite the trend towards globalization in recent years, the financial structures and corporate principles of different economies remain diverse. Allen *et al.* (2009b) have illustrated this by conducting a management survey in selected countries, which shows a persistent, striking difference in corporate governance principles. In their research, they asked business executives which of the two following views would be the most prevalent in their firms: one, executives should maintain dividend payments, even if that meant laying off a number of employees; or, two, executives should maintain stable employment, even if that meant they had to reduce dividends. In response, managers from Japan and continental Europe pointed strongly to job security (Japan 97 per cent, Germany 59 per cent, France 60 per cent) in contrast to managers in the UK and the US, where 89 per cent of respondents opted for dividends. Thus, the source of bank foreign capital in CEE banking should matter, in terms of bigger stress on profitability in banks controlled by capital from shareholder-based countries, and more stable results and strategies in banks from stakeholder-based countries. There is also a prevailing view that the Anglo-Saxon system of corporate governance (shareholder system) works well in boom periods but has undesirable macroeconomic consequences in times of crisis, while the stakeholder system works better in downturns (Allen *et al.*, 2009b). The list of largest global banks by assets in 2006 (pre-crisis) and 2009 (post-crisis) seems to support this view (Table 3.1), although US and British-based banks are, on the other hand, more flexible in restructuring and regaining profitability: the best 2006 to 2009 profit differentials were recorded by Wells Fargo, RBS and Citigroup.

There is a substantial body of literature analysing the impact of foreign capital on bank efficiency and the factors that determine the efficiency of foreign and domestic banks. Numerous studies by A. Berger have analysed the sources of competitive advantages of foreign banks. Berger *et al.* (2005) point up the 'benefits of globalization', when banks follow their clients, or enter a country based on the attractiveness of the host market. Berger *et al.* (2000) observe that foreign banks tend to be more efficient than domestic ones in emerging markets, although not necessarily in developed markets. In general, foreign bank penetration is expected to increase competition and bring superior technology and

Table 3.1 Top 10 world banks by total assets and tier-one capital 2006 and 2009, $billion

Total Assets, 2006		Tier-One Capital, 2006		Total Assets, 2009		Tier-One Capital, 2009	
UBS	1,964	Bank of America	91	BNP Paribas	2,965	Bank of America	160
Barclays	1,957	Citigroup	90	RBS	2,750	J.P. Morgan	133
BNP Paribas	1,897	HSBC	88	Credit Agricole	2,441	Citigroup	127
Citigroup	1,882	Credit Agricole	85	HSBC	2,364	RBS	124
HSBC	1,861	J.P. Morgan	81	Barclays	2,235	HSBC	122
Credit Agricole	1,818	Mitsubishi FG	68	Bank of America	2,223	Wells Fargo	94
RBS	1,711	ICBC	59	Deutsche Bank	2,162	ICBC	91
Mitsubishi FG	1,579	RBS	59	J.P. Morgan	2,032	BNP Paribas	91
Deutsche Bank	1,483	Bank of China	52	Mitsubishi FG	2,026	Santander	82
Bank of America	1,460	Santander	47	Citigroup	1,857	Barclays	81

Source: Top 1000 World Banks ranking for 2007 and 2010, www.thebankerdatabase.com. Accessed on 4 April 2011.

efficiency gains (Bonin *et al.*, 2004). Lensink *et al.* (2008) reviewed studies analysing foreign capital impact and then analysed recent evidence in over 100 countries, finding that proper institutional development in host countries is crucial if foreign capital is to bring long-term efficiency gains. He concluded that, if the institutional distance between the host and the home country governance becomes smaller, foreign banks operate more efficiently. His research clearly indicates the importance of well-developed institutions for the efficient operation of foreign banks.

However, many internationally oriented banks enter other countries, particularly fast-growing emerging markets, not so much seeking for efficiency, but rather as market seekers: to find new customers for their products. Principally in a search for growth, they opt to enter fast-growing markets where they can obtain a large market share quickly. Venzin (2009) describes this as a paradox of growth: economies of scale and scope in the retail banking market may in many cases have a neutral effect on bank performance, while unfocused growth may diminish the competitiveness of the firm. Ways and motives of foreign entry are analysed by Naaborg (2007) and Hryckiewicz and Kowalewski (2007), who tested the hypothesis that foreign bank involvement was positively related to foreign client presence, market opportunities, low efficiency of domestic banks and favourable regulations in the CEE countries. The evidence regarding the stability and profitability of banks with different ownership patterns is more ambiguous. Some research indicates that a higher share of government ownership results in higher banking fragility and crisis probability (Barth *et al.*, 2004).

Corporate governance can be analysed both at a macro and at a micro level. In the US, the term governance typically refers to the methods shareholders use to reduce managerial agency costs, such as board composition, voting rules or stakes held by managers. Studies of governance in developing nations often focus on the role of ownership in reducing these agency problems. This chapter does not concentrate on managerial decision and preference – whether firms are run predominantly in the interest of shareholder or stakeholder – but focuses instead on the indirect measurement of corporate governance, related to selection of bank business model and risk/return preferences by major shareholder. Like Williams and Nguyen (2005) and Berger *et al.* (2005), it analyses governance in terms of bank ownership: the business model and corporate principles brought in by the foreign owner.

The term 'business model' is a broad concept, referring to the logic of the firm in the way it operates and how it creates value (profits) for its stakeholders (Casadesus-Masanell and Ricart, 2009). The selection of a proper business model is an important strategic decision, as shown by research by Weill *et al.* (2005), in which they analysed the 1,000 largest US firms by dividing them first into four types of business models: creators, distributors, landlords and brokers; and further dividing them according to the type of asset involved: financial, physical, intangible, or human. Their results indicated that certain business models perform better than others in terms of operating income, return on invested capital and return on assets. For banks, new insights into the selection of bank business model have been provided by Demirguc-Kunt and Huizinga (2009), who analysed sources of bank risk and return in universal and specialized bank business models, based on a group of publicly quoted banks in 101 countries in the period 1995–2007. They focused on the implications of bank activity (business model) and short-term funding strategies for bank risk and return, looking in particular at the traditional bank model (deposit/loans-oriented) versus models based on a large proportion of non-interest income and non-depository sources of funds. Like Stiroh (2004), they found that traditional banks are low-risk, and, although their expansion into non-interest incomes financed by non-depository funds may offer some diversification benefits, it is nevertheless a very risky strategy, as measured by Z-score. Citibank CEO V. Pandit illustrated this by saying that 'being a supermarket is not a strategy', but it took the Citigroup over a decade to realize this (Euromoney, July 2010).

3.3 Macroeconomic characteristics of CEE-5 countries

The term 'Eastern Europe' is very broad and encompasses a number of groups, in many cases largely heterogeneous:

- Central Eastern Europe (CEE): a group of countries that entered the EU in 2004 (Poland, Hungary, the Czech Republic, Slovakia and Slovenia), some of them members of the Eurozone (Slovenia 2007, Slovakia 2009). These countries display the highest GDP per capita and the highest share of foreign investors in the banking sectors, as well as the highest degree of financial intermediation;
- Baltic countries: Lithuania, Latvia, Estonia, members of the EU since 2004;
- South Eastern Europe (SEE): the EU member states of 2007: Romania and Bulgaria, EU candidate Croatia, and the countries of the Western Balkans: Serbia, Bosnia and Herzegovina, Albania and Kosovo;
- Commonwealth of Independent States (CIS): Russia, Ukraine and Belarus.

In the pre-crisis period, the new EU members were perceived as part of a dynamically growing 'emerging world', characterized by spectacular GDP growth. These countries were also given the historical label of 'transition countries', reflecting their aim to move from a state-controlled economy to one which was privately controlled. In the banking sector, this in most cases meant moving from state control to foreign control, as approximately 70 per cent of the CEE banking market is currently controlled by foreign banking groups. In this it is quite distinct from the emerging Asian economies, and comparable only to the Latin American experience. In the post-crisis literature, the most frequently used descriptor is the geographical term 'East European Countries'. This chapter concentrates on the large and relatively homogeneous group of Eastern European Countries CEE-5, which are at a similar stage of institutional and financial development (Table 3.2).

Table 3.2 CEE macroeconomic and banking key figures (2008)

	Population, million	GDP/ cap PPP, Euro	Banking Assets, billion Euro	No. of banks	Bank C5	Loans as % of GDP	Foreign Currency Loans, % of TL	TL as % of TD	NPL % of TL	Market share of foreign banks, %
Czech Republic	10	20,200	154	37	62	56	14	81	2.8	88
Hungary	10	15,200	126	38	54	59	64	136	2.9	83
Poland	38	13,800	262	70	44	46	34	118	4.5	67
Slovakia	5	17,600	63	26	71	47	22	77	2.9	96
Slovenia	2	23,300	47	19	59	90	10*	88	1.6	29

Note: Data for 2007 (entry to Eurozone), in the previous years above 50%.

Source: Data based on central bank figures and CEE Banking Sector Report, Raiffeisen Research, RZB Group, June 2009.

Although the Central and Eastern European banking market is relatively small, it nevertheless has strong growth potential: its low degree of bank intermediation presents an attractive prospect, with the result that foreign banks invested heavily in the CEE banking sector right from the beginning of the transition period. Austrian banks were among the first to enter CEE, followed by Italian and later Belgian and French banks. Now, with most of the banking sectors in CEE already in the hands of international banking groups, there are only a few larger state-owned banks left, mostly in Poland and in Slovenia. However, investment in CEE also carried potential risks, mainly connected with macroeconomic imbalances, exchange rate volatility and credit risk. As a result, major global players, such as Citigroup or HSBC, had a much lower level of involvement in the region than banks from regions with geographic or historical proximity, such as Italy or Austria (Table 3.3).

In the post-EU accession period, CEE countries enjoyed a rapid economic growth until 2007 (Table 3.4) and high bank profitability (Table 3.5), which contributed to the increased well-being of their citizens, as measured by an increase of GDP per capita. As a result of the global crisis of 2007–9, economic growth collapsed, just as it did in highly developed countries (Figure 3.1). The most affected region was the Baltic countries, and among the CEE-5 Slovenia and Hungary. The sharpest decline in output was recorded in Slovakia, which had seen very dynamic growth before the crisis, while Poland managed to maintain positive GDP growth in 2009. Although the forecast for 2010 for most EE countries is positive, some foreign banks active in Eastern Europe have scaled down or sold their operations in the region, in many

Table 3.3 CEE-17* largest players, 2008

	Assets, Euro billion	Countries of presence	CEE-17 % share of group assets
UniCredit, Italy	121.6	19	12
Raiffeisen, Austria	85.4	16	54
Erste, Austria	79.3	7	39
KBC, Belgium	71.6	12	20
SocGen, France	65.9	16	6
Intesa SP, Italy	42.5	11	7
OTP, Hungary	35.2	9	100

Note: *CEE-17: Poland, Hungary, Czech Republic, Slovakia, Slovenia, Lithuania, Latvia, Estonia, Romania, Bulgaria, Croatia, Bosnia-Herzegovina, Serbia, Turkey, Ukraine, Russia and Kazakhstan.

Source: UniCredit Group CEE Strategic Analysis, CEE Research.

Table 3.4 Growth rate of GDP, percentage change on previous year

	2000	2001	2002	2003	2004	2005	2006	2007	2008	2009	2010f
Czech Republic	3.6	2.5	1.9	3.6	4.5	6.3	6.8	6.1	2.5	−4.1	1.6
Hungary	4.9	3.8	4.1	4.0	4.5	3.2	3.6	0.8	0.8	−6.7	0
Poland	4.3	1.2	1.4	3.9	5.3	3.6	6.2	6.8	5.1	1.7	2.7
Slovenia	4.4	2.8	4.0	2.8	4.3	4.5	5.9	6.9	3.7	−8.1	1.1
Slovakia	1.4	3.5	4.6	4.8	5.1	6.7	8.5	10.5	5.8	−4.8	2.7
CEE-5 average	3.7	2.8	3.2	3.8	4.7	4.9	6.2	6.2	3.6	−4.4	1.6
Baltic average	6.7	7.4	7.1	8.3	7.8	9.3	10.2	8.9	−2.1	−15.5	−1.1
South EE average	3.9	2.3	4.0	4.6	5.9	4.7	5.8	6.0	5.2	−4.6	0.4
EU-15 average	3.9	1.9	1.2	1.2	2.3	1.8	3.0	2.8	0.3	−4.3	0.9

Note: f = forecast.

Source: Eurostat, November 2010.

Table 3.5 CEE-5 bank characteristics (percentage)

	ROA			ROE			NPL/TL			C/I ratio		
	2006	2008	2009	2006	2008	2009	2006	2008	2009	2006	2008	2009
Czech Republic	1.2	1.2	1.5	23,4	21.7	26.0	3.7	3.3	5.3	53	54	42
Hungary	1.5	0.8	1.1	23.8	11.6	14.8	2.6	3.0	5.9	54	59	42
Poland	1.7	1.6	1.2	22.5	21.2	11.8	7.4	4.4	7.0	63	57	56
Slovakia	1.3	1.0	0.7	16.6	14.1	8.4	3.2	3.2	4.3	57	60	57
Slovenia	1.3	0.7	0.5	15.1	8.1	6.3	2.5	1.8	2.3	56	55	59
50 largest European banks	0.5	0.4	−0.2	14.5	12.1	−8.4	1.9	3.0	n.a.	60	76	n.a.

Note: ROA (Return on Assets), ROE (Return on Equity), NPL (Non-Performing Loans), TL (Total Loans), C/I (Cost Income Ratio).

Source: EU Banking Sector Stability Reports 2005–10 and IMF GFSR April 2010.

cases as a consequence of domestic problems rather than worries about the host countries' stability.

Foreign banks entered emerging countries in two main ways: either by creating a global network bank with a limited presence in many countries, such as Citigroup or HSBC, or by pursuing a 'go-native' model, with a deep retail presence in selected countries (*The Economist*, 13 May 2010). The latter model was pursued successfully by Santander and BBVA in Latin America, and later replicated by UniCredit (UCG)

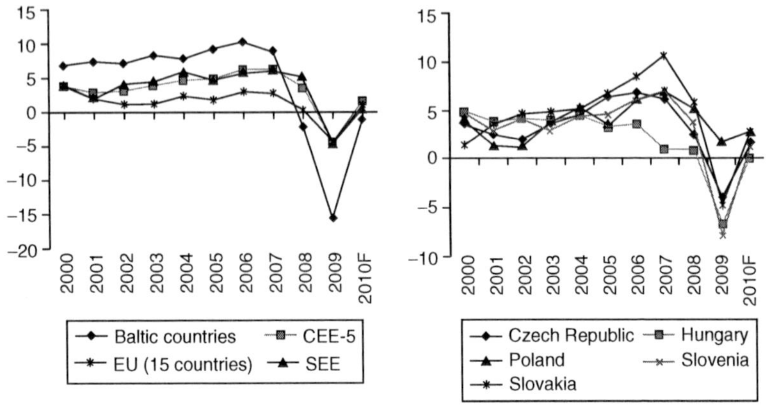

Figure 3.1 EE and CEE-5 countries' growth rate of GDP, percentage change on previous year

Source: Eurostat, November 2010.

Table 3.6 Top three largest banks by assets in CEE-5 (major shareholder)

CEE-5:	1	2	3
Poland	PKO BP/State	PeKaO SA/UCG	BRE/Comerzbank
Hungary	OTP/foreign diverse	K&H/KBC	CIB/Intesa SP
Czech Republic	Ceska Sporitelna/ Erste	Ceskoslovenska Obchodni Banka (CSOB)/ UCG	Komercni Banka/ SocGen
Slovakia	Slov Sporitelna/Erste	VUB/Intesa SP	Tatra/RZB
Slovenia	Nova Ljubljanska Banka (NLB)/State and KBC	Nova Kreditna Banka NKB/ State	Abanka Vipa/ Local priv.

Source: UniCredit Group CEE Strategic Analysis, CEE Research.

in Eastern Europe, which acquired controlling stakes in large retail banks in Poland, the Czech Republic, Bulgaria and Croatia (Table 3.6). The view has been expressed that concentration of assets in one region reduces gains from international expansion; however, this is not supported by case studies of Santander in Latin America or Unicredit in Eastern Europe (Guillen and Tschoegl, 2008). Moreover, Van Hoose (2010) quotes research suggesting that relationship banking is the prime source of banks' comparative advantage in an international context also.

3.4 Research hypothesis, data and methodology

The main goal of the chapter is to analyse whether foreign capital has brought more fundamental, long-term changes to EE banking markets through its use of different strategies, business models and corporate governance principles imported from home countries of foreign owners. To this end, we analysed the following major questions:

- Does the method of bank entry to CEE markets matter? Which business model works better in CEE banking: a retail-based one with partial foreign control, or a wholly foreign-controlled limited subsidiary model?
- Are the remaining state-owned banks and domestic, privately controlled banks less efficient than foreign banks in CEE?
- Which characteristics are more important for a successful bank performance in CEE: home country discipline (corporate governance model) or host country macroeconomic characteristics?
- How is foreign bank performance in CEE related to the global financial crisis?

To assess the importance of macroeconomic environment, banks were grouped by the host CEE-5 markets. To assess the corporate governance models, they were grouped by the ownership structure, distinguishing the following subgroups:

- *state-controlled banks*, where the state was directly or indirectly the major shareholder; special government credit institutions were not included;
- *domestic banks*, where the majority shareholder came from one of the CEE-5 countries;
- *foreign-owned banks*, with a foreign bank as the majority shareholder. This group was further divided into *wholly-owned foreign banks* (F_WO) with the share of the main investor higher than 90 per cent, and *majority-owned foreign banks* (F_MO).

The database contained the bank-level data from the Bankscope database, supplemented with the country-level data. The following selection criteria were used:

- *geographic region*: Central and Eastern European countries: Poland, Hungary, the Czech Republic, the Slovakia Republic, Slovenia;

- *period of time*: 2004–9. Some banks were lacking certain data for 2009. The Z-score in particular was calculated only if the necessary data in three-year rolling time windows were available for three subsequent years;
- *bank specialization*: commercial banks, including some banks wrongly classified in Bankscope as cooperative banks and excluding narrowly specialized mortgage banks;
- *the size of a bank*: a national threshold was imposed of at least 0.25 per cent of the total country assets for 2008, which meant that in Poland banks with assets above 1,000 million Euro were included, while in Slovakia and Slovenia this figure was above 150 million Euro. Banks included in the sample are characterized in Table 3.A1 in the Appendix.

The chapter analyses bank governance in terms of business models and strategies imposed by banks' strategic owners. The analysis focuses on two aspects of bank performance: efficiency and stability. Efficiency is measured by traditional profitability ratios: return on assets and return on equity, non-parametric DEA model and selected regression. Profitability ratios were calculated as arithmetical or weighted averages; for weighted average, the size of bank (i.e. its assets) was used as the weight. To measure bank safety, Z-score, an index of bank sensitivity to risk (default), was used. This points up the riskiness of volatility of returns and is based on the notion that the source of default lies in losses which are not covered by adequate capital. Thus Z-score can be interpreted as the distance from a default, measured by standard deviation of profits expressed by ROA. The value of Z-score is determined by the capitalization (equity capital to assets ratio, CAR) as well as the level and stability of profits. The higher the average ROA and CAR are in a given period, and more stable the returns, the higher the Z-score, and the safer the bank. Z-score was calculated in three-year rolling windows, allowing it to record a gradual decrease in capitalization and a rapid increase in variability of profits in the crisis-related periods.

$$Z - score = \frac{ROA + CAR}{\sigma_{ROA}} \tag{1}$$

where: ROA = return on assets ratio, average calculated in three-year time window; CAR = equity capital to assets ratio, average calculated in three-year time window; σ_{ROA} = standard deviation of ROA, calculated in three-year time window.

To analyse the determinants of bank performance, two econometric regressions were estimated, with explanatory variables including bank-level and country-level data. Bank-level variables included:

- the size of bank, expressed by the logarithm of total assets,
- the growth rate of total assets,
- the level of capitalization, measured by equity capital to total assets ratio,
- the cost efficiency (cost to income ratio),
- the assets structure, expressed by the share of loans in total assets,
- the financing structure, expressed by bank deposits and short-term funding to total assets,
- the profits structure, expressed by non-interest income to gross revenue.

Macroeconomic variables included GDP per capita, the real GDP growth rate, C5 index of concentration in the banking sector, the share of foreign capital in banking sector and the rate of inflation. The macroeconomic data were taken from the IMF (International Monetary Fund), ECB (European Central Bank) and Eurostat databases or publications. In regressions some dummy variables were used, indicating the home country of foreign investors or the type of ownership.

Bank performance was further analysed by employing Data Envelopment Analysis, a non-parametric linear programming method, which seeks out inefficiencies by identifying the best practice production frontier. Efficiency measures generated by DEA are within-sample scores between 0 and 1, calculated relative to the frontier. Constant Returns to Scale (CRS) models measure the technical efficiency (TE), scores assuming that all firms are operating at an optimal scale. TE can be decomposed into two parts: pure technical efficiency (PTE) and scale efficiency (SE), applying Variable Returns to Scale (VRS) models. DEA models can be input-oriented or output-oriented. The former identify technical inefficiency as a proportional reduction in input usage, while keeping output level constant (a concave production frontier), the latter as a proportional increase in output quantities, with input levels held constant (a convex production function) (Coelli *et al.*, 2005). The chapter uses an input-oriented DEA model, which applies an income-based specification of inputs and outputs, following Sturm and Williams (2002, 2005), with interest expenses and non-interest expenses as inputs and net interest income and non-interest income as outputs.

3.5 Empirical results: basic ratios for CEE-5 banks

In the analysis of profitability ratios (Table 3.7), the results for banks in CEE-5 were distinctly higher than in the EU-15 countries, where in 2004–7 ROA was around 0.5 per cent (IMF, 2010). For 2008, bank profitability decreased in CEE countries, but again less than in old Europe.

In the CEE sample (Figure 3.2), Polish and Hungarian banks had the highest ROA, although in 2009 they were outperformed by Czech banks, which had exceptionally stable results throughout the period. In contrast, the Slovenian and Slovakian banks had the lowest ROA. In the last two analysed 'crisis' years in all CEE-5 countries, with the exception of Czech banks, the ROA fell rapidly. Looking at the ownership structure (Figure 3.3), banks controlled by the state (as a major shareholder) appeared to be the least profitable, while the private domestic banks achieved better ROA ratios then foreign-owned ones, both wholly and partially controlled. Following Berger *et al.* (2000), we also analysed the source of competitive advantage of the foreign banks, defined in their paper as global advantage theory not only in an absolute but in a limited version – after decomposition of data according to home country of banks operating in CEE. In this configuration the most profitable (with the advantage disappearing in 2009, however) were banks controlled by American owners, and above average were banks with French and Italian investors, while the worst results were those of Belgian and Dutch-controlled banks.

Analysing CEE-5 bank stability, as measured by Z-score (Figure 3.4), we can clearly see the impact of the global financial crisis: a dramatic decrease of this index in the 2007–9 period for all countries. Before the crisis, Polish banks had the lowest Z-score, while the highest was achieved by Slovakian banks, mainly due to the low variability of ROA. A similar tendency of gradual decrease in the Z-score index can be observed when comparing stability of banks grouped by major shareholders (Figure 3.5), the steepest for state-controlled banks. When it came to the home countries of foreign capital (Figure 3.6), Austrian banks in the CEE had the highest Z-score until 2008, while Italian-controlled ones were most stable and safe during the whole period. In the crisis period of 2007–9, the worst results were recorded by German and Belgium/Dutch banks. Before the crisis, the level of Z-score for banks wholly owned by foreign investors was distinctly superior to that of foreign majority shareholder banks, but decreased to almost the same level in 2007–9 (Figure 3.7).

Table 3.7 Profitability ratios for analysed banks by host countries and by ownership structure (major shareholder), in per cent

	2004	2005	2006	2007	2008	2009	2004	2005	2006	2007	2008	2009
	ROAE – average, %						ROAA – average, %					
1. Host CEE countries:												
- Czech Republic	9.6	14.3	13.5	19.5	17.3	13.0	0.80	1.09	0.95	1.08	1.20	0.93
- Hungary	23.2	18.8	17.3	15.1	9.7	3.5	2.29	1.78	1.44	1.29	0.96	0.33
- Poland	12.6	15.9	16.8	19.3	14.3	4.8	1.54	1.85	2.32	2.37	1.43	0.55
- Slovenia	11.3	7.3	8.4	11.9	5.7	2.0	1.31	0.80	0.82	1.04	0.55	0.30
- Slovakia	9.3	28.4	21.1	14.0	2.2	–2.2	0.79	0.75	0.93	1.00	0.49	–0.10
2. Ownership structure:												
- Domestic_State	10.0	11.0	11.7	9.7	1.5	1.7	0.91	0.99	1.01	0.76	0.34	0.17
- Domestic_Private	7.7	11.4	11.5	16.6	11.4	8.0	1.17	1.28	1.94	2.12	1.26	0.83
- Austria	16.4	12.5	13.3	15.2	14.0	6.1	1.14	0.92	0.97	1.06	0.90	0.42
- Belgium and Netherlands	9.6	29.7	21.1	16.4	–0.5	–0.3	0.67	0.63	0.68	0.94	0.13	0.09
- Germany	8.5	9.4	9.3	14.6	9.5	0.6	1.03	0.93	0.86	1.41	0.77	0.13
- France	22.2	17.3	19.7	28.0	18.5	3.3	2.21	2.07	1.72	1.71	1.61	0.11
- Italy	14.9	15.0	16.6	16.2	17.1	8.6	1.39	1.35	1.47	1.26	1.54	0.85
- the US	24.3	22.9	20.7	19.0	16.0	5.7	3.41	2.91	2.60	2.36	2.06	0.92
- Others	9.6	13.5	12.6	12.4	10.9	3.8	0.98	1.45	1.35	1.31	0.95	0.36
Foreign Wholly-Owned	17.2	18.7	16.2	16.7	12.4	3.8	1.69	1.31	1.21	1.26	1.03	0.35
Foreign Majority-Owned	8.8	15.1	16.4	19.4	7.5	3.8	0.89	1.38	1.50	1.71	0.92	0.42

Note: ROAE = Return on Average Equity, ROAA = Return on Average Assets.

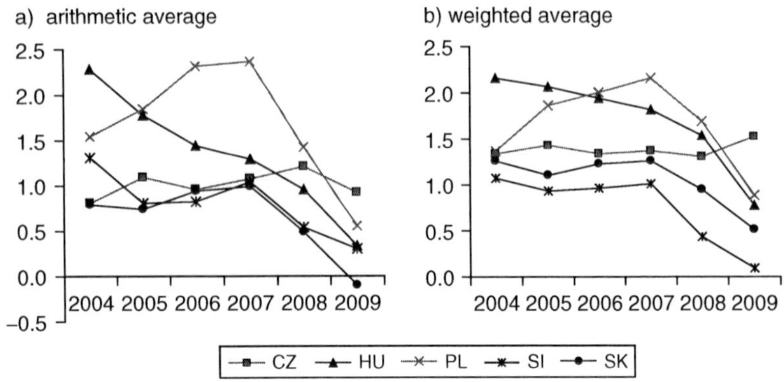

Figure 3.2 ROA averages calculated for banks grouped by host CEE-5 countries
Source: authors' own estimates

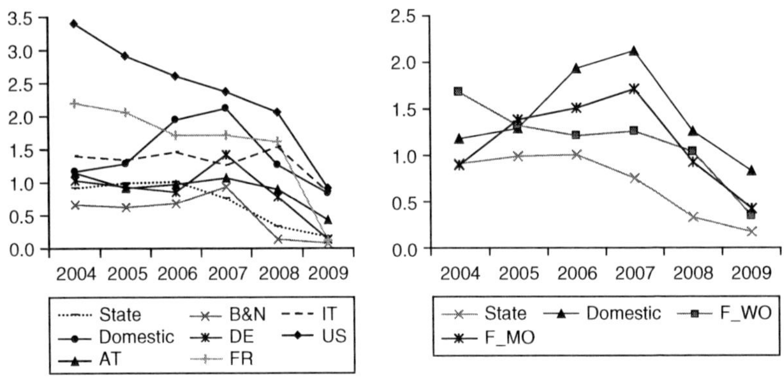

Figure 3.3 ROA averages calculated for banks grouped by ownership structure
Source: authors' own estimates

3.6 Empirical results: CEE bank performance as measured by DEA models and selected regressions

The results of regressions (presented in Tables 3.A2 and 3.A3 in the Appendix) confirm that the opportunity to earn relatively higher profits in fast-growing transition countries was crucial for the massive inflow of foreign banks. The high rate of GDP growth has a positive impact on bank profitability and safety, measured by ROA and Z-score, while the high level of GDP per capita has an adverse impact on both indicators. In models where dummy variables were employed and banks with

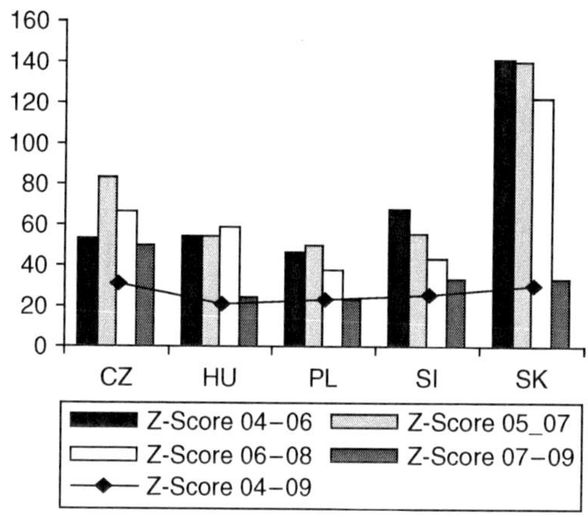

Figure 3.4 Z-score averages calculated for banks grouped by host CEE-5 countries
Source: authors' own estimates

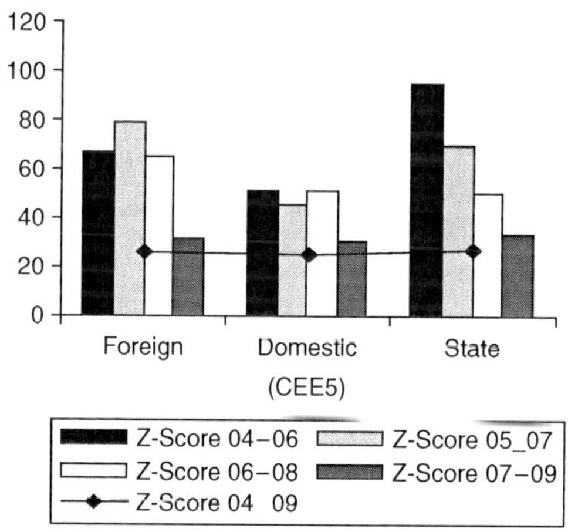

Figure 3.5 Z-score averages calculated for banks grouped by the type of ownership
Source: authors' own estimates

private domestic capital constituted the control group, banks wholly owned by foreign capital achieved the highest Z-score, while banks with foreign major investors were less profitable and more risky. State ownership had a positive impact on safety but a negative one on profitability. These results may suggest that foreign investors enjoying total control can more effectively introduce their home corporate governance and business models with long-term goals, with are more stable

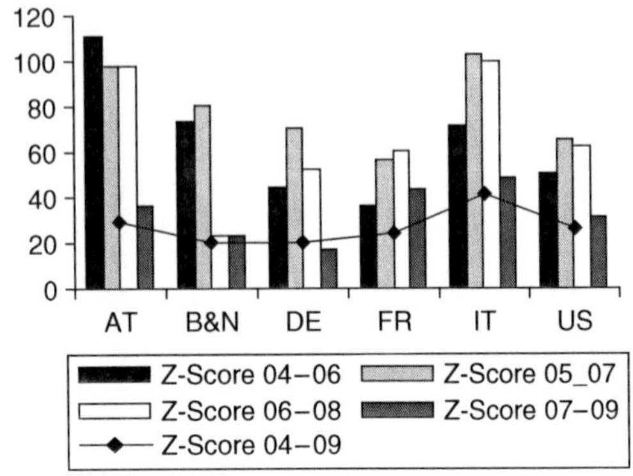

Figure 3.6 Z-score averages for foreign banks grouped by their home countries
Source: authors' own estimates

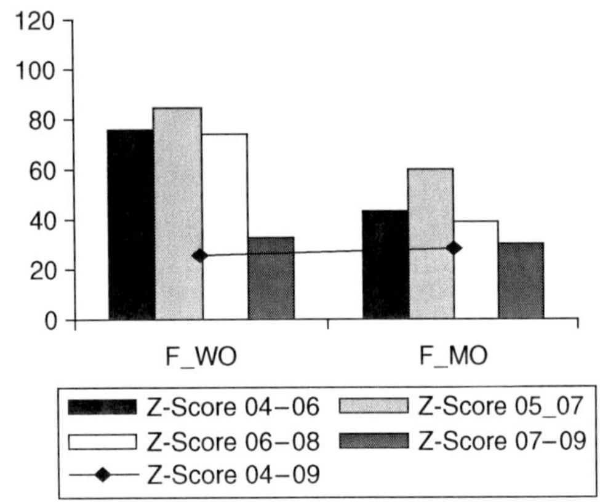

Figure 3.7 Z-score averages for foreign banks grouped by type of ownership
Source: authors' own estimates

and less risky. The foreign majority investor tends to conduct a more risky and less stable strategy, which, however, does not result in higher profits. When we analysed foreign banks according to the home country of their capital, the most successful in terms of profitability turned out to be US banks and, to a lesser extent, French ones. At the other end of the spectrum, banks with Belgian, Dutch and German capital achieved significantly worse results. For bank-level variables, a high rate of asset growth, proper capitalization and usage of short-term funding had a positive impact on profitability, while cost inefficiency (C/I ratio) had a negative impact. The role of the bank size was ambiguous, as the coefficient sign changed in the models used.

The regressions for Z-score indicate that Italian, Austrian and German investors were running the safest banks. Also, a high degree of concentration on the banking sector (C5 index), resulting in lower competitive pressure, had a positive impact on bank Z-scores. Among bank-level variables with a positive impact on Z-score were size of bank (the strongest factor), capital ratio, and share of loans in total assets. Interbank deposits and short-term funds had an adverse impact. The results confirm that in Eastern Europe the most stable banks are also large, well capitalized and traditionally focused (loan–deposit activity), and not dependent on short-term money markets as a source of capital.

The detailed results for DEA models of bank efficiency are presented in Table 3.A4 in the Appendix. The average technical efficiency ranges from 0.475 to 0.642, with pure technical efficiency between 0.629 and 0.745 and scale efficiency between 0.781 and 0.881.

The DEA efficiency estimations generally support the conclusions drawn from the regressions. Figure 3.8 shows that Czech and Polish

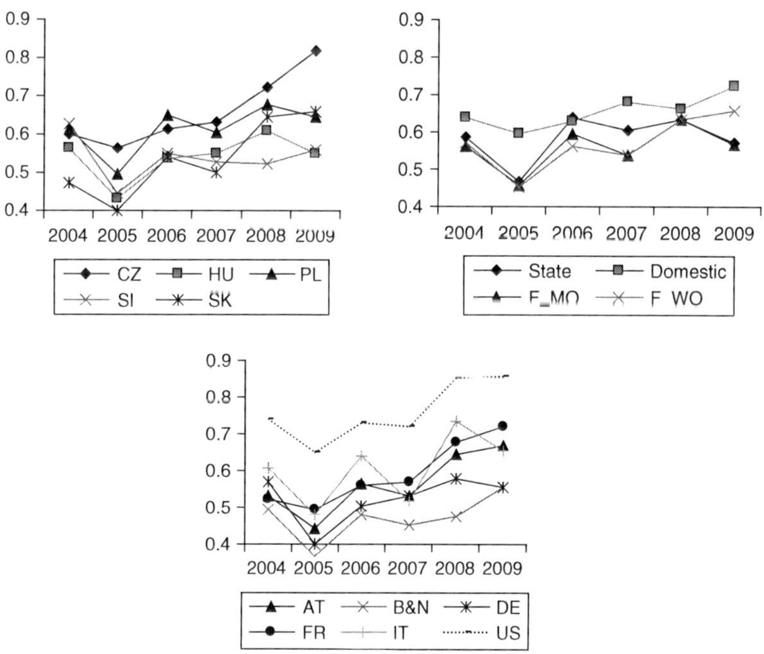

Figure 3.8 DEA results: technical efficiency scores (CRS model)

Source: authors' own estimates

banks achieved the highest technical efficiency scores. For Hungarian banks, the main source of technical inefficiency was scale inefficiency, the highest in the sample. Slovenian and Slovak banks had the highest level of pure technical inefficiency. A striking feature was that domestic banks obtained the highest efficiency scores, not only privately owned (which was consistent with regression results) but also to a lesser extent state-controlled, mainly due to better scale efficiency. After decomposition of foreign banks according to the origin of capital, just as in ratio analysis and regression models, US banks represented the highest efficiency, outperforming even domestic private banks, followed by Italian and French ones, while Belgian, Dutch, German and Austrian banks were the least efficient. This result supports the limited global advantage hypothesis of Berger *et al.* (2000).

3.7 Conclusions

The chapter analyses CEE-5 large commercial banks, in an attempt to discover the most important factors affecting bank performance: home country governance, the business model imposed by the owner or degree of foreign control. Based on the analysed data set, the empirical evidence supports the market-seeking hypothesis: that the opportunity to earn relatively higher profits in fast-growing transition countries was crucial for the massive inflow of foreign banks to CEE-5 countries. When we analyse the importance of the mode of foreign bank entry (retail-based model with partial foreign control, or a wholly foreign-controlled limited subsidiary model), results are less clear. Wholly foreign-controlled banks achieved the highest Z-score, while banks with foreign majority control (go-native model) were less profitable and more risky. The foreign majority investors tend to pursue a more risky and less stable strategy, which, however, does not result in higher profits. These results may suggest that foreign investors enjoying absolute control can benefit not only from market share, but also from efficiency gains.

When foreign banks are analysed according to the home country of their capital, the regressions and ratio analysis used all suggest that the US-based banks are the most profitable (shareholder model), as opposed to banks from Belgium, the Netherlands and Germany (stakeholder model). On the other hand, banks with Belgian, Dutch and German capital achieved the highest Z-score. The DEA efficiency estimations generally support the conclusions drawn from the regressions: US banks represented the highest efficiency, outperforming domestic private

Statistical Appendix

Table 3.A1 Sample characteristics

	No. of observations						Total assets – sum (million Euro)					
	2009	2008	2007	2006	2005	2004	2009	2008	2007	2006	2005	2004
CZ	13	16	20	20	18	16	120,592	134,980	139,633	114,586	97,059	78,937
HU	13	18	17	15	15	14	102,174	110,753	94,665	78,125	61,885	53,057
PL	24	25	22	21	20	16	205,693	210,100	173,799	138,423	119,186	101,472
SI	16	17	17	17	17	11	54,853	51,954	46,814	37,790	32,413	23,594
SK	13	16	14	13	13	10	49,897	60,023	44,775	38,461	36,388	25,566
TOTAL	79	92	90	86	83	67	533,209	567,811	499,686	407,385	346,932	282,625

	Assets of the largest banks (million Euro)						Assets of the smallest banks (million Euro)					
	2009	2008	2007	2006	2005	2004	2009	2008	2007	2006	2005	2004
CZ	32,462	32,025	34,774	27,726	25,392	20,161	1,102	1,175	1,004	783	597	406
HU	36,006	35,821	33,301	28,124	20,701	16,950	214	204	195	201	204	224
PL	38,109	32,663	34,620	26,617	23,812	21,102	1,079	1,359	584	129	498	570
SI	19,606	18,918	18,308	14,411	12,423	9,955	571	702	596	385	112	307
SK	11,486	12,557	10,088	9,889	8,597	7,908	178	182	216	189	181	150

	Ownership (home country of strategic investor) – no. of banks											
	DOMESTIC		FOREIGN – grouped by home country							FOREIGN – by type		
	Private	State-controlled	AT	B&N	DE	FR	IT	US	Others	Wholly owned	Majority-owned	TOTAL
CZ	3	2	5	2	1	3	2	2	0	12	3	20
HU	1	1	4	1	4	2	2	2	1	16	0	18
PL	2	2	1	6	4	2	1	3	4	12	9	25
SI	5	5	3	1	0	1	2	0	0	7	0	17
SK	4	0	4	4	0	1	2	1	0	9	3	16
TOTAL	15	10	17	14	9	9	9	8	5	56	15	96

Table 3.A2 Regression results (ROA)

Variable	MODEL 1	MODEL 2	MODEL 3
Intercept	12.931E***	3.582***	3.606***
	(3.699)	(0.747)	(0.846)
GDP per capita	**–0.061*****	**–0.026*****	**–0.024*****
	(0.022)	(0.008)	(0.009)
Real GDP growth rate	**0.053*****	**0.054*****	**0.059*****
	(0.005)	(0.008)	(0.008)
Inflation HCPI (Harmonised Consumer Price Index)	–0.003	–0.018	–0.033
	(0.026)	(0.026)	(0.031)
Concentration: C5 index	**0.050***	–0.006	–0.012
	(0.026)	(0.021)	(0.023)
Share of foreign capital in banking sector	**–0.034****	–0.006	–0.004
	(0.016)	(0.004)	(0.005)
Ln Total Assets	**–0.478****	**0.111*****	**0.114*****
	(0.195)	(0.014)	(0.014)
Growth rate of Total Assets	**0.006*****	**0.007****	**0.007****
	(0.001)	(0.003)	(0.003)
Equity Capital to Total Assets ratio	**0.097*****	**0.052***	**0.065****
	(0.026)	(0.029)	(0.031)
Cost/Income Ratio	**–0.032*****	**–0.032*****	**–0.033*****
	(0.003)	(0.002)	(0.002)
Loans to Total Assets	0.000	**–0.005****	–0.003
	(0.008)	(0.002)	(0.003)
Non-Interest Income to Gross Revenue	**–0.006***	–0.003	–0.003
	(0.003)	(0.003)	(0.004)
Bank Deposits and Short-term Funding to Total Assets	**0.009*****	**0.004****	0.003
	(0.003)	(0.002)	(0.002)
Ownership dummy: STATE		**–0.352*****	**–0.414*****
		(0.102)	(0.147)
Ownership dummy: F_WO			–0.029
			(0.144)
Ownership dummy: F_MO			**–0.332****
			(0.146)
Foreign Investor's Home Country: AT		–0.078	
		(0.088)	
Foreign Investor's Home Country: B&N		**–0.381****	
		(0.151)	

Continued

Table 3.A2 Continued

Variable	MODEL 1	MODEL 2	MODEL 3
Foreign Investor's Home Country: DE		**–0.263***	
		(0.150)	
Foreign Investor's Home Country: FR		**0.311*****	
		(0.121)	
Foreign Investor's Home Country: IT		–0.013	
		(0.097)	
Foreign Investor's Home Country: US		**0.815*****	
		(0.119)	

Notes: The dependent variable is **Return on Average Assets.** Macroeconomic variables are from IMF database and ECB (C5 index). Bank-level variables are from Bankscope database. All models are Panel Least Square, with White cross-section standard errors and covariance (d.f. corrected). Total panel (unbalanced) observations: 400, includes 96 banks and five periods (2005–9). Model 1 is bank fixed effects model, Model 2 includes dummy variables indicating the ownership structure, while Model 3 includes dummy variables indicating the home country of foreign investors of CEE-5 banks. Standard errors are in parentheses. *, ** and *** denote significance at 10%, 5% and 1%, respectively.

Table 3.A3 Regression results (Z-score)

Variable	MODEL 1	MODEL 2	MODEL 3
Intercept	–564.181**	–236.839**	–271.089***
	(246.215)	(96.657)	(83.693)
GDP per capita	**–3.451*****	**–1.824****	**–1.919***
	(0.644)	(0.925)	(0.993)
Real GDP growth rate	**4.124*****	**3.732*****	**3.943*****
	(0.565)	(0.500)	(0.529)
Inflation HCPI	0.874	2.307	1.822
	(0.812)	(2.076)	(1.953)
Concentration: C5 index	2.725	**4.623*****	**4.834*****
	(2.539)	(1.504)	(1.497)
Share of foreign capital in banking sector	0.048	–0.412	–0.499
	(0.336)	(0.284)	(0.312)
Ln Total Assets	**45.516****	**8.551****	**11.183****
	(19.795)	(4.206)	(4.490)
Growth rate of Total Assets	–0.121	–0.131	–0.167
	(0.121)	(0.103)	(0.143)

Continued

Table 3.A3 Continued

Variable	MODEL 1	MODEL 2	MODEL 3
Equity Capital to Total Assets ratio	2.547	**1.738*** **	**1.660*** **
	(2.387)	(0.408)	(0.094)
Cost/Income Ratio	**−0.848** **	0.104	−0.028
	(0.393)	(0.269)	(0.222)
Loans to Total Assets	**0.683*** **	**0.235*** **	**0.255*** **
	(0.228)	(0.055)	(0.079)
Non-Interest Income to Gross Revenue	0.196	−0.020	0.066
	(0.242)	(0.113)	(0.148)
Bank Deposits and Short-term Funding to Total Assets	**−0.277** **	−0.114	**−0.118* **
	(0.129)	(0.077)	(0.069)
Ownership dummy: STATE		**22.928** **	**22.165** **
		(10.603)	(8.847)
Ownership dummy: F_WO			**23.172*** **
			(5.408)
Ownership dummy: F_MO			**−9.991** **
			(4.314)
Foreign Investor's Home Country: AT		**27.105*** **	
		(7.291)	
Foreign Investor's Home Country: B&N		−5.154	
		(13.987)	
Foreign Investor's Home Country: DE		**17.202* **	
		(10.183)	
Foreign Investor's Home Country: FR		2.541	
		(3.356)	
Foreign Investor's Home Country: IT		**28.316*** **	
		(7.971)	
Foreign Investor's Home Country: US		1.465	
		(1.653)	

Notes: The dependent variable is **Z-score**, calculated over three-year periods. The explanatory variables come from the last year of the three-year periods. Macroeconomic variables are from IMF database and ECB (C5 index). Bank-level variables are from Bankscope database. Both models are Panel Least Square, with White cross-section standard errors and covariance (d.f. corrected). Total panel (unbalanced) observations: 303, includes 87 banks and four periods (2006–9). Model 1 is bank fixed effects model, Model 2 includes dummy variables indicating the ownership structure, while Model 3 includes dummy variables indicating the home country of foreign investors of CEE-5 banks. Standard errors are in parentheses. *, ** and *** denote significance at 10%, 5% and 1%, respectively.

Table 3.A4 DEA results: average efficiency scores

	TECHNICAL EFFICIENCIES CONSTANT RETURNS TO SCALE						PURE TECHNICAL EFFICIENCIES VARIABLE RETURNS TO SCALE						SCALE EFFICIENCIES					
	2004	2005	2006	2007	2008	2009	2004	2005	2006	2007	2008	2009	2004	2005	2006	2007	2008	2009
HOST COUNTRY																		
CZ	0.599	0.565	0.613	0.632	0.723	0.820	0.749	0.687	0.708	0.757	0.802	0.849	0.817	0.839	0.870	0.838	0.902	0.961
HU	0.563	0.434	0.538	0.548	0.609	0.551	0.751	0.643	0.744	0.805	0.744	0.707	0.751	0.695	0.728	0.691	0.825	0.801
PL	0.613	0.496	0.650	0.603	0.675	0.644	0.800	0.696	0.743	0.768	0.746	0.737	0.783	0.742	0.884	0.800	0.907	0.883
SI	0.628	0.445	0.551	0.529	0.521	0.557	0.679	0.559	0.664	0.669	0.623	0.642	0.919	0.828	0.847	0.811	0.863	0.885
SK	0.474	0.400	0.539	0.502	0.647	0.657	0.702	0.520	0.688	0.712	0.773	0.776	0.730	0.796	0.823	0.746	0.857	0.871
TOTAL	0.581	0.475	0.585	0.569	0.637	0.642	0.743	0.629	0.711	0.745	0.737	0.738	0.799	0.781	0.837	0.781	0.873	0.881
OWNERSHIP type																		
State	0.587	0.465	0.638	0.606	0.632	0.570	0.748	0.609	0.747	0.769	0.696	0.629	0.806	0.790	0.865	0.803	0.909	0.917
Domestic	0.640	0.597	0.627	0.679	0.660	0.725	0.839	0.696	0.744	0.838	0.794	0.820	0.783	0.867	0.851	0.818	0.844	0.889
Foreign_ Majority-owned	0.563	0.457	0.594	0.540	0.631	0.569	0.766	0.681	0.713	0.755	0.732	0.703	0.761	0.707	0.853	0.744	0.878	0.835
Foreign_ Wholly owned	0.572	0.454	0.564	0.540	0.633	0.658	0.710	0.601	0.696	0.712	0.731	0.749	0.816	0.782	0.823	0.778	0.873	0.886
TOTAL	0.581	0.475	0.585	0.569	0.637	0.642	0.743	0.629	0.711	0.745	0.737	0.738	0.799	0.781	0.837	0.781	0.873	0.881

Continued

Table 3.A4 Continued

	TECHNICAL EFFICIENCIES CONSTANT RETURNS TO SCALE						PURE TECHNICAL EFFICIENCIES VARIABLE RETURNS TO SCALE						SCALE EFFICIENCIES					
	2004	2005	2006	2007	2008	2009	2004	2005	2006	2007	2008	2009	2004	2005	2006	2007	2008	2009
OWNERSHIP – home country																		
AT	0.534	0.440	0.567	0.532	0.646	0.667	0.671	0.566	0.680	0.706	0.731	0.736	0.811	0.806	0.839	0.769	0.887	0.905
BN	0.495	0.367	0.480	0.452	0.476	0.556	0.689	0.595	0.651	0.706	0.628	0.708	0.759	0.686	0.797	0.694	0.806	0.818
DE	0.571	0.399	0.502	0.534	0.581	0.554	0.708	0.543	0.601	0.703	0.684	0.618	0.799	0.775	0.834	0.772	0.858	0.896
FR	0.525	0.493	0.558	0.568	0.680	0.723	0.717	0.636	0.744	0.768	0.781	0.862	0.788	0.797	0.772	0.772	0.881	0.856
IT	0.608	0.478	0.641	0.518	0.733	0.654	0.772	0.693	0.775	0.727	0.824	0.766	0.797	0.717	0.831	0.738	0.900	0.876
US	0.738	0.652	0.731	0.719	0.854	0.856	0.845	0.778	0.812	0.796	0.895	0.945	0.864	0.839	0.905	0.892	0.950	0.904
Other countries	0.538	0.401	0.577	0.496	0.575	0.487	0.690	0.577	0.686	0.641	0.651	0.580	0.810	0.734	0.851	0.809	0.892	0.856
TOTAL	0.581	0.475	0.585	0.569	0.637	0.642	0.743	0.629	0.711	0.745	0.737	0.738	0.799	0.781	0.837	0.781	0.873	0.881

banks, followed by Italian and French ones, while Belgian, Dutch, German and Austrian banks were the least efficient.

More generally, our findings suggest that both owners' home country governance models and host country macroeconomic and institutional characteristics are important factors in overall bank performance. For profitability, home country source of capital (and governance model) seemed to be of the most importance, particularly for US banks; and for safety (Z-score) local host country environment tended to be very important. The degree of foreign control was not of major importance; and, although US banks, mostly wholly controlled subsidiaries, were the most profitable, the retail network-based Italian banks followed closely behind.

References

Allen, A., Babus, E. and Carletti, E. (2009a) 'Financial Crises: Theory and Evidence', *Annual Review of Financial Economics*, 1, 97–116.

Allen, F., Carletti, E. and Marquez, R. (2009b) 'Stakeholder Capitalism, Corporate Governance and Firm Value', *Wharton Research Paper*, no. 05–27.

Barth, J.R., Caprio, G. and Levine R. (2004) 'Bank supervision and regulation: what works best?', *Journal of Financial Intermediation*, 13, 205–248.

Berger, A.N., DeYoung, R., Genay, H. and Udell, G.F. (2000) 'Globalization of Financial Institutions: Evidence from Cross-Border Banking Performance', *Brookings-Wharton Papers on Financial Services*, no. 3.

Berger, A., Clarke, G., Cull, R., Klapper, L. and Udell, G. (2005) *Corporate Governance and Bank Performance: A Joint Analysis of the Static, Selection, and Dynamic Effects of Domestic, Foreign, and State Ownership.* World Bank Policy Research Paper No. 3632 (Washington DC: World Bank).

Bikker, J. and Bos, J. (2008) *Bank Performance, A theoretical and empirical framework for the analysis of profitability, competition and efficiency* (London: Routledge).

Bonin, J.P., Hasan, I. and Wachtel, P. (2004) 'Privatisation Matters: Bank Efficiency in Transition Countries', The World Bank Conference on Bank Privatisation, Washington DC.

Casadesus-Masanell, R. and Ricart, J. (2009) *Competing through Business Model*, http://ssrn.com/abstract=1115201 (accessed 14 April 2011).

Coelli, T.J., Rao, D.S.P., O'Donnell, C.J. and Battese, G.E. (2005) *An Introduction to Efficiency and Productivity Analysis* (New York: Springer).

Demirguc-Kunt, A. and Huizinga, H. (2009) 'Bank Activity and Funding Strategies: the Impact on Risk and Return', *CEPR Discussion Paper* no. 7170.

The ECB (2005–9): *EU Banking Sector Stability Reports* (Frankfurt: European Central Bank).

The Economist (2010) 'A special report on innovation in emerging markets: What makes emerging-market companies run?', 15 April.

Euromoney (2010): *Award for Excellence, Banker of the Year*, July.

Guillen, M. and Tschoegl, A. (2008) *Building a Global Bank: The Transformation of Banco Santander* (Princeton, NJ: Princeton University Press).

Hryckiewicz, A. and Kowalewski, O. (2007) 'Economic Determinants and Entry Modes of Foreign Banks into Central Europe', XVI International Tor Vergata Conference on Banking and Finance, www.economia.uniroma2.it (accessed on 4 April 2011).

IMF (2010) *Global Financial Stability Report*, April (Washington DC: International Monetary Fund).

Lensink, R., Meesters, A. and Naaborg, I. (2008) 'Bank efficiency and foreign ownership: Do good institutions matter?', *Journal of Banking and Finance*, 32, 834–844.

Naaborg, I.J. (2007) *Foreign Bank Entry and Performance with a Focus on Central and Eastern Europe* (Netherlands: Rijksuniversiteit Groningen).

Raiffeisen Research (2009) *CEE Banking Sector Report*, RZB Group, June.

Stiroh, K.J., (2004) 'Diversification in banking: Is non-interest income the answer?' *Journal of Money, Credit and Banking* 36, 853–882.

Sturm, J.E. and Williams, B. (2002) 'Deregulation, Entry of Foreign Banks and Bank Efficiency in Australia', *CESIFO Working Paper* No. 816.

Sturm, J.E. and Williams, B. (2005) 'What Determines Differences in Foreign Bank Efficiency; Australian Evidence', *CESIFO Working Paper*, No. 1587.

UniCredit Group (2010) *CEE Strategic Analysis*, CEE Research.

Van Hoose, D. (2010) *The Industrial Organization of Banking: Bank Behavior, Market Structure and Regulation* (Heidelberg: Springer).

Venzin, M. (2009) *Building an International Financial Services Firm* (Oxford: Oxford University Press).

Weill, P., Malone, T.W., D'Urso, V.T., Herman, G., and Woerner, S. (2005) 'Do some Business models perform better than others? A study of the 1000 largest US Firms', *MIT Center for Coordination Science Working paper* 226, p. 39 (Boston: MIT).

Williams, J. and Nguyen, N. (2005) 'Financial liberalisation, crisis, and restructuring: A comparative study of bank performance and bank governance in South East Asia', *Journal of Banking and Finance*, 29, 2119–2154.

4

Financial Crisis and Bank Profitability

Ted Lindblom, Magnus Olsson and Magnus Willesson

4.1 Introduction

The recent turmoil in money and capital markets around the world has clearly shown the vulnerability of highly interconnected financial systems in times of recession. This paper examines the impact of the financial crisis on the profitability and risk-taking of Swedish banks. At the beginning of the crisis many banks experienced liquidity problems due to a mismatch in their funding of loans. These banks had for a number of years been financing an increasing long-term (mortgage) lending with short-term borrowing on the market. The financial crisis radically changed the risk premiums on both money and capital markets, and banks' refinancing on these markets became extremely expensive and more or less impossible to accomplish. Without resolute intervention by the Government, issuing general banking guarantees, and the Central Bank, fuelling the market with liquidity to ever lower interest rates, the financial system might have collapsed totally. These prompt actions moved the focus from liquidity risk to credit risk. Even though Swedish banks seem to comply well with the new Basel accord (Lindblom and Willesson, 2010), three of the four largest commercial banks issued new equity in connection with the crisis in order to strengthen their capacity to absorb anticipated credit losses, primarily on the Baltic markets, in a 'worst case scenario'.[1]

The authorities' intervention to rescue the financial system has been positively acknowledged both by analysts and in the public debate. The opinions on how financial institutions, particularly the banks, have responded to the Central Bank's stepwise reduction of the repo rate[2] tend to be less affirmative, however. The major criticism is that most banks appear to be very alert in reflecting repo rate cuts in their offered interest rates on deposit products but more reluctant to fully adjust their lending rates. If this criticism is justified, the result for the single bank should be a widening of its net interest margin without a corresponding increase of its exposure to interest rate risk; that is, the wider interest margin is due to an increase of either the bank's funding spread or its credit spread (or both). This suggests that loan loss provisions that are made for absorbing realized and expected losses in foreign businesses are covered by higher net interest margins in the home market. This can only be the case if the financial crisis did lead to less competition in Sweden. If the financial crisis, instead, increased the banks' exposure to credit risk domestically as well, their seemingly asymmetrical response to repo rate cuts does not necessarily reflect weaker bank competition, but only an adjustment by the banks to a changed trade-off between risks and returns.

The analysis of the profitability and risk-taking of the banks will put particular emphasis on whether there are differences between different types of banks in terms of association form, size, business operations and competitive environment (regional sub-markets). Comparisons will also be made with the previous financial crisis in 1992.

4.2 Measurement of bank profitability and risk

A substantial share of the literature on banking profitability is related to either economies of scale, economies of scope or market concentration. In profitability comparisons between banks, special attention is also paid to growth opportunities (Goddard *et al.*, 2004a), capitalization (García-Herrero *et al.*, 2009), balance sheet structure (Demirgüç-Kunt and Huizinga, 1998), ownership and management (García-Herrero *et al.*, 2009), regional differences (Hannan and Prager, 2009) and bank size.

Intuitively, a bank with low *capitalization* may benefit from leverage effects in terms of a higher return on equity (*ROE*). This is a theme for many empirical studies and is used by, for example, Molyneux and Thornton (1992) for explaining differences in returns between privately owned and state-owned banks. However, several studies (Demirgüç-Kunt and Huizinga, 1998; Goddard *et al.*, 2004b; García-Herrero *et al.*, 2009) argue that the opposite relationship occurs. García-Herrero *et al.* (2009) explain this relationship by the fact that equity capital can be used to raise the share of risky assets if facing profitable opportunities, to raise cheaper financing and to signal effects on creditworthiness. It also requires banks to borrow less in order to support a given level of assets.

It is evident that the *balance sheet structure* on the asset side is vital for the trade-off between profitability and risk-taking of the bank. For instance, higher levels of loans to total assets should be reflected in a higher profit due to the higher risk. In particular, a high ratio of non-interest-earning assets to total assets is shown to impact bank profitability negatively (Demirgüç-Kunt and Huizinga, 1998).

Profitability differences between banks may also be explained by both their *ownership* and their *management* styles (García-Herrero *et al.*, 2009). In comparisons between private and state-owned banks, the ownership question arises from the fact that the latter banks are often found to be less efficient than the former. On the one hand, this is attributed to the fact that state-owned banks generally hold assets of poorer quality (La Porta *et al.*, 2002). On the other hand, Molyneux and Thornton (1992) state that one reason for private banks' higher return is lower capitalization, which arises from the government's implicit underwriting of the state-owned banks.

The environment in which the bank operates does not only relate to the policy standpoint of banks. Instead, it is shown that *regional aspects* matter to banks (Hannan and Prager, 2009). For instance, the profitability of banks operating in less competitive local markets is affected positively when more diversified banks enter their market. One explanation may be that the geographically diversified bank does not adopt the prices of the local market. However, this effect is not totally clear, since it also relies on scale of operations and differs between rural and urban areas.

We study the banks' profitability in terms of *ROE*, which is considered as the core measure in accounting-based studies (cf. Frazer and Zhang, 2009). The reason is threefold. First, we want to be able to derive details about the banks' development of their return from a variety of risk exposures and bank strategies. Second, the majority of the Swedish banks are not listed on the stock exchange, so market data is non-existent. Third, we aim to make longitudinal comparisons with two previous studies (Lindblom, 1994, 2001).

In the Dupont model, a bank's *ROE* is broken down into an equity multiplier and its return on assets (*ROA*), which is further decomposed into asset utilization and profit (and net interest) margin. We use a similar approach, developed by Alberts (1989) and applied by Lindblom (1994, 2001), which captures the trade-off between the bank's return and risk. In this approach, *ROE* is broken down into two components: return on invested funds (*ROIF*) and return on financial leverage (*ROFL*):

$$ROE = ROIF + ROFL.$$

ROFL is derived from the following relationship:

$$\text{ROFL} = (\text{ROIF} - k_d)*D/E,$$

where
k_d = average cost of debt,
D = debt,
E = equity.

This approach allows a detailed study of the impact of the banks' capitalization, balance sheet structure, ownership and size as well as regional differences. The *ROIF* component measures the bank's profitability on the asset side (yield + net non-interest income over assets) and is primarily dependent on its exposures to credit and liquidity risks. The higher the exposure to any of these risks, the higher is the expected interest income and, thus, *ROIF*. The *ROFL* component is a measure of how well the bank has been financing the funds invested, and is primarily related to the bank's exposure to interest rate risk and capital risk. The former directly affects the expected leverage spread ($ROIF-k_d$), whereas the latter is linked to the leverage multiplier (*D/E*).

The analysis is based on the quarterly financial reports of 74 banks from 2007 to 2009.[3] This period also covers the good times before the crisis. The four biggest Swedish banks (SEB, SHB (Handelsbanken), Swedbank and Nordea) are the main targets for the analysis. In terms of total assets these banks account for more than 80 per cent of the banking market in Sweden. In addition, they operate in the other Scandinavian countries and the Baltic States. These banks are compared with more domestically oriented commercial banks, including the niche-oriented Länsförsäkringar bank (LF), which is the fifth largest bank, and three smaller commercial banks that are merged together into one category (CBs) in the analysis. The peers also include two categories of savings banks. On the one hand, there are independent savings banks (ISBs) that are members of the Swedish Savings banks association (63 banks at the end of 2009[4]). These banks are primarily presented and analysed on an aggregated level. The other savings bank category consists of three non-member savings banks (SBs).[5] As these three banks and the three CBs report only twice a year, they can be analysed only on a half-yearly basis. The analysis will partly be based also on results from other recent studies and investigations. Of particular interest are the monthly reports presented by Financial Institutions (FI) on the effects of the government stability measures that have been launched in order to reduce the risks for depositors and other creditors to banks and other financial institutions. These measures consist of (see FI, 2010, pp. 2–3):

i) *the liquidity-supporting activities* initiated by the Swedish National Debt Office and the Swedish Central bank (18 September 2008),
ii) *the extension of the deposit insurance to SEK 0.5 million (≈ EUR 50,000)* (19 September 2008),
iii) *the bank guarantee programme* for facilitating borrowing of banks and mortgage institutions (29 October 2008),
iv) *the fee-based stability fund* allowing the government to support participating Swedish financial institutions that get into trouble in order to mitigate serious disturbances in the financial system (29 October 2008), and
v) *the capital infusion programme,* linked to the stability fund, to which individual banks can apply for capital reinforcement in the form of share capital or hybrid capital (3 February 2009).

These stability measures, possibly with the exception of the deposit insurance extension, are only to be regarded as very temporary measures. Both the guarantee programme and the capital infusion programme have, however, been prolonged several times by the Swedish parliament/government.

4.3 Results and analysis

The financial crisis has not left any of the banks unaffected, but it is clear from Table 4.1 that some banks have been more affected than others.

The profitability of Swedbank in terms of *ROE* before tax stands out as being most affected by the crisis, but also SEB seems to have been suffering from credit losses. The negative *ROE*s of the ISBs at the end of 2008 and the beginning of 2009 are linked to their ownership in Swedbank. Many ISBs made loss provisions after Swedbank's issuance of new equity at the end of 2008. These provisions were partly recovered in 2009, which explains the extra-high profitability in the second quarter. During 2009 the ISBs appear to have managed their banking business about as well as Nordea, SHB and the three small CBs. The three former SBs that are now operating as provincial limited banks independently of Swedbank seem to have been less affected than the ISBs by the crisis. Their low *ROE* in the second half of 2007 is due to the fact that one of these banks invested in a new IT system.

Table 4.1 The overall profitability of the Swedish banks during 2007–9

Measure	Bank	2007				2008				2009			
		Q1	*Q2*	*Q3*	*Q4*	*Q1*	*Q2*	*Q3*	*Q4*	*Q1*	*Q2*	*Q3*	*Q4*
ROE before tax	*Nordea*	22.5%	**25.2%**	22.8%	25.1%	19.9%	20.5%	19.0%	17.5%	18.0%	15.5%	15.2%	10.6%
	SEB	25.2%	**25.9%**	20.4%	23.9%	12.5%	18.8%	13.3%	19.2%	7.3%	2.5%	2.0%	2.3%
	SHB	19.9%	23.5%	19.0%	16.7%	15.6%	18.3%	20.1%	**27.8%**	18.3%	16.6%	15.7%	15.5%
	Swedbank	24.0%	25.7%	22.7%	24.1%	21.1%	**26.1%**	17.0%	11.1%	–16.2%	–19.1%	–13.4%	–7.4%
	LF	6.3%	6.7%	6.9%	**7.0%**	6.6%	6.1%	6.2%	5.4%	6.3%	5.9%	5.3%	5.3%
	ISBs	8.1%	15.6%	8.1%	7.6%	6.5%	11.1%	11.5%	–27.6%	–1.6%	**17.8%**	12.2%	10.2%
	SBs	**14.3%**		1.0%		13.1%		9.0%		8.4%		8.4%	
	CBs	17.9%		11.2%		20.8%		**25.6%**		16.6%		15.7%	

The observation that the commercial banks seem to have managed the crisis relatively better than the ISBs is likely to be explained by the intervention of the Central Bank and the Government. Figure 4.1 shows that the government stability measures, in the form of the guarantee programme, have been of great importance, particularly for the four large commercial banks. The programme does, to a major extent, explain why many banks were able to operate without major constraints even after experiencing credit losses. It was utilized right from the beginning by Swedish banks in general and by one of the four large commercial banks in particular. Swedbank borrowed the largest amounts, and also utilized this opportunity quite steadily over the whole period. SHB only utilized the programme until the first half of 2009.

The funding cost is, of course, crucial for the banks. Figure 4.2 displays how the Central Bank's stepwise cutting of the repo rate affected interest rates on the market. Evidently all market rates were affected, but, most importantly for the banks at the time of the crisis, the short-term STIBOR (Stockholm Interbank Offered Rate) was particularly affected.

As shown in Table 4.2, the decreasing interest rates on the markets appear to have resulted in lower funding costs for the banks.[6] With the exception of the niche bank LF, the banks' average cost of debt (*kd*) started to decline slowly after the third quarter of 2008 and thereafter more rapidly in 2009 along with the ever lower short-term market rates.

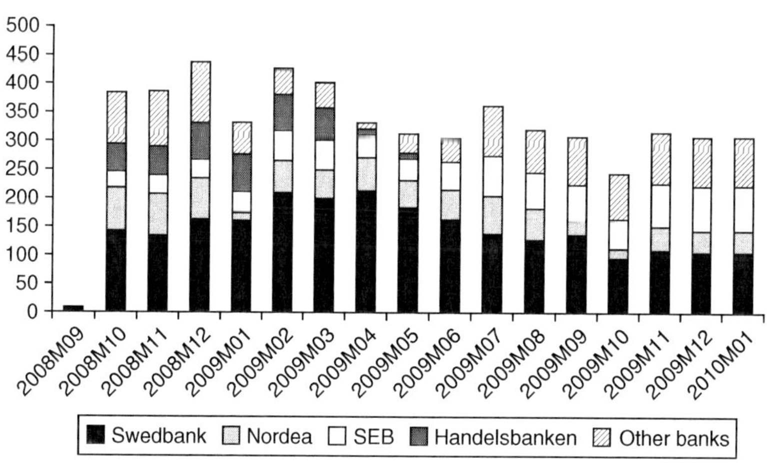

Figure 4.1 Swedish banks' utilization of the guarantee programme (bSEK)
Source: FI (2010, p. 6) and SCB 'Statistics Sweden'.

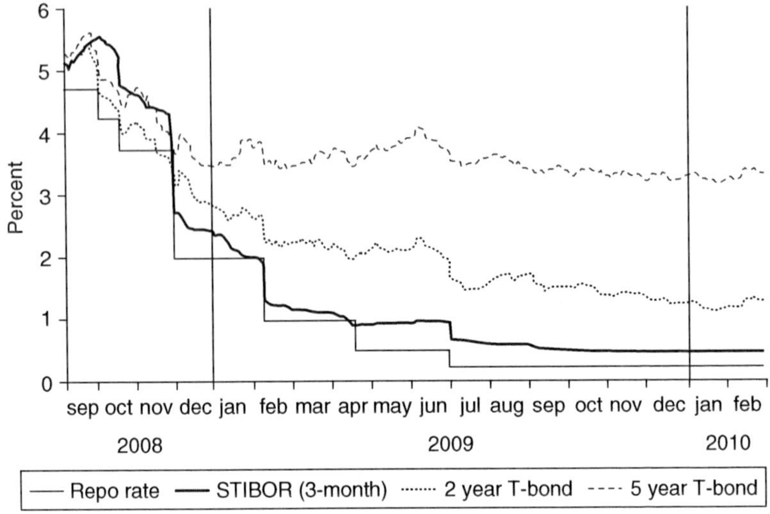

Figure 4.2 Development of market interest rates and the repo rate
Source: FI (2010, p. 5) and Reuters Ecowin.

The rather low average interest costs of the ISBs are interesting, since many of these banks are small. On the other hand, some of these banks operate the only branch in the local market. A more detailed analysis of the 21 smallest ISBs, of which eight banks operate the only local branch and the remaining 13 banks face competition on the local market (not shown in any table), fails to lend support to the idea that the former banks are able to take advantage of operating the only local branch. On the contrary, their interest cost was on average 5–15 basis points higher than the interest cost of the banks explicitly exposed to local competition. However, their interest cost was still lower than that of the average ISB.

The observation that the banks' funding costs have become substantially lower since the financial crisis is in line with the observation of FI (2010) that the average bank adjusted its deposit rates in accordance with the declining market rates. However, the reported adjustment is not as large as the decline of short-term market rates. The average spread between the three-month-based STIBOR and the banks' offered interest rates on transaction (demand) deposits (funding spread) fell from over two percentage units in 2008 to less than a quarter of a percentage unit in 2009/10.

Table 4.2 The banks' average cost of debt during 2007–9

Measure	Bank	2007				2008				2009			
		Q1	*Q2*	*Q3*	*Q4*	*Q1*	*Q2*	*Q3*	*Q4*	*Q1*	*Q2*	*Q3*	*Q4*
Average cost of debt (kd)	*Nordea*	2.22%	2.42%	2.34%	2.57%	2.62%	2.74%	2.88%	2.81%	1.71%	1.28%	0.98%	**0.90%**
	SEB	3.38%	3.31%	3.37%	3.09%	3.42%	3.51%	3.34%	3.24%	2.38%	1.92%	1.65%	**1.65%**
	SHB	2.51%	2.55%	2.70%	3.36%	2.83%	2.88%	3.44%	3.17%	2.12%	1.48%	1.13%	**1.02%**
	Swedbank	2.89%	3.18%	3.29%	3.61%	3.50%	3.50%	3.57%	3.51%	2.58%	2.02%	1.86%	**1.78%**
	LF	4.02%	4.58%	5.18%	5.74%	6.16%	4.68%	7.34%	8.83%	4.73%	3.30%	3.17%	**2.74%**
	ISBs	2.04%	2.11%	2.34%	2.79%	2.99%	3.20%	3.25%	2.97%	1.47%	0.91%	**0.57%**	0.72%
	SBs	2.31%		4.67%		3.37%		3.52%		1.48%		**0.64%**	
	CBs	1.16%		1.26%		1.61%		1.99%		1.25%		**0.83%**	

A major part of the observed convergence of STIBOR and bank deposit rates can be explained by the fact that negative interest rates are not explicitly offered on deposits. Hence, the spread is bound to diminish as STIBOR reaches interest levels below 1 per cent, and at the end of 2009 even half a per cent. One way for the banks to compensate for this is to charge higher fees for services attached to deposit accounts, like payments transactions. Such fees are part of the non-interest income of banks and reported as (net) fees and commission income (FCI) in the income statement.

Table 4.3 shows how the banks' FCI has developed during 2007–9 in relative terms with respect to operating income and net interest income. The higher the ratio, the larger share of the income comes from fees and commissions.

The banks seem to have been unable to compensate themselves for the lower funding spread between market rates and deposit rates by increasing the FCI share. In most banks the ratio between FCI and operating income (OI) has been rather stable, declining slightly, in the commercial banks in particular, after having peaked in the second half of 2007 or at the beginning of 2008. The niche bank, LF, is differentiated from other banks. Except for the last quarter of 2009, the bank has been unable to fully cover its own fee payments by customer charges. The major part of these fee payments consists of inter-bank charges for access to the payment system. The ratio between FCI and net interest income (NII) follows a similar pattern, in which the tendency of relatively less dependence of charge-based income in commercial banks is also discernible.

In principle, two ways remain for the banks to compensate themselves for the lower funding spread. They can either improve their operating efficiency or increase their credit spread on lending. As can be seen in Table 4.4, the banks' interest income also displays a substantial decline after the crisis, even though most banks seem to have been reluctant to decrease their interest levels at the beginning of the crisis. In contrast, the average interest income was increased in the fourth quarter of 2008 for the majority of the banks. A closer look at the small ISBs (not shown in any table) reveals that the interest income of these banks is on average higher than that of other ISBs. Moreover, the eight banks having no local competition show the highest interest income, implying that they were able to utilize their local monopoly on lending.

When the financial crisis began, the banks apparently did increase their credit spread, that is, the difference between their lending rates and the corresponding market rates. Observations presented in FI (2010)

Table 4.3 The relative development of net fees and commission income

Measure	Bank	2007				2008				2009			
		Q1	*Q2*	*Q3*	*Q4*	*Q1*	*Q2*	*Q3*	*Q4*	*Q1*	*Q2*	*Q3*	*Q4*
FCI/ Operating Income	*Nordea*	**29%**	28%	28%	25%	25%	26%	24%	17%	17%	17%	19%	21%
	SEB	42%	42%	43%	41%	**43%**	38%	41%	30%	28%	29%	37%	39%
	SHB	28%	26%	**30%**	30%	29%	24%	23%	18%	21%	23%	23%	25%
	Swedbank	29%	31%	**31%**	29%	26%	25%	27%	19%	15%	21%	27%	28%
	LF	−3%	−4%	−4%	−5%	−8%	−9%	−14%	−14%	−20%	−7%	−4%	**1%**
	ISBs	29%	21%	31%	**46%**	30%	25%	28%	33%	26%	30%	28%	31%
	SBs	**28%**		26%		23%		22%		26%		28%	
	CBs	26%		**35%**		28%		20%		23%		24%	
FCI/Net Interest Income	*Nordea*	**53%**	53%	49%	46%	42%	42%	37%	28%	28%	32%	33%	36%
	SEB	114%	**115%**	105%	94%	90%	88%	82%	69%	54%	71%	79%	105%
	SHB	49%	**52%**	49%	49%	40%	38%	34%	31%	32%	33%	32%	37%
	Swedbank	51%	**56%**	52%	48%	42%	45%	42%	35%	24%	38%	44%	48%
	LF	−3%	−5%	−4%	−5%	−9%	−10%	−13%	−13%	−21%	−8%	−5%	**1%**
	ISBs	45%	47%	44%	**76%**	38%	40%	36%	37%	36%	55%	54%	66%
	SBs	53%		49%		42%		42%		51%		**54%**	
	CBs	40%		**66%**		42%		33%		37%		49%	

Note: FCI, fees and commission income.

Table 4.4 Average interest income of the banks during 2007–9

Measure	Bank	2007				2008				2009			
		Q1	*Q2*	*Q3*	*Q4*	*Q1*	*Q2*	*Q3*	*Q4*	*Q1*	*Q2*	*Q3*	*Q4*
Average interest income	*Nordea*	3.93%	4.23%	4.10%	4.44%	4.53%	4.69%	4.85%	5.27%	3.78%	3.05%	2.67%	**2.51%**
	SEB	4.17%	4.11%	4.17%	3.98%	4.19%	4.36%	4.15%	4.26%	3.41%	2.98%	2.44%	**2.34%**
	SHB	3.62%	3.69%	3.87%	4.59%	4.22%	4.30%	5.02%	4.85%	3.56%	2.89%	2.49%	**2.32%**
	Swedbank	4.25%	4.58%	4.71%	5.13%	5.00%	4.98%	5.20%	5.22%	4.15%	3.40%	3.17%	**3.01%**
	LF	5.34%	5.84%	6.81%	7.66%	8.1%	8.4%	9.01%	8.39%	6.31%	4.78%	4.24%	**3.70%**
	ISBs	4.54%	4.62%	4.72%	5.40%	5.42%	5.82%	5.78%	6.25%	3.56%	3.04%	**2.58%**	2.86%
	SBs	4.9%		5.8%		6.1%		6.2%		3.8%		**2.9%**	
	CBs	6.6%		7.0%		7.8%		7.9%		6.4%		**5.1%**	

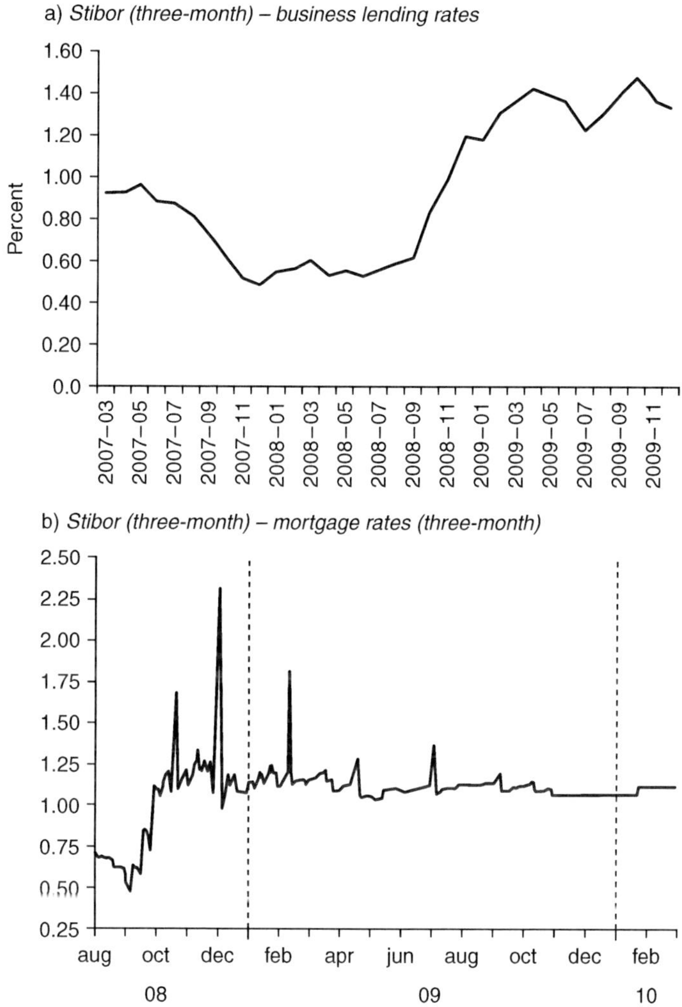

Figure 4.3 The spread between STIBOR and banks' lending rates

Source: FI (2010, pp. 10–11).

also lend support to this interpretation. The two diagrams in Figure 4.3 reveal that the average bank has been taking out a higher premium on both business lending and mortgage loans since the crisis.

The impact of the financial crisis is evident for both business customers and owners of real property. When the crisis began after the summer of 2008 the premium added by the average bank was more than doubled on both types of lending. The interest rates on mortgage loans to property owners seem more volatile than the lending rates to business firms, but this is probably explained by the fact that the short-term STIBOR is compared with the corresponding short-term mortgage rate and not with any of the fixed long-term mortgage rates. Certainly, lending rates on business loans are often floating, but to some extent these rates are likely to be fixed for a longer period than three months. This may also be the reason why the premium observed tends to be higher on business loans.

Table 4.5 shows that the banks have been successful in increasing their profit margin before credit losses since the crisis despite the lower funding spread and decline of fee-based income.

The lower funding spread of the banks seems to have been counterbalanced by their higher lending premiums, that is, their credit spread. Table 4.6 reveals that for a majority of the banks the NII in relation to both OI and operating profit before credit losses did not drop, but even increased, in the third quarter of 2008. With the exception of SEB and the ISBs, both these NII ratios have since been kept by the banks at a similar or higher level than before the crisis.

Not shown in any table, SHB has been the most successful bank in improving the net interest income (more than 42 per cent over the whole period) despite decreasing interest income. The corresponding development was close to 30 per cent for Nordea, 24 per cent for LF, 13 per cent for the ISBs and 5 per cent for Swedbank. In SEB the net interest income declined by almost 2 per cent. The SBs and CBs vary between –3 per cent and 24 per cent, with the exception of the mentioned niche bank, which increased NII by more than 400 per cent.

As shown in Table 4.7, the net interest margin of the banks peaked in the second half of 2008, but in one bank alone – Handelsbanken (SHB) – the higher margin has been maintained over the whole period. Still, the ISBs, the SBs and, particularly, the CBs display a substantially higher margin.

In Table 4.8 the banks' return on equity before tax has been broken down into two components: return on invested funds (*ROIF*) and return on financial leverage (*ROFL*).

The table shows that compensating a declining *ROIF* with a high reliance on *ROFL* is prevalent in commercial banks, but not in ISBs. Since they have no owners, the primary objective of ISBs is not to generate a high *ROE* but rather to minimize risk in order to survive and contribute to a positive development in the local area in which they operate (Olsson, 2009). Despite this, some of the ISBs were, at the

Table 4.5 The banks' profit margins before loss provisions

Measure	Bank	2007				2008				2009			
		Q1	*Q2*	*Q3*	*Q4*	*Q1*	*Q2*	*Q3*	*Q4*	*Q1*	*Q2*	*Q3*	*Q4*
Profit margin *before loss provisions*	*Nordea*	23.4%	23.0%	22.6%	23.6%	19.9%	19.0%	18.6%	20.2%	27.7%	32.6%	**34.9%**	28.9%
	SEB	15.7%	17.1%	14.4%	15.1%	9.7%	13.2%	11.3%	17.7%	16.4%	17.3%	19.2%	**19.8%**
	SHB	20.5%	22.8%	19.1%	15.1%	13.3%	18.0%	15.9%	22.7%	24.5%	27.8%	**30.5%**	29.7%
	Swedbank	21.4%	20.9%	19.1%	19.1%	17.7%	21.4%	17.3%	21.5%	23.2%	**27.0%**	22.3%	23.6%
	LF	**7.4%**	6.5%	6.2%	5.5%	4.7%	5.5%	4.2%	3.0%	5.5%	5.5%	6.1%	5.5%
	ISBs	28.7%	42.1%	27.9%	23.9%	18.5%	24.8%	20.5%	13.2%	22.0%	32.2%	**42.4%**	37.1%
	SBs	**22.2%**		2.5%		18.1%		19.1%		18.6%		21.4%	
	CBs	13.7%		23.0%		13.5%		20.3%		10.9%		**28.0%**	

Table 4.6 The relative development of net interest income (NII)

Measure	Bank	2007				2008				2009			
		Q1	*Q2*	*Q3*	*Q4*	*Q1*	*Q2*	*Q3*	*Q4*	*Q1*	*Q2*	*Q3*	*Q4*
NII/ Operating Income	*Nordea*	54%	53%	57%	53%	60%	62%	**65%**	62%	59%	55%	58%	60%
	SEB	37%	37%	41%	44%	48%	43%	49%	43%	**52%**	41%	46%	37%
	SHB	58%	51%	62%	61%	**73%**	62%	68%	58%	64%	69%	72%	67%
	Swedbank	58%	56%	60%	59%	62%	56%	**66%**	55%	62%	57%	62%	59%
	LF	90%	92%	93%	92%	97%	99%	102%	**103%**	97%	87%	86%	83%
	ISBs	66%	45%	69%	60%	77%	63%	78%	**89%**	71%	55%	52%	47%
	SBs	52%		54%		**55%**		54%		51%		51%	
	CBs	**68%**		62%		78%		64%		68%		59%	
NII/ Operating Profit *before loss provisions*	*Nordea*	114%	110%	119%	107%	130%	134%	**138%**	126%	114%	105%	111%	138%
	SEB	86%	81%	100%	107%	152%	112%	140%	96%	141%	129%	121%	99%
	SHB	103%	90%	112%	123%	160%	112%	122%	93%	115%	129%	136%	**137%**
	Swedbank	117%	112%	123%	121%	131%	106%	138%	105%	121%	109%	**139%**	128%
	LF	354%	368%	338%	346%	351%	381%	368%	**463%**	341%	384%	346%	432%
	ISBs	160%	81%	159%	164%	236%	155%	207%	**397%**	233%	142%	108%	110%
	SBs	164%		**1146%**		184%		170%		210%		210%	
	CBs	246%		–149%		270%		276%		280%		**284%**	

Note: NII, net interest income.

Table 4.7 The development of net interest margin

Measure	Bank	2007				2008				2009			
		Q1	*Q2*	*Q3*	*Q4*	*Q1*	*Q2*	*Q3*	*Q4*	*Q1*	*Q2*	*Q3*	*Q4*
Net interest margin	*Nordea*	1.18%	1.18%	1.18%	**1.25%**	1.22%	1.20%	1.24%	1.24%	1.18%	1.16%	1.14%	1.10%
	SEB	0.73%	0.75%	0.76%	0.81%	0.73%	0.80%	0.79%	0.93%	**1.01%**	0.98%	0.78%	0.68%
	SHB	0.91%	0.92%	0.91%	0.97%	1.00%	1.00%	1.04%	1.08%	1.01%	1.14%	**1.16%**	1.10%
	Swedbank	1.26%	1.28%	1.27%	**1.37%**	1.30%	1.32%	1.35%	1.32%	1.31%	1.21%	1.15%	1.10%
	LF	1.43%	1.41%	1.45%	1.46%	1.32%	1.29%	1.37%	1.42%	1.16%	1.02%	0.92%	0.92%
	ISBs	3.00%	2.97%	2.84%	2.85%	2.93%	3.12%	2.97%	**3.49%**	2.60%	2.48%	2.32%	2.20%
	SBs	2.7%		2.8%		2.7%		2.8%		2.3%		2.2%	
	CBs	4.2%		3.8%		5.4%		**8.3%**		7.9%		7.5%	

Note: NIM, net interest margin.

Table 4.8 Return on invested funds and on financial leverage before tax

Measure	Bank	2007				2008				2009			
		Q1	*Q2*	*Q3*	*Q4*	*Q1*	*Q2*	*Q3*	*Q4*	*Q1*	*Q2*	*Q3*	*Q4*
ROIF	*Nordea*	3.1%	3.4%	3.2%	**3.6%**	3.4%	3.4%	3.5%	3.4%	2.3%	1.9%	1.6%	1.3%
	SEB	4.1%	4.0%	4.0%	3.7%	3.7%	4.0%	3.6%	3.8%	2.6%	1.9%	1.7%	1.7%
	SHB	3.1%	3.2%	3.2%	3.9%	3.6%	3.9%	**4.4%**	4.0%	2.6%	2.0%	1.7%	1.6%
	Swedbank	3.8%	4.1%	4.1%	4.5%	4.2%	4.4%	4.1%	3.9%	1.7%	1.5%	1.2%	1.3%
	LF	6.5%	4.7%	5.3%	5.8%	6.2%	6.9%	7.3%	6.8%	4.8%	3.4%	3.2%	2.8%
	ISBs	3.2%	**4.7%**	3.4%	3.6%	3.6%	4.4%	4.3%	−0.8%	1.1%	3.0%	2.2%	2.0%
	SBs	7.7%		7.9%		8.7%		9.7%		6.7%		6.7%	
	CBs	8.9%		7.1%		4.1%		21.0%		12.4%		8.5%	
ROFL	*Nordea*	19.4%	**21.8%**	19.6%	21.6%	16.5%	17.1%	15.5%	14.2%	15.7%	13.6%	13.6%	9.2%
	SEB	22.5%	**22.2%**	16.9%	18.2%	8.8%	14.8%	9.7%	15.5%	4.8%	0.6%	0.3%	0.6%
	SBH	16.7%	20.2%	15.6%	12.8%	9.5%	14.9%	16.1%	**23.8%**	15.6%	14.5%	14.0%	13.9%
	Swedbank	20.2%	21.6%	18.6%	19.6%	16.9%	**21.6%**	12.8%	7.3%	−17.9%	−10.6%	−14.6%	−8.8%
	LF	44.9%	2.0%	1.6%	1.2%	0.4%	49.4%	−1.1%	−47.4%	1.5%	2.5%	2.1%	2.5%
	ISBs	4.9%	10.9%	4.7%	4.0%	2.9%	6.8%	7.2%	−26.3%	−2.7%	**14.8%**	10.0%	8.2%
	SBs	48.1%		30.1%		50.2%		59.8%		49.1%		48.2%	
	CBs	74.1%		40.0%		7.5%		206.8%		130.4%		91.4%	

Note: ROFL, return on financial leverage; ROIF, return on invested funds.

end of 2008, strongly negatively affected by the crisis due to ownership engagement in Swedbank. If these banks had been poorly capitalized, they would have had no owners to turn to in order to avoid bankruptcy.

Before the financial crisis in 1992, banks were, in general, generating high returns well in line with those achieved in 2007 (Lindblom, 1994). Also at that time a considerable part of this return was attributable to returns on financial leverage. As found by Lindblom (2001), such a high reliance on *ROFL* was also the case for Swedish commercial banks a decade ago – although on a slightly lower level than now.

ROFL is related not only to the exposure to capital risk, but also to the interest rate risk exposure. Table 4.9 gives an indication of the dependence of banks' overall profitability on exposures to interest rate risk and capital risk by displaying the variations in the leverage spread and the leverage multiplier for each bank during 2007–9.

Evidently, the large commercial banks are balancing their relatively narrow leverage spread with a considerably higher leverage multiplier, implying that these banks are very much exposed to capital risk. Lindblom (2001) reported a similar leverage spread (0.7 per cent, $\sigma = 0.2$ per cent) a decade ago (1997–9) for the average commercial bank, but a lower leverage multiplier 20.5 ($\sigma = 5.5$). The corresponding figures for ISBs were 1.7 per cent ($\sigma = 0.4$ per cent) and 6.2 ($\sigma = 2.2$). This suggests that the risk profile of ISBs is more or less unchanged, whereas commercial banks display a higher capital risk. This need not be regarded as unreasonable, since the banks should be better equipped for identifying, assessing and controlling risk exposures after the implementation of the Basel II accord. However, clearly the effect on ROFL of the negative leverage spreads of Swedbank in 2009 was highly amplified by the bank's leverage multiplier.

A more detailed analysis reveals that the shrinking leverage spread of most banks was, to a large extent, caused by credit losses. On average the leverage spread before credit losses was rather stable during the whole period (not shown in any table). A majority of the banks did actually increase the leverage spread before credit losses in connection with the crisis, but towards the end of 2009 it was decreased substantially in most banks. This is a likely effect of the fact that about 85 per cent of consumer loans were changed from fixed to floating rates (FI, 2010). This implies a better matching of the banks' lending and borrowing, and thus a reduced interest rate risk exposure.

The 'riskiness' of the banks may also be analysed based on their actual capital in relation to the regulatory requirement. This relation

Table 4.9 The banks' leverage spread and leverage multiplier

Measure	Bank	2007				2008				2009			
		Q1	*Q2*	*Q3*	*Q4*	*Q1*	*Q2*	*Q3*	*Q4*	*Q1*	*Q2*	*Q3*	*Q4*
Leverage spread (ROIFkd)	*Nordea*	0.90%	0.94%	0.87%	**1.00%**	0.75%	0.71%	0.65%	0.55%	0.62%	0.63%	0.64%	0.43%
	SEB	0.72%	**0.74%**	0.59%	0.62%	0.29%	0.49%	0.31%	0.53%	0.20%	0.02%	0.01%	0.03%
	SHB	0.69%	0.81%	0.63%	0.53%	0.37%	0.60%	0.63%	**0.86%**	0.60%	0.59%	0.56%	0.57%
	Swedbank	0.90%	0.94%	0.80%	0.87%	0.73%	**0.95%**	0.58%	0.36%	−0.85%	−0.50%	−0.65%	−0.46%
	LF	2.43%	0.10%	0.08%	0.06%	0.02%	2.18%	−0.05%	−2.04%	0.06%	0.09%	0.08%	0.09%
	ISBs	1.16%	**2.58%**	1.04%	0.83%	0.57%	1.17%	1.05%	−3.72%	−0.38%	2.13%	1.59%	1.27%
	SBs	5.41%		3.23%		5.29%		6.18%		5.20%		5.06%	
	CBs	6.43%		4.21%		0.55%		17.09%		10.63%		7.47%	
Leverage multiplier (*D/E*)	Nordea	21.46	23.12	22.66	21.67	22.10	24.05	23.70	**25.63**	25.33	21.52	21.27	21.64
	SEB	**31.36**	30.12	28.45	29.56	30.13	29.80	30.88	28.99	23.86	23.02	30.16	22.16
	SHB	26.71	**28.67**	27.59	23.96	23.81	26.29	26.53	27.80	28.19	26.93	25.92	24.55
	Swedbank	22.35	23.04	**23.37**	22.54	23.05	22.79	22.16	19.95	21.05	21.13	22.60	18.95
	LF	18.49	19.38	20.97	21.25	22.76	22.68	21.85	23.27	25.18	28.70	26.31	26.97
	ISBs	4.24	4.24	4.50	4.85	5.12	5.76	6.86	**7.06**	7.01	6.95	6.27	6.49
	SBs	8.88		9.32		9.47		9.65		9.46		9.42	
	CBs	13.67		13.22		15.65		14.97		16.01		15.39	

Table 4.10 Average own funds ratio of savings and commercial banks

Bank category	2007				2008				2009			
	Q1	Q2	Q3	Q4	Q1	Q2	Q3	Q4	Q1	Q2	Q3	Q4
Savings banks	2.30	2.23	2.21	2.30	2.20	2.17	2.13	2.13	2.14	2.05	2.04	2.10
Commercial banks	2.80	2.47	2.48	2.60	2.23	2.25	2.22	2.37	2.22	2.39	2.39	2.42

Source: data from Swedish Financial Supervisory Authority.

is referred to as the bank's 'own funds ratio'. Table 4.10 displays the development of this ratio.

On average the banks seem to be highly capitalized, holding more than twice as much capital as required. Only one bank barely met the regulatory requirement, displaying a ratio close to one. This suggests that the banks in general have control over their capital risk – at least according to the second Basel accord.

4.4 Conclusions

The analysis of the profitability and risk-taking of Swedish banks during the financial crisis shows that the banks, in general, performed well domestically. If it had not for been credit losses due, as it appears, to over-aggressive lending by commercial banks, first of all in the Baltic States, the average profitability of the banks would have been only marginally affected by the crisis, given the stability measures assumed by the government and the Central Bank. In that respect this crisis is different from the one in the early 1990s. On that occasion the financial crisis was domestically driven and primarily caused by over-lending into one sector in the economy: real estates. Despite the issuance of a general bank guarantee, several banks were bailed out and thereafter either restructured or closed down (Lindblom, 1994). The public trust in incumbent banks deteriorated (Lindblom and Andersson, 1997), which paved the way for new banks. This time the outcome of the crisis seems to be the opposite.

We find that losses in foreign lending have been covered to a large extent by higher lending premiums on the home market, implying lessened domestic competition. We also observe that ISBs that operate the only branch in a local market display higher average interest income than other ISBs. This does not exclude the possibility that the increase in banks' lending premiums is caused by greater uncertainty and exposures to credit risk also on the Swedish market also. However, we cannot identify any such signs in the data. We do find indications that the banks' interest rate risk has been reduced. Since the crisis, banks in general, and commercial banks in particular, do not rely as heavily on a high interest rate risk spread as they did previously, when they put a lot of effort into trying to benefit from the concavity of the yield curve. In combination with a declining funding spread, this appears to be a more plausible explanation of their increasing credit spread.

As in earlier studies, we find that the four big commercial banks rely heavily on low capitalization. Their debt-to-equity ratio is even higher today. However, the banks seem to have their exposure to capital risk under control, as their own funds ratio is on average more than twice as high as required by the Basel II capital adequacy framework.

Acknowledgement

We wish to thank 'Jan Wallanders and Tom Hedelius Stiftelse' for financial support.

Notes

1. FI (2010) reports that about half of the credit losses of the four large commercial banks in 2009 occurred in the Baltic States.
2. The repo rate peaked at 4.75 per cent (deposit rate = 4 per cent and lending rate 5.5 per cent) on 10 September 2008. Beginning in mid-October, the Swedish Central Bank has been cutting the repo rate stepwise to a level as low as 0.25 per cent (deposit rate = –0.25 per cent and lending rate = 0.75 per cent) on 8 July 2009. (www.riksbank.com/templates/Page.aspx?id=12182). Accessed on 14 April 2011.
3. The number of banks under the supervision of the Swedish Financial Supervisory Authority was, at the end of the year, 99, 89 and 90, respectively, for the three years. There have been mergers and acquisitions of savings banks, and new investment-type banks have entered the market. The analysis is not affected, as investment-type banks are not included and the M and As take place within the same bank category (ISBs). The analysis further excludes two banks categorized as member banks, 13 banks mainly providing customer credits and one bank lacking available data since it is part of a retail group.
4. Fifty-two ISBs are savings banks and 11 are former savings banks that have converted to limited companies.
5. Two are limited companies and one a savings bank that became a member of the association in 2010.
6. In 1992 the financial crisis resulted in an increase of average funding costs. The credit losses of the banks were too massive for them to manage, which is why their average cost of debt was increasing rather than declining.

References

Alberts, W.A. (1989) 'A New Look at Calculating ROE', *The Bank Magazine*, 172(March–April), 37–42.

Annual and quarterly reports from Swedish banks during 2007–9.

Demirgüç-Kunt A. and Huizinga, H. (1998) 'Determinants of Commercial Bank Interest Margins and Profitability', *World Bank Policy Research Working Paper*, No. 1900. (Washington DC: World Bank).

FI (2010) 'Effekterna av de statliga stabilitetsåtgärderna – första rapporten 2010', *Finansinspektionen rapport 2010-03-11*, Finansinspektionen, Stockholm.

Frazer, D.R. and Zhang, H. (2009) 'Mergers and Long-Term Corporate Performance: Evidence from Cross-Border Bank Acquisitions', *Journal of Money, Credit and Banking*, 41(7), 1503–13.

García-Herrero, A., Gavilá, S. and Santabárbara, D. (2009) 'What explains the low profitability of Chinese banks?', *Journal of Banking and Finance*, 33(11), 2080–92.

Goddard, J., Molyneux, P. and Wilson J.O.S. (2004a) 'Dynamics of Growth and Profitability in Banking', *Journal of Money, Credit and Banking*, 36(6), 1069–90.

Goddard, J., Molyneux, P. and Wilson, J.O.S. (2004b) 'The Profitability of European Banks', *The Manchester School*, 72(3), 363–81.

Hannan, T.H. and Prager, R.A. (2009) 'The profitability of small single-market banks in an era of multi-market banking', *Journal of Banking and Finance*, 33(2), 263–71.

La Porta, R., López-de-Silandes, F. and Shleifer, A. (2002) 'Government ownership of banks', *Journal of Finance*, 57(1), 265–301.

Lindblom, T. (1994) 'Credit Losses in Nordic Banks', in Revell, J.R.S. (ed.), *The Changing Face of European Banks and Securities Markets* (Basingstoke, UK: Palgrave Macmillan), pp. 174–90.

Lindblom, T. (2001) 'Att analysera bankers lönsamhet och finansiella risktagande med nyckeltal', in Landström, H., Mattsson, J. and Helmersson, H. (eds.), *Ur en forskarhandledares örtagård – En vänbok till Bertil Gandemo* (Sweden: Lund Business Press), pp. 101–20.

Lindblom, T. and M. Andersson (1997) 'Recent Developments in Retail Banking in Scandinavia: narrow vs. universal banking', in Revell, J.R.S. (ed.), *The Recent Evolution of Financial Systems* (Basingstoke, UK: Palgrave Macmillan), pp. 181–202.

Lindblom, T. and Willesson, M. (2010) 'Banks' Measurement of Operational Risk and the Effect on Regulatory Capital', in Fiordelisi, F., Molyneux, P. and Previati, D. (eds), *New issues in financial institutions and markets* (Basingstoke, UK: Palgrave Macmillan).

Molyneux, P. and Thornton, J. (1992) 'Determinants of European bank profitability: A note', *Journal of Banking and Finance*, 16(6), 1173–8.

Olsson M. (2009) *Fast rotad är den trygghet som bygges på sparade slantar – En analys av sparbankernas värdeskapande på den avreglerade bankmarknaden i Sverige* (Sweden: BAS).

5

Asset-Backed Securitization and Financial Stability: The Downgrading Delay Effect

Mario La Torre and Fabiomassimo Mango

5.1 Introduction

Asset-backed securitization (ABS) may contribute to generating instability in financial markets both through an 'inside effect' in the banking system – facilitating progressive deterioration of bank assets' quality – and through an 'outside effect' – favouring credit risk transfer from balance sheets of banks acting as originators to investors in asset-backed securities (ABS). The rating assigned to ABS has the function of indicating to the market the credit risk borne by investors. This depends on the quality of assets and of guarantees lent by originators and by any third-party guarantor, as well as on the trend of macroeconomic determinants which may compromise the capacity of principal debtors to honour their debts.

The underlying hypothesis on which this work is based is that rating models do not correctly embody the impact of macroeconomic variables on debtors' solvency, determining a lag in downgrading. In particular, it is considered that any variations in interest rates and GDP have an impact on ABS performances, but that such an impact is not picked up in a timely fashion by rating models. Essentially, in pre-crisis periods, when interest rate increases as well as decreases are recorded in growth rates of GDP, rating assessments fail to register risk increases in ABS securities, only proceeding to downgrade later, when variations in macroeconomic variables have generated negative effects on the flow of ABS funds.

We verify this hypothesis specifically with reference to ABS transactions active during the recent financial and economic crisis. We then proceed to test information on ABS rating, assessing it in relation to the timing of downgrading on a sample of transactions which took place between 2000 and 2009. The conclusions reached confirm the theoretical hypothesis, demonstrating that, in the pre-crisis period, when macroeconomic variables suggested the need for a downgrading judgement, agencies delayed downmarking, making the announcement only at a later stage, after the crisis had taken place and the transaction criticalities were already displayed. The chapter is related to the literature analysing relations between the financial crisis and asset-backed securitization, bringing an innovative contribution to empirical and theoretical studies, aimed at defining an interpretational model for relations between ABS and financial crises.

5.2 Objective, methodology and structure

ABS has often been mentioned as one of the financial techniques which most contributed to the creation and diffusion of the recent financial crisis. It is, in fact, considered that the low quality of securitized assets, and the use of inappropriately set-up ABS structures, resulted in the introduction into the financial market of asset-backed securities (ABS) which contained a high risk factor, not perceived by investors. Rating agencies also contributed to the process, unable as they were to accurately perceive through their assessments the implicit risk in ABS transactions and the following developments.

In this framework, the objective of this chapter is to measure the contribution of ABS to the current systemic crisis, the first signs of which emerged around 2007. With this aim, the reporting efficiency of ABS rating was assessed in relation to the timing of downgrading. At the root of this methodology is the evidence that ABS transactions, for which rating downgrading revision is considered to have occurred late compared with the display of signs of the deteriorating quality of ABS securities, contributed most to the financial crisis.

The anomaly of an ABS transaction is the necessary condition for its contribution to systemic instability. From this point of view, downgrading represents the most explicit indicator to be used to test the contribution of asset securitization to the financial crisis.

On an empirical basis, the rating assigned to ABS securities may represent a measure of the contribution of asset securitization to the economic–financial instability experienced by financial markets. ABS rating judgement should, in fact, summarize and indicate on an ongoing basis any anomalies and criticalities in the transaction.

Downgrading is an alarm signal and a leading indicator of a possible default in the transaction. From this perspective, the number of ABS transactions subjected to downgrading may be considered an indicator of the potential contribution of asset securitization to system instability.

However, reduced information efficiency in financial markets may determine a lag in downgrading, or rather postponement of ABS downgrading compared with the moment when possible determinants of deterioration are expressed. In this case, downgrading loses all or part of its predictive value, representing only ex post the increased risk associated with ABS securities; to the 'primary negative effect' of ABS on systemic stability, therefore, must be added the 'secondary derivative effect' of a missed warning to financial markets of the real risk in the transaction.

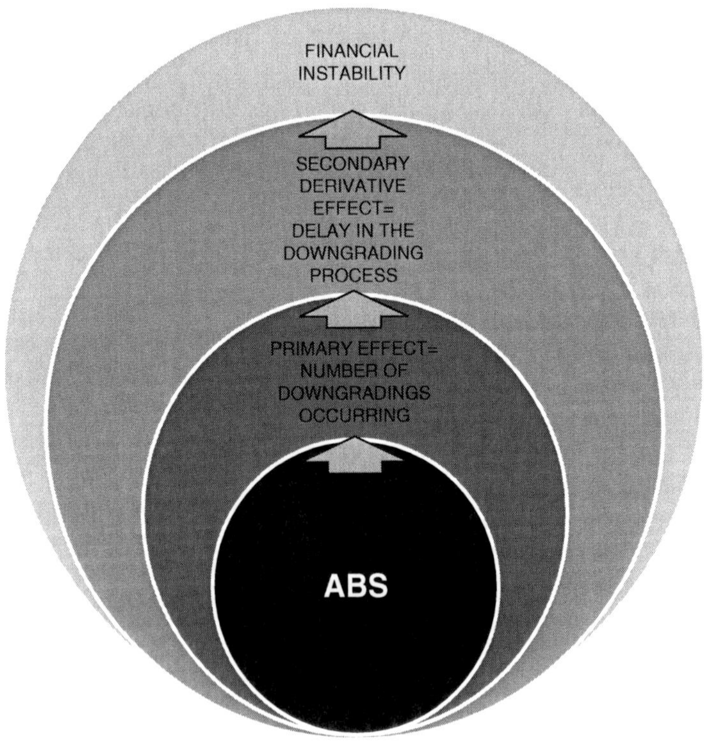

Figure 5.1 ABS and financial instability

Two logical links connect ABS with the financial crisis (Figure 5.1). The first, leading to a 'primary effect', assumes that the degree of downgrading of ABS securities – independently of the timely quality of their occurrence – represents a significant measure of the contribution made by asset securitization to the systemic crisis. The more numerous the downgradings, the greater was the contribution of ABS to financial instability. The second, which can be described as a 'secondary derivative effect', presupposes that a lack of promptness in downgrading increases the significance of ABS' contribution to the diffusion of the crisis; the more numerous the delayed downgradings compared with the expression of determinants of asset quality deterioration, the less is the capacity of the market and of ABS investors to assess and correctly manage the risk associated with their exposure.

As rating judgements are related to microeconomic and macroeconomic variables, when these are not correctly incorporated in rating models it is possible to determine a lag in downgrading. The hypothesis at the core of this chapter is that, before the diffusion of the present crisis, some variables – in particular those of a macroeconomic nature – were not correctly incorporated in rating judgements, determining a sigma effect between the 'primary effect' and the 'secondary derivative effect', increasing the negative impact of ABSs on system stability. Such a 'secondary derivative effect' – not investigated to date in the literature – may represent a highly significant variable in the contribution of ABS to financial and economic instability; particularly if it can be demonstrated that securitization deals which were active during the financial crisis and underwent downgrading, and for which downgrading came late, were numerous and significant.

It is interesting to verify whether, among recently downgraded ABS, a significant number underwent delayed markdown judgement, or, rather, if the conditions had not been met for downgrading to take place earlier. For this reason, the present chapter – after theorizing a conceptual framework explaining the link between ABS and financial stability – verifies on an empirical basis, with selected samples from ABS programmes, the number of transactions subjected to downgrading and the rating efficiency in signalling deterioration in a timely fashion. The test for timely downgrading is preceded by a descriptive analysis of the sample of ABS chosen, and in particular of those which, having undergone downgrading, were able to create negative effects on financial markets in periods of crisis, due to both a 'primary effect' and a 'secondary derivative effect'.

In particular, the analysis concentrates on a sample of securitization transactions including residential mortgages (Residential Mortgage Backed Security – RMBS) carried out in some of the major European countries (UK, Holland, Italy, Portugal and Spain). With reference to the observation period, in order also to capture pre-crisis factors, transactions were considered which were created between 2000 and 2008 and still active. For the selected samples we proceeded to:

- classify ABS for each country and building up the sample;
- identify micro and macro variables considered to explain rating judgement;
- acquire the value of selected variables;
- apply a regression model (panel data) to measure market efficiency in terms of frequency and timing of downgrading intervention.

In the second section of this chapter the contribution of our work is discussed, followed by a description of essential characteristics of an ABS programme. We then outline causal variables of ABS downgrading which can be attributed to the behaviour of both microeconomic variables (micro-determinants) and macroeconomic variables (macro-determinants). We then discuss connections between ABS and economic–financial stability, report the estimates of various models, and finally conclude.

5.3 ABS and financial crisis: the chapter's contribution to the literature

Asset securitization literature is born of a theoretical approach, focusing mainly on two aspects analysed from the originator's perspective: potential benefits, on the one hand, and potential risks and relations with financial regulations, on the other (Pavel, 1986; Greenbaum and Thakor, 1987; Hess and Smith, 1988; Rosenthal and Ocampo, 1988; Norton and Spellman, 1991; La Torre, 1995, 2004; Giannotti, 2004; Affinito and Tagliaferri, 2010).

The ABS market's progressive development has subsequently nurtured empirical investigation, which may be summarized as two trends: one verifying determinants illustrating transactions carried out (Pavel and Phillis, 1987; Donato and Shaffer, 1991) and one concentrating on microeconomic effects, in particular on risk stored in the originator's balance sheet (Loutskina and Strahan, 2006; Demyanyk and van Hemert, 2007; Dell'Ariccia *et al.*, 2008; Keys *et al.*, 2008;

Mian and Sufi, 2008) and on capital requirements (Altunbas *et al.*, 2007). The financial crisis of these last few years has, in conclusion, stimulated a third investigative plan – of an empirical nature – dedicated to links between ABS and financial crisis (Fender and Mitchell, 2005; Allen and Carletti, 2006; BIS, 2008; Borio, 2008; Ibanez and Scheicher, 2009).

The main objective of empirical testing generally concerns relations between ABS and risk borne by originators. Even the link between ABS and systemic crisis is usually tested by verifying whether, and to what degree, originator banks that systematically take recourse to securitization programmes present more risky balance sheets in the middle period. In fact, even if ABS technique allows the originator to reduce the risk exposure it derives from securitized assets, in the case of principal debtors' insolvency there is always the originator bank's moral obligation, which involves for the latter an actual risk which is higher than nominal exposure.

From this perspective, empirical assessment privileges testing of determinants and effect of ABS on the originator; particular attention has been placed on leverage and on the quality of loans in the originator's portfolio following ABS transactions, as well as the overall risk in the originator's balance sheet. Moreover, the results reached are often contradictory, stressing in some cases a drop in risk for originators resorting to asset securitizations (Carey, 1998; Dionne and Harchaoui, 2003; Cebenoyan and Strahan, 2004; Jiangli and Pritsker, 2008; Keys *et al.*, 2008; Mian and Sufi, 2008; Purnanandam, 2010), and in others an opposite or controversial effect (Cantor and Rouyer, 2000; Calomiris and Mason, 2004; Ambrose *et al.*, 2005; Franke and Krahnen, 2005; Haensel and Krahnen, 2007; Sarkisyan *et al.*, 2009). Naturally, as one would expect, the net effect on the originator of one or more ABS programmes is strongly dependent on the transactions' specific structure and, in particular, on the protection the originator itself offers on transferred assets (Casu *et al.*, 2010).

The literature too date is rather limited in investigating the impact of securitization on systemic risk although there has been work investigating the increased exposure of risks to investors in ABS (Ashcraft et al, 2010) and the influence of bank credit policies on securitization activity (Madalone and Alcade, 2009).

The purpose of the present chapter is precisely the contrary: to test the contribution of asset-backed securitization to financial stability through the assessment of the risk distributed on investors in ABS, whether originators or external investors.

In the literary framework, this chapter will make an innovative contribution, both on a methodological plane and in relation to results obtained. From a methodological perspective, the study is intended to contribute to the current debate on the link between ABS and the financial crisis, carrying out an accurate analysis of mechanisms with which ABS may contribute to the creation and spreading of crises. It has been necessary, therefore, in the first place to propose an interpretation model of the link between ABS and economical–financial stability which could offer a logical map of the contribution made by asset securitization to financial and economic crises. On a methodological plane, therefore, this chapter offers an interpretation model for relations between ABS and systemic crises which has proved efficient in building a taxonomy of the variables used for empirical assessment.

On an empirical verification basis, the chapter offers innovative indications, as it measures the contribution of ABS to systemic crisis, considering the riskiness of ABS negotiated in the market rather than the risk retained by originators. Assuming that all programmes downmarked in rating judgements represent *per se* an explicit indicator of ABS' negative impact on market stability, the chapter tests the occurrence of downgrading delays. In this way, the analysis offers results which are not limited to explicating mere descriptive primary effect indicators, but also measure effects that have been defined in the context of 'secondary derivative effects', never before investigated in the literature.

5.4 ABS structure: flow of funds and investors' protection

Asset securitization is a financial technique through which firms transfer portfolios of assets present in their balance sheets to a vehicle company set up for that purpose (Special Purpose Vehicle or SPV); the peculiarity of ABS compared with traditional loan selling lies in the fact that the transferee finances assets acquisition through securities sales on the capital market for an amount corresponding to the transfer price which must be paid by the same. Thus, securitization's distinctive characteristic is the creation of a link between a firm's financial assets and third-party investors active on the capital market.

Specifically (Figure 5.2), and with reference to a banking firm, a typical securitization programme foresees the setting up on the part of the bank (originator) of a portfolio of homogeneous loans, the transfer of the portfolio to the SPV, the issuing on the part of the SPV of ABS securities and the acquisition of the latter by institutional investors. If opportunely structured, the transaction allows the transferee bank to obtain an off-balance sheet treatment for transferred assets, which will therefore disappear from the originator's balance sheet. Normally, parties providing guarantees participate in the transaction (credit enhancers), as well as one or more rating agencies whose task it is to offer a judgement on securities issued. Securities are normally divided into three classes: senior securities, with a low degree of risk, and mezzanine and junior securities, which incorporate rising degrees of risk. It is important to note at this juncture that rating companies' judgements refer to single tranches of securities and not to transferred assets.

The cash flow of an ABS programme (Figure 5.3) allows understanding of the economic ratio underlying the transaction, as well as the key variable of its sustainability and, in the end, of the rating judgement. The securitized portfolio generates flows of funds coming from interest rates and capital reimbursed by the principal transferred debtors. Such flows, net of operational costs, represent investors' yield in ABS. So, any event interrupting or limiting the passage of flows of funds from

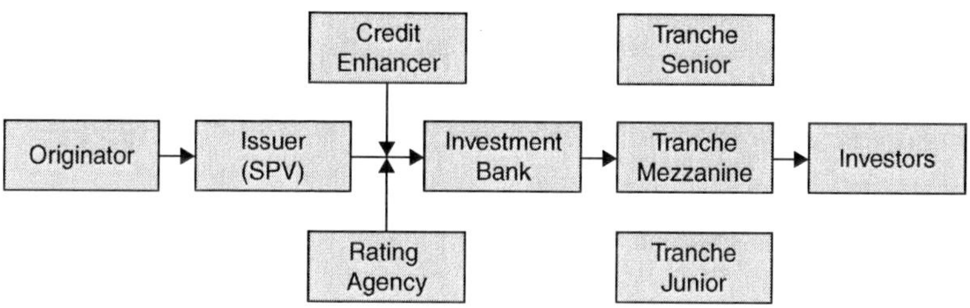

Figure 5.2 The structure of an ABS transaction

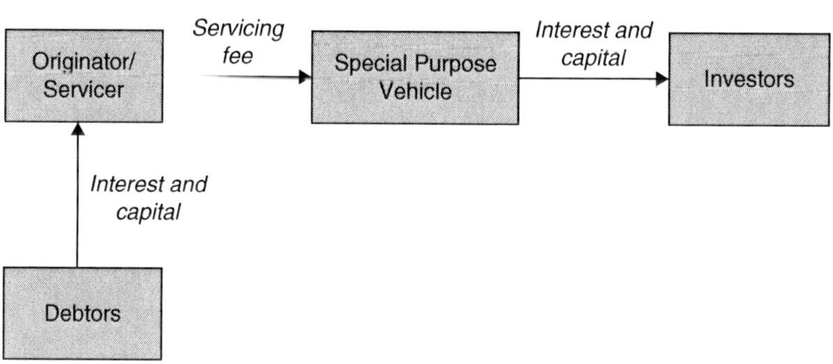

Figure 5.3 The flow of funds of an ABS transaction

principal debtors to final investors represents a risk to the successful outcome of the transaction. Rating judgement, referring to securities and single tranches issued, precisely assesses ABS securities' capacity to ensure the yield promised to investors.

5.5 ABS rating: micro and macro determinants

ABS securities rating judgement is, therefore, related not only to transferred assets quality but also to transaction structure, in particular guarantees offered by the originator itself (internal guarantees) and by third-party guarantors (external guarantees) whose purpose is to protect ABS investors' yield in case of default. For this reason, rating judgement is not referred to the originator, nor can it be attributed only to transferred assets quality; instead, it represents a judgement on securities' capacity to provide the yield promised to external investors. Rating differs for every single tranche issued, because every single tranche, in relation to the transaction structure, withstands differing degrees of risk; for this reason separate ratings are carried out for senior, mezzanine and junior securities in a single ABS programme.

Rating adjustment during the life of an ABS programme is largely connected to specific events which explain a risk variation in ABS securities. Securitization transactions generally foresee clauses which contemplate triggers, or clauses which allow the creation of precautionary actions in the case of contractually predefined events taking place, capable of interrupting the normal transfer of funds from transferred debtors to investors in ABS securities. Such events are considered in rating adjustment of asset-backed securities through constant monitoring of specific ratios whose performances are generally described in three-quarterly reports published by issuers. Among the most used indicators, we find Default Ratio, Disequilibrium Event and Liquidity Agreement Event. ABS transactions' solvency is, in fact, threatened by delinquencies or defaults, by mismatching or commingling of cash flow, in the case of prepayments, and by originator or servicer bankruptcy.

Triggers are events which see their own determinants in microeconomic and macroeconomic variables (Table 5.1); with such prospects, ratings should incorporate elements leading to the quality of securitized assets, the standing of single parties participating in the transaction, the structure of the programme itself (micro-determinants), and also macroeconomic variables capable of impacting the regular trend of the flows of funds (macro-determinants).

Table 5.1 Micro and macro determinants in rating of ABS

Micro Determinants (specific risk)
1. Quality of portfolio (state of anomaly in loans, average duration, technical form, sector and geographical diversification)
2. Structure of ABS transaction (contracts, cash flow, guarantees, etc.)
3. Aim of the operation (transfer of credit risk, liquidity needs, capital requirements, etc.)
Macro Determinants (system risk)
4. Gross Domestic Product
5. Interest rates level (EURIBOR, LIBOR, BCE)
6. Market liquidity (EONIA volatility)
7. Inflation growth level
8. Real estate prices level on the market
9. ABS regulation

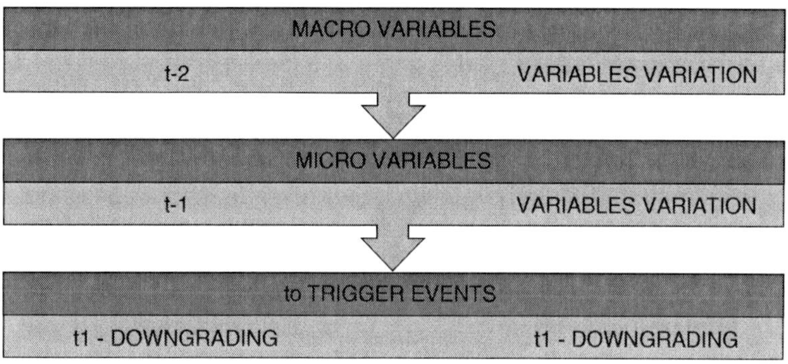

Figure 5.4 The timing lag of the downgrading process

According to the hypothesis at the basis of the empirical investigation carried out in this chapter, the correlation between some macro variables and financial flows of ABS transactions incorrectly incorporated in rating judgement is what determines a delayed rating adjustment. The explanation lies in a different time link between the manifestation of trigger events and the variations in micro and macroeconomic variables that determine them (Figure 5.4).

Rating agencies participate from the start, together with the originator, in setting up the programme; for this reason, the choice of assets constituting the pool of the securitized portfolio, as well as the definition of internal and external guarantees foreseen by the ABS programme, is made according to the rating which the originator desires to obtain on the different tranches of securities in the issuing phase. Microeconomic variables, moreover, are those most directly connected to trigger events. Ongoing variations of micro variables may determine an immediate occurrence of trigger events and a subsequent sudden rating adjustment. Essentially, the timeline reaction connecting variations in microeconomic variables to trigger events and to rating variation is relatively short. We do not, therefore, consider that microeconomic determinants justify a significant downgrading lag.

A less direct time link connects macro determinants to ABS securities' capacity to ensure promised yield to final investors, as variations in macroeconomic variables may generate effects on the regular trend of flows of ABS funds, even with large time lags. Among macro variables, particular significance must be attributed to the relation existing between principal debtors' settlement capacity, on the one side, and the trend of GDP, of the interest rate, of the market liquidity, of the rate of inflation and – particularly in case of securitizations of residential mortgages – of the level of prices on the real estate market, on the other. The increase in the cost of money, or the cost of primary consumptions, may induce a contraction in financial availability of transferred debtors, necessary to fulfil obligations deriving from loans taken up, with the consequent deterioration of the quality of the securitized portfolio. In the case of mortgages, by the way, one must also consider the presence of speculation bubbles, which cause over-assessment of estates and consequently the depreciation of the guarantee from the moment in which a realignment of prices to the real value takes place.

Finally, current ABS regulation could be a highly significant variable, as it is in a position to influence the structure of the programme through prudential ratios imposed on the originator, the guarantors and ABS investors. This chain mechanism of effects of variations in macroeconomic variables on trigger events and on flows of funds in an ABS transaction is longer than the one attributable to micro variables. ABS ratings adjustments, therefore, when justified by macro variables, may take place only with significant delay compared with the occurrence of the justifying cause.

5.6 Asset securitization and financial stability: an interpretative model

There are two transmission channels through which asset securitization may contribute to feeding systemic crises: by favouring the concentration of the credit risk incorporated in balance sheets of single banks, and by facilitating the transfer of the credit risk on institutional investors. The two conditions, moreover, may take place at the same time.

Concerning single banks, the greatest exposure to credit risk occurs when the latter – thanks to ABS transactions – recomposes its loan portfolio, substituting good high-quality assets with riskier loans; especially when, to meet the favour of the market, ABS transactions are built selecting the highest-quality loans present in the originator bank portfolio. The effect is even more significant when, as generally happens, the originator buys part of the junior securities issued – reabsorbing in its own balance sheet the most dangerous tranche issued – or offers important guarantees on securities placed on investors. In those markets where asset securitization is widely used, this scenario may apply to a high number of originator banks. The result is an overall deterioration of bank asset quality.

Concerning investors, the mechanism is fulfilled by placing risky ABS securities on the markets, generally attributable to mezzanine and a portion of junior tranches. This can take place, in the first place, due to the explicit goal of the originating bank, via securitization, to clear its balance sheet of highly risky loans. In the second place, placement on the market of high-risk ABS securities may be the result of the abovementioned deterioration in the credits portfolio, also explained by a negative trend of the macroeconomic variables. The more numerous banks systematically resorting to securitization are on the market, the more this result is realized. In such cases, in fact, credit portfolio restructuring, together with a moral hazard attitude, results in a physiological quality deterioration of assets stored in banks' balance sheets. If these assets are destined to feed revolving portfolios of ABS transactions, or new securitization programmes, the implicit risk in single debt exposures is transferred by originators to investors in ABS securities, thus increasing systemic risk.

It is possible, therefore, to discern asset securitization's contribution to systemic risk due both to an 'inside effect' in the banking system – when ABS favours quality deterioration in bank assets present on the market, both due to the low quality of new loans issued and in relation to the quotas of junior securities held and guarantees lent – and to what can be recognized as 'outside effect' – when the loans risk present in bank balance sheets is transferred, thanks to asset securitization, to final investors in ABS and to third guarantors (Figure 5.5). Both effects may be generated by microeconomic or macroeconomic variables.

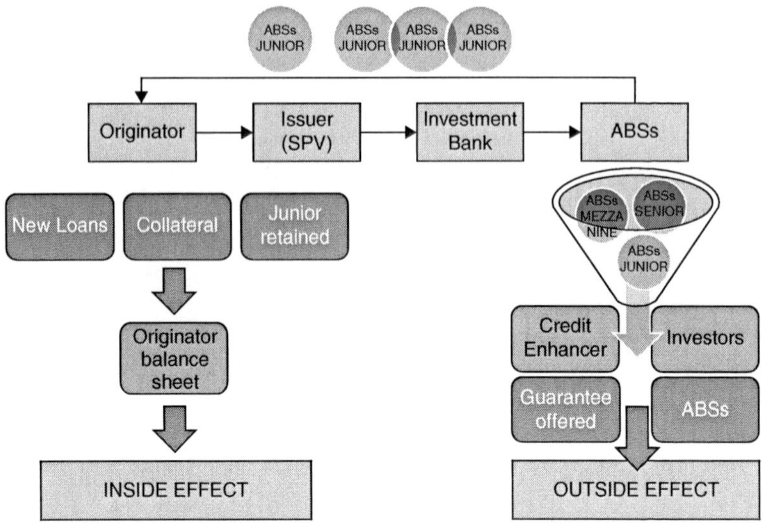

Figure 5.5 ABS and financial stability: inside and outside effect

5.6.1 ABS and systemic crisis: micro variables

In the ABS – financial crisis chain reaction, microeconomic variables which have an impact on ABS optimum performance are related to quality and typology of securitized assets. The portfolio's capacity to generate flows regularly, and not to record a high rate of prepayments, is strictly connected to the characteristics of loans selected, in terms of technical forms, of sector and geographic diversification, of average residual life, and of level of riskiness at the moment of securitization (Figure 5.6). Literature analysing relations between determinants and ABS effects has highlighted connections between the quality of securitized assets and the standing of the originator. Various studies indicate that the riskiest banks have greater incentives in resorting to securitization and transfer of risky assets to external investors. In a nutshell, it is supposed that higher-risk banks use ABS most and, thanks to this technique, improve their balance sheets, securitizing risky loans and investing the derived liquidity in less risky activities.

This mechanism would indicate, as a result, an improvement in banks' balance sheets and, at the same time, a greater diffusion on the capital market of the risk implicit in securitized assets. However, not all empirical tests reach results consistent with this hypothesis, nor do they point to a transfer from inside to outside effect.

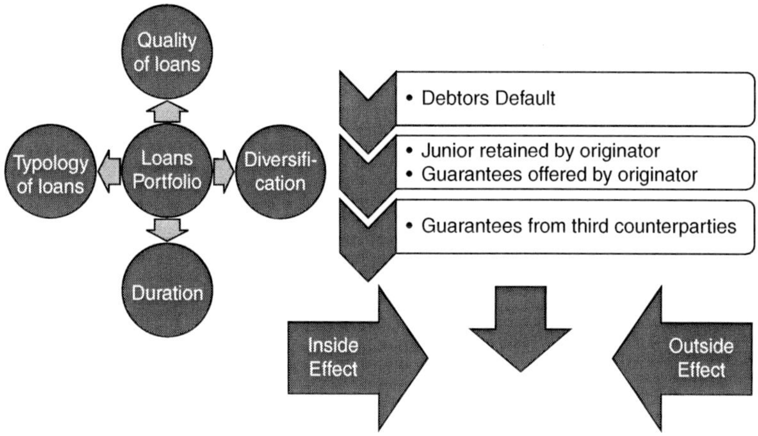

Figure 5.6 ABS and financial crisis: micro determinants

The reason for this lies in the fact that the single ABS transaction structure may determine a different final distribution of risk from securitized loans. Investors and credit enhancers find appropriate protection mechanisms in the ABS program. Originators, in fact, do not only usually repurchase relevant percentages of junior tranches issued, limiting the risk quota transmitted to investors, but also often offer other forms of internal guarantees. For the bank, restructuring its loans portfolio to operate in favour of less risky credits is juxtaposed with a withholding of part of the risk of securitized assets and an increased risk in the portfolio of securities, with a net effect on the balance sheet which is not always positive. Moreover, it must be noted that, in recession phases, the single originator finds more difficulty in substituting securitized loans with good-quality ones.

Underwriting of junior securities, and other inside guarantees provided by the originator, have precisely the purpose of protecting ABS investors and outside guarantors from the possibility of debtors' defaults being transferred; such a phenomenon has been termed in the literature the 'recourse hypothesis'. A kind of barrier against risk would therefore be created to protect final investors and, in part, third-party guarantors. The contribution of asset securitization to system crises, therefore, naturally oriented towards an 'outside effect', may find in the structure of the specific ABS operation a channelling 'inside effect' (Figure 5.7).

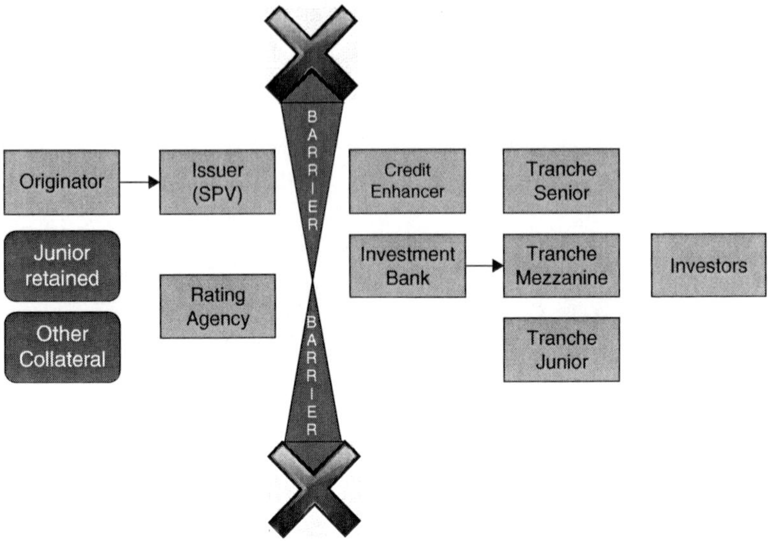

Figure 5.7 Internal recourse and barrier protection

5.6.2 ABS and systemic crisis: macro variables

The chain reaction between macro variables and securitized portfolio quality may be summed up as a logical sequence typically used in literature to explain financial instability. Expansive economic scenarios, typical of pre-crisis phases, usually show low interest rates and, importantly, sustained growth rates of the GDP; in these phases financial intermediaries and banks normally adopt pro-cyclical loan policies. The abundance of liquidity present on the market, the rise in demand for credit, and the need to compensate for decrease in margins due to low interest rates and to an increase in competition determine a general expansion in offers of credit. In this scenario, ABS becomes the perfect tool to go along with expansive credit policies: it provides additional liquidity deriving from the transfer of non-negotiable assets – and which can be used for granting new loans – and it releases the pressure on banks' profitability, both through the restructuring of flows of capital and interests, due to the substitution of old loans with new ones, and through commissions deriving from the ABS programme. Such conditions, however, may favour an attitude of moral hazard on the part of the banks and, in this way, an adverse selection of clients, ultimately causing an increase in the credit risk of the banks' loan portfolios.

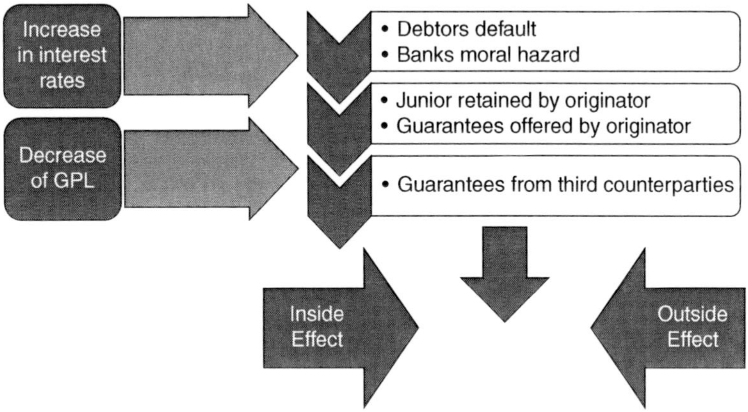

Figure 5.8 ABS and financial crisis: macro determinants

Now, when the economic cycle presents the first signs of inversion, reverting from an expanding cycle to a recessive cycle, interest rates and GDP change sign and measures; interest rates register upward trends and growth in GDP slows down. It is precisely at that point that the logical chain described, which connects ABS to the systemic crisis, brings about its effects with the utmost potency (Figure 5.8).

In the first place, interest rate increases compromise the capacity of transferred debtors to reimburse their debts to the SPV in a timely fashion, negatively impacting ABS investors' returns. In the second place, the decrease in growth rates of domestic product may expose debtors to contractions in their income and consequent difficulties in repaying debts. The negative trend of GDP, however, carries with it a lower demand for credit, stimulating moral hazard policies in those banks which – lacking an alternative – aim at keeping the same growth rhythms in their activity. Even in this case, the distribution between 'inside effect' and 'outside effect' depends on the specific structure of the transaction, and in particular on collaterals offered by the originator and by credit enhancers. There is, however, a further element to consider: criticalities are determined also by those assets which, at the moment of the securitization launch – in the expanding cycle phase – did not reveal problems, but which highlighted criticalities due to macroeconomic factors.

5.6.3 ABS and systemic crisis: downgrading delays

The hypothesis at the basis of the empirical test is that rating judgements are not adjusted in a timely fashion following macro variables;

specifically, they are late in embodying possible 'inside' and 'outside effects' dictated by variations in interest rates and GDP. It would appear that downgradings explained by macro factors do not take place until a later stage, when ABS programmes start to experience some default. Ratings, therefore, would not result in being predictive of the risk potentially affecting ABS securities due to the variation of macroeconomic variables. In a nutshell, according to the theoretical hypothesis illustrated in this chapter, because downgrading intervenes whenever a delay or default in the regular trend of the flows of the transaction takes place, and since variations in macroeconomic variables determine effects on flows in a delayed fashion, the result is that – above all in phases of economic crisis, when the weight of macro determinants is more significant in explaining default events – downgradings are significantly delayed from the appearance of the factors that cause worsening of the risk, further increasing the contribution of securitization to systemic instability.

5.7 Empirical analysis: methodology and sample selected

5.7.1 Selected variables

5.7.1.1 Micro determinants

From a microeconomic perspective, the state of health of securitization transactions may be affected by specific events which could negatively impact transfer of funds: among them the occurrence of debtors' defaults, the violation of what had been declared and guaranteed in agreements by originator and third parties participating in the programme, the originator's bankruptcy, or any other judiciary procedures which could be attributed to it.

Such events have an impact on the programme's performance and are monitored through various indicators, including the number of past due on the amount of the initial portfolio, the average number of past due over a predetermined period in time, and the number of past due beyond a period in time predetermined on the total of the first loss piece. The latter is made up of junior tranches, or from the reserve account, and it is representative of the credit enhancement level from which tranches with more seniority benefit.

Such microeconomic variables, 'captured' by trigger events, are all connected to the financial structure and participating subjects and, for the purpose of this chapter, are excluded from the empirical analysis.

This is because of the fact that, as already explained, it is considered that they are correctly incorporated in rating judgements.

5.7.1.2 Macro determinants

Assessment of the existence of connections between macro variables and ABS performances, and of whether they are correctly considered in the rating judgements of securitized securities, therefore forms the area of investigation of the present work.

It is maintained in the literature, and in many empirical studies, that there is a positive correlation between the increase in the cost of money, inflation, average price of real estate, low level of liquidity, and deterioration of mortgage quality ABS.

The increase in the cost of money and inflation, particularly in times of stagnation of GDP, does in fact reduce debtors' spending capacity; they find it more difficult to honour debts, with consequent repercussions on the quality of the securitized portfolio.

Deterioration of a mortgage portfolio is recorded even in the case of, as happened during the recent financial crisis, an unjustified increase in the price of real estate. In fact, the formation of speculative 'bubbles' in the real estate sector, combined with high interest rates, has the effect of amplifying the deterioration of the quality of the portfolio and reducing recovery rate deriving from estates sales.

Finally, poor liquidity, in periods of financial turmoil, reduces negotiation of credit lines given and collateral lent on the inter-bank market. In the light of these factors, the macroeconomic variables chosen for the investigation relate to:

- GDP;
- EURIBOR growth rate;[1]
- LIBOR growth rate;[2]
- average growth rate of prices in real estate for every nation;
- EONIA volatility growth rate;[3]
- inflation growth rate for every nation.

5.7.2 Estimated model

From the methodological perspective it has been decided to use the rating of a single primary bond issue, deriving from RMBS operations, as a dependent variable, taking this as an assessment assigned by agencies to express the capacity of a debtor to pay fully and on time the interest and reimbursement of capital on the debt; independent variables, chosen to support the hypothesis that there are macro determinants for downgrading, have been selected from variables considered to be expressions of the level of gross product, the cost of money, liquidity and inflation rate of single countries forming the sample. The estimate model for variables chosen is represented in the following expression:

Expression 5.1 The Estimate Model

$$\text{Rating} = \beta_0 + \beta_1 \text{PILn}az + \beta_2 EURrate + \beta_3 LIBORrate + \beta_4 BCErate + \beta_5 EONIArate + \beta_6 IMMrate + \varepsilon$$

which sets a model of multiple regression, fed by panel data, referred to macro variables selected, and that allows the problem of the possible presence of disturbances from omitted variables to be overcome.

5.7.2.1 *The sample*

Data used for empirical analysis were related to RMBS transactions set up between 2000 and 2009, still active at the time of the analysis, quoted on the market, provided with ratings and related to five European nations:[4] the United Kingdom (UK), the Netherlands (NL), Italy (IT), Portugal (P) and Spain (E). It is a sample (Table 5.2) of 502 deals related to asset securitization of residential mortgages (66 per cent of the total of RMBS set up in the nations considered), for which the rating evolution of tranches 'A' and 'B'[5] over the period in time considered for a total of 1,004 observations. Data related to ratings has been collected by drawing on Moody's Corporation website (www.moodys.it and www.moodys.com), while data related to independent variables has been collected through the telematics platform 'Bloomber'.[6]

Table 5.2 The sample selected for the test

	Nation	No. active transactions taken a census of (population)	% of active transactions (population)	No. transactions considered (sample)	No. issues considered (sample)
1	United Kingdom	245	32.5	164	328
2	Netherlands	136	18.0	90	180
3	Italy	79	10.5	52	104
4	Portugal	35	4.6	24	48
5	Spain	259	34.4	172	344
	Total	754	100.0	502	1004

Table 5.3 Distribution of rating for the sample

Moody's rating observed	Percentage observations	Cumulative observations (%)
Aaa	49.67	49.67
Aa1	4.26	53.93
Aa2	8.06	61.99
Aa3	11.70	73.69
A1	6.78	80.47
A2	15.11	95.58
A3	0.77	96.36
Baa1	0.19	96.55
Baa2	1.51	98.06
Baa3	0.85	98.92
Ba1	0.15	99.07
Ba2	0.19	99.26
Ba3	0.08	99.34
B1	0.19	99.54
B2	0.00	99.54
B3	0.04	99.57
Caa1	0.15	99.73
Caa2	0.04	99.77
Caa3	0.15	99.92
C	0.08	100.00

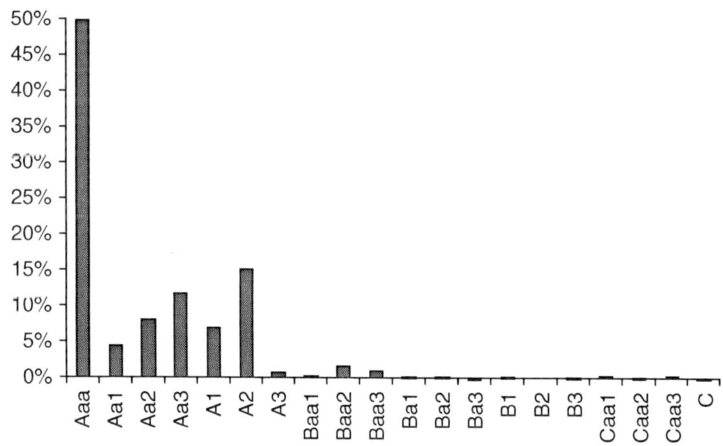

Figure 5.9 Sample rating distribution

It is noted that the sample presents an important concentration of synthetic assessments (about 50 per cent) in the highest class of the rating scale and that distribution of the rating revision appears to be concentrated in the higher classes (Table 5.3). In fact, more than 96 per cent of ratings concerning the sample, considering both downgradings and upgradings of every single issue in the period considered, are placed between 'Aaa' and 'A3' on Moody's scale.

In other words, it is a sample of issues of ABS characterized by an elevated theoretical degree of solvency (Figure 5.9) and, for this reason, capable of highlighting with greater clarity the occurrence of significant and/or concentrated downgrading/upgrading.

ABS and systemic crisis: primary effect. The first result to highlight is that in the RMBS sample observed, on a total of 1,004 issues, 120 downgradings[7] were recorded (about 12 per cent of all issues which suffered downgrading), among which 92 (9.16 per cent of issues concerned with downgrading and 76.6 per cent of the total of downgradings) were connected only to 2009 (Table 5.7). Moreover (Table 5.8), an obvious concentration of downgradings can be seen in the three nations which have carried out ABS transactions more than the rest (Holland, Spain and the UK). It is confirmed, therefore, that asset securitization contributes to the systemic crisis in what we term a 'primary effect'.

5.8 Findings of the test

Correlations between the dependent variable and selected independent variables

In order to verify the existence of the 'secondary derivative effect', a regressive analysis was adopted. To be able to investigate the correlation between chosen independent variables (of a numeric nature) and rating (of an alphanumeric nature), it was necessary to convert Moody's scale into a numerical vector (Table 5.4). It is noticeable that the sample does not show, as it is logical to expect, a number of deals sufficient to cover the complete distribution of Moody's rates scale. In fact, the ABS transactions considered are distributed within only 20 classes of rating.

For this reason the rating scale is represented, in the statistical elaboration, by 20 whole increasing numbers at the deterioration of credit. In other words, the whole number '1' was attributed to the highest class, the whole number '2' to the second class, and so on, until arriving at number 20, attributed to the lowest class (class 'C'). This choice,

Table 5.4 Rating conversion matrix

Moody's ratings observed	Aaa	Aa1	Aa2	Aa3	A1	A2	A3	–
Whole number assigned	1	2	3	4	5	6	7	
	Baa1	Baa2	Baa3	Ba1	Ba2	Ba3	B1	B2
	8	9	10	11	12	13	14	15
	Caa1	Caa2	Caa3	C	–	–	–	–
	17	18	19	20				

Table 5.5 Correlations hypothesized by the model

Independent variable	Dependent variable (*Rating*)	Correlation between dimensions considered	Sign foreseen from angular coefficient of the regression line without distortions induced by *rating agencies*
PIL*naz*	(↑[i]-↑[ii]); (↓-↓)	+	–
EUR*rate*	(↑-↓); (↓-↑)	–	+
LIBOR*rate*	(↑-↓); (↓-↑)	–	+
BCE*rate*	(↑-↓); (↓-↑)	–	+
EONIA*rate*	(↑-↓); (↓-↑)	–	+
IMM*rate*	(↑-↓); (↓-↑)	–	+

Notes: [i]The arrow pointing upwards indicates an improvement in the growth rate of GDP. [ii]The arrow pointing upwards indicates an improvement in the judgement of merit.

necessary to elaborate qualitative data, will allow us to verify the hypothesis (Table 5.5), specifically whether an increase in:

- national GDP corresponds to an average improvement in the rating of ABS (positive correlation between the two dimensions and negative coefficient of the intercept);
- EURIBOR growth rate corresponds to a deterioration in the rating of ABS (negative correlation between the two dimensions and positive coefficient of the intercept) (see Figure 5.10);
- LIBOR growth rate corresponds to a deterioration of the rating of ABS (negative correlation between the two dimensions and positive coefficient of the intercept);
- BCE growth rate corresponds to a deterioration of the rating of ABS (negative correlation between the two dimensions and positive coefficient of the intercept);
- EONIA growth rate corresponds to a deterioration of the rating of ABS (negative correlation between the two dimensions and positive coefficient of the intercept);

- growth rate of the average cost of real estate corresponds to a deterioration of the rating of ABS (negative correlation between the two dimensions and positive coefficient of the intercept).

Correlation hypotheses are amply shared by literature and numerous empirical analyses and justify how, with the increase of the cost of money and in periods of recession of the economic cycle, the capacity to fulfil obligations and the quality of both the securitized portfolio and associated ratings deteriorate.

Test for possible correlations existing among the chosen independent variables

The first test carried out has been the search for any possible correlations among the chosen independent variables, with the purpose of avoiding alterations induced by possible correlations existing between the observed variables. The analysis, carried out using the 'z statistic' to verify the hypothesis, gave significant results for all variables, except between growth rate of cost of real estate and growth rate of EURIBOR and LIBOR; such a result can probably be attributed to the lack of a complete series of data on the trend of the cost of real estate in the nations chosen for the sample. In other words, an obvious degree of correlation between all the chosen independent variables has been considered (Table 5.6), which allowed three variables at most to be considered simultaneously in the successive regressions.

Secondary derivative effect

Evidence for the existence of a contribution from ABS to the systemic crisis in the form of a 'secondary derivative effect' is seen in the results

Table 5.6 Significance of relevant correlations among independent variables

Correlations	*natGDP*	EUR*rate*	LIBOR*rate*	BCE*rate*	EONIA*rate*	*RErate*
natGDP	–	Z=62.91; P>|z|= 0.00	Z=62.92; P>|z|= 0.00	Z=49.65 P>|z|=0.00	Z=35.53 P>|z|=0.00	Z= 57.73 P>|z|=0.00
EUR*rate*		–	Z=max P>|z|=0.00	Z=772.82 P>|z|=0.00	Z=355.08 P>|z|=0.00	Z=0.41 P>|z|=0.685
LIBOR*rate*			–	Z=773.53 P>|z|=0.00	Z=355.28 P>|z|= 0.00	Z= 0.40 P>|z|= 0.687
BCE*rate*				–	Z=490.54 P>|z|=0.00	Z=7.73 P>|z|=0.00
EONIA*rate*					–	Z=19.94 P>|z|=0.00
RErate						–

Table 5.7 Downgrading occurring

Wrap-up	Sample	% compared with total of issuances
ABS issuances which underwent at least one *upgrading*	32	3.19
ABS issuances which underwent *downgrading*	120	11.95
Total *downgrading* for tranche A	50	4.98
Total *downgrading* for tranche B	70	6.97
Total ABS issuance downgraded (A and B) in 2009	92	9.16
Total ABS issuance downgraded (A and B) in 2005–8	16	1.59

Table 5.8 Downgrading occurring in each country

	Down	Down %	Up	Up %	No. issuances	No. issuances (%)
Tot. UK	52	43.3	12	37.5	328	32.6
Tot. NL	22	18.3	16	50.0	180	18.0
Tot. IT	6	5.0	0	0.0	104	10.4
Tot. P	0	0.0	0	0.0	48	4.9
Tot. E	40	33.3	4	12.5	344	34.2
Tot	120	100.0	32	100.0	1,004	100.0

of econometric analysis carried out for the independent variables considered singly (Table 5.9).

The estimated correlation of four of the independent variables with rating (EURrate, LIBORrate, EONIArate, RErate) is negative, opposite to what is expected when ratings correctly incorporate variations in macro variables (in this case the sign of the angular coefficient of the intercept of the regression rate is positive). In other words, as the starting premise is the existence of a negative correlation between variables and rating– by virtue of the choice made when converting Moody's scale – a positive angular coefficient of the regression lines is expected. As this does not happen, and angular coefficients have a negative sign, the analysis confirms the theoretical hypothesis, namely that rating judgements are invalidated by a delay in downgrading.

Test for the significance of the chosen variables

The statistical significance of the chosen independent variables was then tested. L'R2 'correct' (0.5008), which gives a synthetic measure

Table 5.9 Regression results

Regressor	Sign of theoretic coefficient	Estimated coefficient	Test	$\bar{R}^2$ (with fixed effects on tranches A and B, and temporal effects)
natGDP	–	−0.0395	Z=−6.21; P>|z|=0.000	0.5008
EUR*rate*	+	−0.0355	Z=−2.53; P>|z|=0.011	0.5019
LIBOR*rate*	+	−0.0355	Z=−2.53; P>|z|=0.011	0.5038
BCE*rate*	+	0.0775	Z=+2.94; P>|z|=0.003	0.4988
EONIA*rate*	+	−0.0370	Z=−2.20; P>|z|=0.028	0.4607
RErate	+	−0.0115	Z=−3.44; P>|z|=0.001	0.4280

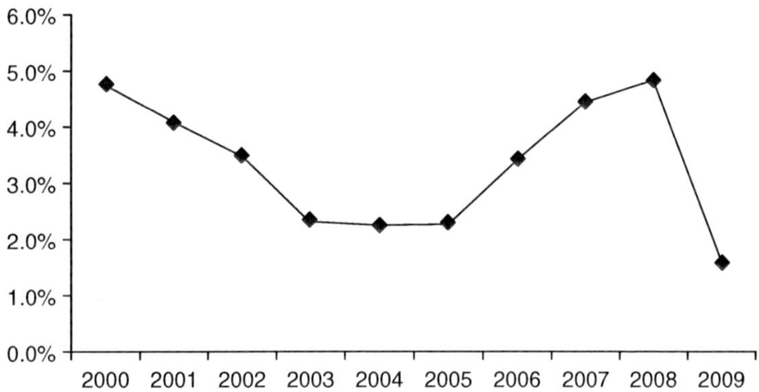

Figure 5.10 Evolution of EURIBOR rate (2000–9)

Table 5.10 Results of regression in a 'downgrading shift scenario'

Regressor	Sign of theoretic coefficient	Estimated coefficient	Test	$\bar{R}^2$ (with fixed effects on tranches A and B, and time effects)
natGDP	–	−0.0141	Z=−2.20; P>|z|=0.027	0.5087
EUR*rate*	+	0.0497	Z=3.53; P>|z|=0.000	0.5076
LIBOR*rate*	+	0.0496	Z=3.52; P>|z|=0.000	0.5076
BCE*rate*	+	0.1538	Z=6.09; P>|z|=0.000	0.5043
EONIA*rate*	+	0.0431	Z=2.52; P>|z|=0.012	0.4653
RErate	+	−0.0119	Z=−3.63; P>|z|=0.000	0.4334

of the significance of the regression, or rather the degree to which the dependent variable is explained by independent variables, turned out to be sufficiently elevated for all variables considered singly (Table 5.9).

Double check analysis: downgradings shift

In the period of time observed, the downgradings occurred after a period of consistent interest rate increases (2005–8), in which 16 separate downgradings were recorded (Figure 5.4).

Bearing this in mind, to complete the analysis, the hypothesis was made that rating agencies had announced the downgradings occurring in 2009 at least a year earlier, or, rather, before the recent financial crisis. In this way econometric analysis should give coherent signs of correlations between variables mentioned, or rather the positivity and/or negativity of angular coefficients of regression lines, in harmony with the hypothesized theoretical correlations. From this perspective, recalibrating the panel data with the downgradings of 2009 moved back to 2008 gives results compatible with the theory expounded: angular coefficients of −0.0141 for GDP, +0.0497 for EURIBOR rate, +0.0496 for LIBOR rate, +0.0153 for BCE rate and +0.0431 for the volatility of the EONIA rate, as well as a R2 'correct' sufficiently significant for every independent variable considered individually (Table 5.10).

5.9 Conclusions

The chapter's objective has been to verify the promptness of downgrading of ABS securities in the context of the recent financial crisis, selecting a European sample of securitization programmes of residential mortgages. More specifically, we tested the hypothesis that variations in macroeconomic variables are not incorporated promptly in ratings and that this determines a downgrading lag, producing what has been defined as a 'secondary derivative effect' on the stability of the financial system. Results of the descriptive analysis indicate, in the first place, the presence of a 'primary effect', highlighting the fact that ABS contributed to the systemic crisis due to the significant number of downgradings. The regressions undertaken, moreover, also show a positive result in terms of 'derivative secondary effect', significantly confirming the theoretical hypothesis that, in pre-crisis periods, rating agencies tend to delay downgradings, announcing them only at a later stage, when the crisis is already under way.

The chapter offers an innovative contribution to the literature on relations between asset securitization and financial crises, both by proposing a theoretical framework of the connections between ABS and financial stability and by highlighting, thanks to empirical analysis, a low degree of information efficiency in ABS ratings and, therefore, a significant contribution made by ABS to the systemic crisis.

Notes

1. Euro interbank offered rate, reference rate for transactions on the inter-bank market on funds in Euros and used as an index parameter for variable rate mortgage loans, calculated daily as a simple average of info quotes received at midday on a sample of banks with an elevated credit selected periodically by the European Banking Federation.
2. London Interbank Offered Rate, reference rate for transactions on the inter-bank market, the market where banks exchange short-term funds, as an average of the eight central values provided by 16 major banks.
3. European OverNight Index Average, a parameter representating the average of overnight rates of financing applied by the main European banks and transmitted daily to the European Central Bank (BCE).
4. The choice of nations is justified by the greater number of RMBS set up compared with other European nations.
5. It has been chosen to monitor the state of health of only tranches 'A' and 'B' as, often, tranches with a greater risk are subscribed by the originator.
6. It has not been possible to consider the EONIA volatility growth rate from 2000 to 2004 and growth rate of real estate prices in Spain and Holland.
7. A single downgrading of each issue was included in the data, as annual data in the sample considered were recorded on the basis of individual downgradings, and in many cases only a single downgrading took place during the period analysed.

References

Affinito, M. and Tagliaferri, E. (2010) 'Why Do (or Did?) Banks Securitize Their Loans? Evidence from Italy', *Bank of Italy, Temi di Discussione (Working Paper)* no. 741.

Allen, F. and Carletti, E. (2006) 'Credit Risk Transfer and Contagion', *Journal of Monetary Economics*, 53, 89–111.

Altunbas, Y., Gambacorta, L. and Marqués, R. (2007) 'Securitization and the Bank Lending Channel', *Banca d'Italia, Temi di Discussione* no. 653 and *ECB Working Paper Series* no. 838 (Frankfurt: European Central Bank).

Ambrose, B.W., Lacour-Little, M. and Sanders, A.B. (2005). 'Does Regulatory Capital Arbitrage Reputation or Asymmetric Information Drive Securitisation?', *Journal of Finance Service Research*, 28(1), 113–133.

Ashcraft, A., Goldsmith, P.P. and Vickery, J. (2010) 'MBS Ratings and the Mortgage Credit Boom', Federal Reserve Bank of New York Staff Reports No 449, (New York: Federal Reserve Bank of New York).

BIS – Bank for International Settlements (2008) *78th Annual Report* (Basel: Bank for International Settlements).

Borio, C. (2008) 'The Financial Turmoil of 2007? A Preliminary Assessment and some Policy Considerations', *BIS Working Papers*, no. 251 (Basel: Bank for International Settlements).

Calomiris, C.W. and Mason, J.R. (2004) 'Credit Card Securitization and Regulatory Arbitrage', *Journal of Financial Service Research*, 26(5), 5–27.

Cantor, R.M. and Rouyer, S. (2000) 'Another Perspective on Risk Transference and Securitization', *Journal of Risk Finance*, 1, 37–47.

Carey, M. (1998) 'Credit Risk in Private Debt Portfolios', *Journal of Finance*, 53, 1363–87.

Casu, B., Clare, A., Sarkisyan, A. and Thomas, S. (2010) 'Does Securitization Reduce Credit Risk Taking? Empirical Evidence from US Bank Holding Companies', *Centre for Banking Research, Cass Business School, Working Paper Series*, no. WP 02/10 (London: Cass Business School).

Cebenoyan, S.A. and Strahan, P.E. (2004) 'Risk Management, Capital Structure and Lending at Banks', *Journal of Banking and Finance*, 28, 19–43.

Dell'Ariccia, G., Igan, D. and Laeven, L. (2008) 'Credit Booms and Lending Standards: Evidence From The Subprime Mortgage Market', *CEPR Discussion Papers* 6683 (London: Centre for European Policy Research).

Demyanyk, Y. and Van Hemert, O. (2007) 'Understanding the Subprime Mortgage Crisis', New York University, Stern School of Business, mimeo.

Dionne, G. and Harchaoui, T.M. (2003) 'Banks' capital, securitization and credit risk: An empirical evidence for Canada', *Working Paper* no. 03-01, HEC Montréal.

Donato, K.K. and Shaffer, S. (1991) 'Capital Requirements and the Securitizations Decision', *Quarterly Review of Economics and Business*, 31(4), 12–23.

Duffie, D. (2008) 'Innovations in Credit Risk Transfer: Implications for Financial Stability', *BIS Working Paper*, no. 255 (Basel: Bank for International Settlements).

Fender, I. and Mitchell, J. (2005) 'Structured finance: complexity, risk and the use of rating', *BIS Quarterly Review*, June (Basel: Bank for International Settlements).

Franke, G. and Krahnen, J.P. (2005) 'Default Risk Sharing Between Banks and Markets: The Contribution of Collateralized Debt Obligations', *NBER Working Papers* 11741, National Bureau of Economic Research, Inc. (Washington DC: NBER).

Giannotti, C. (2004) *La cartolarizzazione dei crediti: rischi e regolamentazione* (Milano: FrancoAngeli).

Greenbaum, S.I. and Thakor, A.V. (1987) 'Bank funding modes: securitization versus deposits', *Journal of Banking and Finance*, 11, 379–401.

Haensel, D.N. and Krahnen, J.P. (2007) 'Does Credit Securitization Reduce Bank Risk?', Evidence from the European CDO Market, Available at SSRN: http://ssrn.com/abstract=967430, Accessed on 14 April 2011.

Hess, A.C. and Smith, C.W. (1988) 'Elements of mortgage securitization', *The Journal of Real Estate Finance and Economics*, 1, 331–46.

Ibanez, D.M. and Scheicher, M. (2009) 'Securitization. Instruments and Implications', in *The Oxford Handbook of Banking* Eds., A.N Berger, P. Molyneux and J.O.S Wilson (Oxford: Oxford University Press), 599–629.

Jiangli, W. and Pritsker, M.G. (2008) 'The Impacts of Securitization on US Bank Holding Companies', mimeo.

Keys, B., Mukherjee, T., Seru, A. and Vig, V. (2008) 'Did Securitization Lead to Lax Screening? Evidence from Subprime Loans', *Quarterly Journal of Economics*, 125, 307–362.

La Torre, M. (1995) *Securitisation e Banche. La titolarizzazione degli attivi bancari* (Il Mulino).

La Torre, M. (2004) 'Securitisation e vigilanza dopo Basilea 2: la normativa italiana', *Bancaria*, 10.

Loutskina, E. and Strahan, P.E. (2006) 'Securitization and the Declining Impact of Bank Finance on Loan Supply: Evidence from Mortgage Acceptance Rates', *NBER Working Paper*, W11983 (Washington DC: NBER).

Maddaloni, A. and Alcade, J.L.P. (2009) 'Bank Risk-Taking, Supervision and Low Interest Rates: Evidence from lending Standards', in *Business Models in Banking: Is there a Best Practice?*, CAREFIN, Università Luigi Bocconi (Milan: Universita Luigi Bocconi).

Mian, A. and Sufi, A. (2008) 'The Consequences of Mortgage Credit Expansion: Evidence from the 2007 Mortgage Default Crisis', *NBER Working Paper*, no. W13936 (Washington DC: NBER).

Norton, J.J. and Spellman, P.R. (1991) *Asset Securitization. International Financial and Legal Perspectives* (London: Blackwell Finance).

Pavel, C.A. (1986) 'Securitization', *Federal Reserve Bank of Chicago Economics Perspective*, 10, 16–31.

Pavel, C. and Phillis, D. (1987) 'Why commercial banks sell loans: an empirical analysis', *Federal Reserve Board of Chicago, Economic Perspectives*, May–June, 11, 3–14.

Purnanandam, A.K. (2010) 'Originate-to-Distribute Model and the Sub-Prime Mortgage Crisis', (April 2010). AFA 2010 Atlanta Meetings Paper. Available at SSRN: http://ssrn.com/abstract=1167786.

Rosenthal, J.A. and Ocampo, J.M. (1988) *Securitisation of Credit. Inside the New Technology of Finance* (New York: Wiley & Sons).

Sarkisyan, A., Casu, B., Clare, A. and Thomas, S. (2009) 'Securitization and Bank Performance', *Centre for Banking Research, Cass Business School, Working Paper Series*, no. WP 04/09 (London: Cass Business School).

6
A Revenue-Based Frontier Measure of Banking Competition

Santiago Carbó-Valverde, David Humphrey and Francisco Rodríguez Fernández

6.1 Introduction

Standard indicators of banking competition frequently used in empirical studies have been: (a) the structure–conduct–performance (SCP) paradigm, which focuses on the degree of banking market concentration, usually a Herfindahl–Hirschman index (HHI) of deposit/loan market concentration; (b) the Lerner Index, which is a price mark-up measure as in (price – marginal cost)/price; and (c) the H-statistic, which indicates the degree to which changes in funding/factor input costs are associated with changes in output price. In practice, academic analyses have almost always applied only one of these three indicators to assess banking competition. While there is disagreement about which of these measures may 'best' reflect market competition, the expectation is that, since they purport to measure the same thing, they are strongly and positively correlated. Unfortunately, this expectation is not always met.

These three standard measures are almost unrelated when compared across European countries over time and can be negatively related within the same country over time. To illustrate: with data on 14 European countries over 1995–2001 covering 1,912 banks, the R^2 between the Lerner Index and the H-statistic was only 0.06. Similarly, the R^2 between the HHI concentration measure and the Lerner Index and H-statistic was, respectively, 0.09 and 0.05 (Carbó *et al.*, 2009). In addition, when we look at each of the 14 countries separately over time, the relationship between the Lerner Index and the H-statistic was positive in only eight out of 14 countries.[1] The relationship between the HHI and these two measures was positive in only eight and five countries, respectively. As shown below, similar inconsistencies apply to Spain. As the choice of an existing banking competition measure may affect the results obtained, a different procedure in which choice among these current measures is not necessary may prove useful.

Our competition measure borrows from the cost/profit efficient frontier literature and is applied to Spain to assess banking competition over 1992–2005. We use revenue (since price data are quite limited) and measure competition for two broad categories of banking services: traditional loan–deposit spread activities and non-traditional non-interest income fee-generating activities. Non-interest income is significant in European and US banks, and for Spain in 2005 it was 46 per cent of loan–deposit spread revenues and 144 per cent of securities revenues.

In what follows, inconsistencies in identifying competition among the HHI, Lerner Index and H-statistic measures are illustrated for Spain in Section 2. Our revenue-based competition measure is set out in Section 3, while Section 4 contains our empirical results and how they differ from the standard competition indicators. Identifying why competition may have changed over time is covered in Section 5, along with outlining the characteristics of the most and least competitive banks. Conclusions are presented in Section 6.

6.2 Inconsistencies among standard measures of bank competition

The HHI, Lerner Index and H-statistic have all been used to assess the degree of market competition, and one would expect them to consistently differentiate those banks experiencing more competition from those experiencing less of it. Table 6.1 presents these three measures for different aggregations of Spanish banks over 1992–2005.[2] The average HHI for all banks is 978. This is a relatively low level of market concentration and suggests that competition is likely 'reasonable'.[3] However, the H-statistic at 0.20 suggests weak competition, since the relationship between changes in output and input prices is low. On average, a 10 per cent change in input prices is associated with only a 2 per cent change in output prices, suggesting that other influences on output prices are much more important than costs. This conclusion is seemingly supported by the average 25 per cent mark-up of price over marginal total cost from the Lerner Index. This mark-up is rather large considering that marginal cost here includes funding as well as operating cost and the total cost scale economies are on the order of 0.95.[4]

If we look at quartiles of the largest versus the smallest banks, there is a dramatic difference in market concentration, as large banks have

Table 6.1 Standard competition efficiency measures: Spain, 1992–2005

	HHI	Lerner Index(%)	H-statistic
All 75 Banks	978	25	0.20
Quartile of Largest Banks	2,970	25	0.27
Quartile of Smallest Banks	97	26	0.29
Savings Banks (45)	714	27	0.25
Commercial Banks (30)	1,375	23	0.17
Pre-Euro Period 1992–7	968	25	0.26
Savings Banks	691	27	0.43
Commercial Banks	1,384	23	0.22
Post-Euro Period 2000–5	993	22	0.22
Savings Banks	740	23	0.21
Commercial Banks	1,373	20	0.35

an average HHI of 2,970 versus only 97 for smaller banks. While this suggests that smaller banks operate in more competitive markets while large banks do not, there is no real difference in the Lerner Index or the H-statistic, suggesting no difference in competition between large and small institutions. However, although the Lerner Indices for large and small banks are equal to the average for all banks, the H-statistic for these two groups is larger (at 0.27 and 0.29) than the overall average of 0.20. Thus the H-statistic suggests that the middle two size quartiles are less competitive than either the largest or the smallest banks.

When savings banks are compared with commercial banks, the HHI would suggest that savings banks operate in more competitive markets than commercial banks. This conclusion would be supported using the H-statistic, as savings banks have a higher H-statistic, but is not consistent with the Lerner Index, since savings banks have a marginally higher mark-up.

When these measures are contrasted over time, there is little change in the HHI six years before the Euro was implemented (1992–7) relative to the six years during and after implementation (2000–5). This holds for the average of all banks as well as for savings and commercial banks averaged separately. The Lerner Index gives essentially the same result as the HHI – little change pre- or post-Euro – as does the H-statistic for all banks in these two periods (rows 6 and 9). However, when savings and commercial banks are considered separately, competition is considerably reduced for savings banks but apparently improves for commercial banks between these two periods.[5]

Another way to contrast these three standard competition measures concerns their degree of correlation across individual banks over 14 years.[6] The R^2 between the HHI and the Lerner Index or the H-statistic across banks was, respectively, 0.04 and 0.01 over 1992–2005. That is, the conclusion here would be that there is no relationship. And, while there is a positive relationship between the Lerner Index and the H-statistic across banks, it is quite weak since the $R^2 = 0.15$. For these reasons, it may be useful to investigate a different way to measure banking competition.

6.3 A revenue-based frontier indicator of banking competition

Prior to the adoption of the Euro, European banks are estimated to have saved some $32 billion in operating costs over 1987 to 1999 due to the realization of scale economies, such as non-cash payment volume expanded, combined with the technology-associated shift from paper-based to cheaper electronic payment methods plus the increased use of lower-cost ATMs rather than branch offices for cash acquisition (Humphrey *et al.*, 2006). For Spain, these changes in payments and cash delivery services are estimated to have reduced bank operating costs by 37 per cent compared to what they otherwise would have been and to have saved some €4.5 billion or 0.7 per cent of GDP over 1992–2000 (Carbó *et al.*, 2006). Over a longer time period (1987–2004), cost savings at European banks are evident from a 34 per cent reduction in the average ratio of operating costs to asset value. For Spain, this reduction was even greater at 50 per cent (Bolt and Humphrey, 2007).

If European and Spanish banking markets are reasonably competitive, such large unit cost reductions should be correlated over time with lower unit revenue flows from loan–deposit rate spreads and non-interest income activities. This is because banking revenues are fundamentally a function of underlying input costs and factor productivity. Indeed, differences in input costs; factor productivity; scale economies; bank risk; temporary demand variations associated with the business cycle; and the degree of price competition in the market for banking services are the six major determinants of revenue flows among banks and over time. As detailed cost accounting and other data are not available by specific banking service category either currently or over time, statistical procedures can be used to 'subtract' the influence of the first five revenue determinants from observed revenue flows across banks such that the remaining or residual differences in revenues are likely associated with differences in price competition – the sixth influence. In simple terms, this is our approach to measuring banking competition: namely, as residual revenues after accounting for costs and other influences. This approach is broader than the typical procedure used in applications of the H-statistic or the Lerner Index in that it does not require information on specific unit revenues (prices), which, for payment and other non-spread activities, is simply not available.[7]

While our procedure borrows from the efficient frontier literature to estimate a competition frontier, the framework is not very different from the theoretically based industrial organization approach of Boone (2008a, b). Specifically, Boone proposes to rely upon a firm's balance sheet to compute the difference between reported total revenues and reported total variable costs, a spread that contains total fixed cost plus extra revenues associated with the degree of price competition (along with other influences). As we are interested in revenues for particular subsets of banking services, statistical cost analysis is used to identify the associated (but unallocated) variable and fixed costs, along with other influences on revenues, leaving the effect of price competition on revenues as an average residual.

In our approach, if the variation in cost, productivity, scale, risk and demand variation over the business cycle explains most of the variation in revenues, then, in a manner similar to when the H-statistic (∂ ln price/∂ ln cost) is close to 1.0, we would conclude that competition is strong. Here the R^2 of the H-statistic equation would be high and the (average) unexplained variation would be small, just as it would be in our approach.

6.3.1 A revenue-based frontier model

There are at least four ways to determine a competition frontier. The approach used here is the composed error Distribution Free Approach or DFA (Berger, 1993).[8] This approach assumes that averaging each bank's residuals from the relationship estimated in Equations (1) and (2) (below) across separate annual cross-section regressions (containing two six-month observations on each bank) reduces normally distributed error to minimal levels, leaving only the average effect of competition on bank revenues relative to a single (or set of) frontier bank(s) having the lowest averaged revenue residual.

In applying frontier analysis to the measurement of competition, it is maintained that the most important determinants of loan–deposit spread revenues and non-interest income revenues are the underlying unit operating costs of producing these services, the productivity of the factor inputs used to produce these services, the scale of bank operations, the level of bank risk, the variation in demand over the business cycle, and the degree of price competition. Two unit revenue functions are specified. One is the ratio of revenues from the loan–deposit rate spread times the value of deposits (*SPREAD*) to production or operating cost (*SPREAD/OC*).[9] A second function reflects the ratio of non-interest income (*NII*) to operating cost (*OC*) and reflects how income from priced services (payment transaction fees, debit/credit card fees, ATM fees, deposit account maintenance charges, loan fees, compensating balance requirements, loan commitment fees, and so on, as well as certain trading income) varies with production costs (*NII/OC*). These two revenue sources, along with revenue from securities operations (which are excluded since these rates of return are set in competitive national and international markets), sum to total bank revenues.[10]

The variation of each dependent variable is a function of bank asset composition of loans (*LOAN*) and securities (*SEC*), factor input costs composed of the average price of labour (*PL*) and implied cost of physical capital (*PK*), which reflects cost function influences. Factor productivity is assessed using a labour/branch ratio (*L/BR*) and a deposit/branch ratio (*DEP/BR*). A bank's productivity rises when less labour is used per branch office and/or when each branch on average generates/supports a greater value of deposits.[11]

Scale economies are associated with processing greater payment volumes and having a larger network of ATMs and branch offices. Scale estimates for Spain (Bolt and Humphrey, 2007) are used to devise an index of unit payment costs (*PC*) and an index of unit ATM/branch service delivery costs (*ATMBRC*).[12] The variation in bank revenues due to risk is reflected in each bank's equity capital/asset ratio (*CAPITAL*), its loan loss ratio (*LLR*), and an indicator of funding or liquidity risk reflected in the ratio of deposits to loans (*DEP/LOAN*).[13] Finally, temporary business cycle and macroeconomic effects on loan demand and deposit supply are reflected in the level of regional GDP in Spain (*GDPR*), the growth of bank assets relative to the general level of regional economic activity (*TA/GDPR*), and the national three-month interest rate (*INTRATE3*). In summary, our two equation translog functional form model in logs is:

$$\ln(SPREAD/OC) = \theta_0 + \sum_{i=1}^{12} \theta_i \ln X_i + 1/2 \sum_{i=1}^{11}\sum_{j=1}^{11} \theta_{ij} \ln X_i \ln X_j + \sum_{i=1}^{11}\sum_{k=1}^{2} \psi_{ik} \ln X_i \ln P_k + \sum_{k=1}^{2} \phi_k \ln P_k + 1/2 \sum_{k=1}^{2}\sum_{m=1}^{2} \phi_{km} \ln P_k \ln P_m + \ln e_{SPREAD} + \ln u_{SPREAD} \quad (1)$$

$$\ln(NII/OC) = \alpha_0 + \sum_{i=1}^{12} \alpha_i \ln X_i + 1/2 \sum_{i=1}^{11}\sum_{j=1}^{11} \alpha_{ij} \ln X_i \ln X_j + \sum_{i=1}^{11}\sum_{k=1}^{2} \delta_{ik} \ln X_i \ln P_k + \sum_{k=1}^{2} \beta_k \ln P_k + 1/2 \sum_{k=1}^{2}\sum_{m=1}^{2} \beta_{km} \ln P_k \ln P_m + \ln e_{NII} + \ln u_{NII} \quad (2)$$

where:

$X_{i,j}$ = LOAN, SEC, L/BR, DEP/BR, PC, ATMBRC, CAPITAL, LLR, DEP/LOAN, GDPR, TA/GDPR, INTRATE3;

$P_{i,j}$ = *PL, PK,* and have been defined above.[14]

Equations (1) and (2) are related in that banks may choose to increase revenues over time (in response to higher costs or weak competition) by altering their loan–deposit rate spread (raising loan rates and/or lowering deposit rates), or they can instead increase revenues by instituting or raising the fees they charge on various banking services (affecting NII). Since errors in explaining the variation of revenues from the loan–deposit rate spread in (1) may be correlated with errors in explaining the variation of non-interest revenues in (2), these two revenue equations are estimated jointly in a seemingly unrelated regressions (SUR) framework.[15]

6.3.2 A competition frontier

In a composed error framework, the regression relationship (2) can, for illustration, be truncated and re-expressed simply as:

$$\ln(NII/OC) = f(\ln \text{Cost}, \ln \text{Productivity}) + \ln e + \ln u \quad (3)$$

The total residual (ln e + ln u) reflects the unexplained portion of the revenue-dependent variable remaining after cost and productivity influences have been accounted for. Here ln e represents the value of random error, while the maintained hypothesis is that ln u represents the effect of price competition on revenues. The DFA concept relies on the assumption that ln e will average to a value close to zero when the total residual in (3) is averaged across a number of separate cross-section estimations, leaving the average of $\ln u_i$ to reflect the average effect of competition ($\ln \bar{u}_i$).

The ith bank (or set of banks) with the lowest average residual ($\ln \bar{u}_{min}$) is also the bank where the variation in underlying cost, productivity, and risk explains the greatest amount of the variation in revenues and hence the smallest variation in revenues attributed to price competition.[16] This minimum value defines the competition frontier, and the relative competition efficiency (CE_i) of all the other i banks in the sample is determined by their dispersion from this frontier:

$$CE_i = exp\ (\ln \bar{u}_i - \ln \bar{u}_{min}) - 1 = (\bar{u}_i / \bar{u}_{min}) - 1 \qquad (4)$$

As the term u_i is multiplicative to the dependent variable in an unlogged equation (3), the ratio $(NII/OC)_i$ equals R (Cost, Productivity)$_i$ u_i. Thus the ratio $\bar{u}_i / \bar{u}_{min}$ is an estimate of the ratio *NII/OC* for the ith bank, for a given level of underlying cost, service productivity and risk, to the value of the ratio $(NII/OC)_{min}$ for the bank facing the greatest price competition and having the same underlying cost, service productivity and risk.[17]

If $CE_i = 0.25$, then $\bar{u}_i$ is 25 per cent larger than $\bar{u}_{min}$, so the unexplained portion of the revenue-dependent variable in (3) is 25 per cent larger than its minimum value at another bank. This difference reflects the unspecified influence of competition. Thus, the larger is CE_i, the weaker is the ability of market competition to restrain revenues.[18]

A limitation is that CE only indicates the relative level of competition: it cannot determine the absolute level of competition even for the most competitive bank. Consequently, it is important to examine the fit of the estimating equation, since, if the R^2 is high (e.g. 0.80 or above), the difference in relative competition measured by CE may not be very economically significant, since the residuals $\bar{u}_i$ and $\bar{u}_{min}$ would themselves be absolutely small (regardless of their percentage difference).[19]

6.4 Banking competition in Spain

6.4.1 Competition efficiency by bank type, size and time period[20]

Separate cross-section SUR estimations of (1) and (2) were made for each of the 14 years over 1992–2005. Each annual estimation includes two six-month observations on 45 savings and 30 commercial banks that were in continuous operation over the period.[21] These banks accounted for 93 per cent of deposits and 94 per cent of banking assets in Spain in 2005. Residuals from these cross-section estimations were then averaged for each bank separately and Equation (4) was used to obtain the competition efficiency (CE) measures shown in Table 6.2.

Table 6.2 Competition efficiency in Spain: 1992–2005

	CE_{SPREAD}	CE_{NII}
Single Frontier Over 1992–2005:		
All 75 Banks	0.40	0.11
Quartile of Largest Banks	0.38	0.10
Quartile of Smallest Banks	0.34	0.11
Savings Banks (45)	0.42	0.10
Commercial Banks (30)	0.38	0.11
Separate Frontier For Each Period:		
Pre-Euro Period 1992–7	0.21	0.13
Savings Banks	0.23	0.13
Commercial Banks	0.17	0.13
Post-Euro Period 2000–5	1.40	0.22
Savings Banks	1.42	0.21
Commercial Banks	1.37	0.24

Looking at all 75 banks over the entire 1992–2005 period, the average unit revenue dispersion of banks from the competition frontier was 40 per cent for the loan–deposit rate spread (CE_{SPREAD}) but only 11 per cent for non-interest income activities (CE_{NII}). As a lower CE value indicates a smaller average dispersion of revenues associated with price competition, SPREAD activities appear to have experienced less price competition than NII fee-based activities over the 14-year period. That is, a smaller variance in residual unit revenues is equated with a smaller dispersion of price competition effects on revenues once other plausible influences have been accounted for.[22]

When all banks are separated into asset size quartiles, banks with the largest assets are about equally competitive with those with the smallest assets in each of the two activities separately. While there is little difference in competitive efficiency by bank size within a given activity, which also illustrates the difference between banks in urban areas (large banks) versus rural areas (smaller banks), SPREAD activities remain less competitive than fee-based NII activities. The same results apply when savings banks are separated from commercial banks. In sum, there is little difference in competition efficiency between banks by size or type of institution for either SPREAD or NII activities separately, but there is a consistent difference between the two activities, with SPREAD activities experiencing less price competition.

To compare competitive efficiency over time, the 14-year time frame was split into pre- and post-Euro periods and separate frontiers were estimated for each period. Both sets of activities appear to have worsened in the second period. In the pre-Euro period (1992–7), CE values were relatively low – 21 per cent for SPREAD and 13 per cent for NII activities – indicating stronger price competition compared with the average for the entire period. In the post-Euro period (2000–5), however, CE values are markedly higher – rising by a factor of six for SPREAD activities and almost doubling for NII activities – suggesting less price competition. Importantly, this deterioration was experienced for both savings and commercial banks to about the same degree in each activity.

The reason for this reduction in competitive efficiency is directly related to the marked change in the distribution of the averaged residuals between the pre- and post-Euro periods shown in Figure 6.1. The distribution of residuals, in turn, is directly related to the ability of Equations (1) and (2) to explain the variation in unit revenue in the two periods. While the average R^2 for the two sets of six separate yearly cross-section regressions for fee-based activities rose somewhat (from 0.62 pre-Euro to 0.71 post-Euro), the average for spread activities fell from 0.76 to 0.54, indicating a reduction in explanatory power in the post-Euro period.[23]

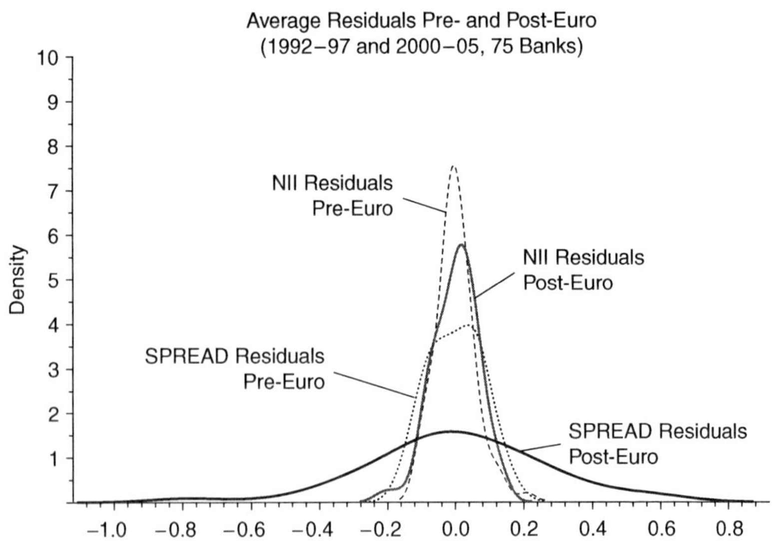

Figure 6.1 Distributions of averaged residuals pre- and post-Euro

As seen in Figure 6.1, there is a slight expansion in the range of averaged residual values for the post-Euro period for NII fee-based activities.[24] The rise in dispersion accounts for the doubling of CE values for NII activities in the post-Euro period, even though the change in the range in Figure 6.1 seems rather small. This illustrates the sensitivity of CE values to what appear to be small changes in minimum values of averaged residuals. Thus not too much should be read into the magnitude of the CE changes. The main point is that price competition appears to have worsened and that spread activities appear to have worsened more than fee-based activities.

The conclusion that price competition deteriorated in the post-Euro period conflicts with two standard indicators of competition. The average HHI only rose by 3 per cent over its pre-Euro value of 968, while the average Lerner Index fell by three percentage points in Table 6.1. While both of these results suggest little change in competition, the H-statistic fell for savings banks (falling from 0.43 to 0.21) while it rose for commercial banks (from 0.22 to 0.35), suggesting worsening competition for the former and improvement for the latter.[25]

6.4.2 Why do standard and CE competition measures give different results?

As shown earlier, the HHI, Lerner Index and H-statistic can differ in identifying the most and least competitive banks for Spain. The HHI, for example, only suggests the possibility of a lack of price competition leading to a larger mark-up of price over cost when market concentration is 'high', while the Lerner Index is a direct measure of the mark-up itself. In contrast, the H-statistic is concerned with how strongly changes in costs are reflected in output prices. The presumption is that, if $\partial \ln price/\partial \ln cost$ is close to 1.0, then competition induces firms to reflect increases or decreases in input costs directly in the output prices being charged. In such a regression, the residual – the unexplained variation in output price – would be small, and the percentage difference across residuals would also likely be small. This result suggests that our CE measure has more in common with the H-statistic than the Lerner Index or the HHI, and that the main difference is the use of additional independent variables to hold constant revenue changes that are not directly related to price competition but, rather, reflect other influences.

Some examples may make this distinction clearer. If either the Lerner Index or the H-statistic is not adjusted for differences in factor productivity or ATM/branch network economies of scale across banks and over time, the observed factor prices (the average cost of labour and physical capital) will not be an accurate representation of their 'true' cost. That is, observed factor prices will be higher than their true value for banks with greater productivity, and need not reflect the full benefit from scale economies. With stable output prices, this would generate a lower Lerner Index, suggesting greater competition, when in fact the difference between more and less productive banks is not in competition but in productivity. What if more productive and scale-efficient banks pass on some (not all) of this cost reduction to users by lowering their output prices? These banks will appear to be even more competitive because their observed mark-up is even lower, when, if input prices had been properly adjusted, the mark-up need not have changed much even if output prices had been reduced. These same problems arise with the H-statistic, since it is based on the sum of partial derivatives measuring the change in output prices with respect to changes in input prices, and the input and output prices can be mismeasured.[26] Since opinions may differ on just what influences may bias the measurement of competition, this can be accommodated in the decision on what to include/exclude in the CE frontier model.

6.5 Changes in competition and characteristics of competitive banks

6.5.1 Identifying why competition appears weaker in the post-Euro period

One reason why our competition efficiency measure suggests that competition is weaker in the post-Euro period may be because the Lerner Index is higher. As shown in Table 6.1, however, the Lerner Index did not rise, but instead fell by three percentage points in the post-Euro period.[27] Alternatively, perhaps the H-statistic is lower. This would indicate that price changes are less closely related to underlying cost changes, suggesting that other influences on prices are stronger, so cost changes are weaker.[28]

It is more instructive to look at the raw data. The pre-Euro difference between the average price of loans (11.7 per cent) and deposits (6.1 per cent) was 5.6 percentage points. Post-Euro, the loan and deposit rates both fell (to 6.9 per cent for loans and 4.5 per cent for deposits) and the difference was only 2.4 percentage points. The change in rate spreads pre- to post-Euro is –3.2 percentage points, close to the –3 percentage point reduction in the Lerner Index of Table 6.1 which was estimated for the entire bank. Over the same period the three-month market interest rate fell from an average 9.2 per cent pre-Euro to 3.5 per cent post-Euro, a reduction of –5.7 percentage points.

As average loan and deposit rates largely mirror changes in market rates over time, the reduction in the loan–deposit rate spread and the Lerner Index is not surprising, but a conclusion that the reduction in these spreads necessarily indicates an improvement in competition would be misleading. Using the average three-month market rate as an interest cost index, it would be 1.00 pre-Euro (from 9.2 per cent/9.2 per cent) but falls to 0.38 post-Euro (from 3.5 per cent/9.2 per cent). Deflating the average nominal loan–deposit rate spreads gives a 'real' spread of 0.056/1.00 = 0.056 pre-Euro and 0.024/0.38 = 0.063 post-Euro. This suggests that the real spread may have increased by perhaps 13 per cent, rising from 0.056 to 0.063.[29]

One reason why the real spread may have increased, even as the nominal spread fell, is the fact that there was a 147 per cent rise in loan demand between the two periods. Indeed, loan growth was so large that it far outstripped the growth of deposits, evident by the fall in the ratio of deposits to loans from 1.28 pre-Euro to 0.95 post-Euro. In such an environment it would not be surprising to find that some (many) banks adjusted their loan/deposit pricing behaviour to raise real margins, reducing competition and generating greater dispersion of CE values from the competition frontier.

While the competition efficiency measure for fee-based activities in Table 6.2 also suggests weaker competition in the post-Euro period, the change here is considerably smaller than for spread activities. Merchant unhappiness with high bank credit and debit card fees as well as fees paid for other banking services may be the reason for our finding a small decrease in competition for fee-based activities. The existence of strong scale economics associated with rapidly growing volumes of electronic non-cash payment transactions should have correspondingly reduced payment and other banking service fees if competition in the post-Euro period had been strong.[30]

6.5.2 Characteristics of most and least competitive banks

What aspects of a bank are associated with being more or less competitive than the average institution? Contrasting the most competitive CE quartile of banks with institutions in the least competitive quartile, the most competitive banks experienced 31 per cent lower profits (ROA), 20 per cent lower spread revenues and 17 per cent lower loan–deposit spread revenues relative to operating cost, received a 4 per cent lower loan rate and paid an 11 per cent higher deposit rate. These differences would be expected to be associated with greater price competition even after accounting for cost, productivity, scale and risk differences. The most competitive banks were also more productive (holding 44 per cent more deposits per office) and somewhat larger (holding 23 per cent more assets).[31]

A comparison of most with least competitive banks in non-interest-income (fee-based) activities suggests that competitive banks have 15 per cent lower profits, have 16 per cent less non-interest income relative to operating cost, are smaller (holding 36 per cent fewer assets), employ slightly more workers per office, pay about the same annual average wage, and support the same level of deposits per office.[32]

So what do these comparisons tell us? First, that the quartile of most competitive banks in spread activities using the CE indicator receive lower profits, pay higher deposit rates, generate more deposits per branch office, and (because they are larger) likely realize greater scale economies from their ATM/branch networks and in their payment activities. Second, although these banks also have a lower average Lerner Index and higher H-statistic, they are not always the same banks that would be identified as most or least competitive using only either one of these two standard measures to judge their competitive position. As both the Lerner Index and the H-statistic effectively only indicate the spread or correlation between output and input prices, if these two measures were adjusted to account for differences in factor productivity, scale economies and risk, their correspondence with the CE measure and with each other would likely become stronger and more consistent.

6.6 Conclusions

The three main indicators of banking market competition in empirical analyses have been the HHI, Lerner Index and H-statistic. Unfortunately, conclusions regarding competition among individual banks, between savings and commercial banks, or over time can differ depending of which of these measures are chosen to indicate competitive behaviour. Some inconsistencies occur for Spain (Table 6.1 in this chapter) and within and across 14 European countries (Carbó *et al.*, 2009).

Our approach to measuring price competition borrows from frontier cost and profit function analysis but is closer in concept to the H-statistic approach than to the other two methods. The approach is quite flexible and allows one to specify what influences on unit revenues are not directly, or are only weakly, associated with competition. When these influences are statistically 'subtracted' from banks' unit revenues, the average unexplained residual is assumed to reflect unspecified price competition.

Conceptually, our approach would be similar to computing a Lerner Index or an H-statistic and adjusting the resulting values for the list of influences enumerated above. For example, neither of these standard measures makes any allowance for differences in productivity among banks, so the input prices used to estimate the mark-up (Lerner Index) or correlation of input prices with output prices will not reflect the true underlying cost. The same holds for output prices not adjusted for differences in risk. It also applies to differences in operating cost not reflected in factor prices, which occur among different-sized institutions when scale economies are important, and differences in wages across regions, which are the result of cost-of-living differences and not competition.

Using our revenue-based frontier approach, we found no important difference in competition between large and small banks in Spain or between savings and commercial banks. However, when we divide our 1992–2005 time span into pre- and post-Euro periods, banking competition appears to have been reduced for both traditional loan–deposit spread and non-traditional fee-based activities. For spread activities, the 'real' spread seems to have increased even as it fell in nominal terms. This is likely associated with the 147 per cent rise in loan demand between the two periods and the fact that loan growth far outstripped the growth of deposits, resulting in a 26 per cent reduction in the ratio of deposits to loans. For fee-based activities, bank credit and debit card fees paid by merchants are not yet fully cost-based, so they may not have fallen as rapidly as scale economies realized from expanding electronic payment volumes. Overall, differences in cost, productivity and risk explain 60 per cent to 70 per cent of unit revenue 'price' variation across banks. Competition differences account for the rest.

Notes

Financial support from the Fundacion de las Cajas de Ahorros Confederadas para la Investigación Economica y Social is acknowledged and appreciated, as well as comments from Joaquin Maudos and seminar participants at the Federal Reserve Bank of Philadelphia.

1. In this analysis, the H-statistic was multiplied by –1.0 so that a larger value of the H-statistic, the Lerner index and the HHI would all indicate less competition.
2. The HHI is computed for each bank for each six months and averaged for the time periods or set of banks shown in the table. The Lerner Index and

H-statistic are estimated separately for the time period or set of banks shown. For example, only savings banks (row 4 in Table 6.1) or only commercial banks (row 5) are used in the estimation models outlined in the Appendix of our working paper (same title). The difference in procedures – six-month estimates for each bank, which are then averaged, or separate estimations for each row shown in the table – generate almost identical results for the Lerner Index, but one difference for the H-statistic (which is noted below).

3. For example, in the US Department of Justice merger guidelines an HHI < 1,000 would represent an unconcentrated market.
4. Funding costs essentially have no scale economies, but operating costs do. If marginal operating cost were considered instead, the associated operating cost scale economies would be close to 0.30, far from 0.95.
5. The two ways of estimating the Lerner Index and H-statistic only affected the H-statistic. Estimating the H-statistic for each bank in each six-month period and then averaging over the different time periods or sets of banks in Table 1 resulted in lower post-Euro period results – showing less competition – for all banks together as well as commercial and savings banks separately. All of the other H-statistic conclusions were unchanged. An H-statistic robustness test indicating competitive equilibrium is outlined in our working paper.
6. This involves estimating all three measures using all banks and then evaluating the results for each bank, giving 2,100 observations (14 years times 75 banks observed every six months). This is the second estimation method noted earlier and in the previous footnote.
7. The limited availability of pricing data is why the Lerner Index and the H-statistic use computed average loan and deposit rates along with factor prices and deposit/funding average or (statistically estimated) marginal costs.
8. An alternative Stochastic Frontier Approach typically assumes a half-normal distribution for inefficiencies (or in our case competition inefficiencies) in order to separate unknown inefficiencies from normally distributed error in a panel regression. Two other approaches concern Data Envelopment Analysis (DEA) and Free Disposal Hull. These are linear programming approaches that assume error is zero but have the advantage that no functional form is imposed to fit the data.
9. Operating cost rather than total cost is the basis for our two unit revenue-dependent variables. Although the average deposit/funding interest cost varies across banks, the vast majority of this variation is due to different funding compositions, as specific funding rates are quite similar across banks and over time. This suggests that the focus should be on revenues relative to operating expenses rather than total costs. Funding costs, of course, are directly reflected in the loan–deposit *SPREAD* variable.
10. There are no differences in regulation between commercial and savings banks, and the revenue and cost data used here refer only to operations within Spain, not (for example) Latin America, where some of the largest institutions have subsidiaries.
11. The labour/branch ratio is similar to a labour/capital ratio, while the deposit/branch ratio is equivalent to an output/capital ratio. While banks also make and monitor loans, the vast majority of production cost is associated with deposits and payments between deposit accounts.

12. Bank-specific payment volume data are not available for any European country except Norway. However, over the last 20 years in Spain (1987–2006), the R^2 between the value of aggregate bank deposits and the number of aggregate country-level non-cash transactions (cheque, debit and credit card, paper and electronic giro transactions) was 0.92. Consequently, the value of each bank's deposits was used to approximate the unknown non-cash payment volume for each bank in the payment cost index *PC*. Bank-specific information does exist for the number of ATMs and branches in Spain, and the service delivery cost index *ATMBRC* is a weighted average of unit cost indices of the realized scale economies of these two networks for each bank. While some internet banking exists in Spain, it is currently small (and effectively did not exist in the early portion of our time period).
13. The loan loss ratio is expressed as (loan value – losses)/loan value, since logs of all variables are used in the estimating equations. A simple ratio of losses to loan value can be negative or positive depending on recoveries recorded in periods after losses were first recorded. The *DEP/LOAN* variable reflects funding stability (and hence liquidity and funding risk) since deposits are the most stable form of funding for loans (as opposed to short-term market or inter-bank borrowings). Although credit ratings also exist for most banks, they vary less over time than changes in loan losses or any other risk indicator and so have not been used here.
14. Each variable has an own and squared term, but the interaction terms are limited to 12 in each equation (versus a possible 78). This trades off a minor improvement in fit for less multicollinearity, which reduces our ability to gauge significance of the RHS variables. Interaction terms are specified within the cost group (*LOAN, SEC, PL, PK*), productivity group (*L/BR, DEP/BR*), scale group (*PC, ATMBRC*), risk group (*CAPITAL, LLR, DEP/LOAN*) and business cycle group (*GDPR, TA/GDPR, INTRATE3*), but not between groups. The exception is the three-month interest rate (*INTRATE3*), which only has an own term. This variable is sometimes the same for all banks, even though it is observed over the two six-month periods that comprise each annual cross-section estimation (hence the 12 own terms but 11 squared terms shown in the summations).
15. Homogeneity of degree 1.0 in input prices is not imposed. A doubling of input prices need not double revenues (but would double costs in a cost function).
16. In the context of an H-statistic, this would be the bank with an H-statistic closest to 1.0.
17. The ratio $\bar{u}_i / \bar{u}_{min}$ = $[(NII/OC)_i/R\ (Cost,\ Productivity)_i]/[(NII/OC)_{min}/R\ (Cost,\ Productivity)_{min}]$ and, when evaluated at the same mean level of underlying cost and service productivity, the predicted values of R (Cost, Productivity)$_i$ and R (Cost, Productivity)$_{min}$ are equal, as both are at the same point on the estimated unit revenue curve, leaving the ratio $(NII/OC)_i/(NII/OC)_{min}$.
18. The cost efficiency literature reports efficiency (EFF) and inefficiency (INEFF) values. If efficiency is 80 per cent (EFF = 0.80), then inefficiency is INEFF = (1 – 0.80) / 0.80 = 0.25, or 25 per cent. In Equation (4), CE reflects the relative weakness of competition in restraining revenues, and is equivalent to INEFF, which reflects relative weakness of cost efficiency.

19. This qualification is not well understood in the frontier literature. Absolute differences in residuals need to be considered along with their relative size, so goodness of fit should be an additional consideration (Carbó *et al.*, 2007).
20. A similar model was applied to aggregate country-level data on 11 European countries, finding very little difference in competition efficiency across countries (Bolt and Humphrey, 2010). The Spanish sample concerns individual banks and is a much larger and richer data set.
21. The data set includes all savings banks, all but the very smallest commercial banks (which were excluded due to missing data), and no cooperative banks (which also had missing data). Banks that merged or were acquired during the period were treated as being merged/acquired for the entire period via backward aggregation. For example, if bank 1 merged with or was acquired by bank 2 in 2001, the data for both banks are aggregated backward in time to 1992. Thus bank 1 is reflected in the data for bank 2 for the entire 1992–2005 period. This yields a balanced panel that does not neglect merged/acquired banks.
22. Truncating the 4 per cent highest and lowest unaveraged residual values reduces the mean CE value for spread activities by 40 per cent, so 0.40 falls to 0.24. For fee-based activities, the CE value only falls from 0.11 to 0.10. Truncating extreme values of residuals has little effect on the ranking of which banks are more versus less competitive, since the R^2 between truncated and un-truncated spread CE values is 0.91, while it is 0.99 for fee-based values.
23. For fee-based activities in the post-Euro period, the yearly R^2 ranged from 0.63 to 0.76, but was 0.76 to 0.38 for spread activities, with the lowest values occurring during 2003–5.
24. These residual values are estimated separately and averaged separately in the pre- as well as the post-Euro periods, as separate frontiers apply to each period.
25. Estimating an H-statistic for all banks and averaging the results for these separate time periods suggests that both savings and commercial banks experienced weaker competition in the post-Euro period (0.15 and 0.11, respectively, versus 0.34 and 0.17 pre-Euro). This result is consistent with the competition efficiency results of Table 2.
26. The regression used to derive the H-statistic includes the level of output, so if revenues are the dependent variable the partial derivatives reflect the relation between output and input prices.
27. Maudos and Fernández de Guevara (2004) identified reductions in operating cost and credit risk as important reasons for the decline in the loan–deposit interest margin over 1993–2000, as well as an increased emphasis in obtaining fee-based revenues to offset a lower mark-up.
28. The H-statistic in Table 1 fell only for savings banks in the post-Euro period (suggesting weaker competition) while it rose for commercial banks (suggesting the reverse).
29. Deflating the nominal deposit/loan rate spread by the cost-of-living index (COL), rather than an index of the market interest rate, is not appropriate. Banks buy deposits and sell loans at interest rates: they do not buy housing, food, clothing, and so forth, which comprise the COL indicator of consumer purchasing power.

30. While merchant payment fees that do not reflect lower bank costs are the main merchant complaint, an additional concern is the perception that merchants' sales are unlikely to be larger from accepting cards when the vast majority of merchants already accept them. That is, the real beneficiary of bank card use is no longer merchant sales, but rather card users, who are effectively subsidized, since they do not pay the full cost of their card use that generates bank revenues.
31. The 31 per cent lower profits for competitive banks are associated with a 17 per cent higher HHI, a 32 per cent lower Lerner Index and a 30 per cent higher H-statistic.
32. In contrast to spread activities, the HHI is lower for competitive banks (as would be expected). Also, the Lerner Index shows a lower mark-up and the H-statistic a higher value for the set of most competitive banks identified using the frontier model.

References

Berger, A. (1993) '"Distribution Free" Estimates of Efficiency in the US Banking Industry and Tests of the Standard Distributional Assumptions', *Journal of Productivity Analysis*, 4, 261–92.

Bolt, W. and Humphrey, D. (2007) 'Payment Network Scale Economies, SEPA, and Cash Replacement', *Review of Network Economics*, 6, 453–73.

Bolt, W. and Humphrey, D. (August 2010) 'Bank Competition Efficiency in Europe: A Frontier Approach', *Journal of Banking and Finance*, 34(8), 1808–1817.

Boone, J. (2008a) 'A New Way to Measure Competition', *Economic Journal*, 118, 1245–61.

Boone, J. (2008b) 'Competition: Theoretical Parameterizations and Empirical Measures', *Journal of Institutional and Theoretical Economics*, 164, 587–611.

Carbó, S., Humphrey, D. and Lopez, R. (2006) 'Electronic Payments and ATMs: Changing Technology and Cost Efficiency in Banking', in Balling, M., Lierman, F. and Mullineaux, A. (eds), *Competition and Profitability in European Financial Services. Strategic, Systemic and Policy Issues* (Abingdon, UK: Routledge), pp. 96–113.

Carbó, S., Humphrey, D. and Lopez, R. (2007) 'Opening the Black Box: Finding the Source of Cost Inefficiency', *Journal of Productivity Analysis*, 27, 209–20.

Carbó, S., Humphrey, D., Maudos, J. and Molyneux, P. (2009) 'Cross-Country Comparisons of Competition and Pricing Power in European Banking', *Journal of International Money and Finance*, 28, 115–34.

Humphrey, D., Willesson, M., Bergendahl, G. and Lindblom, T. (2006) 'Benefits from a Changing Payment Technology in European Banking', *Journal of Banking and Finance*, 30, 1631–52.

Maudos, J. and Fernández de Guevara, J. (2004) 'Factors Explaining the Interest Margin in the Banking Sectors of the European Union', *Journal of Banking and Finance*, 28, 2259–81.

7
Regulation and Bank Performance in Europe

Georgios E. Chortareas, Claudia Girardone and Alexia Ventouri

7.1 Introduction

A complex net of regulations permeates the financial systems of most developed and emerging economies. The various rationales emphasize the implications of fragile financial structures for social welfare, especially those that materialize when financial crises occur. Given their specialness, banks are typically more heavily regulated than non-banking financial institutions. Bank regulation, that is, the rules governing banks' behaviour, is complemented by bank supervision, which refers to the oversight which ensures that banks comply with those rules.[1] Both financial and bank regulation are highly controversial issues, and the debate has become more intense, especially since the 2008 financial crisis. The extent of financial regulation in the pre-crisis period has been considered inadequate by some analysts and excessive or misplaced by others. The financial crisis in itself is a manifestation of the failure of the existing regulatory framework, rendering the reconsideration of the existing arguments and policy institutions necessary.

The case for bank regulation and supervision, as well as their implications for systemic stability, typically relies on arguments which stress the special role of banks in the economy. The banks have a pivotal role in clearing and payment systems and constitute the sole source of finance for a large fraction of business and households. Banking regulation aims to mitigate systemic risk, protecting consumers, and ultimately the industry, from opportunistic behaviour (e.g. unfair pricing polices) and achieving some social objectives, including stability (see, e.g. Llewellyn, 1999). Bank regulation is not cost-free, however. Elliehausen (1998) surveys the findings of various studies and reports that the total compliance costs can be up to 13 per cent of the banks' non-interest operating expenses. Moreover, regulation can impact on the efficient operation of the banking industry, as it directly affects the bankers' incentives and thus the banks' conduct of business. For example, tight limitations and restrictions on particular bank activities can induce banks to engage in riskier behaviour (e.g. Jalilian *et al.*, 2007). Moreover, banks may engage in investment practices that attempt to circumvent regulation. Such behaviour typically has adverse effects on the real economy.

Many emerging markets have faced serious financial crises within the last two decades, such as south-east Asia, Latin America and Russia. In recent years a number of advanced economies have also experienced banking crises. The 2007–8 US subprime crisis and the current global financial turmoil have set in motion a new round of debates. On the one hand, advocates of more effective regulation and supervision attribute the financial crisis to the excesses of the broader deregulation movement in general and the deregulation of structural and conduct rules of banks in particular. Inherent in this approach is the view that 'unfettered markets are neither efficient nor stable', as the Nobel Laureate J. Stiglitz (2010) suggests. On the other hand, analyses adhering to the Chicago political economy tradition (e.g. the 'free banking' school) result in a different interpretation of the crisis, blaming inefficient regulation. Financial liberalization was accompanied by a strengthening of regulation influencing prudential concerns, particularly in relation to the setting of minimum capital requirements. A number of studies, prior to the recent financial crisis, emphasized the role of capital standards in preventing bank failure and in safeguarding customers and the economy from potential externalities (e.g. Gorton and Winton, 1995; Hovakimian and Kane, 2000; Rochet, 1992). Nevertheless it is widely accepted that the framework for controlling and monitoring banks has been proven inadequate. Basel II is the Accord that revised and extended the first (Basel I) of 1988 and is based on three main pillars: minimum capital requirements, supervisory review, and market discipline. Well before the release of Basel II, heated discussions on bank regulation have been reactivated. The International Monetary Fund (IMF) and the World Bank (WB) recommended the adoption of Basel II to all their member states, as it was expected to produce significant benefits by helping banks and supervisors to assess and manage risks and improve stability (e.g. Molyneux, 2003). Basel II's framework, however, was designed in a way that would maintain Basel I's 8 per cent minimum capital requirement. In the EU the implementation of Basel II started in 2007, just before the global financial crisis and recession.

While the debate on the costs and benefits of the Basel II framework remains open (Herring, 2005), another 100 countries or so also plan to adopt it by 2015, and a new proposal is under preparation.

The Basel committee response to the lessons of the crisis included measures to strengthen the Basel II framework. A package of proposals to strengthen global capital and liquidity regulations aiming to increase the resilience banking systems has been approved for consultation. The latest proposals from the Basel Committee, which have been dubbed 'Basel III', urge regulators to better equip banks against various catastrophe scenarios. The IMF has also stressed the need for rethinking bank regulation, and criticized the current practices of bank regulation and supervision. Thus, the current global financial crisis highlights further the need for reassessing the prudential rules of regulation.

While regulation can take the form of detailed and precise prescriptive rules, its accuracy is often questionable. Capital adequacy rules, for example, may specify how much capital each bank should hold, but if such rules do not truly reflect the risks involved they could unintentionally induce banks to hold either too much or not enough capital. Excessive capital imposes unnecessary costs on banks and their customers, with adverse implications for the efficiency of the banking system. Insufficient capital increases the danger of bank failure. Furthermore, economic theory provides conflicting predictions about the impact of regulatory and supervisory policies on bank performance (e.g. Barth *et al.*, 2004, 2008a).

This chapter considers the relationship between bank regulation, supervision and performance for a sample of European Union countries in the early new millennium. We also compare the efficiency scores between the New Member States (NMSs) and selected countries from the 'old' EU15 bloc. To do so we split our sample into these two banking groups. The data required to construct the indices related to bank regulatory and supervisory practices are drawn from Barth *et al.* (2001, 2006, 2008b) and the WB database. Our exploratory results show that there is a strong link between various forms of banking regulation and supervision and bank performance and efficiency. In particular, strengthened regulatory practices on Pillars I and II appear to be associated with lower inefficiencies, whereas more demanding regulation on Pillar III decreases the efficient operation of banks. The next section provides a review of the relevant literature; Section 3 presents the methodology and data used for the analysis; Section 4 discusses the main findings and Section 5 concludes.

7.2 Regulation and banking sector performance

Theoretical models have been developed focusing on the relative importance of capital adequacy requirements in bank regulation (Dewatripont and Tirole, 1993). In such models capital is a buffer against losses which could otherwise lead to a bank failure. No consensus exists, however, as to whether minimum capital requirements actually reduce banks' incentives for taking excessive risk (Blum, 1999). By monitoring and disciplining banks, official supervision can improve the functioning of banks as intermediaries and weaken corruption in bank lending, thus affecting the probability of market failures (Beck *et al.*, 2006). A more sceptical view suggests that the concerns of powerful supervisors for their own private welfare dominate over concerns for social welfare. In this context, regulation becomes a form of wealth transfer and can negatively affect bank performance (Becker, 1983; Shleifer and Vishny, 1989). Moreover, the existing evidence on the relative effectiveness of official supervisions and capital requirements as compared with market monitoring is inconclusive (Herring, 2004).

To analyse the three Basel II pillars, Barth *et al.* (2004) use survey data from more than 150 countries on bank regulations and supervisory practices for 107 countries in relation to bank development, performance and stability. They produce empirical evidence on each of the three pillars showing that no statistically significant relationship exists between capital stringency, official supervisory power and bank performance, on the one hand, and stability, on the other. Instead, results suggest that bank performance is most decisively affected by private monitoring. In general these findings appear to suggest that restrictions on bank activities can negatively affect bank efficiency. Moreover, such policies can increase the probability of banking crises. In other words, empowering supervisors or strengthening capital standards is ineffective in promoting bank efficiency, reducing corruption in lending and lowering banking system fragility. This set of results constitutes a serious challenge for the current practice of bank regulation and supervision. Instead, the authors urge reforms that would shift focus onto greater disclosure and transparency in the banking sector as well as better private sector monitoring of banks.

Demirguc-Kunt *et al.* (2004) also investigate the impact of bank regulations, market structure, and national institutions on the cost of intermediation using the net interest margin and overhead costs. They use the databases of Barth *et al.* (2001, 2003a) for a sample of 1,400 banks operating in 72 countries from 1995 to 1999. The evidence provided suggests that tighter banking services regulation raises the costs of financial intermediation. These findings are broadly consistent with the findings by Beck *et al.* (2006), which show that strengthening the power of supervisory agencies can reduce the integrity of bank lending with adverse implications for the efficiency of credit allocation. Consequently, private monitoring can have a positive impact on the banking industry in terms of efficient operations and bank soundness. The above findings emerge from the analysis of firm-level data on 2,500 firms across 37 countries to examine the relationship between supervisory strategies and corporate financing obstacles. Focusing on the period 1995 to 1999 for a sample of stock exchange-listed banks, Fernandez and Gonzalez (2005) find that bank managers' risk-taking behaviour is moderated in countries with low accounting and auditing requirements and more powerful official supervisory authorities. They also indicate that tighter restrictions on bank activities diminish the probability of banking crises.

The existing evidence on the relationship between different types of regulations, supervisory practices and bank performance is subject to various limitations, including the focus on the experience of individual countries (Barth *et al.*, 2004; Beck *et al.*, 2006; Berger *et al.*, 2008) and reliance on traditional measures of bank efficiency and performance which are constructed from accounting ratios (Barth *et al.*, 2003a, b; Demirguc-Kunt *et al.*, 2004). Barth *et al.* (2006) investigate the impact of a broad range of regulatory and supervisory practices on bank development, performance, stability and the degree of corruption in bank lending for over 150 countries. They provide a detailed account of such practices, including an analysis of the three pillars of Basel II: official supervision, capital regulations and market discipline (see Section 3 for more detail).

The Basel Core Principles for effective banking supervision (BCPs) have recently become the focus of empirical research. These studies consider whether the degree of bank soundness can be explained by compliance with the BCPs. Das *et al.* (2005) and Demirguc-Kunt *et al.* (2008) find that improved bank regulation and supervision are associated with more sound financial institutions. Consequently, policymakers should give priority to information provision over the elements of the core principles in order to upgrade regulatory governance. The findings of a more recent study by Demirguc-Kunt and Detragiache (2010), however, question the current emphasis on these principles as key to effective supervision. In particular, Demirguc-Kunt and Detragiache (2010) find no evidence of a relationship between BCP compliance and systemic risk.

All the studies reviewed above rely on accounting measures to infer the performance and efficiency of the banking sector. Recent developments, however, suggest the use of efficiency estimates that emerge from frontier analysis as an alternative and theoretically consistent bank efficiency measurement. Frontier-analysis-based efficiency measures are considered superior to the traditional accounting-ratio-based efficiency measures (Berger and Humphrey, 1997). Only very recently have some papers attempted to consider the relationship between regulation and frontier-analysis-based efficiency measures (e.g. Fries and Taci, 2005; Grigorian and Manole, 2006; Pasiouras, 2008; Pasiouras *et al.*, 2009; Chortareas *et al.*, 2010). For instance, Pasiouras (2008) uses a cross-country Tobit regression model to assess the impact of several regulations on bank-specific data envelopment analysis (DEA) technical efficiency scores. The sample covers 715 commercial banks in 95 countries for 2003, and the results reveal that market discipline is positively related to commercial banks' technical efficiency. The relationship between banking regulation and parametric cost and profit efficiency measures is the focus of Pasiouras *et al.* (2009), who consider 615 publicly quoted commercial banks operating in 74 countries during the period 2000–4. The results produced corroborate those of Pasiouras (2008) regarding the role of market discipline. The findings on capital requirements and restrictions on bank activities are mixed, but supervisory powers appear to have positive effects on both cost and profit efficiency. Chortareas *et al.* (2010) focus on how the dynamics between bank regulatory and supervisory policies associated with Basel II's three pillars are related to various aspects of banks' technical efficiency and performance for a sample of EU commercial banks during 2000–8. The authors use both traditional accounting ratios and frontier analysis to measure bank efficiency. Their results suggest that strengthening capital restrictions and official supervisory powers can improve the efficient operations of banks. With a focus on Pillar III, however, the results suggest that interventionist supervisory and regulatory policies such as private sector monitoring and restricting bank activities can impact negatively on bank efficiency levels.

In general, the existing empirical literature on the relationship between bank regulation and efficiency is still at an early stage, especially given the challenges that the recent financial crisis poses for researchers, policymakers and bank managers. The evidence highlights the role of market discipline. The results on the impact of different aspects of regulations on bank performance and efficiency are mixed. Most studies, however, tend to cover vast international cross-country data samples.

The present study advances the existing literature by examining alternative measures of bank performance, using both accounting ratios and frontier-based measures to proxy bank efficiency, and by investigating the relationship by means of correlation analysis between efficiency estimates, calculated performance ratios and Basel II pillars on regulation and supervision. In our analysis we distinguish between selected countries from the 'old' EU15 block and the 10 NMSs.

7.3 Main methodological issues and data sample

As discussed above, while the extant literature on bank efficiency and regulation relies mostly on accounting ratios for measuring bank performance, there are advantages to using frontier analysis in the calculation of bank performance (see, e.g. Berger and Humphrey, 1997). In this study we employ an input-oriented DEA framework to compute the bank-specific efficiency scores. DEA employs linear programming and makes some fairly general assumptions about the production technology in order to provide an estimate of the Farrell (1957) efficiency measure for each bank in the sample.[2] In the generic situation of n banks, with each of them consuming m different inputs to produce s different outputs and constant returns to scale, this translates into the following linear programming problem being solved n times (each time for a different bank in the sample).

$$\begin{aligned} &Min_{\theta,\lambda}\ \theta, \\ &st \qquad \theta x_i - X\lambda \geq 0, \\ &\qquad\quad -y_i + Y\lambda \geq 0, \\ &\qquad\quad \lambda \geq 0, \end{aligned} \tag{1}$$

where θ is a scalar, λ is a vector of ones and finally X and Y are the $m \times n$ input and $s \times n$ output matrices respectively. In this context θ is the efficiency score of each bank and is measured relative to an estimate of the true production frontier, which is known as the best practice frontier. When the value of θ is unity the bank operates on the efficient frontier and is therefore deemed efficient.

The efficiency scores are estimated relative to a common best practice frontier by pooling the data across countries. In particular, our sample comprises commercial banks operating in the EU. We compute a common frontier under the assumption that the banks operating in these countries share the same technology. Our analysis adopts the 'intermediation approach' (Berger and Humphrey, 1997), which views banks as institutions that employ labour, physical capital and deposits to produce loans and other earning assets. Accordingly, we consider personnel expenses, total fixed assets, and deposits and short-term funding as inputs, and total loans and other earning assets as outputs. Capturing the non-traditional activities of banks is essential, especially when dealing with banking institutions in the European area characterized by a wide scope of activities. Hence, we consider the fee-based financial services as a third output.

The data set used in this study consists of individual bank data sourced from financial statements of banks operating in selected European countries available in the BankScope database by Bureau van Dijk. We consider banks operating in 22 EU countries (10 of which are NMSs) over 2000–8, namely: Austria, Belgium, Cyprus, Czech Republic, Denmark, Estonia, France, Germany, Hungary, Italy, Latvia, Lithuania, Luxembourg, Malta, the Netherlands, Poland, Portugal, Slovakia, Slovenia, Spain, Sweden and the United Kingdom.[3]

The EU22 sample used in this study is comprised of institutions classified as commercial banks. The data have undergone substantial editing to void inconsistencies, reporting errors and double counting of institutions. Moreover, in order to obtain a relatively homogeneous dataset and further detect and remove the potential outliers from the sample, we apply the Jackstrap methodology.[4] Implementing the aforementioned screening methods results in an unbalanced panel of 5,286 commercial bank observations.[5] Details of the number of bank observations by country and year are provided in Table 7.1. Germany and France have the largest groups of banks in the sample (approximately 19 per cent and 16 per cent of the total, respectively), followed by Luxembourg with the third biggest group (about 11 per cent). The average bank size in our sample in terms of total assets as at the end of 2008 is over €11.3 billion, with the largest average bank being in Sweden and the smallest located in the United Kingdom.

In our analysis we also examine the relationship between estimated technical efficiency scores for our sample of commercial banks and alternative regulatory practices. The main aim is to verify the degree of association between bank regulatory and supervisory policies associated with Basel II's three pillars and various aspects of banks' technical efficiency and performance.

Data for regulatory and supervisory variables are collected from Barth *et al.* (2001, 2006, 2008b). In particular we specify two groups of variables. The first group contains bank regulatory and supervisory

Table 7.1 Data frequency distribution by country and year

	Austria	Belgium	Cyprus	Czech Republic	Denmark	Estonia	France	Germany	Hungary	Italy	Latvia	Lithuania	Luxembourg	Malta	Netherlands	Poland	Portugal	Slovakia	Slovenia	Spain	Sweden	UK	Total
Number of bank observations	288	157	50	105	373	38	825	986	98	557	140	71	563	43	59	163	66	70	75	186	133	240	5,286
Observations by year																							
2000	33	22	6	9	46	4	113	126	10	33	15	8	86	5	6	19	6	7	8	21	6	17	606
2001	33	13	5	12	43	5	111	109	9	32	14	6	74	5	8	14	6	5	5	14	17	17	557
2002	37	16	7	10	38	5	98	105	9	19	15	7	66	5	7	15	7	7	5	15	16	17	526
2003	34	21	5	10	42	4	91	109	10	19	18	7	64	5	6	14	6	6	6	11	15	23	526
2004	36	22	6	14	45	4	92	103	10	68	18	9	61	7	10	22	7	6	6	12	16	35	609
2005	33	20	5	15	49	5	87	114	13	134	16	9	57	4	8	24	8	14	14	34	16	36	715
2006	29	15	4	13	52	3	82	114	15	98	15	10	63	3	5	20	10	8	12	41	17	32	661
2007	29	15	6	13	46	5	84	104	12	89	16	10	56	6	4	19	10	9	11	22	15	32	613
2008	24	13	6	9	12	3	67	102	10	65	13	5	36	3	5	16	6	8	8	16	15	31	473
Total Assets on average (as of end 2008 in € million)	4,335	20,094	5,388	8,776	13,625	1,806	9,426	8,841	4,835	11,256	2,039	2,346	8,102	1,962	2,130	4,969	18,387	2,875	3,670	17,983	21,274	1,335	11,337

Figures are in million Euros.

Source: BankScope and own calculations.

indicators, focusing on Official Supervisory Power, Capital Regulatory Index, Private Monitoring and Activity Restrictions. The second group includes institutional and country-specific factors that are expected to influence banks' efficiency. We also include the Z-score, which is a bank-specific variable measuring the risk of insolvency (higher values of the Z-score are associated with lower probabilities of failure).[6] We obtain information on bank regulation and supervision from the WB database by Barth *et al.* (2001) Version I, and updated by Barth *et al.* (2006, 2008b) with Versions II and III. We discuss these regulatory variables, and we provide detailed information on the regulatory variables of Basel II's pillars in Table 7.2. The broad interpretation for these indexes should be that higher values are associated with greater regulatory, supervisory and monitoring powers.

Tables 7.3 and 7.4 report the descriptive statistics for the inputs and outputs used in the DEA efficiency measurement and the explanatory variables used, respectively.

7.4 Efficiency and regulatory practices in EU banking

Figure 7.1 illustrates the average DEA efficiency scores by country. Overall, the results show relatively high average technical inefficiency levels of about 22 per cent, which is broadly in accordance with previous bank efficiency studies for Europe (e.g. Goddard *et al.*, 2001; Lozano-Vivas *et al.*, 2002; Casu and Molyneux, 2003; Fethi and Pasiouras, 2010). The (commercial) banking sectors that achieved the highest average operating efficiency scores during the early millennium recession are those of Luxembourg, Portugal and Italy.

Furthermore, our evidence shows that, on average, the estimated technical inefficiency scores are generally higher for the NMSs than the 'old' EU countries included in our sample, implying better cost management for commercial banks operating in EU12 (Figure 7.2, panel a). On the other hand, costs (relative to income) appear to increase more in the EU12 than in the NMSs, especially in the last year of the studied period. This broadly reflects a bigger impact of the 2007–8 financial crisis in the EU12 than in the NMSs, as illustrated in Figure 7.2 (panel b). It is noticeable that, in terms of net interest margins, the NMSs appear to have higher interest margins across all years compared with their EU12 counterparts (Figure 7.2, panel c). This could be explained, on the one hand, by their greater focus on traditional banking activities, derived from lending and borrowing. On the other hand, high interest margins could also signal greater market power for

Table 7.2 Details on regulatory and supervisory variables included in the empirical analysis

Variable	Category	Description
CAPRQ	Capital Regulatory Index	The sum of (a) Overall Capital Stringency and (b) Initial Capital Stringency. This variable takes values between 0 and 9, with higher values indicating greater stringency. It is determined by adding 1 if the answer is yes to questions 1–7 and 0 otherwise, while the opposite occurs in the case of questions 8 and 9. (1) Is the minimum capital–asset ratio requirement risk weighted in line with the Basel guidelines? (2) Does the minimum ratio vary as a function of market risk? (3) Are market values of loan losses not realized in accounting books deducted? (4) Are unrealized losses in securities portfolios deducted? (5) Are unrealized foreign exchange losses deducted? (6) What fraction of revaluation gains is allowed as part of capital? (7) Are the sources of funds to be used as capital verified by the regulatory/supervisory authorities? (8) Can the initial disbursement or subsequent injections of capital be done with assets other than cash or government securities? (9) Can initial disbursement of capital be done with borrowed funds?
SPOWER	Official Supervisory Power	This variable indicates whether the supervisory authorities have the authority to take specific actions to prevent and correct problems, with higher values indicating higher power. It is determined by adding 1 if the answer is yes and 0 otherwise, for each of the following questions: (1) Does the supervisory agency have the right to meet with external auditors to discuss their report without the approval of the bank? (2) Are auditors required by law to communicate directly to the supervisory agency any presumed involvement of bank directors or senior managers in illicit activities, fraud or insider abuse? (3) Can supervisors take legal action against external auditors for negligence? (4) Can the supervisory authority force a bank to change its internal organizational structure? (5) Are off-balance-sheet items disclosed to supervisors? (6) Can the supervisory agency order the bank's directors or management to constitute provisions to cover actual or potential losses?
ACTRS	Activity Restrictions	The score of this variable is determined on the basis of the level of regulatory restrictiveness for bank participation in: (1) securities activities, (2) insurance activities, (3) real estate activities, (4) bank ownership of non-financial firms. These activities can be unrestricted, permitted, restricted or prohibited, which are assigned the values of 1, 2, 3 or 4 respectively. We use an overall index by calculating the average value over the four categories.

Continued

Table 7.2 Continued

Variable	Category	Description
PRMONIT	Private Monitoring	This variable takes values between 0 and 10, with higher values indicating policies that promote private monitoring. It is determined by adding 1 if the answer is yes and 0 otherwise, for each of the following 10 questions: (1) Does accrued, though unpaid, interest/principal enter the income statement while loan is non-performing? (2) Are financial institutions required to produce consolidated accounts covering all bank and any non-bank financial subsidiaries? (3) Are off-balance-sheet items disclosed to supervisors? (4) Are off-balance-sheet items disclosed to public? (5) Must banks disclose their risk management procedures to the public? (6) Are directors legally liable for erroneous/misleading information? (7) Is an external audit compulsory? (8) Are these specific requirements for the extent of audit? (9) Are auditors licensed or certified? (10) Do regulations require credit ratings for commercial banks?

Source: WB (Barth *et al.* 2001; 2006; 2008b).

Table 7.3 Descriptive statistics of banks' inputs and outputs used to compute DEA efficiency

	Full sample: EU22				
Variable	**Mean**	**Std. dev**	**Minimum**	**Maximum**	**Median**
Inputs					
Personnel Expenses	80.65	374.07	0.08	7,107	10.3
Total Fixed Assets	47.96	197.93	0.01	3,686.95	5.55
Deposits and Short-term Funding	8,533.39	46,798.51	0.20	1,167,853	814.55
Outputs					
Total Loans	4,670.28	22,464.75	0.5	585,157	418.78
Total Other Earning Assets	5,379.65	31,139.71	0.05	657,637	335.16
Fee-based Income	121.27	787.39	0.01	15,508	9.90

Figures are in million Euros.

Source: BankScope and own calculations.

Table 7.4 Descriptive statistics for the variables employed in the empirical analysis[a]

Symbol	Definition	Mean	St. dev.	Minimum	Maximum	Median
Dependent Variables						
INEFF	Technical Inefficiency measure using the Data Envelopment Analysis (DEA) methodology (VRS)	0.22	0.15	0.16	0.84	0.23
NIM	(Interest Income – Interest Expenses) / Interest-Bearing Assets	0.03	0.02	0.00	0.49	0.02
C/I	Cost / Income Ratio	0.63	0.17	0.03	0.99	0.63
Regulatory and Supervisory Variables						
CAPRQ (Pillar I)	Capital Regulatory Index	5.87	1.73	3.00	9.00	6.00
SPOWER (Pillar II)	Official Supervisory Power	9.38	2.26	5.00	14.00	9.00
ACTRS (Pillar III)	Activity Restrictions	7.22	2.60	3.00	12.00	7.00
PRMONIT[b] (Pillar III)	Private Monitoring	7.89	0.94	5.00	9.00	8.00
Country-Specific and Institutional Variables						
Z-SCORE	Risk of Insolvency	8.90	5.60	2.42	78.38	8.42
ΔGDP	Annual Growth rate of per capita GDP	0.03	0.02	–0.04	0.12	0.02
VOICE	Voice and Accountability	1.26	0.20	0.71	1.78	1.32
CORR	Control of Corruption	1.47	0.67	0.11	2.39	1.77
GOVER	Government-Owned Banks	10.81	13.40	0.00	42.20	3.90
FINDEV	Deposit Money Bank Assets / GDP	1.78	0.38	0.18	2.49	1.78

Sources: WB (Barth *et al.* 2001, 2006, 2008b), Governance Matters VIII, WB financial structure database (Beck *et al.*, 2009), AMECO, BankScope and own calculations.

[a] All financial variables measured in million Euros. Annual GDP growth is measured at constant 2000 market prices.
[b] Data for the PRMONIT variable refer to the EU16 subsample, due to data unavailability.

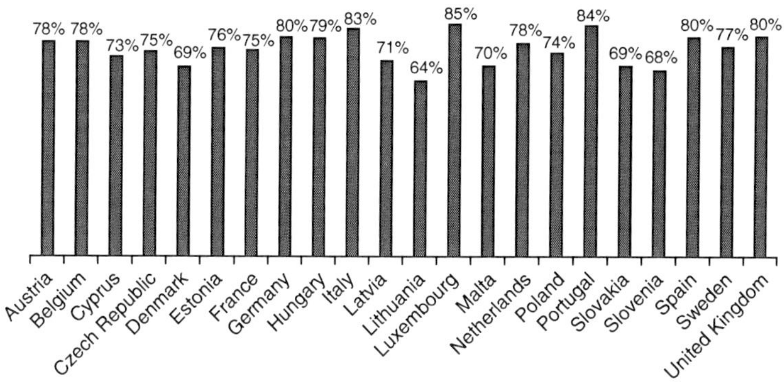

Figure 7.1 Technical efficiency scores in selected EU countries (2000–8)

banks. This latter interpretation implies that high margins signal inefficient intermediation.

Table 7.5 reports the estimated Pearson correlation coefficients, together with their significance levels, between the estimated technical efficiency scores, performance measures, and regulatory and institutional variables. Net interest margins and cost–income ratios are positively and significantly correlated with inefficiency, suggesting that, as expected, inefficient banks also have high interest margins and costs, which might signal inefficient intermediation and greater market power. Where significant, the results for the relationship between INEFF, NIM, C/I and our chosen regulatory variables are typically negative for Pillar I (CAPRQ) and II (SPOWER). This broadly suggests that lower capital regulation and supervision are associated with more inefficiency. The coefficients, however, are relatively small. Conversely, the relationship between inefficiency and Pillar III is positive and significant in most cases, indicating that greater activity restrictions and private monitoring are associated with higher bank inefficiencies.

In addition, it appears that the probability of bank failure is higher for inefficient banks (although the coefficients are small) and significantly lower in more regulated and supervised environments. Finally, concerning the institutional and country-specific factors, in the vast majority of cases the relationships with the alternative measures of inefficiency are negative and significant, suggesting that lower bank

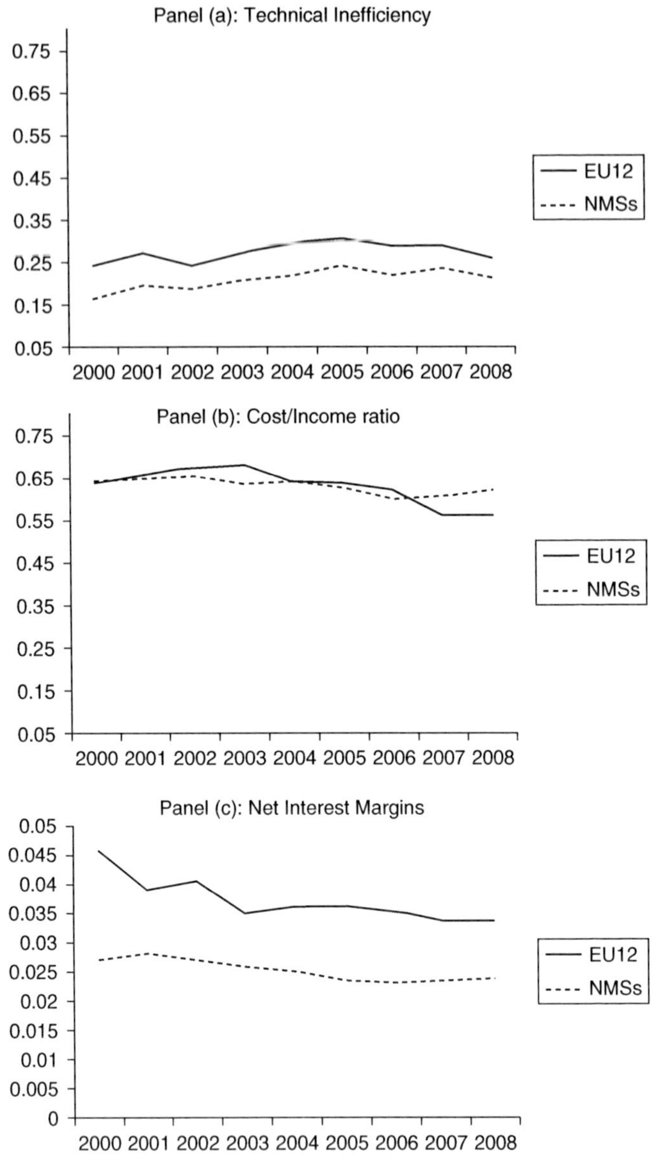

Figure 7.2 Efficiency and performance measures by groups of countries over 2000–8[a]

Panel (a): Technical Inefficiency; Panel (b): Cost/Income ratio; Panel (c): Net Interest Margins

[a] EU12 includes Austria, Belgium, Denmark, France, Germany, Italy, Luxembourg, the Netherlands, Portugal, Spain, Sweden, the United Kingdom.
NMSs includes Cyprus, Czech Republic, Estonia, Hungary, Latvia, Lithuania, Malta, Poland, Slovakia, Slovenia.

Table 7.5 Correlation matrices for Basel II pillars on regulation and institutional characteristics

	INEFF	NIM	C/I	CAPRQ (pillar I)	SPOWER (pillar II)	ACTRS (pillar III)	PRMONIT[a] (pillar III)	Z-SCORE	ΔGDP	VOICE	CORR	GOVERN	FINDEV
Inefficiency and performance measures													
INEFF	1												
NIM	0.17***	1											
C/I	0.28***	−0.04***	1										
Basel II pillars on Regulation and Supervision													
CAPRQ (pillar I)	0.01	−0.05***	−0.07***	1									
SPOWER (pillar II)	0.02*	−0.04***	−0.11***	0.38***	1								
ACTRS (pillar III)	0.10***	0.07***	−0.02	−0.19***	−0.15***	1							
PRMONIT[a] (pillar III)	0.11***	0.14***	−0.03	0.05**	−0.16***	0.06***	1						
Institutional environment													
Z-SCORE	−0.01	−0.03**	−0.05***	0.16***	0.16***	0.13***	−0.12***	1					
ΔGDP	0.05***	−0.03**	−0.09***	−0.02	0.44***	−0.06***	0.02	0.04***	1				
VOICE	−0.003	−0.13***	−0.10***	0.21***	−0.09***	−0.23***	0.11***	0.01	−0.19***	1			
CORR	−0.04***	−0.14***	−0.08***	0.28***	−0.03*	−0.49***	−0.03*	−0.03*	−0.20***	0.87***	1		
GOVERN	−0.08***	−0.01	0.09***	−0.04***	−0.17***	−0.11***	0.04**	0.07***	−0.22***	0.12***	0.14***	1	
FINDEV	−0.03**	−0.14***	−0.13***	0.25***	−0.15***	−0.08***	0.08***	0.11***	−0.42***	0.62***	0.64***	0.13***	1

*, **, *** means statistically significant at the 10 per cent, 5 per cent and 1 per cent level respectively.

[a] Results for the PRMONIT variable refer to the EU 16 subsample.

inefficiencies – however defined – are more likely to arise in more developed and open institutional frameworks.

7.5 Conclusions

This study focuses on the relationship between bank performance and regulatory and supervisory practices under Basel II's three pillars, for a sample of banks operating in 22 EU countries (10 of which are NMSs) over 2000–8. Efficiency scores are computed with an input-oriented DEA methodology, while performance measures are calculated using traditional accounting ratios, namely net interest margin and cost-to-income. We also carry out an exploratory analysis on the relationship between these variables and institutional factors and a measure of bank-specific risk of insolvency (Z-score). We find that banks' average inefficiency levels are relatively higher for NMSs than for their 'old' EU counterparts (in this study, EU12). As expected, the performance ratios of our banks operating in the EU12 have been more significantly affected than NMSs by the 2007 financial crisis.

Concerning this study's main research questions, our calculated correlation coefficients give some evidence of a significant association between different forms of banking regulation and supervision and bank performance and efficiency. Although this study provides a preliminary data analysis, some interesting relations can be identified, which should be corroborated using sophisticated econometric methods. Specifically, our evidence suggests that strengthened regulatory practices on Pillars I and II appear to be associated with lower inefficiencies, whereas more demanding restrictions and monitoring (Pillar III) seem to decrease the efficient operation of banks. Evidence also shows that bank inefficiency is generally correlated with higher probability of failure and lower regulatory burden. Lastly, it appears that degree of openness and development are important factors in lowering bank inefficiencies, however defined.

Notes

1. In the literature it is possible to identify three types of financial regulation: systemic, prudential and the conduct of business regulations. For more discussion on the different types of regulation, see, among others, Llewellyn (1999).
2. For a systematic introduction to DEA methodology, see among others, Ray (2004).

3. Due to unavailability of data or/and missing values for a significant number of banks we had to exclude Bulgaria, Finland, Greece, Ireland and Romania from our EU data set.
4. This methodology combines Bootstrap and Jackknife re-sampling techniques, to reduce the effect of outliers and possible errors in the dataset (De Sousa and Stosic, 2005).
5. The banks we consider are those of Austria, Belgium, Cyprus, the Czech Republic, Denmark, Estonia, France, Germany, Hungary, Italy, Latvia, Lithuania, Luxembourg, Malta, the Netherlands, Poland, Portugal, Slovakia, Slovenia, Spain, Sweden and the United Kingdom.
6. The Z-score is estimated as (ROA [Return on Assets] + equity/assets)/sd(ROA). The standard deviation of ROA, sd(ROA), is estimated as a five-year moving average.

References

Barth, J.R., Caprio, G. and Levine, R. (2001) 'The Regulation and Supervision of Banks around the World: A New Database', in Litan, R.E. and Herring, R. (eds), *Integrating Emerging Market Counties into the Global Financial System*, Brookings-Wharton Papers in Financial Services (Brooking Institution Press), pp. 183–240.

Barth, J.R., Nolle, D.E, Phumiwasana, T. and Yago, G. (2003a) 'Across-Country Analysis of the Bank Supervisory Framework and Bank Performance', *Financial Markets, Institutions and Instruments*, 12, 67–120.

Barth, J.R., Caprio, G. and Levine, R. (2003b) 'Bank Regulation and Supervision: Lessons from a New Database', in Garza, J.A.M. (ed.), *Macroeconomic Stability, Financial Markets, and Economic Development* (Mexico City: Banco de Mexico).

Barth, J.R., Caprio, G. and Levine, R. (2004) 'Bank Regulation and Supervision: What Works Best?', *Journal of Financial Intermediation*, 13, 205–48.

Barth, J.R., Caprio, G. and Levine, R. (2006) *Rethinking Bank Regulation: Till Angels Govern* (Cambridge: Cambridge University Press).

Barth, J.R., Caprio, G. and Levine, R. (2008a) 'The Microeconomic Effects of Different Approaches to Bank Supervision', in Haber, S., North, D. and Weingast, B. (eds), *The Politics of Financial Development* (Stanford University Press), 156–188.

Barth, J.R., Caprio, G. and Levine, R. (2008b) 'Bank Regulations are Changing: But for Better or Worse?', July, World Bank, available at: http://go.worldbank.org/SNUSW978P0, World Bank Policy Research Working Paper Series, No4646. Available at SSRN: http://ssrn.com/abstract=1149579, Accessed April 18 2011.

Beck, T., Demirguc-Kunt, A. and Levine, R. (2006) 'Bank Supervision and Corruption in Lending', *Journal of Monetary Economics*, 53, 2131–63.

Beck, T., Demirguc-Kunt, A. and Levine, R. (2009) 'Financial Institutions and Markets across Countries and over Time: Data and Analysis', *World Bank Policy Research Working Paper*, No. 4943, available at: http://econ.worldbank.org/programs/finance

Becker, G. (1983) 'A Theory of Competition among Pressure Groups for Political Influence', *Quarterly Journal of Economics*, 98, 371–400.

Berger, A.N. and Humphrey, D.B. (1997) 'Efficiency of Financial Institutions: International Survey and Directions for Further Research', *European Journal of Operational Research*, 98, 175–212.

Berger, A.N., Klapper, L.F. and Turk Ariss, R. (2008) 'Banking Structures and Financial Stability', Mimeo, Wharton Financial Institutions Working Paper No 08/13.

Blum, J. (1999) 'Do Bank Capital Adequacy Requirements Reduce Risks', *Journal of Banking and Finance*, 23, 755–71.

Casu, B. and P. Molyneux (2003) 'A Comparative Study of Efficiency in European Banking', *Applied Economics*, 35(17), 1865–76.

Chortareas, G., Girardone, C. and Ventouri, A. (2010) 'Bank Supervision, Regulation, and Efficiency: Evidence from the European Union', Paper presented at the EWG-EPA Efficiency and Productivity Analysis conference, Chania, Crete, July.

Das, U.S., Iossifov, P., Podpiera, R. and Rozkhov, D. (2005) 'Quality of Financial Policies and Financial System Stress', *IMF Working Paper*, 05/173 (Washington: International Monetary Fund).

De Sousa, M.C. and Stosic, B. (2005) 'Technical Efficiency of the Brazilian Municipalities: Correcting Nonparametric Frontier Measurements for Outliers', *Journal of Productivity Analysis*, 24, 157–81.

Demirguc-Kunt, A. and Detragiache, E. (2010) 'Basel Core Principles and Bank Soundness: Does Compliance Matter?', *Journal of Financial Stability*, forthcoming.

Demirguc-Kunt, A., Laeven, L. and Levine, R. (2004) 'Regulations, Market Structure, Institutions, and the Cost of Financial Intermediation', *Journal of Money, Credit and Banking*, 36, 593–622.

Demirguc-Kunt, A., Detragiache, E. and Tressel, T. (2008) 'Banking on the Principles: Compliance with Basel Core Principles and Bank Soundness', *Journal of Financial Intermediation*, 17, 511–42.

Dewatripont, M. and Tirole, J. (1993) *The Prudential Regulation of Banks* (Cambridge: Cambridge University Press).

Elliehausen, G. (1998) 'The Cost of Bank Regulation: A Review of the Evidence', *Staff Study* 171, Board of Governors of the Federal Reserve System (Washington DC: Federal Reserve System).

Farrell, M.J. (1957) 'The Measurement of Productive Efficiency.' *Journal of the RoyalStatistical Society* 120, 253–290.

Fernandez, A.I. and Gonzalez, F. (2005) 'How Accounting and Auditing Systems Can Counteract Risk-Shifting of Safety-Nets in Banking: Some International Evidence', *Journal of Financial Stability*, 1, 466–500.

Fethi, D.M. and Pasiouras, F. (2010) 'Assessing Bank Efficiency and Performance with Operational Research and Artificial Intelligent Techniques: A Survey', *European Journal of Operational Research*, 204, 189–98.

Fries, S. and Taci, A. (2005) 'Cost efficiency of banks in transition: Evidence from 289 banks in 15 post-communist countries', *Journal of Banking and Finance*, 29, 55–81.

Goddard, J.A., Molyneux, P. and Wilson, J.O.S. (2001) *European Banking: Efficiency, Technology, and Growth* (Chichester: John Wiley).

Gorton, G. and Winton, A. (1995) 'Bank Capital Regulation in General Equilibrium', *Working Paper*, Wharton Financial Institutions Centre.

Grigorian, D. and Manole, V. (2006) 'Determinants of commercial bank performance in transition: An application of Data Envelopment Analysis', *Comparative Economic Studies*, 48, 497–522.
Herring, R. (2004) 'How Can the Invisible Hand Strengthen Prudential Regulation? And How Can Prudential Supervision Strengthen the Invisible Hand?', in Borio, C., Hunter, W., Kaufman, G. and Tsatsaronis, K.J. (eds), *Market Discipline across Countries and Industries* (Cambridge, MA: MIT Press), pp. 363–80.
Herring, R. (2005) 'Implementing Basel II: Is the Game Worth the Candle?', *Financial Markets, Institutions and Instruments*, 14, 267–87.
Hovakimian, A. and Kane, E.J. (2000) 'Effectiveness of capital regulation at U.S. commercial banks, 1985 to 1994', *Journal of Finance*, 55, 451–68.
Jalilian, H., Kirkpatrick, C. and Parker, D. (2007) 'The Impact of Regulation on Economic Growth in Developing Countries: A Cross-Country Analysis', *World Development*, 35(1), 87–103.
Llewellyn, D. (1999) 'The Economic Rationale for Financial Regulation', *FSA Occasional Papers in Financial Regulation*, Occasional Paper Series 1.
Lozano-Vivas, A., Pastor, J.T. and Pastor, J.M. (2002) 'An Efficiency Comparison of European Banking Systems Operating Under Different Environmental Conditions', *Journal of Productivity Analysis*, 18, 59–77.
Molyneux, P. (2003) 'Regulation and Financial Innovation Trends in European Banking and the Impact on the Supply and Demand for Financial Services in Europe', United Nations University, Institute for New Technologies, *EIFC – Technology and Finance Working Papers*, No. 16.
Pasiouras, F. (2008) 'International Evidence on the Impact of Regulations and Supervision on Banks' Technical Efficiency: An Application of two-stage Data Envelopment Analysis', *Review of Quantitative Finance and Accounting*, 30(2), 187–223.
Pasiouras, F., Tanna, S. and Zopounidis, C. (2009) 'The Impact of Banking Regulations on Banks' Cost and Profit Efficiency: Cross-Country Evidence', *International Review of Financial Analysis*, 18, 294–302.
Ray, S.C. (2004). *Data Envelopment Analysis: Theory and Techniques for Economics and Operations Research* (New York: Cambridge University Press).
Rochet, J. (1992) 'Capital Requirements and the Behavior of Commercial Banks', *European Economic Review*, 36(5), 1137–70.
Shleifer, A. and Vishny, R.W. (1989) 'Management entrenchment: The case of manager-specific investments', *Journal of Financial Economics*, 25, 123–39.
Stiglitz, J. E. (2010) 'Financial Re-Regulation and Democracy', *Project Syndicate*, 4 June, http://www.project-syndicate.org/commentary/stiglitz126/English
Stosic, B. and Sampaio de Sousa, M.C. (2003) 'Jackstrapping DEA Scores for Robust Efficiency Measurement', *Anais do XXV Encontro Brasileiro de Econometria SBE*, 1525–40.

8 The Italian Popular Banks and Their Behaviour after the Recent Financial Crisis

Pierluigi Morelli and Elena Seghezza

8.1 Introduction

In this work we intend to understand whether Italian Popular Banks' particular corporate governance has implications for the profitability and efficiency of these banks and for the behaviour of these banks across economic cycles, like the recent financial crisis. Part of the literature comprises the peculiarity of Popular Banks in the wider panorama of local banks: being near to the customers allows banks which operate in a limited geographical area to enjoy advantages as regards information. Such advantages can be traced back to the fact that local bank managers can take account of a large range of factors, such as the loanholder's personal characteristics and those of the local markets, when evaluating the creditworthiness of small businesses.

Conversely, executives of large banks, when evaluating local customers, tend to fall back on impersonal methods, such as scoring techniques (Cole *et al.*, 2004; Berger *et al.*, 2002). Nevertheless, if Popular Banks were not distinguishable from other local banks, their particularity would be nothing to do with their particular corporate governance. Current literature traces the origins and existence of cooperative banks to the possibility of exploiting peer monitoring. Moreover, because peer monitoring assumes critical importance where the state is weak and is not able to fully guarantee property rights, as happens, for example, in developing countries, cooperative banks would be expected to be linked to a particular historical and geographical context. When property rights became established in an economy, there would be no further reason for having cooperative banks. The aspects just mentioned above are detailed in Section 1. In the same section it is shown that, differently from other cooperative banks, Popular Banks are based on the principle of shareholders' limited liability. This principle, and that of 'one head, one vote', makes these banks specific. After all, this specificity derives from the particular Popular Banks governance. Given the extreme fragmentation of their shareholding, these banks are similar to public companies. However, the principle 'one head, one vote' shields Popular Banks from takeovers. The way in which the managers are induced to pursue high profitability and efficiency stems from the informal commitment of banks to guarantee a predetermined rate of return on shares, that is, a high stability of the dividends.

This informal commitment constrains managers to achieve a level of profits at least sufficient to pay the expected dividends. In this way they are discouraged from any form of short-termist behaviour and expense preference. A formal presentation of these arguments is given by an analytical model in Section 2. The model is empirically tested in the last two sections, comparing, with regard to Italy, the behaviour of Popular Banks and of Stock Banks after the recent financial crisis. In particular, in Section 3 we focus on the cyclical effects on incomes and profits of these two types of banks. In Section 4, we analyse the cyclical sensitivity of operating expenses of Italian banks. Lastly, in the Conclusions, there is a summary of the topics dealt with in the previous paragraphs, and some policy indications are given.

8.2 Popular banks, *peer monitoring* and customer relationships

A large strand of the literature shows that, in contexts where property rights are not guaranteed, debt repayment can be induced by resorting to peer monitoring (Stiglitz, 1990; Varian, 1990; Arnott and Stiglitz, 1991). The latter consists of control over one member of the group by other members of the group. In the Stiglitz–Varian models, peer monitoring within groups reduces moral hazard behaviours of individual group members. In this context monitoring activity is delegated to group members, reducing the cost of lending and therefore the interest rate borrowers have to pay.

Varian (1990) and Banerjee *et al.* (1994) single out many forms of group incentives, for example responsibility of the other members if there are losses on the credit issued, obligation that a loan is partially financed by the other members as well, and sequential distribution of loans so that the other members' financing depends on the loan repayment of members financed previously.

Some forms of cooperative banks exploit peer monitoring in this way. Others make use of borrowers' links to their social community as an incentive to avoid moral hazard behaviour. The willingness to maintain strong social links with a certain community (mainly a socio-economic community) makes borrowers increase their efforts to honour their commitments. Links with the socio-economic community are highly important for the borrower because they allow him to have credit again in the future, and he also gains contacts (with clients, suppliers, etc.) useful for developing his business.[1] In cooperative banks, like credit unions, given the unlimited liability of their members, peer monitoring represents the main instrument to relieve problems of moral hazard behaviour by individual borrowers.

However, as Luzzatti (1952) writes: 'Unlimited liability would have kept away from the bank all those wealthy people who, fearful of having to pay out on behalf of less well-off members, would have risked disaster without any advantage to themselves if the bank went bankrupt'. The insistence with which Luzzatti championed the opportunities of limited member liability mainly derived from his conviction that this way would allow Popular Banks to enlarge their size and their financial activities. Obviously, the principle of limited liability reduces the involvement of every member in the outcome of the loans granted. The Italian Popular Banks, being based on the principle of limited liability, cannot by definition resort to peer monitoring in order to disincentivize forms of moral hazard. Problems of adverse selection and moral hazard are solved by Popular Banks using two means: by exploiting forms of 'long-term interaction' among entrepreneurs and establishing long-term customer relationships.

The first means consists of information that an entrepreneur gets by having relationships with other entrepreneurs who perform similar or complementary business activities. This information is useful for a good screening of borrowers; hence the importance given to the inclusion of entrepreneurs in Popular Banks' executive boards. It's no simple coincidence that a conspicuous number of entrepreneurs in the local community take part in them.

The second means allowing Popular Banks to overcome problems of moral hazard is represented by the establishment of long-term relationships with customers. The literature explain in different ways how long-term customer relationships can relieve, if not solve, the problem of asymmetric information. In a seminal article Fama (1985) showed that a bank acquires a large amount of information not only when it initially evaluates a customer's creditworthiness, but also when it performs monitoring on the management behaviour of the firm being financed. However, a large part of the literature (see, among others, Fama, 1985), insists on the fact that customer relations influence a firm's ability to gain funding initially from banks and subsequently from the market.

The theory on which this conclusion is based is as follows. Bank loans are a form of short-term financing. Every time the bank renews its credit to the company it publicly 'accredits' the company with the ability to deal with its contractual obligations and hence to deserve the credit. As highlighted by some of the empirical literature, the announcement that a loan has been granted or renewed to a firm reduces the cost for that firm to raise funds on the market. Diamond (1989) highlights the fact that the existence of long-term relationships allows better screening of customers. More precisely, in a context of repeated games, a bank can select customers through the solvency reputation that they acquire. The theory mentioned above, however, leads us to think that banks have the role of informing the market: at the end of the screening process, in fact, the banks' customers with least risky projects can ask for financing directly on the market. All the contributions just quoted conclude that banks screen their customers and, in so doing, allow the best-quality customers to raise funds through financial market instruments. This does not seem to be the path taken by Popular Banks' customers. Actually, the structure of these banks' customers is stable over time.

A different way of considering long-term relations between Bank and customer hinges on the fact that such relationships allow relief of problems arising from the existence of incomplete contracts, which do not take account of all possible future circumstances. In this framework, incentives to honour contractual clauses can arise from the possibility of revising loans' contractual terms. Von Thadden (1995), for example, showed that relations between bank and customer allow the period of investments to be lengthened: thanks to the existence of long-term relations, a bank can single out 'good'-quality entrepreneurs and subsequently guarantee them financing of their project for a longer time. Boot and Thakor (1994), instead, show that banks, when they issue a long-term loan contract, tend to ease the contract's terms if the customer is seen to comply with his obligations. Customer relations allow contractual terms to be revised not only ex ante, but also ex post. When a firm finds it difficult to satisfy its contractual obligations, the bank can adjust the loan contractual terms as long as the company undertakes certain strategies when times are difficult. In this way, due to their

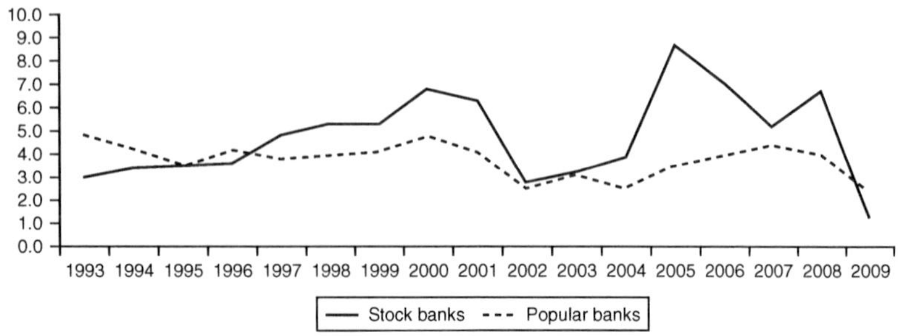

Figure 8.1 Bank share dividends

long-term relationships, banks, on the one hand, can support firms hit by negative shocks (Hoshi *et al.*, 1990; Ferri *et al.*, 2000), and exert some form of control over managers' choices (Rajan, 1992; Petersen and Rajan, 1994; Longhafer and Santos, 1998); on the other hand, they maintain the possibility of not renewing the credit (Berle, 1926; Stiglitz, 1985) and renegotiating the loans' contractual terms (Hart and Moore, 1988).

Popular Banks are well fitted to entertain long-term relationships with customers, given the feature of their corporate governance. The principle of 'one head, one vote' shields these banks from takeovers. However, in order to attract a large number of small shareholders, Popular Banks guarantee a stable return on invested capital.

Figure 8.1 shows that, in Italy, dividends paid out by Popular Banks are markedly more stable than those paid out by Stock Banks.[2] Therefore, the shares of Popular Banks can be assimilated to assets with a predetermined rate of interest, like bonds.[3]

The informal commitment of Popular Banks to pay out stable dividends determines a set of incentives for managers, who are induced, on the one hand, to refrain from short-termism and, on the other hand, to avoid expense preference behaviour. A formal presentation of these arguments will be given through an analytical model in the next section.

8.3 Corporate governance and short-termism in banks

As is well known, the principal/agent approach applied to firms' corporate governance focuses on agency costs which derive from the separation between management and ownership: in fact, managers are tempted to pursue their own objectives, which often aim at greater prestige and higher salary (Marris, 1964). The opportunistic behaviour of managers can jeopardize a firm's profitability, and the consequent fall in share price makes likely a takeover and the replacement of management. Wherever the capital market is working well, the threat of takeover represents the main incentive for managers to maximize profit and share prices.

Current literature's arguments about firm's takeovers can be transposed, with some marginal distinctions, to banks. However, as the experience of the recent financial crisis shows, the threat of takeover can in fact induce short-sighted behaviour in managers. It can thus be the case that bank managers also suffer from short-termism when there is an efficient stock market. To show how this could come about, let us suppose that the stock market uses dividends to make a rational estimate of a bank's value; that is, it is assumed that highest dividends today are linked with highest dividends in the future. Taking this into account, managers try to trick the market by inflating current dividends to increase the bank's expected value. In equilibrium, the market is efficient and does not get caught out: investors have rational expectations, correctly predict the inflation of dividends and take account of this when inferring about the bank's future value. On the basis of this hypothesis, it could be considered that managers concerned with keeping the shares' current price high to avoid takeovers tend to invest in short-term assets, while managers not worried about the shares' current price invest in long-term assets and favour the establishment of long-term relationships with borrowers.

As is well known, the threat of takeover represents a means of discipline for managers. It could thus be considered that, where such a risk is weak, managers' time horizon gets longer, but the bank's efficiency suffers. In reality, takeovers represent one of the various types of incentives for managers in order to help efficient running of the bank. Commitment to keep dividends (and thus profits) stable over time may represent an alternative form of incentive to takeovers: following this type of commitment, managers have no option but to increase their efforts to reach ever higher efficiency levels. What has just been explained above can be shown better by means of a formal model.[4] Let us consider a bank which operates for two periods. In the absence of short-sighted behaviour and efforts on the manager's part, the bank's profit in the first period is given by:

$$e_1 = y_1 + u_1 \qquad \text{where } y \in (e_H, e_L) \quad \text{and} \quad e_H > e_L \tag{1}$$

As Equation (1) shows, profits are made up of two parts. The first part, y, is the bank *potential* profit, and can assume only two values, e_H or e_L: if

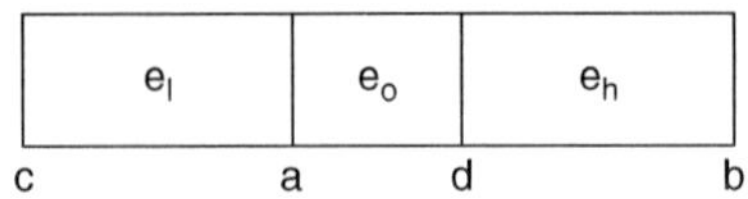

Figure 8.2 First period profits distribution

the bank is *good*-quality it will have *potential* profits equal to e_H, if it is *bad*-quality it will have a *potential* profit of e_L. We assume that if in the first period y is low (= e_L) it will also be in the second (or if it is high it will stay that way in the second). The second section, u, represents the transitory component: this component is independent from one period to another and is uniformly distributed with zero mean. Neither y nor u is observable. Neither the bank nor the market knows whether the potential profits of the banks are high or low, that is to say, whether the bank is type e_H or e_L, so an ex-ante probability of 50 per cent is assigned to both outcomes. At the end of the first period the bank's profits become known to the public. The market uses this information to update the probability that the bank's potential profits are good-quality, and, based on this, assigns a price to the bank's shares.

To render analysis easier, let us suppose that the profit range for a good-quality bank is $[a, b]$, while for a poor-quality bank it is $[c, d]$, with $d-c=b-a$, e $b>d>a>c$, which means that first period profits do not always reveal the type of bank. Figure 8.2 shows this situation.

First period profits can be:

- Greater than d; in this case they show that the bank's potential profit is high (and remain the same also in the second term);
- Between a and d, inclusive; in this case the profits do not show the bank's potential profit. This because a profit between a and d, inclusive, can be gained both by a poor-quality bank (a poor-quality bank's profits fall between c and d), and also by a good-quality bank (a good-quality bank's profits fall between a and b).
- Less than a; in this case they show that the bank's potential profit is low.

The bank's ex-ante expected share price is therefore:[5]

$$E(P_1) = \frac{1}{2}\frac{b-d}{b-a}e_H + \frac{1}{2}\frac{d-a}{b-a}e_0 + \frac{1}{2}\frac{d-a}{b-a}e_0 + \frac{1}{2}\frac{a-c}{b-a}e_L = e_0 \qquad (2)$$

where $e_H = \dfrac{a+b}{2}$, $e_L = \dfrac{c+d}{2}$, $e_0 = \dfrac{e_H + e_L}{2} = \dfrac{a+b+c+d}{4}$

Up to now, banks' efficiency has been considered exogenous. Now let us introduce the hypothesis that it is affected by managers' behaviour. Managers, by increasing their efforts, can improve the screening of a bank's clients and thus reduce the chance of obtaining low profits. In particular, we assume that manager's effort (S) shifts the profit distribution function: if the bank is poor-quality, profits fall between $c+S$ and d; if the bank is good-quality, profits fall between $a+S$ and b.[6] As Figure 8.2 shows, the profit distribution function is defined on a more restricted range of values and, consequently, is higher. If managers make the effort, expected profits increase in every period[7] by $\frac{S}{2}$.

The effort, S, is not visible to the market. Given the market's 'effort' expectations, S^e, the bank's expected share price increases. Figure 8.4 illustrates the situation.

By using Figure 8.3, the expected share price can be calculated:[8]

$$\begin{aligned} E(P_1^S) &= \frac{1}{2}\frac{b-d}{b-a-S^e-S}\left(e_H+\frac{S^e}{2}\right)+\frac{1}{2}\frac{d-a-S^e-S}{b-a-S^e-S}\left(e_0+\frac{S^e}{2}\right) \\ &\quad +\frac{1}{2}\frac{d-a-S^e}{b-a-S^e-S}\left(e_0+\frac{S^e}{2}\right)+\frac{1}{2}\frac{b-d-S}{b-a-S^e-S}\left(e_L+\frac{S^e}{2}\right) \\ &= \frac{S^e}{2}+\frac{1}{8(b-a-S^e-S)}\big(2(b-a)(a+b+c+d) \\ &\quad -S(a+b+3c+3d)-2(a+b+c+d)S^e\big) \end{aligned} \qquad (3)$$

Let's now suppose that managers, as well as having the chance of improving profit distribution through their efforts, have the chance to perform short-termistic actions: a manager can create an additional flow of current income by borrowing from next period profits at an unfavourable interest rate. In the case of banks, a short-termistic action is disinvesting long-term loans. In particular, if we indicate with an 'X' the amount of this loan, profit flows increase by X, while second-term profits fall by RX^2. This formula[9] has been chosen to show that the cost of short-termism goes hand in hand with the amount of short-termism. Of course, the amount X of the loan cannot be observed.[10]

A manager may be interested in undertaking such an action in order to increase the chance that the bank is considered good-quality

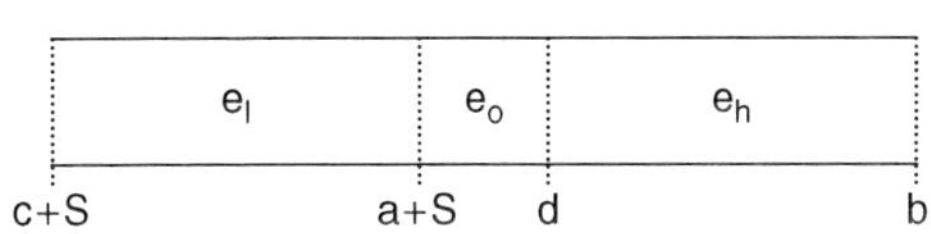

Figure 8.3 Firms' profits with managers' effort

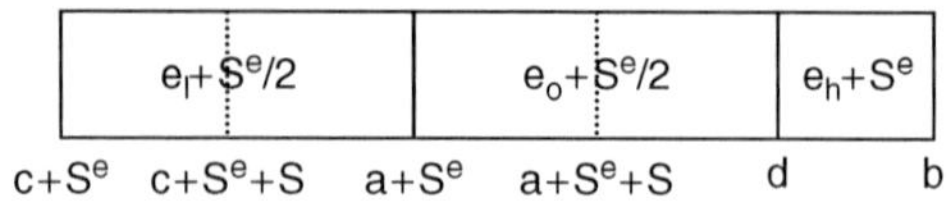

Figure 8.4 Firms' profit and market's expected effort

and hence to see the share price increased. Given the market's expectations, if a manager were to put into practice both his 'efforts' and short-termism, the expected price for the bank's shares would increase. Figure 8.5 shows the situation.

The expected price for shares is now:

$$\begin{aligned} E(P_1^{SX}) &= \frac{1}{2}\frac{b+X-d}{b-a-S^e-S}\left(e_H+\frac{S^e}{2}-R\left(X^e\right)^2\right) \\ &+\frac{1}{2}\frac{d-a-S^e-S-X}{b-a-S^e-S}\left(e_0+\frac{S^e}{2}-R\left(X^e\right)^2\right) \\ &+\frac{1}{2}\frac{X}{b-a-S^e-S}\left(e_H+\frac{S^e}{2}-R\left(X^e\right)^2\right) \\ &+\frac{1}{2}\frac{d-a-S^e}{b-a-S^e-S}\left(e_0+\frac{S^e}{2}-R\left(X^e\right)^2\right) \\ &+\frac{1}{2}\frac{b-d-S-X}{b-a-S^e-S}\left(e_L+\frac{S^e}{2}-R\left(X^e\right)^2\right) \end{aligned} \tag{4}$$

Which simplifies to:

$$E(P_1^{SX}) = \frac{S^e}{2} - R(X^e)^2 + \frac{\begin{array}{c}[3(a+b-c-d)X+2(b-a)(a+b+c+d) \\ -S(a+b+3c+3d)-2(a+b+c+d)S^e]\end{array}}{8(b-a-S^e-S)} \tag{5}$$

Up to now, managers' behaviour has not been taken into account. As in other articles, it can be assumed that managers are interested in both the banks' long-term returns and current share values. Managers' interest in the current value of share price can arise from the possibility of takeover. The greater the likelihood of takeover, the greater is managers' interest in the shares' current price.

Furthermore, it is assumed that the manager's utility depends negatively on the variability of profits in time (VP). This assumption has been included to take account of the fact that Popular Banks tend to stabilize their profits.

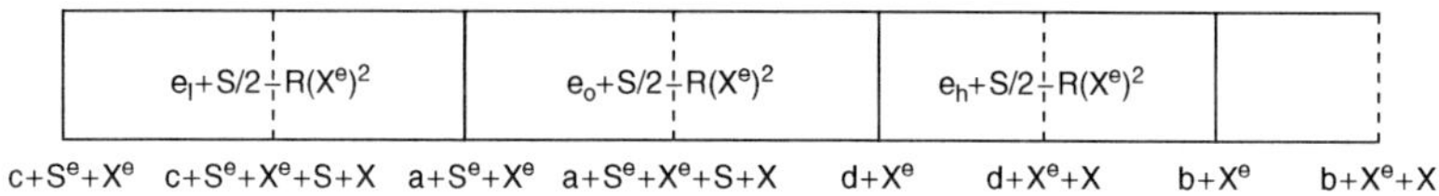

Figure 8.5 Firms' profit, manager effort and *shortermism*

A way of measuring profit variability is the variation range. To stabilize ex-ante profits in time it is necessary to reduce both the range of profit variation in every single period and the range of profit variation between periods. If the managers make efforts and practice short-termism, the profit variation range in any given term is given by $b–c–S$, while the variation range between terms is given by the expected value of $(e_1–e_2)=X+RX^2$. The variation of profits in time is hence given by:

$$VP = b - c - S + X + RX^2. \tag{6}$$

Managers' utility function is thus the following:

$$U_m = e_1 + \lambda P_1 + e_2 - \beta S^2 - \gamma VP \tag{7}$$

where λ represents the chance of takeover, γ the importance given by managers to stabilizing profits and β the cost of managers' efforts. Managers choose the level of effort and the level of short-termism which maximize expected value of (7). Bearing in mind that $e_1^e = e_0 + \frac{S}{2} + X$ and $e_2^e = e_0 + \frac{S}{2} - RX^2$ and using (5) and (6), the first conditions are obtained:

$$\begin{aligned} \frac{\partial U^e}{\partial X} &= -2RX(1+\gamma)+1-\gamma+\lambda\frac{3(a+b-c-d)}{8(b-u-S^e-S)}=0 \\ \frac{\partial U^e}{\partial S} &= 1-2\beta S+\gamma+\lambda\frac{(a+b-c-d)(b-a+3X-S^e)}{8(b-a-S^e-S)^2}=0 \end{aligned} \tag{8}$$

Now we can distinguish Popular Banks from Stock Banks and solve the problem for both types of banks to see whether, and in what way, they can be differentiated. As observed in the text, Popular Banks are subject to a minimal takeover risk, and to the stabilization of their profits over time. They can be associated with a λ value of zero and a positive value of γ. Stock Banks, on the other hand, are subject to the risk of takeover, but have no profit stabilization policy. They feature a positive value of λ and a γ value of nil.

By replacing $\lambda = 0$ in (8), the value of short-termism and efforts of managers of Popular Banks can be obtained:

$$X^{pop} = \frac{1-\gamma}{2R(1+\gamma)}; \quad S^{pop} = \frac{1+\gamma}{2\beta} \tag{9}$$

If the Popular Banks' shareholders, being averse to risk, force managers to stabilize profits, forms of short-termism are avoided. From (9) it can be deduced that for popular banks the level of short-termism falls when γ increases. The assumption just made regarding shareholders' risk aversion seems to correspond to the fact that the holders of Popular Banks' shares are generally small savers who thus have limited wealth. Stabilizing profits, as well as corresponding to shareholders' preferences, is a tool to motivate managers to achieve minimum profit levels. In this model, therefore, shareholders exercise a form of control similar to creditors in the free cash-flow approach. Essentially, stabilizing profits forces managers into efficient behaviour: as the emphasis on stabilizing profits grows, so do the efforts made by managers. For a high enough value of γ,[11] the efforts made by managers reach a maximum.

Let's move on to Stock Banks. Replacing $\gamma = 0$ in Equation (8a) and bearing in mind that expectations are rational ($S^e = S$), we get:

$$X = \frac{1}{2R}\left(1+\lambda\frac{3(a+b-c-d)}{8(b-a-2S)}\right) \tag{10}$$

As Equation (10) shows, the managers of a Stock Bank will always choose a certain amount of short-termism (there is no way of getting $X=0$[12]). Moreover, for any value of γ and λ, (10) is higher than (9), so managers of a Stock Bank perform more acts of short-termism compared with managers of a Popular Bank. Replacing (10), $S^e = S$ e $\gamma = 0$ in (8b) we get:

$$-128R(b-a-2S)^3(1-2\beta S) =$$
$$\lambda(a+b-c-d)\left[16R(b-a-S)+24\right](b-a-2S)+9\lambda^2(a+b-c-d)^2 \tag{11}$$

The equation above is a fourth grade equation, and studying it is rather complex. However, we are only interested in knowing whether, for the range of possible values for S, $S \in (0, \frac{d-a}{2})$ has a solution, and whether the solution, S^*, is an increasing or diminishing function of λ. The solutions for Equation (11) are those values of S for which the curve corresponding to the first term of (11), a bell-shaped curve, meets the curve corresponding to the second term of (11), the decreasing side of a parabola (in Figure 8.6 approximated by a decreasing line).

As Figure 8.6 shows, the two curves meet up at two points. However, only the first point is economically relevant; it corresponds, in fact, to a maximum point, and the second to a minimum point. As λ increases, the line moves higher. As the likelihood of takeover grows, manager's optimal effort increases. When the line rises completely above the first curve, the optimum effort becomes the maximum.[13]

Note that the straight line is always found in the positive quadrant; thus a Stock Bank manager's efforts are always greater than a Popular Bank manager's efforts, should the latter not stabilize its profits ($S = \frac{1}{2\beta}$). Should the Popular Bank, however, stabilize its profit ($S = \frac{1+\gamma}{2\beta}$), which type of bank is more efficient is not clear; the result depends on parameters.

This model leads us to conclude that Stock Banks carry out actions of short-termism more extensively than Popular Banks and that the stabilizing of profits allows managers in Popular Banks to reach more efficient behaviour levels, in particular:

a) For high enough values of γ (importance given to profit stability), Popular Bank managers do not practice short-termism and they

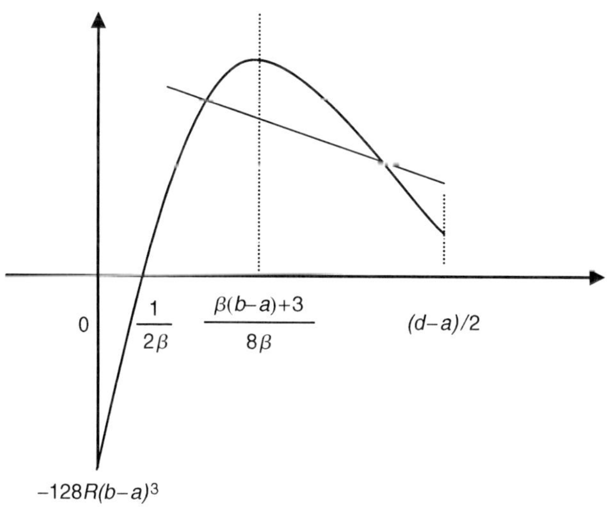

Figure 8.6 Stock banks' efforts and probability of takeovers

behave efficiently. In any case, as γ grows, short-termism actions decrease and efficiency increases.

b) For high enough values of λ (likelihood of takeover), Stock Banks' managers practice short-termism and they behave efficiently. In any case, short-termism is always practised, and increases with λ.
c) For intermediate values of γ and λ Popular Banks practice less short-termism than Stock Banks, but it is not clear which type of bank is more efficient.
d) The market correctly predicts managers' behaviour and takes this into account when fixing the current share price.

The model just presented allows us to conclude that the informal commitment of Popular Banks to guarantee a predetermined rate of return on shares constrains managers:

1. To achieve a stable level of profits. This way they are discouraged from any form of short-termism. This implies that Popular Banks, on one hand, are in a better condition to establish long-term relationships with their customers and, on the other hand, are more devoted than Stock Banks to traditional banking activity.
2. To expand incomes and to contain operating expenses and losses in order to achieve an amount of profits at least sufficient to pay the expected dividends. In this way a high level of profitability and efficiency can be attained.

These conclusions are empirically tested in the following paragraphs.

8.4 Italian banks' revenues and profits during the recent financial crisis

The recent financial crisis is a topical moment to verify the propositions set out in the model for two reasons. First, the crisis was largely caused by several banks' exploitation of an excessive leverage, and therefore by a typical short-termist behaviour. The necessary balance sheets adjustment after the crisis was inevitably more intense for the banks that had been involved in such behaviour.

Second, since the crisis dramatically hit financial markets, particularly for some instruments, such as derivatives, the recomposition of revenue structure should have been less sharp for those banks characterized by a management less conditioned by forms of short-termism. To check the two conclusions of the model, the FAST data bank has been used, comparing the Profit and Loss Accounts of 43 Popular

Banks with those of 72 Stock Banks and those of 61 mutual banks and savings banks within the time frame 2006–9, more precisely the two years before the financial crisis and the two years following it. From the comparison of the profitability of the various categories of banks (Table 8.1) emerges the basic stability of Popular Banks' profitability, measured by both ROE (Return on equity) and ROA (return on assets).

On the contrary, Stock Banks suffered a significant reduction in profitability in the two years 2008–9: these banks seem to have suffered from the short-termist behaviour of their management. The ANOVA test confirms the significance of these results for ROE. The ROA values are at the limit of significance (Table 8.2).

A further support of this argument comes from teh changes in gross income individual components. As shown in Table 8.3, the value of Popular Banks' gross remained substantially stable even after the

Table 8.1 ROE and ROA of Italian banks (2006–9)

	Years			
Categories of bank	**2006**	**2007**	**2008**	**2009**
ROE (Return on Equity)				
Stock Banks	6.86	5.30	–1.57	1.19
Popular Banks	6.61	6.73	6.53	7.67
Other Banks	8.46	5.96	4.91	4.24
ROA (Return on Assets)				
Stock Banks	0.55	0.66	–0.04	0.11
Popular Banks	0.66	0.63	0.58	0.69
Other Banks	0.77	0.61	0.42	0.44

Source: FAST data bank.

Table 8.2 Changes in profitability (difference between 2006–7 and 2008–9 values)

Bank Categories	**Number of Banks**	**ROE**	**ROA**
Stock Banks	72	–6.27	–0.58
Popular Banks	43	0.43	–0.02
Other Banks	61	–2.64	–0.26
ANOVA Test	F	5.42	2.5
	significance	97.9%	91.5%

Source: FAST data bank.

financial crisis. Conversely, Stock Banks' gross income shows a significant decrease in the two years 2008–9 in comparison to the preceding two years.

The decrease in public company banks' gross income has entirely derived from the behaviour of 'Other incomes', which has remained practically stable in the case of Popular Banks (Table 8.4). It is interesting to note that, conversely to what is argued by a large part of the literature, in the case of Italian Stock Banks the 'Other incomes' have contributed to increasing, instead of reducing, revenues and profit volatility. It is important to note that Popular Banks, having been less exposed to forms of short-termism, have registered a very low decrease of 'Other incomes' after the crisis (Table 8.4).

After the recent financial crisis both Popular Banks and Stock Banks have increased the share of net interest income, that is, from traditional bank activities, in their gross income formation. The importance of this item of the profit and loss account on total assets is increased in a similar way in the two categories of banks (Table 8.5).

Popular Banks' higher stability of gross income with respect to public company banks has been due not only to the lower incidence and volatility of 'Other revenues' but also to a higher importance in banks of this kind of traditional bank activity, that is, deposit and loan activities

Table 8.3 Gross income on capital (percentage values)

	2006–7	2008–9	Variation
Stock Banks	49.59	46.98	–3.61
Popular Banks	45.08	46.67	+1.59
Other Banks	45.14	47.10	+1.96
ANOVA Test F	0.94	0.004	1.19
significance	60.8%	0.4%	69.4%

Source: FAST data bank.

Table 8.4 Other incomes on capital (percentage values)

	2006–7	2008–9	Variation
Stock Banks	26.90	22.32	–4.58
Popular Banks	16.38	15.45	–0.93
Other Banks	15.53	16.30	0.76
ANOVA F	9.33	2.76	2.34
significance	99.9%	93.4%	90.1%

Source: FAST data bank.

Table 8.5 Net interest income on total assets (percentage values)

	2006–7	2008–9	Variation
Stock Banks	22.69	24.65	1.96
Popular Banks	28.70	31.22	2.52
Other Banks	29.61	30.81	1.20
ANOVA F	5.78	4.58	0.31
significance	99.6%	98.8%	26.4%

Source: FAST data bank.

(Table 8.5). This confirms the particular attention paid by Popular Banks to customer relationships.

8.5 Popular Banks' efficiency and cyclical sensitivity of their operating costs

It has been stated that the principle of 'one head, one vote', inhibiting forms of takeover and making managers difficult to remove, might discourage them from high levels of profitability. A basic assessment of the traditional literature is that the possibility of takeovers induces managers to maximize profits and efficiency (Jensen, 1988). Berle and Means (1932) maintain that in modern business there is a direct relationship between concentration of ownership and company performance. This conclusion derives from the assertion that, where a large number of shareholders exist, the typical shareholder does not have enough power to exercise control over managers. Similar conclusions are reached by the principle–agent approach (Fama and Jensen, 1983; Shleifer and Vishny, 1986, Brickley *et al.*, 1988, Jensen, 1989, Zwiebel, 1995), according to which, when the ownership of a firm is fragmented, monitoring of management is loose, given that for individual owners it is not convenient to exert this form of control. In this context, managers, since their objectives are different from those of the owners, may use resources in a way that does not maximize the share value. A conflict of interest between owners and managers arises: it can happen that managers have an expense preference, so that they aim at targets such as maximization of size or expenditure.

On the other hand, given the low concentration of their shareholding, Popular Banks should be more prone to forms of expense preference, and thus less efficient than other banks, in particular the majority of Stock Banks. The lower efficiency of Popular Banks should result in

Table 8.6 Operating expenses on total assets (percentage values)

	Operating Expenses on gross income		**Operating Expenses on total assets**	
	2006–7	**2008–9**	**2006–7**	**2008–9**
Stock Banks	71.99	75.17	3.05	2.49
Popular Banks	61.56	62.66	2.49	2.47
Other Banks	60.04	62.47	2.43	2.40
Anova Test F	3.71	3.12	2.85	0.09
significance	98.3%	95.3%	93.9%	8.4%

Source: FAST Data Bank.

a higher level of operating expenses. However, Table 8.6 shows that the level of Popular Banks' operating expenses is lower than those of Stock Banks, both before and after the crisis. This seems to confirm the thesis of the model that Popular Banks' managers, being incentivized to achieve a predetermined level of profits, are meanwhile constrained to contain the operating expenses.

Table 8.6 gives also evidence that Popular Banks' operating costs are less cyclical sensitive than Stock Banks': it is possible to suppose that there is a bi-directional causality between long-term relationships with customers and stable relationship with employees.

8.6 Conclusions

Most literature that focuses on Popular Banks examines forms of cooperative banks, and considers the features of peer monitoring and other advantages of being a local bank. However, the specificity of these banks stems above all from their corporate governance. In Stock Banks, the main device for controlling managers is the threat of takeover. This principle dictates that if a bank's profitability decreases so does the price of its shares, and therefore there is an increased chance that ownership will change. Being conscious of this fact, managers, in order to prevent a possible takeover, can resort to forms of short-termism. Conversely, in the case of Popular Banks, given the principle of 'one head, one vote' on which they are based, takeovers are unlikely.

The way managers are induced to pursue high levels of profitability and efficiency stems from the informal commitment of Popular Banks to guarantee a predetermined rate of return on shares, that is, a remarkable stability of dividends. This informal commitment constrains managers to achieve a stable level of profits; that is, to avoid any form of short-termism. To this end they favour long-term customer relationships and limit the banks' activity to traditional fields. This argument has been tested, considering the Italian banks' profit and loss accounts across the recent financial crisis. From this test it emerges that the returns on capital of Popular Banks are stable even after the crisis, while those of Stock Banks are extremely volatile.

The informal commitment of Popular Banks to grant their shareholders a predetermined rate of return on capital constrains managers to expand incomes and to contain operating expenses, that is, to pursue a high level of efficiency. This assessment is empirically confirmed by the experience of the recent financial crisis, during which Popular Banks have held their operating expenses significantly more stable and lower than Stock Banks. The arguments and the empirical tests put forward in this chapter allow us to conclude that the profitability and efficiency of banks can be assured not only by takeovers, but also by other schemes of incentives.

Notes

Although the work is the fruit of a joint project, Sections 1 and 2 are to be attributed to E. Seghezza and Sections 3 and 4 to P. Morelli. The views expressed in the chapter are those of the authors and do not represent the views of their institutions.

1. Relaxing the assumption of costless peer monitoring implicit in the Stiglitz–Varian models, some scholars have emphasized the role of social ties in reducing moral hazard behaviour by individual borrowers (see Floro and Yotopoulos, 1991; Besley and Coate, 1995; Wydick, 1999, 2001).
2. A discussion of this aspect can be found in Pittaluga *et al.* (2004).
3. It is possible that the small shareholders of Popular Banks demand risk-free assets.
4. The model's structure is based on the plan proposed by Stein (1989) and its development proposed by Nolan (1998).
5. The first term of Equation (2) is the product of the probability the bank is of good quality (1/2) that it has profit in the first period greater than d, $(b-d/b-a)$, and that it can be recognized as a good-quality bank, multiplied by the profits of a good-quality bank, e_H. The second term is the product of the probability the bank is of good quality (1/2) and that it has profit in the first period (1/2) between a and d $(d-a/b-a)$, and thus is not recognizable as a good-quality bank, multiplied by its average profit value. The third term is the product of the probability that the bank is poor-quality and has a first term profit which falls between a and d, multiplied by its average profit value. The fourth term is the product of the probability that the bank is poor-quality and has first term profits less than a, multiplied by the profits of a poor-quality bank.

6. Effort, *S*, cannot be greater than ba(d–a)/2. This assumption has been introduced because, even with efforts and short-termism, first term profits are not certain indicators of the bank's quality.
7. It is assumed that, if managers decide to make an effort, they must do it in both terms.
8. In Equation (3) the fact is used that $b - d = a - c$.
9. Also followed by Stein (1989).
10. $X < (d - a)/2$
11. $\gamma = \beta(d - a) - 1$
12. Note that $b - a - 2S$ is always greater than 0 because $S < (d - a)/2$.
13. Because the first derivate is always positive.

References

Arnott, R. and Stiglitz, J.E. (1991) 'Moral hazard and nonmarket institutions: dysfunctional crowding out or peer monitoring?', *American Economic Review*, 81, 179–90.

Banerjee, A.V., Beslie, T. and Guinnane, T.N. (1994) 'The neighbor's keeper: the design of a credit cooperative with theory and a test', *Quarterly Journal of Economics*, 84, 490–515.

Berger, A.N., Miller, N., Petersen, M., Rajan, R. and Stein, J. (2002) 'Does function follow organizational form? Evidence from the lending practice of large and small banks', *NBER working paper* 63 (Washington DC: NBER).

Berle, A. (1926) 'Non voting stock and bankers' control', *Harvard Law Review*, 39, 679–93.

Berle, A. and Means, G. (1932) *The modern corporation and private property* (New York: Palgrave Macmillan).

Besley, T. and Coate, S. (1995) 'Group lending, repayment incentives and social collateral', *Journal of Development Economics*, 46, 1–18.

Boot, A.W.A. and Thakor, A.V. (1994) 'Moral hazard and secured lending in an infinitely repeated credit market game', *International Economic Review*, 35, 899–920.

Brickey, J.A., Lease, R.C. and Smith, C.W. (1988) 'Ownership structure on corporate restructuring', *Strategic Management Journal*, 14, 15–31.

Cole, R.A., Goldberg, L.G. and White, L.J. (2004) 'Cookie-cutter versus character: the micro structure of small business lending by large and small banks', in Federal Reserve System (ed.), *Business Access to Credit. Journal of Financial and Quantitative Analysis*, 39, 227–251.

Diamond, D.W. (1989) 'Reputation acquisition in debt markets', *Journal of Political Economy*, 97, 828–62.

Fama, E.F. (1985) 'What's different about banks?', *Journal of Monetary Economics*, 15, 5–29.

Fama, E.C. and Jensen, M.C. (1983) 'The separation of ownership and control', *Journal of Law and Economics*, 26, 301–28.

Ferri, G., Kang, T.S. and Kim, I.J. (2000) The value of relationship banking during financial crises: evidence from the Republic of Korea. World Bank Working Paper No 2553. Washington DC: World Bank.

Floro, S.L. and Yotopoulos, P.A. (1991) *Informal credit markets and the new institutional economics: the case of the Philippine agriculture* (Boulder: West View Press).

Hart, O. and Moore, J. (1988) 'Incomplete contracts and renegotiation', *Econometrica*, 56, 755–86.
Hoshi, T., Kashyap, A. and Scharfstein, D. (1990) 'The role of banks in reducing the costs of financial distress in Japan', *Journal of Financial Economics*, 27, 67–88.
Jensen, M.C. (1988) 'Takeovers, their causes and consequences', *Journal of Economic Perspectives*, 2, 21–48.
Jensen, M.C. (1989) 'Eclipse of the public corporation', *Harvard Business Review*, 67, 67–74.
Longhafer, S.D. and Santos, J.A.C. (1998) 'The importance of bank seniority for relationship lending', *BIS working paper*, 58 (Basel: Bank for International Settlements).
Luzzatti, E. (1952) *Opere* (Bologna: Zanichelli).
Marris, R. (1964) *The economic theory of managerial capitalism* (London: Palgrave Macmillan).
Nolan, D. (1998) 'Capital structure and short term decisions', *Royal Holloway University of London discussion papers in economics*, 9810.
Petersen, M.A. and Rajan, R.G. (1994) 'The benefits of firm-creditor relationship: evidence from small business data', *Journal of Finance*, 49, 3–38.
Pittaluga, G.B., Morelli, P. and Seghezza, E. (2004) 'Fondamenti teorici della Corporate governance e comportamento delle Banche Popolari', in De Bruyn, R. and Ferri, G. (eds), *Le Banche Popolari nel localismo dell'economia italiana*, Quaderni, Rivista Credito Popolare 3/4, 53–123.
Rajan, R. (1992) 'Insiders and Outsiders: the Choice between Relationship and Arm's-Length Debt', *The Journal of Finance*, 47, 1367–400.
Shleifer, A. and Vishny, R. (1986) 'Large shareholders and corporate control', *Journal of Political Economy*, 94, 461–88.
Stein, J.C. (1989) 'Efficient capital markets, inefficient firms: a model of myopic corporate behavior', *Quarterly Journal of Economics*, 104, 655–69.
Stiglitz, J. (1985) 'Credit markets and the control of capital', *Journal of Money, Credit and Banking*, 17, 132–52.
Stiglitz, J. (1990) 'Peer monitoring and credit markets', *The World Bank Economic Review*, 4, 351–66.
Varian, H. (1990) 'Monitoring agents with other agents', *Journal of Institutional and Theoretical Economics*, 146, 153–74.
Von Thadden, E.L. (1995) 'Long-term contracts, short-term investment, and monitoring', *Review of Economic Studies*, 62, 557–75.
Wydick, B. (1999) 'Can social cohesion be harnessed to repair market failures? Evidence from group lending in Guatemala', *Economic Journal*, 109, 463–75.
Wydick, B. (2001) 'Group lending under dynamic incentives as a borrower discipline device', *Review of Development Economics*, 5, 406–20.
Zwiebel, J. (1995) 'Block investment and partial benefits of corporate control', *Review of Economic Studies*, 62, 161–85.

9
Access to Equity for New, Innovative Companies in Italy

Luciana Canovi, Elisabetta Gualandri and Valeria Venturelli

9.1 Introduction

Numerous studies have revealed the ability of innovative companies, as a category, to positively affect a country's economic growth.[1] This explains why the topic of innovation and the growth of innovative firms is not only at the centre of national and international economic policy, but is also destined to acquire greater importance in the context of exit strategies for the current economic crisis.

This chapter investigates the subject of finance for the growth of small and medium enterprises (SMEs) in one of the Italian Provinces: the Province of Modena. The aim is, first, to analyse the means by which start-ups are financed, especially in the form of equity, and attempt to identify any financial constraints which restrict the growth and development of firms of this kind. Second, attention will be focused on the roles of the various financial players in financing new firms, and the obstacles they encounter in accessing equity investments. This financial channel is crucial in today's economic crisis, since the banks, which tend to ignore start-ups even during normal market circumstances, have generally tightened their lending criteria and business owners will need to look elsewhere for financing.

Compared with the empirical evidence already available, the study conducted on innovative start-ups in the Province of Modena offers a number of original features. In particular, as far as we are aware, this study is one of the first attempts in Italy to measure the main demand-side constraints, both financial and managerial, on the birth and growth of innovative new firms.

The work is structured as follows. The first section reviews the theoretical and empirical literature on the existence of an equity gap (e.g. a shortage of equity investments), especially during the initial stages of firms' life cycle. The section that follows presents the research method used. The third section presents the main results of the survey; these are followed by the work's main conclusions.

9.2 Financing gap and equity gap

In the literature and the empirical studies conducted at national and international levels,[2] one significant topic with regard to the financing of SMEs is the existence or otherwise of the *financing gap*, the term used to describe situations in which, due to market failings, deserving firms are unable to obtain the volume of investments which they would receive in an efficient market. In the case of innovative SMEs, the literature and the studies conducted in a variety of contexts specifically refer to a possible *equity gap*, meaning a shortage of risk capital investments, especially during the initial stages of firms' life cycle.[3] The interest in the existence of a specific gap on the equity side arises from the fact that this form of financing has been found to be the most suitable for innovative SMEs during their birth and growth stages,[4] in view of the high risk level of innovative businesses and the information asymmetries which make traditional forms of debt financing, and borrowing in particular, poorly suited to firms of this kind.

The first indications of the existence of an equity gap date from the United Kingdom in the 1930s, with the Macmillan Report.[5] Subsequent studies,[6] in various contexts, have revealed that this situation derives from both the demand and supply sides with regard to risk capital – in other word, private equity, provided above all by venture capital investors and business angels. Moreover, the characteristics of the equity gap, in terms of the type of firm and life-cycle stage affected, its dimensions, and the size of the amount concerned, depend on the level of development of the individual national financial systems, and especially on the presence of informal investors/business angels and venture capital investment firms. Another factor that tends to affect the equity gap is the presence and functioning of financial markets on which these investments can be traded, necessary to provide a satisfactory response to inventors' need for disinvestment strategies.

During the last few years, numerous studies have been conducted in various national contexts, aiming to ascertain whether such a gap exists and to trace its outlines, in terms of amount thresholds, any geographical/regional dimensions, and the types/sectors of firms and stages in the life cycle affected. Although the evidence is generally inconclusive, particular attention is paid to the possibility of equity gaps occurring for innovative SMEs (mainly in the high-tech sector), especially during the early stages of their life cycle: seed, start-up and early/sustained growth. The studies performed reveal an additional factor which generates difficulties in obtaining funds, the so-called *knowledge gap*, a genuine cultural and managerial gap typical of innovative small entrepreneurs, which is a hindrance to dialogue with potential equity investors.[7]

The problem of measuring the equity gap is not easily overcome: since this gap is generated by market failures, it is necessary first to establish what conditions would be needed to allow supply and demand to come together in an efficient market. Moreover, it is difficult to prove the existence of a financing gap using statistical data sets, since they do not reflect unsatisfied demand for funds.

For this reason, studies are generally qualitative and are conducted by means of interviews and/or questionnaires, on both the demand and the supply side of equity investment. On the demand side, questions are addressed to innovative entrepreneurs, while from the supply side they target informal investors, mainly business angels, venture capital and private equity firms, banks, government agencies, and so on. On the supply side in particular, this type of study tends to be adversely affected by the composition of the panel/sample, which has a fatally strong influence on replies, and by anecdotal convictions. It is also particularly difficult to monitor the business angel segment, and that of informal investors in general, due to the lack of specific information about their operations.

9.3 Methodology and research design

To analyse the means by which innovative start-ups are financed, especially in the form of equity, and attempt to obtain empirical proof of the presence or otherwise of an equity gap at the local level, a questionnaire was drawn up and sent to a suitably selected sample of firms.[8] The use of a questionnaire was necessary since, as already explained, the very concept of an equity gap means that the qualitative method is the only way of quantifying the gap between the supply and demand of risk capital.

The study was conducted in 2008 on the innovative new firms in the Province of Modena. The analysis is developed on SMEs located in one of the Italian Provinces; Modena was chosen because the qualitative approach used necessarily required the selection of a limited number of firms, and the firms located in Modena can be considered an adequate proxy of 'average' Italian innovative SMEs. Moreover, the supply of finance in this Province is similar to that in the rest of the country.

In the context of our research, the term *new* firms refers to those incorporated during the period from 1 January 2003 to 30 June 2008. The firms' *degree of innovation* was assessed using the Italian industry classification ATECO coding system, which the literature[9] approves as meeting the relative requirements in terms of product or process innovation. The chosen sectors were Information and Communication Technology (ICT), the biomedical industry, aircraft and aerospace services, experimental R&D and the pharmaceutical sector.

The three criteria used – geographical, temporal and sectorial – allowed the selection of a universe of 470 firms (Table 9.1), more than 80 per cent of them operating in the ICT sector. This group is followed in order of importance by firms working in the biomedical industry (12.8 per cent) and experimental R&D (5.3 per cent), with the remainder belonging to the aircraft and pharmaceutical sectors. When the 470 firms' period of incorporation is examined, it can be seen that the majority were formed between 2004 and 2007, with an average age around 2.5 years.

Sixty-two questionnaires were received, giving a response rate of 13.2 per cent (Table 9.1), in line with that of other surveys on this topic.[10]

As for the universe, in more than 75 per cent of cases, the 62 sample firms were active in the ICT sector. This is followed in order of importance by firms working in the biomedical industry (12.9 per cent) and

Table 9.1 Structure of the universe and sample

	Universe (no.)	Sample (no.)	Universe (%)	Sample (%)
Sectors	470	62	100.0	100.0
ICT	382	47	81.3	75.8
Biomedical	60	8	12.8	12.9
Experimental R&D	25	6	5.3	9.7
Aircraft and aerospace services	2	1	0.4	1.6
Pharmaceuticals	1	0	0.2	0.0
Year of incorporation	470	62	100.0	100.0
2003	39	4	8.3	6.5
2004	85	10	18.1	16.1
2005	105	16	22.3	25.8
2006	84	17	17.9	27.4
2007	124	13	26.4	21.0
1st half 2008	33	2	7.0	3.2

Source: Our data processing.

experimental R&D (9.7 per cent), with a very small number belonging to the aircraft sector (1.6 per cent). None of the pharmaceutical sector firms replied to the questionnaire (Table 9.1).

As required by the aims of the survey, the sample studied consisted of very young companies; more than three-quarters of them were less than 3.5 years old (Table 9.1). This finding also emerges from the analysis of the firms' growth stage (Table 9.2), which reveals that firms in the early phases of their life cycle predominate. Specifically, more than 40 per cent of firms were in one of the initial phases (seed/start-up) and thus in the planning phase or prototype stage rather than that of actual operating launch. Twenty-eight firms, representing 45.2 per cent of the sample, were in the phase immediately above (early/sustained growth), while 14.5 per cent of firms were in the consolidation phase, in which an enterprise's business is considered to have reached maturity.

The sample also appears to meet the requirements of the aims of the study in terms of the firms' size. More than 80 per cent of firms were in the very small enterprise category, with 2007 sales below 2 million euro, a finding confirmed by the average number of staff, which was less than five. The very small size of the firms in the sample is also reflected by the local character of their business: more than 80 per cent of the companies interviewed stated that the market they served was local or, at the most, national.

Verification that our choice of ATECO codes really enabled us to identify firms with a high degree of business innovation is a more complex matter. To investigate this aspect more thoroughly, firms' degree of innovativeness was also assessed by considering R&D expenditure as a percentage of operating costs (Table 9.3). From this point of view,

Table 9.2 Firms' growth cycle stages

	Sample (no.)	**Sample (%)**
Planning stage	3	4.8
Prototype production	0	0.0
Start-up	22	35.5
Total seed/start-up	**25**	**40.3**
Early growth	13	21.0
Sustained growth	15	24.2
Total early/sustained growth	**28**	**45.2**
Consolidation	**9**	**14.5**
Total	**62**	**100.0**

Source: Our data processing.

Table 9.3 R&D expenditure as a percentage of total operating costs and firm's development stage (number of firms)

	S1	S2	S3	Sample
0%	6	6	6	18
0–20%	2	10	1	13
20–50%	4	3		7
50–75%	2	1		3
> 75%	3			3
Respondents (no).	17	20	7	44
Missing values (n.)	*8*	*8*	*2*	*18*

S1, Seed/start-up; S2, Early/sustained growth; S3, Consolidation.

Source: Our data processing.

the enterprises in which R&D expenses accounted for more than the sample's average proportion of total operating costs (20 per cent) were classified as having the highest innovation content. Thirty-one companies in our sample had a rate of R&D expenditure of 20 per cent or less. The 13 firms with the highest innovative content were concentrated mainly in the first phase of the life cycle (nine) and the follow-on phase of early/sustained growth (four), while all seven companies in a stage of maturity for which information was available had a R&D expenditure rate statistically below the average for the sample.

9.4 Main findings of the study

The section that follows presents the study's main findings. First, the main barriers and constraints which firms encountered as they started their operations are described. We then move on to analyse the importance of equity investment and the sources of finance used to cover investments in fixed assets and working capital. Finally, the prospects for and restrictions on the firm's future growth will be described.

9.4.1 Barriers and constraints encountered at the start of activity

To analyse the problems in accessing finance, we first assessed the difficulties encountered by innovative SMEs in the Province of Modena as they set up their businesses. In general terms, the firms interviewed do not seem to have had serious difficulties at the time of their birth (Table 9.4). Only 27.8 per cent of firms described the obstacles they

Table 9.4 Obstacles encountered at the start of operations (percentage frequency)

	Sample	F1	F2	F3	HHT	MHT
None	32.8	24.0	33.3	55.6	23.1	35.5
Some	39.3	32.0	48.1	33.3	38.5	38.7
Quite a lot	18.0	32.0	7.4	11.1	23.1	16.1
Large number	9.8	12.0	11.1	0.0	15.4	9.7
Respondents (no).	61	25	27	9	13	31
Missing values (n.)	*1*	*0*	*1*	*0*	*0*	*0*

F1, Seed/start-up; F2, Early/sustained growth; F3, Consolidation; HHT, highly innovative; MHT, fairly innovative.

Source: Our data processing.

encountered at the outset as fairly or very numerous. The breakdown of the replies by life-cycle stage and degree of innovation reveals that obstacles were higher for highly innovative firms (HHT) in the initial phases of the life cycle (F1).

The replies received to the question about the extent of the individual types of difficulties encountered (Table 9.5) gave the highest rating to obstacles of a bureaucratic type (average 3.43 on a scale of 7) followed by problems in accessing borrowed capital (average 2.83). The significance of difficulty in obtaining equity investments received a lower rating (average 2.60).

To reduce the various constraints firms encountered at the start of their operations to uniform subsets, factorial analysis was used (Table 9.5). This technique was applied to the seven items relating to the barriers to growth on incorporation of the firm. The items were measured using the Likert scale, which runs from 1 to 7, where 1 refers to a factor of low significance, while a score of 7 indicates that the factor under consideration has a high level of importance. Then, a principal component factor analysis with a varimax rotation was used to determine the factor loadings and communalities. A summated scale or score was calculated for each factor to determine which factor had the greatest importance. Each summated scale is an average of the Likert scores on the variables included in that factor. The Mann–Whitney test was used to determine whether one factor was significantly different from another.

The factorial analysis allowed identification of three main factors, which together account for 78.7 per cent of the total variance; the first factor is the one which explains more variance than any of the others

Table 9.5 Barriers to growth at the time of incorporation (average values on scale 1–7)

	Sample	F1	F2	F3	HHT	MHT
Obstacles of a bureaucratic nature	3.43	3.33	3.64	3.00	2.92	3.46
Lack of management expertise	2.71	2.83	2.70	2.20	3.31	2.71
Poor infrastructure	2.63	2.61	2.70	2.40	2.31	2.75
Lack of suitable advisory services	2.43	2.36	2.58	2.20	3.00	2.17
Management/environmental shortcomings	**2.71**	**2.68**	**2.81**	**2.45**	**2.88**	**2.74**
Difficulties in accessing borrowed capital	2.83	2.65	3.35	1.60	2.31	3.00
Difficulties in acquiring equity investments	2.60	3.32	2.11	1.00	3.54	2.04
Lack of financial resources	**2.67**	**2.96**	**2.66**	**1.13**	**2.92**	**2.43**
Lack of technical expertise	**2.15**	**2.59**	**1.79**	**1.60**	**2.15**	**2.13**

F1, Seed/start-up; F2, Early/sustained growth; F3, Consolidation; HHT, highly innovative; MHT, fairly innovative.

Source: Our data processing.

(32.8 per cent) and the others cover gradually decreasing amounts (23.3 per cent and 22.6 per cent). The first factor groups together elements of a non-financial nature, the second the availability of financial resources, and the third technical expertise.

For barriers of a management/environmental nature (lack of management expertise, bureaucratic obstacles, poor infrastructures and lack of suitable advisory services), the average value obtained (2.71) was higher than that generated by combining the financial factors (difficulty in accessing borrowed capital and difficulty in acquiring equity investment), which was an average of 2.67. The barrier relating to a lack of technical expertise was even less significant, with an average value of 2.15.

When the data are broken down by life-cycle stage and degree of innovation, the picture obtained is relatively similar overall. However, financial barriers, especially the difficulties encountered in obtaining equity capital, were above average for firms in the seed/start-up phase, and were the main obstacle for those with a high level of innovation.

The data seem to indicate that overall the degree of difficulties was fairly low, and, among the problems encountered, those relating to management factors in the broad sense were most prevalent. This suggests that investors need to combine their provision of capital with the supply of managerial inputs. In other words, those contributing capital should become actively involved in the company in a way which helps it to overcome the problems arising both from the surrounding context (too much bureaucracy, poor infrastructure and lack of advisory services) and from the company's own shortcomings.

9.4.2 The importance of equity investment

To obtain a better understanding of the reason for the relative insignificance of financial constraints at the time of the firm's foundation, we decided to assess the sources of finance used by firms, on incorporation and subsequently.

The main source of financing when the business was started up consisted of the founding partners' own resources (Table 9.6). Of the 59 firms which answered the question, 57 used this source of financing, and for 39 of them it was the only source.

The second largest source of funds, although a considerable distance behind, was bank debt, with short-term debt slightly ahead (six replies) of medium–long-term borrowing at ordinary or low interest rates (five replies). Therefore the banking system plays an absolutely marginal role during the start-up of firms in innovative sectors.

Table 9.6 Sources of finance used at the time of incorporation (number of replies)

Total number of sources of finance	**1**	**2**	**3**	**Total**
Founding partners' own funds	39	17	1	57
Ordinary short-term bank debt		5	1	6
Ordinary and low-interest medium-term bank debt		5		5
Investment by other firms	1	3	1	5
Venture Capital investment		1	1	2
Business Angel investment		2		2
Equity investment by friends and relatives			1	1
Investment by incubators/universities				
Investment by other financial intermediaries				
Public incentive schemes		1		1
Others			1	1
Total	**40**	**17**	**2**	**59**

F1, Seed/start-up; F2, Early/sustained growth; F3, Consolidation; HHT, highly innovative; MHT, fairly innovative.

Source: Our data processing.

Table 9.9 Reasons for equity investors' lack of interest: firms' opinions (number of replies)

	Sample	F1	F2	F3	HHT	MHT
Investment too low	3	0	3	0	0	3
Investment too high	1	1	0	0	1	0
Lack of interest in enterprise's sector of business	8	4	2	2	4	3
Difficulty in assessing the enterprise's business	10	6	2	2	3	3
Investor's time horizon too short for the enterprise's requirements	3	2	1	0	2	1
Investor's time horizon too long for the enterprise's requirements	0	0	0	0	0	0
Total replies	**25**	**13**	**8**	**4**	**10**	**10**
Respondents (no).	15	7	5	3	5	6
Missing values (n.)	*47*	*18*	*23*	*6*	*8*	*25*

F1, Seed/start-up; F2, Early/sustained growth; F3, Consolidation; HHT, highly innovative; MHT, fairly innovative.

Source: Our data processing.

enterprise. The set of replies shows the clear prevalence of 'real' factors (Table 9.9).

In 10 out of 25 cases, according to the firms' opinions, the problems lay in difficulties in assessing the business on the part of the investor, and, in eight cases, in a low level of interest in the firm's sector of operations. Factors of a strictly financial nature (investment too small/large in four cases), or problems of the investor's time horizon (too short for the company's needs in three cases) were involved only marginally. Although this must be stated with caution, due to the small number of comments received, it appears that the firms are fairly critical of equity investors, for two main reasons. The first is that investors are accused of prejudice against strongly innovative, and thus risky, sectors, and thus of failing to fulfil the 'mission' assigned to equity investors by financial theory. The second factor is that investors appear to have difficulty in assessing the firm's business.

The data also indicate that firms are not well informed about the dimensional aspect of equity investors' contributions. Most firms in the sample were unaware of the differences between the roles of business angels and venture capitalists as providers of investments.

However, if we restrict our analysis to venture capitalists alone, the small size of the investment was an obstacle to the acquisition of venture capital in more than 25 per cent of the replies given by the firms interviewed. This is in line with the modus operandi of a formal equity investor, of the kind normally involved in a venture capital investment, who generally makes investments of a considerable size. Confirming this, in reply to a question intended to ascertain the existence or otherwise of an investment threshold below which venture capitalists no longer become involved, the range identified by the firms interviewed was from 300,000 to 1 million Euro. Similarly, the investment thresholds above which business angels are no longer prepared to invest were set in the range 100,000 to 1 million Euro.

The difficulties of acquiring equity investment are aggravated by the entrepreneurs' low level of knowledge of this opportunity. If we take a more detailed look with regard to venture capital only, the firms interviewed appear incapable of assessing the level of supply available in the Italian region (Emilia Romagna) in which the Province of Modena is located (Table 9.10).

Of the firms which replied to the question, 48.3 per cent were unable to give an opinion. The level of 'don't knows' remained high when the sample was broken down by life-cycle stage and degree of innovation,

Table 9.10 Availability of venture capital for innovative SMEs in Emilia Romagna (number of firms)

	Sample	F1	F2	F3	HHT	MHT
Very low	3	3	0	0	2	0
Low	17	6	8	3	4	7
Satisfactory	9	2	5	2	2	6
Good	1	0	1	0	0	1
Very good	0	0	0	0	0	0
Don't know	28	14	11	3	5	16
Respondents (no).	58	25	25	8	13	30
Missing values (n.)	*4*	*0*	*3*	*1*	*0*	*1*

F1, Seed/start-up; F2, Early/sustained growth; F3, Consolidation; HHT, highly innovative; MHT, fairly innovative.

Source: Our data processing.

Table 9.11 Frequency of contacts with venture capital investors (number of firms)

	Sample	F1	F2	F3	HHT	MHT
Never	13	5	5	3	3	9
Rarely	24	10	11	3	7	9
Often	2	0	2	0	0	2
Don't know	20	10	8	2	3	10
Respondents (no).	59	25	26	8	13	30
Missing values (n.)	*3*	*0*	*2*	*1*	*0*	*1*

F1, Seed/start-up; F2, Early/sustained growth; F3, Consolidation; HHT, highly innovative; MHT, fairly innovative.

Source: Our data processing.

varying from 56.0 per cent for seed/start-up firms to 37.5 per cent for firms in the consolidation stage. It is worth noting that not one company assessed the availability of venture capital in the region as very good. Entrepreneurs' low level of knowledge is confirmed by the low frequency of contacts and the high level of inability to reply to the question about this aspect (Table 9.11).

9.4.3 The sources of finance used by firms

A brief look at Table 9.12 reveals that the sample's preferences appear to provide a good fit with the pecking order theory,[11] even though this theory refers to companies of a completely different kind.

Self-financing is considered the most important form of cover for fixed asset investments, followed by medium–long-term bank loans at normal or low interest rates. Fresh equity investment, either by the company's owner or, above all, by third parties, is much less significant. This appears to point to a preference for managing investment processes internally or with bank partners. Firms' tendency not to involve new equity investors in order to avoid jeopardizing the owner's control of the company may be the main reason for their marginal role in entrepreneurs' preferences.

However, companies' ownership structures are not completely closed to new investors; the entry of new partners is more likely as a means of solving problems relating to a lack of expertise than as a strategy for obtaining new financial resources (Table 9.13).

As one would have expected, the role of equity in covering working capital requirements is even more limited (Table 9.12). The preference

Table 9.12 Sources of finance for fixed asset and working capital investments (average values on scale 1–7)

	Fixed asset investments	Working capital investments
Self-financing	5.02	4.92
Medium–long-term bank loans	3.98	3.21
Low-interest loans	3.96	3.45
Short-term bank loans	3.56	3.98
New equity investments by owners	3.43	3.02
Indebtedness to suppliers	2.51	2.79
New equity investments by third parties	2.19	1.89

Source: Our data processing.

Table 9.13 Firms' willingness to accept new partners (average values on scale 1–7)

	Sample	F1	F2	F3	HHT	MHT
The main reason for involving new partners is not the need to obtain new investments	4.96	4.69	5.23	4.86	4.62	5.26
The main reason for the entry of new partners is the need to acquire their technical expertise	4.79	4.61	5.12	4.14	5.00	4.93
The disadvantages of the entry of new partners exceed the potential benefits	3.04	3.09	3.12	2.57	2.31	3.07
Bank debt is preferable to the acquisition of new partners	2.44	2.25	2.15	4.14	2.54	2.59
It is better to sell the firm than to bring in new partners	2.40	2.35	2.27	3.00	1.85	2.50

F1, Seed/start-up; F2, Early/sustained growth; F3, Consolidation; HHT, highly innovative; MHT, fairly innovative.

Source: Our data processing.

is to obtain working capital from internal resources, short-term bank debt and low-interest loans. What does seem rather surprising, when these findings are compared with firms' normal business practice, is the low level of importance assigned to indebtedness to suppliers, which in these companies appears to be accepted as a necessary evil rather than adopted as a strategic choice, probably due to the lack of alternatives.

9.4.4 Prospects for and barriers to firms' growth

When interpreting our data, we must bear in mind that the questionnaires were compiled before the gravity of the current economic crisis had clearly emerged. Of the firms that replied to the related question, 52.8 per cent predicted a growth rate for the following year (2009) of more than 10 per cent. Firms' relative optimism also clearly emerges when we examine their assessment of the likelihood of barriers to their growth: 17.5 per cent of firms believed there were no constraints on their expansion, and 50.9 per cent assessed the level of constraints as only limited (Table 9.14).

A survey of the main barriers to growth perceived by the firms interviewed reveals that overall they are of limited significance (Table 9.15).

The factorial analysis allowed the identification of four main factors which together account for 70.5 per cent of the total variance. Specifically, firms do not appear to be afraid of serious obstacles arising from a lack of technical expertise (lack of expertise in the development and marketing of products), nor do they envisage major managerial/environmental barriers (difficulty in hiring qualified staff, lack of managerial expertise, organizational problems, poor infrastructure or lack of suitable advisory services). Neither do financial barriers to growth seem to play a significant role. In spite of this, the most important constraint of this kind is a lack of working capital, followed by the possible

Table 9.14 Barriers to growth in coming years

	Number	%
None	10	17.5
Some	29	50.9
Quite a lot	14	24.6
Large number	4	7.0
Respondents	57	100.0
Missing values (n.)	5	

Source: Our data processing.

Table 9.15 Barriers to future growth (average values on scale 1–7)

	Sample	F1	F2	F3	HHT	MHT
Weak image due to small size	3.92	4.45	3.83	2.71	3.69	4.15
Low profitability	3.77	3.95	3.38	4.57	3.15	3.93
Image and profitability	**3.83**	**4.18**	**3.6**	**3.64**	**3.42**	**4.06**
Lack of working capital	3.47	3.71	3.35	3.14	2.85	3.70
Difficulties in acquiring equity investments for amounts of over 100,000 Euro	3.27	3.74	3.08	2.50	3.92	3.00
Difficulties in accessing bank credit	3.18	3.45	3.04	2.86	3.31	3.00
Difficulties in acquiring equity investments for amounts of less than 100,000 Euro	2.57	2.74	2.50	2.33	2.54	2.32
Excessive indebtedness	2.36	2.73	1.96	2.57	2.46	2.37
Financial constraints	**2.91**	**3.16**	**2.77**	**2.67**	**3.02**	**2.87**
Difficulty in hiring qualified staff	3.78	3.05	4.38	3.86	3.08	4.12
Lack of managerial expertise	2.83	3.10	2.88	1.86	2.15	2.92
Organizational problems	2.76	2.80	2.96	2.00	2.38	2.88
Poor infrastructure	2.53	2.50	2.54	2.57	2.15	2.65
Lack of suitable advisory services	2.27	2.25	2.29	2.29	1.92	2.38
Management/ environmental shortcomings	**2.83**	**2.73**	**3.01**	**2.51**	**2.34**	**2.99**
Lack of expertise in the marketing of products	3.06	3.30	3.17	2.00	2.69	2.38
Lack of expertise in the development of products	2.39	2.55	2.33	2.14	1.69	2.77
Lack of technical expertise	**2.73**	**2.93**	**2.75**	**2.07**	**2.19**	**3.08**

F1, Seed/start-up; F2, Early/sustained growth; F3, Consolidation; HHT, highly innovative; MHT, fairly innovative.

Source: Our data processing.

lack of equity investments for amounts of over 100,000 Euro. Therefore, although they had assigned only marginal importance to this form of financing in their classification of the types sought, firms still envisaged a risk (even if not a serious one) that they might not be able to acquire equity investments. The fact that the amount was above and not below 100,000 Euro may indicate that firms associated an increase in equity with the involvement of new partners, assuming that capital increases of lower amounts could more easily be covered from within the existing ownership.

The constraints arising from the weak image that a small enterprise presents to the market, and to a lesser extent from the firm's low level of profitability, were considered to be more important. In any case, firms saw few obstacles in their path to future growth.

9.5 Conclusions

The main aim of this study has been to use a qualitative method to analyse the means of financing innovative new firms in the Province of Modena, attempting on the one hand to identify any financial constraints which may affect their birth and/or growth, and on the other hand to analyse the current and possible future role of various financial players in equity investment to finance operations.

To analyse the problems in accessing finance, we first assessed the difficulties encountered by our sample of 62 innovative SMEs in the Province of Modena as they set up their businesses. In general, the level of difficulty firms encountered in their start-up phases was fairly low, and, among the problems encountered, those relating to management factors in the broad sense prevailed over financial constraints. The breakdown of the replies by life-cycle stage and degree of innovation reveals that obstacles were higher for highly innovative firms and those in the initial phases of the life cycle. This suggests that investors need to combine their provision of capital with the supply of managerial inputs. In other words, those contributing capital, and equity in particular, should become actively involved in the company in a way which helps it to overcome the problems arising both from the surrounding context and from the firm's own shortcomings.

An assessment of the sources of finance used by firms, both on incorporation and in the subsequent periods, provides a better understanding of the reasons for the relative insignificance of financial constraints at the time of a firm's foundation.

The main source of financing at business start-ups was the founding partners' own resources; the banking system was found to play a marginal role in the birth of firms in innovative sectors. Overall, the involvement of equity investors was very low. A survey of the modes of finance used by firms in the post-start-up phases reveals a picture which is little changed from the above. The data show that the sample's preferences tended to fit the pecking order theory: self-financing was the form of cover for fixed asset and working capital investments assigned the greatest importance, followed by bank loans. Fresh equity investment, either by the company's owner or, above all, by third parties, was much less significant.

The analysis of the sources of finance used by firms appears to point to a preference for managing investment processes internally or with bank partners. The entry of new partners into the company's ownership structure is more likely as a means of solving problems relating to a lack of expertise than as a strategy for obtaining new financial resources.

An examination of the causes that explain the lack of involvement of equity investors allows the clear identification of factors linked to the demand side (which predominate) and others on the supply side. Of the factors affecting the demand side, it strongly emerges that firms have little interest in equity financing: no fewer than 60 per cent of the replies given indicate that firms consider it unimportant. It appears probable that this result arises from a basic lack of in-depth knowledge about the role of equity investors on the part of firms, and/or other causes, such as the founding partners' individualism and their reluctance to allow outsiders into the management of their firm. This interpretation is backed up by the fact that the fear of investors playing an excessively large role in the company's management was reported as the main barrier to the acquisition of venture capital on the part of the firms interviewed.

On the supply side, only 18 per cent of firms referred to problems, claiming that equity investors had shown little interest in investing in their businesses; this is linked to the investor's difficulty in assessing the business, and an unwillingness to invest in the firm's sector of business. Factors of a strictly financial nature (investment too small/large), or problems of the investor's time horizon (too short for the company's needs) emerge only to a marginal extent.

The survey also revealed that no firms had a positive opinion with regard to the availability of venture capital in the Emilia Romagna region. The limited availability of venture capital is also confirmed by the low frequency of contacts.

Turning to future prospects, and in the awareness that the replies refer to a situation in which the crisis had not revealed its scale or the extent of its effects, firms saw the obstacles to their growth as limited. Of the various barriers, the most significant appear to be those arising from the weak image a small enterprise presents to the market, and to a lesser degree from the firm's low level of profitability. In any case, obstacles of a financial nature do not seem to play a significant role.

In conclusion, two main findings have emerged from this study. The first is the fact that investors need to combine their financial contribution with the supply of managerial inputs. In other words, it would be advisable for those who provide firms with capital, especially in the form of equity, to become actively involved in their operations. The second finding is that the survey described is unable to solve the long-standing question as to why new equity investors are rarely drawn into the ownership structures of Italian enterprises. From the demand side, this low degree of involvement may be due to the chronic fear on the part of firms' owners of losing control of their business, while on the supply side there may be a problem with equity investors' attitude, since they systematically complain of the low quality of the demand. Evidence in the former direction can be traced in the replies to the questionnaire, but it is not possible to obtain any indication of equity investors' perception of the quality of demand, since our survey method was specifically designed to assess the perceptions of enterprises and not those of potential financiers.

Notes

1. For a survey of the main studies, see Gualandri and Venturelli (2008) and Landi and Rigon (2006).
2. For further details, see Gualandri and Schwizer (2008) and Gualandri and Venturelli (2008).
3. See, in particular, Bank of England (2001), European Commission (2005) and OECD (2004, 2006).
4. See Berger and Udell (1995, 1998). For a survey, see Hall (2002).
5. Report of the Committee on Finance and Industry (1931), also known as the 'Macmillan Report'.
6. For a detailed analysis see Gualandri and Schwizer (2008).
7. See Harding (2002).
8. The questionnaire was drafted and administered with the assistance of the research centre of the Modena Chamber of Commerce. The complete questionnaire is available from the authors upon request.
9. For further details see Cavallo *et al.* (2002).
10. For a recent survey see Cenni and Ferretti (2010).
11. Originally proposed by Myers (1984) and Myers and Majluf (1984).

References

Bank of England (2001) *The Financing of Technology-Based Small Firms* (London, February).

Berger, A.N. and Udell, G.F. (1995) 'Relationship Lending and Lines of Credit in Small Firm Finance', *Journal of Business*, 68, 351–82.

Berger, A.N. and Udell, G.F. (1998) 'The economics of small business finance: The roles of Private Equity and Debt Markets in the financial growth cycle', *Journal of Banking and Finance*, 22, 613–73.

Cavallo, C., Lazzeroni, M., Patrono, A. and Piccalunga, A. (2002) 'Osservatorio sulle imprese high-tech della provincia di Pisa', *Rapporto annuale*, May.

Cenni, S. and Ferretti, R. (2010) 'Le scelte di finanziamento e il rapporto banca-impresa secondo le imprese', in C. Bisoni (ed.), *Finanza e credito per le imprese del territorio* (Bologna: Il Mulino), 253–263.

Committee on Finance and Industry (1931) *Macmillan Report*, Cmd. 3897 (London: HMSO).

European Commission (2005) *Best Practices for Public Support for Early Stage Equity Finance*, Final Report of the Expert Group, Directorate-General for Enterprise and Industry, September, Brussels.

Gualandri, E. and Schwizer, P. (2008) 'Bridging the equity gap: il caso della PMI innovative', *Studi e Note di Economia*, 1.

Gualandri, E. and Venturelli, V. (2008) *Bridging the Equity Gap for Innovative SMEs*, Palgrave Macmillan Studies in Banking and Finance Institutions (Basingstoke: Palgrave Macmillan).

Hall, B.H. (2002) 'The Financing of research and development', *Oxford Review of Economic Policy*, 18: 35–51.

Harding, R. (2002) 'Plugging the Knowledge Gap: International Comparison of the Role for Policy in the Venture Capital market', *Venture Capital: an International Journal of Entrepreneurial Finance*, 4(1), 59–76.

Landi, A. and Rigon, A. (2006) 'Finanza e sviluppo delle PMI in Europa. Banche e intervento pubblico nelle aree svantaggiate', *Rapporti ABI*, 12 (Rome: Bancaria Editrice).

Myers, S.C. (1984) 'The Capital Structure Puzzle', *Journal of Finance*, 39, 575–92.

Myers, S.C. and Majluf, N.S. (1984) 'Corporate Financing and Investment Decisions When Firms Have Information that Investors Do Not Have', *Journal of Financial Economics*, 13, 187–221.

OECD (2004) *Financing Innovative SMEs in a Global Economy* (Paris: OECD).

OECD (2006) *The SME Financing Gap (Vol. I). Theory and Evidence* (Paris: OECD).

10

Can R&D Expenditures Affect Firm Market Value? An Empirical Analysis of a Panel of European Listed Firms

Andi Duqi and Giuseppe Torluccio

10.1 Introduction

The market valuation of R&D expenditures or, in a more general context, the valuation of intangibles is a particularly interesting issue for researchers. Unfortunately, the evaluation of this type of investment is also difficult, and studies are divided on the methods of this process and its incorporation into stock prices.

This research began to take shape in the 1980s with contributions by different scholars. These authors found a relation between the intensity of R&D expenditure and the book-to-market-value variations. Following this strand of research, Green *et al.* (1996) showed that investors evaluated R&D expenditure in the UK stock market as a short-term tangible asset, but in the long-term profits deriving from this kind of investment are higher since the risk for investors is greater. Hall (1999) found a significant link between R&D outlays, patent citation and corporate value. Similar results derived from the contributions of Chambers *et al.* (2002) and Eberhart *et al.* (2004), who generally found a significant positive correlation between stock price abnormal returns and variations in R&D investment plans.

In this chapter we concentrate on a sample of European listed firms (UK and Continental Europe) since only a small number of contributions focus on these, namely Hall and Oriani (2006). Our aim is to test the relationship between the R&D expenditure of these firms and their market value over a five-year period. Although other studies have attempted to capture this relationship using data spanning from 10 to 50 years, we assume that focusing our attention on a shorter period will permit us to use both a larger number of variables (reducing the number of potential missing values) and companies (restraining the survival bias effect) in order to shed light on the impact of each on firm market value over a more homogeneous time horizon. In order to study the relation between market value and R&D expenditure, we control several aspects, such as firm size, R&D industry intensity, financial leverage, accounting standards adopted and firm market power.

Comparing results from different countries has several drawbacks: countries differ by stock market microstructure, investors, corporate governance mechanisms and firm typologies in terms of size, industry and internationalization intensity.

In addition, intangible investments have further specific and intrinsic characteristics. These assets are crucial for the purpose of creating new products or services in the mid-term, with high uncertainty of the final result. Furthermore, it is interesting to see whether these expenditures differ when comparing more stock-market-oriented (i.e. the UK) with other, bank-oriented financial systems (i.e. France or Germany).

To test the abovementioned relationship, this study uses two different econometric models: a pooled cross-section and a fixed-effect panel model. The hypothesis of a positive impact of greater R&D investments on firm market value is not ascertained for every country: some variables such as firm size or industry are decisive in positively valuating firm R&D investments.

The accounting standards used by firms of different countries deserve specific consideration. In fact, in recent years, listed companies have adopted International Accounting Standards (IAS) / International Financial Reporting Standards (IFRS) in accounting total R&D expenditure in the year it is incurred. This was not always the case. Prior to 2004/5, firms had the opportunity to capitalize some of these costs and to depreciate them over five years. We test whether firms that did not adopt these standards in 2004, but continued capitalizing a part of their R&D expenditure for a further two years, had a different market valuation compared with firms that immediately adopted the new IAS standard in 2004.

The study is structured as follows. In the next section, different theoretical and empirical contributions to the market valuation of R&D costs are examined. In the third section, we explain how the sample is constructed and the variables we used to study the phenomenon. The last section explains the econometric models and the main results attained. A brief conclusion and final remarks follow.

10.2 Literature review

Contributions to the relationship between firm market value and innovation require some hypotheses on the behaviour of financial markets, and particularly the issue of their efficiency (Fama, 1970). The theory of financial markets postulates that prices reflect all the information on a certain stock, and the price valuation may only change if investors receive new information that changes their expectations about the firm's future free cash flow (Pakes, 1985).

This branch of research was first developed by the pioneer contributions of Schumpeter (1942) and Solow (1956) and consolidated over the last 20 years of the previous century. A key issue researchers tried to resolve is whether investments in intangibles are relevant to the value of the firm and their degree of intensity. Value creation can be reflected by increased productivity (Griliches, 1995; Mairesse and Hall, 1995) and/or by improved market valuation of the firm stock price or market value (Hall, 2000). The present paper focuses on the market valuation approach, which postulates that in efficient financial markets market value should correctly reflect the future expected returns from R&D investments (and other intangibles such as goodwill, advertising, and so on). In this way, by correlating firm performance with R&D investment, we will indicate the impact of the former on the latter.

Other studies report a positive association between measures of current and recent changes in the level of R&D investment and future abnormal returns (Lev, 2001; Chambers *et al.*, 2002; Penman and Zhang, 2002; Tovainen *et al.*, 2002; Eberhart *et al.*, 2004; Oswald and Zarowin, 2007).

Another strand of research finds a significant positive relationship between R&D expenditure and investors' firm valuation as reflected in stock prices: it is assumed that the firm is evaluated by the market as a bundle of tangible and intangible assets (Griliches, 1981). From this perspective, firm innovation activities create a stock of technological assets that should be consistently evaluated by the stock market. In equilibrium, the market valuation of any asset results from the interaction between firm investment demands and market supply of capital for that specific asset. Following the pioneer contribution of Griliches (1981), other authors have applied this 'hedonic model' based on proxies of Tobin's Q (among others, Hirschey, 1982; Jaffe, 1986; Cockburn and Griliches, 1988; Blundell *et al.*, 1999; Hall and Oriani, 2006). These studies share with previous research the need to use a stock measure of firm R&D technological assets created from year to year by R&D expenditure

(Griliches and Mairesse, 1984). Financial markets positively value this stock of R&D capital, although the valuation changes over both time and industrial cycles, as underlined by Hall (1993).

Another research stream, based mainly on UK accounting data, deals with firm accounting R&D expenditure and market value. These accounting-based studies derive from Ohlson's (1989) and Sougiannis's (1994) residual income model. Among others, Green *et al.* (1996) suggest that the excess of market over book value can be expressed as the sum of a multiple of the book value, capitalized residual income, R&D capital (expressed as a multiple of current R&D expenditure, due to persistence in R&D expenditure, as, for example, in Hirschey and Weygandt, 1985), and the effects of other control variables. The results of this study cast some doubt on the value relevance of R&D expenditure in the UK in the years 1990–2.

It would seem that investors do not find it easy to evaluate the future earnings implications of past and present R&D investments (Wyatt, 2008). However, more recent UK evidence for the 1990–4 (Stark and Thomas, 1998) and 1990–2001 periods (Akbar and Stark, 2003; Shah *et al.*, 2008), found that R&D is value-relevant in the UK setting. Hughes (2008) followed this approach. She found that the value of R&D activities is recognized by the market not only contemporaneously but also in relation to previous R&D expenditure.

Anagnostopoulou and Levis (2008) expanded prior US and UK evidence and found that R&D intensity appears to be associated with an improvement in the persistence of operating growth, but only among firms that engage in R&D as a result of the industry to which they belong. Franzen and Radhakrishnan (2009) extended the residual income model to both profit and loss firms. They found that R&D expenditure is positively (negatively) associated with stock prices for loss (profit) firms. On the other hand, Callen and Morel's (2005) research, in a time series framework, found weak evidence of the value relevance of R&D expenditure on stock prices.

Few scholars have studied this relationship considering Continental European data. Hall and Oriani (2006) found the relative shadow value of R&D to be remarkably similar for France and Germany as well as for the UK and US during the same period. In contrast, R&D in quoted Italian firms is not generally valued by financial markets. Cincera *et al.* (2009) found robust evidence of a positive relationship of a sample of European top R&D investment companies and their stock price performance. Finally, Karjalainen (2007) pointed out that this relationship is stronger in bank-based rather than market-based countries.

As highlighted by previous research, there is an ongoing debate on expensing or capitalizing R&D expenditure. Most researchers agree that capitalizing development expenditure grants a better view of firm assets. The IAS accounting standards, introduced in 2004, imply that firms entirely expense their R&D investments as incurred. Evidence shows that these standards should allow some discretion on whether to capitalize qualifying development expenditure or expense them in the year incurred.[1] Some authors, such as Skinner (2008) and Penman (2006), asserted that this would not impact on UK financial market prices. Oswald (2008) found that the IAS standard, in removing the discretion over the treatment of development expenditure, eliminates a useful way for firms to communicate information to stock markets. Chan *et al.* (2007) found the same results for Australia. As Stark (2008) pointed out, although the IAS approach might be standardized in accounting terms, transparency of accounting may not be an absolute informational value.

10.2.1 Hypothesis development

In literature different models are used that attempt to link R&D costs and, more generally, the firm's efforts to produce innovation to its performance in terms of both market value and return on equity or surplus profit (for a review on this topic see Wyatt, 2008). In particular, the model used in the present study follows the contributions of Ohlson (1989), Green *et al.* (1996) and Stark and Thomas (1998). In these studies, firm market value is depicted as a linear function of its book value (BV), residual income (RI) and research and development expenditure (RD). Generally, the book value of the year in progress (BV)[2] is used as a deflator to try to reduce the scale effect. The main model specification used here is thus:

$$(MV_{i,t} - BV_{i,t}) / BV_{i,t} = \alpha_i + \beta\left(RI_{i,t}/BV_{i,t}\right) + \gamma\left(RD_{i,t}/BV_{i,t}\right) + \epsilon_{i,t} \qquad (1)$$

where $MV_{i,t}$ is the market value of firm *i* at time *t*, $BV_{i,t}$ is the book value of firm *i* at time *t*, $RI_{i,t}$ is the residual income expected by firm *i* at time *t*, and finally $RD_{i,t}$ denotes the firm's research and development expenditure in the year in progress. Residual income is expressed as: $RI_{i,t} = (Ebit_{i,t} - k_{i,t}BV_{i,t-1})$ where $Ebit_{i,t}$ is the operating profit of firm *i* at time *t*, k_{it} is the weighted average cost of capital determined with the CAPM (Capital Asset Pricing Model) method at time *t* and $BV_{i,t-1}$ is the book value of firm *i* at time *t–1*.

Similarly to Sougiannis (1994), Green *et al.* (1996), Tovainen *et al.* (2002) and Akbar and Stark (2003), only research and development costs that appear in the current year are considered: in contributions cited above, it is assessed that past expenditure has already produced tangible assets and is therefore reflected in the remuneration of these assets by the residual income.

The first two hypotheses that we test concern residual income capacities, research and development expenditures and firm market value; they aim to partition out the effects produced by these two variables over the corporate value.

Hp1: Residual income has a positive effect on firm market value
Hp2: Research and development expenditure has a positive effect on firm market value

While the first hypothesis is in line with the main firm valuation theories, the second attempts instead to verify whether research and development expenditure is also value-relevant if incurred in the year in progress. This issue is critical for research: R&D investment could prove positive for the firm, but only after a period of time, and not immediately reflected in market value.

It would also be interesting to capture the impact of R&D expenses on firms in different countries. Green *et al.* (1996), Stark and Thomas (1998) and Hughes (2008) found a positive effect of R&D expenditure in a sample of British companies, even if in the case of Green *et al.* (1996) the impact was not significant for all the years observed. The same effect was confirmed in Cincera *et al.* (2009) for a sample of large European listed firms. Hall and Oriani (2006) instead found that the R&D stock has a positive effect on firm value in countries such as France, Germany, the UK and the US, while not finding evidence of this influence in Italian firms.

Previous studies have highlighted how firm size plays a significant role in terms of both the extent of investment in research and development and its positive valuation by the markets. This coincides with the Schumpeterian view of the predisposition of larger firms to make greater investments and to signal this to the market. On the other hand, many firms that operate in industries with highly intensive R&D investments, even though smaller, invest a significant proportion of their turnover in R&D. This means that the market should not necessarily favour larger firms among those that invest in innovation. The following two hypotheses derive from this reasoning:

Hp 3: Among those firms that invest in research and development, larger firms have greater market value

Hp 4: Firms operating in industries with highly intensive R&D investments should have greater market value

The other variables used help to improve the inference on the main explanatory variables and allow other components to be controlled. The first additional variable is a measure representing the firm's market power, composed of relations that identify the proxies of market power in the industry to which it belongs.

The second variable concerns the firm's financial structure. The level of debt weighs heavily upon the decisions to finance innovative projects, especially for younger or smaller enterprises. This implies verifying the impact that leverage has on the market value of an innovative firm, but clearly in relation to the industry average, that is taken as reference of the optimal capital structure.[3] The theories on financial structure, in the same way as the numerous associated empirical verifications, underline the importance of the debt ratio in explaining different market values. Research does not currently present a univocal hypothesis of the impact of the financial structure on firm market value, given the differences between trade-off theory, pecking order theory and financial flexibility theories.

In general, more innovative firms have more recourse to risk capital, in as much as the greater weight of intangibles entails more risks for external borrowers in terms of information asymmetries and moral hazard (Myers and Majluf, 1984; Himmelberg and Petersen, 1994). It follows that there is a need also to consider debt ratio among the possible explanatory elements of market value. In view of the accounting nature of the data used, the effects that IAS standards have on the balance sheet representation of research and development expenditure must also be considered.[4] This effect is modelled with a dichotomous variable, which takes value 1 if the firm adopted the IAS standards before the compulsory year 2006 or 0 otherwise. The effect of this dummy allows us to understand whether the market appreciates the greater transparency entailed by this regulation.[5]

With the use of dichotomous variables, the model explicitly considered belonging to industries with different levels of technological intensity.[6] The final model thus attained is the following:

$$(MV_{i,t} - BV_{i,t}) / BV_{i,t} = \alpha_0 + \beta\left(RI_{i,t}/BV_{i,t}\right) + \gamma\left(RD_{i,t}/BV_{i,t}\right) + \sum_{j=1}^{6} \lambda_j Z_{i,j,t} + \epsilon_{i,t} \tag{2}$$

where:

α_i represents the individual effects of each firm in the sample
The $Z_{i,j,t}$ variables including the following six variables:
MKTSHARE= market share of firm *i* at time *t*;
LEVERAGE = debt on equity ratio of firm *i* at time *t*;
Ln_Sales = natural logarithm of annual firm sales;
IAS-IFSR Dummy;
Dummy hi_tech, medium_tech, low_tech;
Country Dummies;
$\epsilon_{i,t}$ = error term.

10.3 Sample and methodology

The data set used includes a fixed sample of 416 non-financial listed firms that operated continuously from 2001 to 2007. The firms considered, given the survey objective, have the characteristic of having recorded research and development expenditure in each year. The initial reference allowing the selection was provided by EUROSTAT[7] statistics on the expenditure of the *Top 1000* firms that consistently implemented research and development expenditure.[8]

The European countries considered in this work are the United Kingdom, Germany, France, Sweden and Italy, given that the remaining countries did not have the required sample size to be eligible for consideration.[9] As previously indicated, it is unclear from the studies conducted to date how the financial markets of Continental Europe perceive investments in intangibles, particularly in research and development, while there is ample evidence of such a valuation for firms listed on the financial markets of the United Kingdom and the United States.

This study is focused only on listed companies having a market value for at least seven consecutive years (2001–7).[10] Therefore, the analysis does not concern those firms that were listed after 2001 and those that ceased their activities on equity markets before 2007.

The data found on the EU Industrial Scoreboard was supplemented with market value data derived from DataStream and accounting data from Bureau van Dijk (OSIRIS, AMADEUS).[11] The final fixed sample is made up of 416 companies, of which 136 are British, 122 German, 75 French, 53 Swedish and 30 Italian. The sample contains only those companies that persistently recorded research and development activities in the 2001–7 period for a total of 2,884 observations distributed over five countries.

The sample was entirely composed of listed firms, which could entail a problem of selection bias, given that in some countries, such as Italy for example, listed companies form a very small proportion of national companies, which are generally larger than those that are not quoted. The analysis intends to monitor how the financial markets assess investments in research and development, and therefore the problem is intrinsic to the markets themselves and cannot be eliminated.

In accordance with the methodology used by Green *et al.* (1996), Stark and Thomas (1998) and Hughes (2008), the stock price measured six months after the closing of the financial (calendar) year was considered as the firm market value at time t ($MV_{i,t}$).[12] The market value calculation includes the firm's debt value, while the book value ($BV_{i,t}$) was determined as the sum of the book value of equity plus reserves plus the firm's debt value.[13]

The extra operating profits or residual income was computed as the difference between the firm's operating results and the book value of its assets times the cost of capital.[14] The firm's operating results were calculated by subtracting the costs of production, inclusive of depreciation and provisions for liabilities, from the value of production. To these entries, the research and development costs were then added.

The research and development costs ($RD_{i,t}$) were identified by the particular cost item resulting from the annual expenditure declared in each firm's financial statement.

Ln_sales represents the size impact, which could manifest a different reaction of market value to R&D investments.

Furthermore, a representative variable MRKSHARE was used to indicate the market share of each company within its industry[15] as the ratio between the sales of the company in year t (net sales) and the total sales of the industry to which it belonged.

The indicator of the financial structure of the company, LEVERAGE, was built by means of the relationship between the sum of the long and short-term debt and the book value of the equity.

By means of the variables Dummy_hitech, Dummy_mediumtech and Dummy_lowtech, the study considered the degree of innovation of the industry to check the natural level of innovation expected from each company.[16]

Table 10.1 shows the average and median main variables for the full sample, while Table 10.2 shows the same deflated variables for each country, indicating very little homogeneity among the data of the various countries.[17] The median of the deflated dependent variable does not substantially differ among the different countries.[18] The main

Table 10.1 Univariate statistics, years 2001–7 / full sample

Variable	Variable description	Source	Mean	SD	P5	Median	P95
Dependent variable							
(Mv-Bv)/Bv	Firm market value-firm book value deflated with firm book value	Datastream Int.	24.40	86.40	0.30	3.80	110.80
Independent variables							
RI/BV	Residual income* to book value	Datastream int.	2.10	6.90	−0.20	0.40	9.80
RD/BV	R&D expenditures to book value	EU IIS	1.70	7.00	0.00	0.20	6.90
Mktshare (%)	Firm market share	Datastream int.	1.30	26.40	0.00	0.00	0.50
Leverage (%)	Firm "Debt to equity ratio"	Bureau Van Dijk	55.00	96.40	0.00	1.40	145.70
Lu_Sales (€ /000)	Nat. log of firm Sales	Datastream int.	13.40	2.60	9.50	13.30	17.70
Dummy hi_tech	Hi-tech firm sector = 1	STAN-ANBERD	0.40				
Dummy medium_tech	Medium tech firm sector = 1	STAN-ANBERD	0.36				
Dummy low_tech	Low-tech firm sector = 1	STAN-ANBERD	0.24				
rd_sales (€)	R&D/Bv* Ln_Sales	EU IIS and Datastream int.	20.40	82.90	0.10	2.40	77.90
rd_hitech	R&D/Bv* Dummy_hitech	EU IIS and STAN-ANBERD	1.30	6.70	0.00	0.00	5.10
rd_medtech	R&D/Bv*Dummy_medtech	EU IIS and STAN-ANBERD	0.30	2.00	0.00	0.00	1.00
rd_lowtech	R&D/Bv*Dummy_lowtech	EU IIS and STAN-ANBERD	0.20	1.30	0.00	0.00	0.40

Continued

Table 10.1 Continued

Variable	Variable description	Source	Mean	SD	P5	Median	P95
sales_hitech (€)	Ln_Sales*Dummy_medtech	Datastream int. and STAN-ANBERD	5.10	6.40	0.00	0.00	15.80
sales_medtech (€)	Ln_Sales*Dummy_medtech	Datastream int. and STAN-ANBERD	4.90	6.70	0.00	0.00	16.20
sales_lowtech (€)	Ln_Sales*Dummy_lowtech	Datastream int. and STAN-ANBERD	3.40	6.30	0.00	0.00	16.60
Dummy_Fr	French firm = 1	Datastream int.	0.18				
Dummy_Gr	German firm = 1	Datastream int.	0.29				
Dummy_It	Italian firm = 1	Datastream int.	0.07				
Dummy_Sw	Swedish firm = 1	Datastream int.	0.13				
Dummy_Uk (base)	UK firm = 1	Datastream int.	0.33				

Table 10.2 Univariate descriptive statistics by country, years 2001–7

	France				Germany				Italy				Sweden				United Kingdom			
Variable	Mean	P5	Median	P95	Mean	P5	Median	P95	Mean	P5	Median	P95	Mean	P5	Median	P95	Mean	P5	Median	P95
(Mv–Bv)/Bv	18.53	0.37	3.41	90.53	20.6	0.38	4.17	108.9	10.9	0.23	2.39	56.77	67.61	0.68	7.07	398.09	16.93	0.16	3.30	69.48
RI/BV	1.49	–0.18	0.40	7.97	2.09	–0.24	0.59	12.88	0.75	–0.14	0.27	3.72	4.38	0	0.29	26.03	1.74	–0.27	0.37	10.06
R&D/BV	1.68	0	0.16	8.72	1.18	0.01	0.28	6.02	0.33	0	0.09	1.82	4.79	0.01	0.29	30.56	1.37	0	0.15	6.22
Mktshare	0.15	0	0.02	0.73	0.12	0	0.01	0.48	0.04	0	0	0.20	0.33	0	0.04	0.77	3.60	0	0.01	0.29
Leverage	2.11	0.02	0.63	5.31	173.9	1.54	41.68	299	18.47	0.01	0.37	103.32	6.63	0.06	3.63	16.43	3.15	0.01	0.51	6.18
Ln_Sales	13.77	9.21	13.74	17.61	13.39	9.92	13.16	17.70	13.75	10.9	13.32	17.74	14.66	10.97	14.71	18.27	12.61	8.5	12.54	16.69
rd_sales	19.8	0.06	2.11	103.51	14.14	0.20	3.97	72.51	4.08	0.05	1.19	20.14	58.65	0.18	4.18	350.49	14.87	0.03	1.86	71.6
rd_hitech	1.14	0	0	5.33	0.73	0	0	4.65	0.23	0	0	1.72	4.03	0	0	16.86	1.03	0	0	4.93
rd_medtech	0.24	0	0	0.54	0.32	0	0	1.51	0.06	0	0	0.27	0.60	0	0	1.17	0.15	0	0	0.42
rd_lowtech	0.29	0	0	0.47	0.14	0	0	0.46	0.03	0	0	0.19	0.16	0	0	0.46	0.19	0	0	0.45
sales_hitech	5.17	0	0	16.14	4.77	0	0	15.89	5.79	0	0	16.01	5.27	0	0	15.64	5.09	0	0	14.44
sales_medtech	4.79	0	0	16.46	5.52	0	0	15.7	4.01	0	0	14.5	6.76	0	0	17.82	3.81	0	0	15.15
sales_lowtech	3.81	0	0	16.95	3.10	0	0	16.7	3.95	0	0	17.35	2.63	0	0	16.19	3.71	0	0	16.17
Obs.			75				122				30				53				136	

explanatory variables are almost similar in terms of median values among the countries.[19]

The residual income and research and development outlays, on the other hand, are similar.[20] The sample used here thus requires, in addition to an overall analysis, a deeper investigation of individual countries, as developed below.

10.4 Results

This section examines the relationship between research and development expenditures, firm operating profits, size and participation in industries with a higher or lower propensity to innovation and the firm market value. Table 10.3 shows the correlation matrix between the main variables.

There is a significant correlation between (MV–BV)/BV and the principal independent variables RD/BV and RI/BV (68.7 per cent and 65.8 per cent respectively). Even RD/BV and RI/BV are well correlated with each other (46.9 per cent). The other variables show a weak correlation with each other and with (MV–BV)/BV.

a. Firms of the entire sample; size effect

As described previously, the literature generally found a positive relationship between the first two variables and the market value. We thus initially proceeded with a pooled cross-section analysis of the entire sample using country and industry dummies (Table 10.4) .[21]

The results of this initial analysis appear in line with our first two hypotheses and with the previous literature on the topic. Extending

Table 10.3 Correlation matrix, years 2001–7

	1	2	3	4	5	6	7	8	9	10
1 (MV–BV)/BV	1									
2 RD/BV	0.687*	1								
3 RI/BV	0.658*	0.469*	1							
4 Ln_Sales	−0.151*	−0.158*	−0.075*	1						
5 Mktshare	−0.011	−0.011	−0.012	0.055*	1					
6 Leverage	−0.015	−0.012	−0.015	0.031	−0.002	1				
7 Dummy_IAS	0.059*	0.005	0.036*	0.035	−0.004	−0.029	1			
8 Dummy hi_tech	0.156*	0.168*	0.123*	−0.304*	−0.037*	−0.029	0.005	1		
9 Dummy medium_tech	−0.082*	−0.103*	−0.066*	0.119*	−0.027	0.040*	0.016	−0.614*	1	
10 Dummy low_ tech	−0.088*	−0.079*	−0.068*	0.216*	0.074*	−0.011	−0.024	−0.464*	−0.414*	1

Notes: Stars show 5% level of significance.

Table 10.4 Analysis in pooled cross-section. Dependent variable: (Mv–Bv)/Bv

	(Mv-Bv)/Bv		
	Full sample	**Low sales**	**High sales**
Independent variables	**A**	**B**	**C**
RI/BV	3.464***	2.744***	8.332***
	(4.35)	(2.95)	(6.39)
RD/BV	5.098***	6.637***	–3.465**
	(5.32)	(6.74)	(–2.47)
Mktshare	0.015**	31.57	0.001
	(2.12)	(0.40)	(0.35)
Leverage	0.001	**–0.004***	**0.001***
	(0.06)	(–1.95)	(1.67)
Dummy_IAS	4.466	3.112	3.852
	(1.33)	(0.56)	(1.63)
Ln_Sales	–2.856***		
	(–5.25)		
Dummy hi_tech	4.840**	5.954*	7.292***
	(2.12)	(1.65)	(3.16)
Dummy medium_tech	–0.657	2.715	–0.228
	(–0.36)	(0.71)	(–0.24)
Dummy_Fr	4.607**	4.954	–0.335
	(2.36)	(1.40)	(–0.26)
Dummy_Gr	6.066***	6.244**	–0.903
	(3.49)	(2.34)	(–0.60)
Dummy_It	6.151***	5.686	1.073
	(2.84)	(1.60)	(0.56)
Dummy_Sw	30.46***	66.76***	11.96***
	(3.99)	(2.99)	(3.19)
Intercept	34.57***	–4.045	–3.312*
	(4.36)	(–0.79)	(–1.76)
Number of obs.	2884	1443	1441
R^2	0.51	0.55	0.50
F-test	17.91***	11.78***	10.81***

Notes:
In regressions B and C full sample is divided in two parts by sales median for every country.
Year dummies have been included in every regression.
t-tests in brackets. Stars show levels of significance (*** p< 1%, ** p< 5%, * p< 10%).
$MV_{i,t}$ is market value for firm i six months after the end of financial year. $BV_{i,t}$ is book value for firm i at the end of financial year. $RD_{i,t}$ is RD expenditure for firm i in year t.

the previous literature and empirical analysis, even when considering European countries, both RI/BV and RD/BV have a positive and highly significant impact on the dependent market value variable.

The market share also has an impact on market value; operating in an industry with a high propensity to innovation also contributes positively to market value.

The geographical specificity, already foreseen in the descriptive analysis, required an explicit measurement of its effects, also confirmed in the model: generally, all the country dummies are positive and significant. Given the definition of the dummy variables, we can state that firms that belong to countries of the sample other than the UK have greater market value, other conditions being equal.[22]

The size component in many financial studies has considerable importance, given that the behaviour of larger firms appears to differ from that of others. The impact of Ln_Sales, negative and highly significant in the regression model proposed in Table 10.4, confirms this behaviour for the sample considered here, not following Hypothesis 3. Given the importance and the significance of firm size in the analysis, here approximated by means of the logarithm of sales, we split the sample into two subsamples (Table 10.4 regressions b and c) according to the median[23] of each country's sales. We note that the two main variables remain positive and significant for firms we could call small–medium enterprises, while for the large enterprise sample RD/BV becomes negative and highly significant.

This is further evidence that the market assigns great importance to investments in research and development for small–medium enterprises, while for large firms variables that tend to catch economic value added, such as the RI/BV, may be more significant.

Belonging to an industry with high R&D expenditure contributes to further increasing market value: the Dummy hi_tech is positive and significant for both large and small enterprises.

b. Country and panel analysis

To further investigate country and size effects, firms were analysed according to their country of origin using a longitudinal approach. The methodology used is fixed effects panel data regression (fixed effects panel estimation Tables 10.5a and 10.5b), which has some advantages over the simpler OLS models in Table 10.4.[24]

As our study focuses on different countries, fixed effect panel models seem preferable, given that the non-observable variables are inherent to the contexts of the firms in question and it is unlikely that the environmental conditions changed in the period of study.[25]

Table 10.5a Panel fixed effects regression. Dependent variable: (Mv–Bv)/Bv

	(Mv-Bv)/Bv				
	FR	GR	IT	SW	UK
RI/BV	3.589***	3.274***	4.994***	9.549**	4.790***
	(6.53)	(10.56)	(5.01)	(2.26)	(10.27)
RD/BV	2.064***	7.820***	−6.876**	8.424**	1.992***
	(3.73)	(9.88)	(−2.21)	(2.13)	(3.72)
Mktshare	−14.01*	0.579	27.58	0.711	0.005
	(−1.77)	(0.11)	(0.68)	(0.06)	(0.14)
Leverage	−0.348	0.001	−0.001	−0.054	0.006
	(−0.68)	(0.24)	(−0.09)	(−0.13)	(0.27)
Dummy_IAS	7.514	0.341	−0.406	−9.147	4.909
	(1.45)	(0.09)	(−0.15)	(−0.46)	(1.21)
Ln_Sales	−3.293***	−0.586	0.507	11.44	−0.989
	(−3.16)	(−0.27)	(0.33)	(0.86)	(−0.95)
Dummy hi_tech	2.735	3.422	9.111**	−10.52	−1.48
	(0.51)	(0.76)	(2.55)	(−0.44)	(−0.34)
Dummy medium_ tech	5.608	0.095	13.04***	−3.402	1.406
	(1.00)	(0.02)	(3.65)	(−0.15)	(0.31)
Intercept	55.89***	8.058	−4.509	−96.54	17.11
	(3.91)	(0.28)	(−0.22)	(−0.50)	(1.28)
Number of obs.	527	853	210	371	923
R^2 – overall	0.46	0.64	0.32	0.49	0.41
R^2 – within	0.30	0.45	0.25	0.39	0.34
F – test	13.25***	41.86***	33.86***	11.89**	29.11**

Notes:
Dummy for years has been included.
t-tests in brackets. Stars show levels of significance (*** p<1%, ** p<5%, * p<10%).
$MV_{i,t}$ is market value for firm i six months after the end of financial year. $BV_{i,t}$, is book value for firm i at the end of financial year. $RD_{i,t}$ is RD expenditure for firm i in year t.

The results of the panel analysis (Table 10.5a) essentially confirm Hypotheses Hp1 and Hp2. In line with expectations, the residual income effect is positive and significant for all countries. Residual income seems to be a good factor for increasing the market perception of firm value, and it is positively evaluated by investors. The estimators are all significant at 5 per cent, with higher levels for the Swedish sample, which confirms the specificity of this country. The main variable of our study, RD/BV, presents positive evidence for the UK, Germany, France and Sweden, while it is negative for Italy. All the estimators are significant at 5 per cent, with greater robustness for the German and

Table 10.5b Panel fixed effects regression by country. Dependent variable: (Mv–Bv)/Bv

	(Mv-Bv)/Bv									
	FR		GR		IT		SW		UK	
	Low sales	High sales	Low sales	High sales	Low sales	High sales	Low sales	High sales	Low sales	High sales
RI/BV	2.14**	14.56**	3.21***	4.22***	2.48**	6.70***	13.92**	21.92***	4.91***	6.31***
	(2.03)	(33.48)	(8.28)	(7.17)	(2.11)	(3.33)	(2.23)	(7.40)	(6.36)	(19.88)
RD/BV	3.76***	−12.92***	7.89***	5.30***	−0.824	−13.01	12.42**	−19.81***	2.82***	−0.98***
	(4.06)	(−18.84)	(8.04)	(3.16)	(−0.24)	(−1.35)	(2.15)	(−6.51)	(3.09)	(−2.82)
Mktshare	−1.40**	0.618	39.92	0.671	−276.5	56.02	591.4	−0.241	605.9	0.001
	(−2.31)	(0.37)	(0.21)	(0.22)	(−1.21)	(1.28)	(1.44)	(−0.21)	(0.49)	(0.05)
Leverage	−0.432	0.157	0.01	0.01	−0.153	−0.015	0.22	−0.088	0.006	−0.005
	(−0.60)	(0.64)	(0.51)	(0.16)	(−0.65)	(−0.09)	(0.39)	(−1.22)	(0.18)	(−0.19)
Dummy_IAS	10.34	2.03	2.7	0.634	−3.349	3.033	−20.58	−5.359*	11.6	1.545
	(1.00)	(1.46)	(0.40)	(0.20)	(−0.99)	(0.67)	(−0.49)	(−1.85)	(1.40)	(0.93)
Dummy hi_tech	9.097	−1.689	−0.34	5.294	−1.473	24.43***	−43.34	0.638	−3.075	−0.856
	(0.80)	(−1.44)	(−0.04)	(1.46)	(−0.38)	(3.62)	(−0.76)	(0.19)	(−0.34)	(−0.41)
Dummy medium_tech	13.72	−0.424	−3.662	5.674	−0.969	29.69***	−14.8	−1.272	−1.807	1.215
	(1.26)	(−0.33)	(−0.51)	(1.54)	(−0.23)	(4.92)	(−0.28)	(−0.37)	(−0.17)	(0.71)
Intercept	19.24*	2.433**	6.472	−5.461*	13.39***	−13.28*	108.8**	4.046	6.443	1.123
	(1.96)	(2.04)	(1.01)	(−1.70)	(3.66)	(−1.92)	(2.03)	(1.29)	(0.79)	(0.69)
Number of obs.	266	261	426	427	108	102	189	182	462	461
R^2 – overall	0.53	0.23	0.55	0.77	0.27	0.31	0.29	0.59	0.45	0.41
R^2 – within	0.32	0.88	0.48	0.57	0.29	0.44	0.25	0.69	0.35	0.63
F – test	36.95***	114.53***	24.95***	35.00***	22.4***	34.26***	11.96**	23.44***	15.49***	47.90***

Notes:
Every country sample has been divided in two by sales median. Dummy years have been included.
t-tests in brackets. Stars show levels of significance (*** p<1%, ** p<5%, * p<10%).
$MV_{i,t}$ is market value for firm i six months after the end of financial year. $BV_{i,t}$, is book value for firm i at the end of financial year. $RD_{i,t}$ is RD expenditure for firm i in year t.

Swedish samples. Results confirm Hp2 regarding a positive effect of R&D expenditure on the market value.

For all these countries, investing 1 Euro in research and development has a more than proportional impact on firm market value, with an even more pronounced effect for Swedish and German firms. The results regarding British data are in line with previous studies (Stark, 2008). Green *et al.* (1996) found a positive impact of R&D expenditure on the market value, but this was not always statistically significant. Stark and Thomas (1998) and Akbar and Stark (2003), on the other hand, found more than significant evidence of the importance of the market's reaction to R&D expenditure, and especially that it exploits long-term effects. Hughes (2008) also found similar results, while, in studies of other European markets, Hall and Oriani (2006) found positive evidence of R&D expenditure on the market value of US, British, German and French companies, albeit less significant than in our sample. Furthermore, they did not find significant evidence for Italian data, for which we find a negative correlation.

Considering the entire sample, none of the other variables are significant, with the exception of Ln_Sales for France. The industry dummies are again positive and significant for Germany.

Similarly to what was proposed in the OLS analysis, in Table 10.5b we further split the samples of each country according to the respective median of sales. The results offer support to the thesis that financial markets associate firm size with stable and positive profits: the importance of RI/BV is greater in large companies for all countries. Exactly the opposite occurs for the second regressor: the market value of smaller firms depends largely and significantly on RD/BV, with the exception of the Italian data, for which there is no evidence of this impact.

The results of these tests are in line with some research contributions: Griliches (1990), for example, indicates that on average smaller companies are more efficient in terms of R&D expenditure and number of patents registered, although this may be explained by the sample selection. Chauvin *et al.* (1993), by contrast, found that the effect of the R&D expenditure on market value is much stronger in larger companies than in others. Hall and Oriani (2006) found a positive relationship between market value and size for a sample of British and US companies, while this relation was negative for German, French and Italian firms.

The other variables are not significant, with the exception of MKTSHARE for France and the industry dummies for the larger firms in the Italian sample, in contrast with other countries.

c. Analysis of the sample by industrial sector

As a further analysis of the effect of R&D expenditure on firm market value, we classify the firms by sector. It can be observed that participation in industries with high research and innovation propensity entails a positive impact on corporate value, as implied in Hp 4. Previous literature in the field supports this thesis. Blundell *et al.* (1999) found a higher positive impact of research and development on equity prices of a sample of British firms operating in three top-innovative sectors. Chauvin *et al.* (1993) obtained similar results for firms belonging to the three group sectors that generally have a higher R&D intensity ratio. Our analysis is part of this research strand, considering the specificity of different countries and crossing the size effect with the research and development costs and belonging to highly innovative industries.

The analysis by sector is shown in Table 10.6. In line with Hp 4, companies that are part of industries with high-innovation propensity have a positive and significant RD/BV impact on market value. The market values of firms of other sectors are not susceptible to R&D investments, since other drivers concern them.

Among these is certainly residual income (RI/BV), being positive and significant in all industries but with a much greater impact in low-innovation industries. A joint interpretation of the coefficients therefore allows strengthening the hypothesis that in high-innovation industries it is necessary to maintain a significant R&D intensity to have an advantage in terms of market value: in other industries, residual income components are especially valued. Size estimators highlight the fact that dimension penalizes the market value of hi-tech firms more than others.

The size effect is greater for more innovative firms. In order to better analyse this relation, we inserted into the OLS pooled cross-section regression (Table 10.7) the dummies relating to countries, industries and size. The models represented in Table 10.7 highlight the interactions between some variables. Table 10.7A recalls the model 'a' of Table 10.3, with the addition of the new variables sales_hitech and sales_medtech to consider the statistical interaction of Ln_sales with industry dummy variables. The results on market value confirm a strong negative significance of the joint effect of large size and hi-tech sector. Therefore it seems that large firms in hi-tech industries, *ceteris paribus*, manifest lower market value.

In Table 10.7B we insert two new variables, R&D_Hitech and R&D_Medtech, as interactions between RD/BV and Dummy hi_tech and

Table 10.6 Analysis in pooled cross-section. Dependent variable: (Mv–Bv)/Bv

	(Mv-Bv)/Bv		
	Hi tech	**Med tech**	**Low tech**
RI/BV	1.744*	8.365***	6.377***
	(1.80)	(5.48)	(3.38)
RD/BV	6.611***	–1.076	–0.951
	(6.64)	(–0.28)	(–0.40)
Mktshare	1.224	–0.0235	0.006*
	(0.35)	(–1.29)	(1.78)
Leverage	–0.008	0.001	–0.005
	(–1.18)	(1.56)	(–1.23)
Dummy_IAS	11.06	–0.915	–0.777
	(1.55)	(–0.30)	(–0.36)
Ln_Sales	–3.714***	–2.107***	–1.347**
	(–4.15)	(–3.29)	(–1.98)
Dummy_Fr	5.915*	2.721	5.680**
	(1.71)	(0.98)	(2.52)
Dummy_Gr	14.03***	–2.853	4.335**
	(4.05)	(–1.46)	(2.12)
Dummy_It	11.87***	–0.055	6.024***
	(2.79)	(–0.02)	(2.79)
Dummy_Sw	62.05***	8.533***	16.18*
	(3.54)	(3.05)	(1.83)
Intercept	38.87***	36.84***	22.61**
	(3.37)	(3.57)	(2.28)
Number of obs.	1176	1021	687
R^2	0.53	0.53	0.36
F-test	11.48***	13.64***	17.69***

Notes:
Full sample has been divided into three groups based on propensity to innovate of firms' industry sectors. Dummy years have been included.
t-tests in brackets. Stars show levels of significance (*** p<1%, ** p<5%, * p<10%).
$MV_{i,t}$ is market value for firm i six months after the end of financial year. $BV_{i,t}$, is book value for firm i at the end of financial year. $RD_{i,t}$ is RD expenditure for firm i in year t.

Dummy medium_tech respectively. The first variable is highly significant and shows that firm R&D expenditure in highly innovative industries is appreciated, given that only R&D, without other specifications, is now not significant. Likewise in Table 10.7C, where we inserted the size component, we found confirmation of the previous results, namely that the R&D investments of larger firms are less valued by the market.

Table 10.7 Analysis in pooled cross-section for full sample. Dependent variable: (Mv–Bv)/Bv

	(Mv-Bv)/Bv		
	A	B	C
RI/BV	3.562***	3.552***	3.608***
	(4.48)	(4.37)	(4.47)
RD/BV	5.000***	1.179	1.343
	(5.23)	(0.91)	(1.04)
Mktshare	0.011	0.012*	0.009
	(1.55)	(1.78)	(1.41)
Leverage	0.001	0.001	0.002
	(0.05)	(–0.09)	(–0.07)
Dummy_IAS	4.945	4.496	4.79
	(1.47)	(1.38)	(1.46)
Ln_Sales	–1.216*	–3.119***	–2.039***
	(–1.77)	(–5.91)	(–3.97)
Dummy hi_tech	39.00***	0.544	22.26*
	(2.83)	(0.23)	(1.76)
Dummy medium_tech	24.40*	–2.326	15.65
	(1.89)	(–1.15)	(1.36)
sales_hitech	–2.486***		–1.560*
	(–2.62)		(–1.78)
sales_medtech	1.753**		–1.248
	(–2.03)		(–1.64)
RD_hitech		4.140***	3.913***
		(2.92)	(2.76)
RD_medtech		1.991	1.756
		(0.69)	(0.60)
Dummy_Fr	4.878**	5.392***	5.506***
	(2.53)	(2.85)	(2.95)
Dummy Gr	6.510***	6.318***	6.567***
	(3.76)	(3.65)	(3.82)
Dummy_It	6.514***	5.884***	6.085***
	(3.03)	(2.76)	(2.89)
Dummy_Sw	30.90***	30.88***	31.20***
	(4.01)	(4.06)	(4.06)
Intercept	11.36	41.69***	26.23***
	(1.08)	(5.77)	(3.51)
Number of obs.	2884	2884	2884
R^2	0.51	0.51	0.52
F-test	17.09***	17.87***	16.73***

Notes:
Models with interactive effect between size, industry and R&D expenditures. In regression 'A' interactions between 'size' and 'industry effect' have been analysed. In 'B' there are interactions between R&D expenditures and industry effect. In 'C' all interactions have been included. Dummy years have been included.
t-tests in brackets. Stars show levels of significance (*** p<1%, ** p<5%, * p<10%).
$MV_{i,t}$ is market value for firm i six months after the end of financial year. $BV_{i,t}$, is book value for firm i at the end of financial year. $RD_{i,t}$ is RD expenditure for firm i in year t.

The RD/BV variable remains significant only if associated with companies operating in high-innovation-propensity industries. In regressions 'b' and 'c', only rd_hitech remains positive and significant. The Ln_sales variable is always negatively correlated with market value, but this correlation is stronger when the company operates in one of the hi-tech industries. The sales_hitech dummy is negative and significant in regression 'a'; the same applies to the sales_medtech dummy. It remains confirmed that the RI/BV variable residual income, the de facto control variable, remains substantially stable and significant in all the specifications considered.[26]

10.5 Conclusions

By means of the construction of a data set of 416 listed firms operating in 36 different industries, listed in five European countries (France, Germany, Italy, Sweden and the United Kingdom), the relationship between the market value and investment in research and development of these companies was investigated. There were four basic hypotheses to verify: implementing R&D is a fundamental activity for an innovative firm and is therefore a factor that is positively evaluated by the market, together with the profits, that allow remunerating the capital beyond expectations; size should have a positive impact on firm research and development expenditure, implying that more resources available for investments impact positively on corporate value; and, finally, the firm industry sector is important for the investors' valuation. The results of the econometric analysis, both of the entire sample and when grouped by country, suggest some common conclusions and a few specific caveats.

The results by country are always positive in terms of the impact of R&D expenditure on market value, although with different amplitudes, with the exception of the Italian data, for which the effects of R&D are negatively correlated with corporate value. This result is confirmed by former empirical conclusions.

Other variables, such as financial leverage, market share or the adoption of international accounting standards, do not seem to produce a significant and persistent effect on market valuations.

Surplus profit, or residual income, always has a positive and significant impact on market value, confirming that the revenue indicators, although retrospective, are among the key elements for defining market value. In this context, residual income is an element to verify the different hypotheses in the same way as the statistical interactions between size, sector and R&D variables.

R&D investment has a positive impact on market value, as predicted by the relevant literature. Our third hypothesis is not confirmed: firm size has a negative effect on market value; the valuation of small and medium enterprises positively and significantly depends on their investments in innovation and to a lesser extent on size. The opposite occurs for larger firms, for which the market valuation is more influenced by cash flows, such as residual income, than by new opportunities for future growth and research and development.

Operating in sectors with high-innovation intensity positively affects market value; models show that firms with greater market value not only operate in these sectors, but make higher R&D investments, as expected by market investors.

Notes

1. Lev and Sougiannis (1996); Mohnen *et al.* (2000); Chan *et al.* (2001); Chambers *et al.* (2002).
2. Other authors have used other variables as deflators, such as sales, number of shares or year start book value (Hirschey and Weygandt, 1985; Rees, 1997; Lo and Lys, 2000).
3. For a complete contribution to the debate, see Rajan and Zingales (1995).
4. IAS regulations require firms to consider R&D investments entirely as components of expenditure in the year in progress and not to capitalize them to then amortize them at a rate of 15 per cent.
5. In general, in the countries considered, greater discretion was possible in the choice between entirely expensing or capitalizing part of product/service development investments.
6. Reference is made to the OCSE (Organization for Security and Co-Operation in Europe) (STAN ANBERD [Structural Analysis Database – Analytical Business Enterprise Research and Development Database]) classifications of R&D expenditure in respect of the sales of the firm industry sector.
7. The 2007 EU Industrial R&D Investment Scoreboard.
8. The published data was derived from the EU Industrial Scoreboard available for each year from 2001 to 2007, while all the data on R&D expenditure came from the accounting documents of the firms.
9. In the annual survey carried out by the EU Industrial Scoreboard, the capitalization of companies from the five countries we considered constituted around 80 per cent of the entire sample.
10. The sample does not, therefore, consider companies that were delisted or subject to IPOs in that period. Notwithstanding that the models proposed present a limited number of accounting variables, only companies that had all the necessary data were considered. The presence of some outliers was controlled by winsoring above 1 per cent.
11. Furthermore, a search on the financial statements of firms was carried out to find the missing data related to costs or turnover items.

12. For example, for a company that closes the balance sheet on 31 December 2001, the market value considered for the year 2001 will be equal to that recorded at 1 July 2002 or the trading day closest to this date. This choice has the advantage of identifying the level of market value when the financial statement has for some time been deposited and made available to the investors, who have consequently already absorbed the information contained in this document and will therefore have acted on the stock market based on the various expectations created. The disadvantage, on the other hand, is that the measurement takes place at different times depending on the date of closure, and therefore the entries are not all subject to the same economic conditions.
13. As usual, it is assumed that the market value of debt coincides with its book value.
14. The weighted average cost of capital (WACC) was calculated using as the risk-free rate the yield to maturity of Government bonds for each country. The return of Government bonds with roughly an expiry date closest to 10 years was used as the risk-free rate of return. The annual market rate of return was calculated as the sum of daily returns of the stock markets index. The beta of each firm, when not available, was computed by correcting the DataStream International Industry Beta for the specific firm leverage.
15. The industries were defined using the ICB sectors of the Industry Classification Benchmark.
16. Industry innovativity was obtained from the classification that the OECD draws up each year based on the R&D intensity of firms in each industry (ANBERD Database).
17. This feature is common for accounting data and for variables that cannot become negative and with a non-defined upper limit. Generally, the median is much lower than the average, indicating an asymmetry in the distribution of the data.
18. The exception is Sweden, probably indicating a greater capitalization of firms in the Swedish sample.
19. Also in this case, Swedish firms indicate a substantially higher average than those of other countries. As concerns the non-deflated variables, which have greater skewness, the average for the Swedish sample is nearly double compared with the others, but with a similar order of magnitude as regards the median.
20. The larger size of Swedish firms is also confirmed as regards the median and average number of sales by country.
21. All models include a correction for the heteroscedasticity of residuals.
22. The strong differentiation traits are confirmed for the selected companies belonging to Sweden.
23. We use the median since the samples are highly asymmetric.
24. The panel models allow managing the effect of the non-observable variables and the dynamic effects, elements that in the OLS models could determine distorted estimators.
25. In the FE model it is assumed that the non-observable effects do not change over time and are correlated with the explanatory variables, while in the RE model these effects are part of the regression error and are not correlated

with the explanatory variable with a random walk between one year and the next. The Hausman test offers robust evidence to support fixed effects compared with random effects.

26. Robustness checks were performed on the various relations, going over all the models proposed here but using the (MV–BV)/(Sales) variable instead of the dependent variable (MV–BV)/(BV). The results confirm the estimates here proposed and the main relations described.

References

Akbar, S. and Stark, A.W. (2003) 'Deflators, net shareholder cash flows, dividends, capital: Contributions and estimated models of corporate valuation', *Journal of Business, Finance and Accounting*, 30(9–10), 1211–33.

Anagnostopoulou, S.C. and Levis, M. (2008) 'R&D and performance persistence: Evidence from the United Kingdom', *International Journal of Accounting*, 43(3), 293–320.

Blundell, R., Griffith, R. and Van Reenen, J. (1999) 'Market share, market value and innovation in a panel of British manufacturing firms', *Review of Economic Studies*, 66(3), 529–54.

Callen, J.L. and Morel, M. (2005) 'The valuation relevance of R&D expenditures: Time series evidence', *International Review of Financial Analysis*, 14, 304–25.

Chambers, D., Jennings, R. and Thompson II, R.B. (2002) 'Excess returns to R&D-Intensive firms', *Review of Accounting Studies*, 7(2–3), 133–58.

Chan, L.K.C., Lakonishok, L. and Sougiannis, T. (2001) 'The stock market valuation of research and development expenditures', *Journal of Finance*, 56(6), 2431–56.

Chan, H.W.F., Faff, R.W., Gharghori, P. and Ho, Y.K. (2007) 'The relation between R&D intensity and future market returns: Does expensing versus capitalization matter?', *Review of Quantitative and Financial Accounting*, 29(1), 25–51.

Chauvin, K.W. and Hirschey, M. (1993) 'Advertising, R&D expenditures and the market value of the firm', *Financial Management*, 22(4), 128–43.

Cincera, M., Ortega-Argilés, R. and Moncada-Paternò-Castello, P. (2009) 'The performance of top R&D investing companies in the stock market', *IPTS Working Paper Series*.

Cockburn, I. and Griliches, Z. (1988) 'Industry effects and appropriability measures in the stock markets' valuation of R&D and patents', *American Economic Review*, 78(2), 419–24.

Eberhart, A.C., Maxwell, W.F. and Siddique, A.R. (2004) 'An examination of the long-run abnormal returns and operating performance following R&D increases', *Journal of Finance*, 59(2), 623–51.

Fama, E. (1970) 'Efficient capital markets; A review of theory and empirical work', *Journal of Finance*, 25(2), 383–417.

Franzen, L. and Radhakrishnan, S. (2009) 'The value relevance of R&D across profit and loss firms', *Journal of Accounting and Public Policy*, 28, 16–32.

Green, J.P., Stark, A. and Thomas, H.W. (1996) 'UK evidence of the market valuation of R&D expenditures', *Journal of Finance and Accounting*, 23(2), 191–217.

Griliches, Z. (1990) 'Patent Statistics as Economic Indicators: A Survey.' *Journal of Economic Literature*, 28, 1661–707.

Griliches, Z. (1981) 'Market value, R&D, and patents', *Economic Letters*, 7(2), 183–7.
Griliches, Z. (1995) 'R&D and productivity: Econometric results and measurement issues', in Stoneman, P. (ed.), *Handbook of the economics of innovation and technological change* (Oxford: Blackwell).
Griliches, Z. and Mairesse, J. (1984) 'Comparing productivity growth: An exploration of French and U.S. industrial and firm data', *European Economic Review*, 21(1–2), 89–126.
Hall, B.H. (1993) 'The stock markets valuation of R&D investment during the 1980s', *American Economic Review*, 83(2), 259–65.
Hall, B.H. (1999) 'Innovation and market value', *SSRN Working Papers Series*.
Hall, B.H. (2000) *Innovation, market value and productivity: Innovation and Economic Performance* (Cambridge: Cambridge University Press).
Hall, B.H. and Oriani, R. (2006) 'Does the market value R&D investment by European firms? Evidence from a panel of manufacturing firms in France, Germany, and Italy', *International Journal of Industrial Organization*, 24(5), 971–93.
Himmelberg, C.P. and Petersen, B.C. (1994) 'R&D and internal finance: A panel study of small firms in high-tech industries', *Review of Economics and Statistics*, 76(1), 38–51.
Hirschey, M. (1982) 'Intangible capital aspects of advertising and R&D expenditures', *Journal of Industrial Economics*, 30(4), 375–91.
Hirschey, M. and Weygandt, J.J. (1985) 'Amortization policy for advertising and research and development expenditures', *Journal of Accounting Research*, 23, 326–35.
Hughes, J. P. (2008) 'R&D and dividend payments as determinants of corporate value in the UK', *International Journal of Managerial Finance*, 4(1), 76–91.
Jaffe, A.B. (1986) 'Technological opportunity and spillovers of R&D: Evidence from firms' patents, profits, and market value', *American Economic Review*, 76(5), 984–1002.
Karjalainen, P. (2007) 'Economic relevance and determinants of R&D capital in different financial systems', *International Journal of Accounting, Auditing and Performance Evaluation*, 4(1), 1–15.
Lev, B. (2001) *Intangibles: Management, measurement and reporting* (Washington DC: Brookings Institution Press).
Lev, B. and Sougiannis, T. (1996) 'The capitalization, amortization and value relevance of R&D', *Journal of Accounting and Economics*, 21, 107–38.
Lo, K. and Lys, T. (2000) 'The Ohlson model: Contribution to valuation theory: Limitations, and empirical applications', *Journal of Accounting, Auditing and Finance*, 15, 337–67.
Mairesse, J. and Hall, B.H. (1995) 'Estimating the productivity of research and development in French and United States manufacturing firms', *Journal of Econometrics*, 65(1), 263–94.
Mohnen, P., Nadiri, M. and Prucha, I. (2000) 'R&D, production structure, and productivity growth in the U.S., Japanese and German manufacturing sectors', *SSRN Working Paper Series*.
Myers, S.C. and Majluf, N. (1984) 'Corporate financing and investment decisions: When firms have information that investors do not have', *Journal of Financial Economics*, 13(2), 187–221.

Ohlson, J.A. (1989) 'Accounting earnings, book value and dividends: The theory of the clean surplus equation', *Unpublished working paper*, Columbia University.

Oswald, D. (2008) 'The determinants and the value relevance of the choice of accounting for research and development expenditures in the United Kingdom', *Journal of Business, Finance and Accounting*, 35(1–2), 1–24.

Oswald, D. and Zarowin, P. (2007) 'Capitalization of R&D and the informativeness of stock prices', *European Accounting Review*, 16(4), 703–28.

Pakes, A. (1985) 'On patents, R&D and the stock market rate of return', *Journal of Political Economy*, 93(2), 390–410.

Penman, S.H. (2006) *Financial statement analysis and security valuation* (New York: McGraw-Hill).

Penman, S.H. and Zhang, X. (2002) 'Accounting conservatism, the quality of earnings and stock returns', *Accounting Review*, 77(2), 237–65.

Rajan, R.G. and Zingales, L. (1995) 'What do we know about capital structure? Some evidence from international data', *Journal of Finance*, 50(5), 1421–61.

Rees, W.P. (1997) 'The impact of dividends, debt and investments on valuation models', *Journal of Business Finance and Accounting*, 24, 1111–50.

Shah, S., Stark, A.W. and Akbar, S. (2008) 'Firm size, sector and market valuation of R&D expenditures', *Applied Financial Economics Letters*, 4(2), 87–91.

Schumpeter, J. (1942) *Capitalism, socialism and democracy* (New York: Harper and brothers).

Skinner, D.J. (2008) 'Accounting for intangibles: A critical review of policy recommendations', *Accounting and Business Research*, 38(3), Special Issue, 191–204.

Solow, R. (1956) 'A contribution to the theory of economic growth', *Quarterly Journal of Economics*, 70(1), 65–94.

Sougiannis, T. (1994) 'The accounting based valuation of corporate R&D', *Accounting Review*, 69(1), 44–68.

Stark, A.W. (2008) 'Intangibles and research: An overview with a specific focus on the UK, Plus ça change, plus c'est la même chose', *Accounting and Business Research*, 38(3), 275–85.

Stark, A.W. and Thomas, H.M. (1998) 'On the empirical relationship between market value and residual income in the UK', *Management Accounting Research*, 9, 445–60.

Toivanen, O., Stoneman, P. and Bosworth, D. (2002) 'Innovation and the market value of UK firms, 1989–1995', *Oxford Bulletin of Economics and Statistics*, 64(1), 39–61.

Wyatt, A. (2008) 'What financial and non-financial information for intangibles is value relevant? A review of the evidence', *Accounting and Business Research*, 38(3), 217–56.

11
Value Creation of Internationalization Strategies of Italian Medium-Sized Listed Firms

Ottorino Morresi and Alberto Pezzi

11.1 Introduction

In the last 40 years, the intensity of the internationalization process of Italian firms has been growing. Unlike other developed countries, for which studies on internationalization are mostly related to large multinational corporations, the majority of Italian studies rely on Small and Medium-sized Enterprises (SMEs) (Depperu, 1997; Zucchella and Maccarini, 1999), which are considered to be distinctive of the Italian entrepreneurial base. Italian SMEs are used to going abroad through either non-equity or low-equity entry modes, such as exporting and joint ventures, because of their low confidence in international M&As. The propensity of Italian firms to go international through high-equity entry modes is more recent, and has grown in the last few years. Between 2002 and 2007, the Italian outward Foreign Direct Investments (FDIs) increased by 3.6 per cent if we look at the average growth rate of foreign shareholdings and 5.8 per cent if we look at the number of subsidiaries (ICE, 2009, p. 290). It is worth noticing that medium-sized enterprises contributed the most to the above growth, despite their relatively low incidence on the total FDI stock (Mariotti and Mutinelli, 2009). These data lead us to argue that internationalization strategies of SMEs are likely to be remarkably different depending on the specific size of constituent firms (e.g. micro, small and medium firms).

In the Italian context, the use of SMEs as an undifferentiated concept does not shed any light on the specific behaviour of each dimensional class (Coltorti, 2006; Arrighetti and Ninni, 2008). Medium-sized enterprises can be considered as a hybrid model between smaller and larger firms. On the one hand, they present the same structure as smaller firms; on the other hand, they have already experienced more complex market environments, as have larger firms. Medium-sized listed enterprises can rely upon a more managerial approach toward internationalization, so that they can have easier access than smaller enterprises to international markets. For the purposes of this work a dimensional distinction is needed to highlight what kind of international orientation is consistent with the international path of medium-sized enterprises and in order to investigate the relation between internationalization and performance. From this perspective, medium firms rely on advantages and forces stemming from industrial district affiliation and niche products (Becattini *et al.*, 2009) and, at the same time, they are structured as international networks and thus can also benefit from the advantages of multinationality.

The amount of research focusing on market reaction in response to internationalization announcements made by medium-sized enterprises has been very limited, with a mix of results. The study aims at investigating the market performance of those firms that choose to internationalize, and accordingly we expect to find a positive and significant market reaction in response to internationalization announcements. Internationalization strategies have been observed according to the entry mode, the country of destination, the relative size of the deal, the firm age, the industry R&D intensity, the country risk of the target country, and the changes affecting the information disclosure regulation of listed firms over time. We find results that support our key idea: the market seems to be confident in the capabilities of medium enterprises to extract value from investments in foreign markets. Besides, we find that the country of destination, the entry mode, the deal size, the firm age, the country risk, and the evolution of information disclosure regulation matter in explaining the outcomes.

The remainder of the chapter is organized as follows. Section 11.2 provides the conceptual background according to the principal statements set by both theoretical and empirical contributions, in order to qualify the relationship between the internationalization process of the firm and its performance; Section 11.3 provides the description of the variables that are supposed to affect the value creation of internationalization strategies; Section 11.4 illustrates the sample and research design; Section 11.5 discusses results and limitations of the study; and Section 11.6 attempts to draw some conclusions and policy implications.

11.2 Literature review

In the last decades, the growth of international deals also involving small- and medium-sized firms has led to the expectation that multinationality can generate advantages (Dunning, 1979; Kogut, 1983; Cowling and Sugden, 1987) by reducing the marginal cost of foreign investments of firms already involved in internationalization processes (Ietto Gillies, 2002, 2005). The belief that multinationality is worthwhile has been applied to transnational corporations. As these last are organized as transnational networks, the theory of multinational advantages can be applied to some kind of organizational form structured as international networks, such as medium-sized firms and clusters. Although some literature suggests that foreign activities and country diversification processes do not affect corporate performance (Rugman, 1981), a number of studies (Stopford and Dunning, 1983; Beamish and Newfield, 1984; Rugman, 1986; Lu and Beamish, 2001) found that internationalization choices were linked to performance with different intensity. Specifically, multinational firms were able to increase their competitive advantage by coordinating international activities, achieving benefits in terms of economies of scale and scope and economies of learning (Bartlett and Ghoshal, 1989). Additional value creations came from the ability to exploit different market, employment and tax regulations in the host country.

The empirical results on the link between internationalization and firm performance are diversified. Hsu and Boggs (2003) present a complete review of literature and empirical studies that discuss and find a linear and curvilinear relationship between internationalization and firm performance. They argue that firm financial performance is affected by the degree of international involvement according to an inverted U-shape relationship. Accordingly, the initially increasing trend of performance will retreat as a result of an escalation of risks, costs and organizational problems. The positive relationship between internationalization and performance expected for small-sized firms engaged in international expansion is not inconsistent with the Uppsala school of thought proposing a step-by-step internationalization process with reference to experience, distance and entry mode (Johanson and Vahlne, 1977), or with the framework of born global firms (Oviatt and McDougall, 1994). For born global firms that are engaged in fast-growing internationalization processes, often in innovative industries, a positive link between internationalization and performance was found by Bloodgood *et al.* (1996) and McDougall and Oviatt (1996). The above discussion about theoretical and empirical contributions to internationalization leads us to the following research hypothesis:

> **Hypothesis 1**: Italian medium-sized listed firms are expected to show a positive stock market reaction to announcements of internationalization strategies.

1. Selected variables on value creation

The internationalization–performance relationship is believed to be context-dependent because of the lack of a broad theoretical consensus on the matter. The performance impact of internationalization decisions is typically influenced by factors concerning a firm's external and internal environment. In accordance with existing research, this study will concentrate on several variables that have an impact on the financial performance of the acquiring firm: entry mode, country of destination, deal size, firm age, industry R&D intensity, country risk, and changes of information disclosure regulation.

Equity entry modes

Dunning (1988), in the eclectic paradigm, found a relation between entry modes and the advantages of internationalization (OLI). Subsequent studies found that the ability of firms to enter a market by FDI entry modes was seriously limited by their size, their previous international experience, and risk, and also concluded that high-equity entry modes were not exclusively related to the high potential of markets of destination (Agarwal and Ramaswami, 1992). The choice of the entry mode for a firm is not an economic optimum, but outlines a convenient decision to be taken in conditions of uncertainty and contingency (Kumar and Subramanian, 1997). In short, the level of control associated with the entry mode depends on internal variables, such as resources and size, and external variables related to target country, home country and/or industry. The correct adoption of the entry mode is likely to result in a good economic and financial performance.

Ahern and Weston (2007) point out that value creation through M&A activities results from economies of scale and scope; extending technological capabilities; industry consolidation strategies; industry roll-ups; new capabilities and managerial skills; first mover advantages; customer relationships; and globalization. Value destruction at the expense of shareholders is largely explained by behavioural theories of M&As (i.e., hubris, stock market misvaluations, agency, and integration problems). Moreover, Lu and Beamish (2006) argue that SMEs suffer a trade-off between growth and profitability that is likely to have an adverse effect on shareholders' gains from M&As.

Italian medium-sized enterprises are likely to create value through equity entry modes because they are usually family businesses and their managers are not in the hierarchical position of operating in their own self-interests. Nevertheless, Italian firms are likely to encounter uncertainty in the international environment. Value creation is likely to be dependent on the depth of the international implications according to high-equity and low-equity entry modes.

For the purposes of this study, high-equity entry modes encompass international mergers and acquisitions, and establishment of subsidiaries abroad; low-equity entry modes consist of international equity joint ventures and purchase of minority stakes in foreign companies.

> **Hypothesis 2** (low-equity entry modes): Formation of international equity joint ventures by Italian medium-sized listed firms is positively related to their stock market performance.
>
> **Hypothesis 3** (high-equity entry modes): International mergers and acquisitions, and establishment of subsidiaries abroad by Italian medium-sized listed firms, generate lower shareholders' gains than those shown in joint ventures, when the deal size is very relevant.

Country of destination

In advanced economies, the risk underlying international operations seems to be limited to geographical and cultural problems, and does not involve institutional and political concerns, which are distinctive problems of emerging countries. In advanced economies the infrastructure is more developed, the political situation is usually more stable, and the standard of living and consumption are higher. This evidence leads us to argue that, on the one hand, internationalization in an emerging country benefits from the higher growth rate of the host country and the lower correlation between emerging and advanced markets (Van Agtmael and Errunza, 1982). On the other hand, emerging markets are more likely to be exposed to sudden changes in the political and institutional environment and in the exchange and interest rate policy that make market entrance much more exposed to risk.

From the perspective of empirical findings, the picture seems to be quite diversified, without a clear and sound path. Grant (1987), by using accounting-based performance measures, found that there is no significant difference in firms' profitability depending on the country of destination of FDIs; Janakiramanan *et al.* (2005a) found that the country of destination and its features in terms of risk and institutional variables are not relevant factors in explaining the positive wealth gains from international joint venture announcements. Conversely, other studies show that host country characteristics affect firm performance in different ways. Doukas and Travlos (1988) found that international expansion via acquisitions results in higher abnormal returns when the country of destination is new and less developed than the US market; more recently, Pantzalis (2001) examined the determinants of Tobin's Q on a sample of US multinational companies. He showed that firms with a presence in developing markets perform significantly better than firms that only operate in advanced economies; Janakiramanan *et al.* (2005b) showed that joint venture announcements in high-risk host countries are associated with higher shareholders' gains. Studies that find a lower performance for firms that enter developing economies are not lacking. Collins (1990), relying on a number of risk-adjusted market measures, found that the performance of a sample of US firms engaged in FDIs in advanced economies is better than that of firms running in developing economies. Demos *et al.* (2004) found higher abnormal returns in a sample of Greek firms that operate in advanced economies. Bausch and Van Tri (2007) found a negative relationship between shareholders' gains and internationalization in a sample of German firms entering the Chinese market. Larimo and Pynnönen (2008) found that shares of Finnish firms have a higher price reaction to FDI announcements if the host country is developed and has a low risk.

From the aforementioned empirical and theoretical literature it seems that the mode of entry and level of development of the country can influence value creation. As such we posit the following two hypotheses:

> **Hypothesis 4**: The value creation is higher when the country of destination of the high-equity entry modes is advanced.
>
> **Hypothesis 5**: The value creation is higher when the country of destination of the low-equity entry modes is emerging.

The study adopts the classification provided by the International Monetary Fund (2009), dividing the countries into two groups: Advanced Economies vs. Emerging and Developing Economies.

Relative size of the target

Several studies examined the impact of the relative size of targets to bidders on the acquiring firms' market performance (Asquith *et al.*, 1983; Jensen and Ruback, 1983; Jarrell and Poulsen, 1989; Houston and Ryngaert, 1994). They found that the abnormal returns of the acquiring firm increase with the relative size of the target. Particularly, Fuller *et al.* (2002) show that for public targets, as the relative size of the target increases, returns become more positive for cash offers and less positive for stock offers, and change a little for combination offers. However, for private targets, there is a positive relationship between the target's relative size and the acquirers' positive abnormal returns. The different market reaction to the acquisitions of private targets versus public acquisitions depends on a liquidity effect – private firms cannot be bought and sold as easily as publicly traded firms. This lack of liquidity makes investment in private firms less attractive and less valuable than in public firms. Kiymaz and Baker (2008) found that large and significantly positive returns to announcements of acquisitions are most closely related to the target's relative size and to bidder and target being in a related industry. In the same vein as previous studies, we take into account the relative size of the deal by dividing the purchase price by the market capitalization of the acquiring firm. This variable only applies to mergers and acquisitions.

Hypothesis 6: The value creation is higher for larger deals.

Firm age

Several studies have shown that there is a strong correlation between firm age and performance. Younger, smaller firms are relatively more effective in identifying opportunities than their larger, established counterparts, yet they are less effective in developing competitive advantages in order to seize value from those opportunities (Ireland *et al.*, 2003). Younger and more entrepreneurially oriented firms are flexible enough to face the risk and still remain proactive and innovative (Lumpkin and Dess, 1996; Sapienza *et al.*, 2003).

Generally, it is known that entering a foreign market involves high risks and uncertainties. The high flexibility of younger firms allows them to adapt to the needs set by internationalization. Older firms, which have grown in a domestic setting for a longer period, may not be able to exploit the opportunities in the new markets, or may not be able to turn these into financial performance (Bausch and Van Tri, 2007), whereas younger firms that have not yet developed this rigid mind-set are better able to learn how to deal with the advantage of newness (Autio *et al.*, 2000).

> **Hypothesis 7**: The value creation is higher in foreign operations made by younger firms.

The sample is divided into two groups, representing older companies (age at the announcement of the event higher than or equal to 12 years) and younger companies with stronger entrepreneurial orientation (age at the announcement of the event lower than 12 years). The definition of young and old firms follows the standards of prior research (Covin *et al.*, 1990).

Industry R&D intensity

Numerous empirical studies analysed the relationship between stock market reaction to internationalization operations and R&D intensity of the field of industry. According to the internalization theory, FDIs can help internalize the market of selected intangible assets such as patents, superior production skills, marketing abilities, and so on. The internalization allows firms to overcome transaction difficulties linked to the nature of these assets being largely based on proprietary information. The consequence is that R&D expenditures should be an important factor for multinational firms, which should be able to increase the value of their intangibles by expanding their multinationality (Morck and Yeung, 1991). Morck and Yeung (1992) and Chen *et al.* (1991) found that market performance is positively influenced by the degree of intangible assets accumulated by the investing firm. Although López-Duarte and García-Canal (2007) did not find any significant difference depending on the degree of R&D expenditures in foreign acquisitions made by Spanish firms, we believe that internationalization holds special benefits for high R&D-intensity industries.

> **Hypothesis 8**: The value creation is higher in investments made in high R&D-intensity industries.

The sample is divided into two groups, representing low R&D-intensity industries and high R&D-intensity industries. The definition of low and high R&D-intensity industries follows the standards of prior research. Pavitt (1984) proposed a classification of industrial firms into four groups (supplier-dominated, scale-intensive, specialized suppliers and science-based) depending on the sources of technology, the requirements of the users and the appropriability regime. We consider high R&D-intensity fields to be those included in the science-based category (i.e. industrial and agricultural chemicals, pharmaceutical preparations, electronic computers, aircraft and space vehicle building) and, for non-industrial firms (excluded from the Pavitt taxonomy), those operating in the software industry.

Country risk

When business transactions occur across international borders, they carry additional risks not present in domestic transactions (Brouthers *et al.*, 2003). These additional risks typically include risks arising from a variety of national differences in economic structures, policies, socio-political institutions, geography and currencies. Several studies analysed the risk of target country in investment activity (La Porta *et al.*, 1997; McNamara and Vaaler, 2000; Uhlenbruck *et al.*, 2006; López-Duarte and García-Canal, 2007; Larimo and Pynnönen, 2008). They found that a low country risk means a stable operating environment, lower market uncertainty, lower operational and political risks and higher value creation than a high country risk. Merchant (2002) and Gerpott and Jakopin (2007) did not find empirical support for their assumptions of negative relationship between country risk and wealth creation.

> **Hypothesis 9:** The value creation is higher in foreign operations made in countries with a low country risk.

The country risk is measured by the Standard & Poor's rating scores. We classify the countries into two groups: countries with investment grade ratings (i.e., from BBB– to AAA) and countries with speculative grade ratings (i.e., from BB+ to D).

Besides, we take into account a relative measurement of the country risk, classifying the countries into two groups: countries with country risk lower than or equal to Italy's and countries with country risk higher than Italy's.

> **Hypothesis 10:** The value creation is higher in foreign operations made in countries with country risk lower than or equal to Italy's.

The evolution of information disclosure regulation of listed firms

The Consolidated Italian Law on Financial Intermediation (D.Lgs 58/1998, hereafter 'TUF') has laid the foundations for a model of corporate governance of listed companies in line with the legislation of countries with the most highly developed financial systems. The main purposes of the TUF are to develop the Italian financial market, making it more efficient and accountable and above all ensuring the transparency, disclosure and circulation of information, while at the same time making it easier for Italian firms to gain access to risk capital, thereby reducing their dependence on bank financing (Ulissi, 2000). Despite the fact that SMEs suffer asymmetric information problems, are usually neglected by the investor community, and trade at a discount (Draper and Paudyal, 2008), the huge problems of asymmetric information and lack of visibility of strategies and operations of Italian medium-sized listed firms have been significantly reduced by the TUF.

> **Hypothesis 11**: The value creation is higher in investments made after the enactment of the TUF.

11.3 Sample description and research design

Our sample is composed of 140 announcements of internationalization decisions released by 67 Italian non-financial listed firms. The sample results from a survey on all Italian non-financial listed firms, from 1986 to 2006, with annual sales ranging from 13 to 290 million Euros (i.e., the so-called medium-sized firms). Turnover thresholds for medium-sized firms are in accordance with the definition provided by the Mediobanca–Unioncamere (2009) annual survey on Italian manufacturing medium-sized firms.

We have split internationalization decisions into subcategories according to the degree of international involvement (high-equity entry modes vs. low-equity entry modes), the country of destination (emerging countries vs. advanced countries), the relative size of the deal (small, medium and large deals), the firm age (young firms vs. old firms), the R&D intensity (high R&D-intensity industries vs. low R&D-intensity industries), the risk of the target country (high country risk vs. low country risk) and finally the changes of information disclosure regulation (before entry into force of TUF vs. after entry into force of TUF). High-equity strategies (i.e., mergers, acquisitions, and establishment of subsidiaries abroad) comprise 96 events; low-equity strategies (i.e., purchase of minority stakes in foreign companies and overseas joint ventures) comprise 44 events. With reference to the country of destination, 111 events are related to internationalization strategies in developed countries and 29 events involve internationalization in emerging countries (Tables 11.1 and 11.2). The relative size of the deal is measured by dividing the purchase price by the market capitalization of the acquiring firm.

This variable only applies to mergers and acquisitions according to the following breakdown:

- Small deals (28 events): the ratio between purchase price and market capitalization of the acquiring firm is smaller than the lower quartile.
- Medium deals (54 events): the ratio between purchase price and market capitalization of the acquiring firm is between the lower and the upper quartile.
- Large deals (28 events): the ratio between purchase price and market capitalization of the acquiring firm is bigger than the upper quartile.

The number of events for this variable is lower than the size of the sample of high-equity entry modes because of missing data on the deal price (Table 11.1). Despite the limited number of events involving internationalization in emerging countries, Table 11.2 shows that the degree of development of a country is not necessarily linked to the risk of the country itself: about 45 per cent of announcements in emerging economies involve countries with a low risk, such as China, Poland and Hong Kong. As expected, most announcements occurred after 1998 (Table 11.3), the year in which the TUF entered into force. The result is mainly explained by three factors: first, the confidence of Italian medium-sized firms in internationalization strategies has been growing over time; second, during the internet bubble, a great number of small, young, innovative, fast-growing, entrepreneurially oriented firms carried out waves of acquisitions within a few months; third, before 1998 the quality of information disclosure on strategic operations, and, more broadly, on operations not made in the ordinary course of business, was poorer and the press often released incomplete and outdated details concerning the deal. Besides, it appears that M&As as strategies to go abroad have been largely employed since 1998, while before 1998 Italian medium

Table 11.1 Deal size and distribution of events by country of destination and entry mode

Country of destination	Entry mode	Number of events	Deal size		
			Mean	Median	Std. Deviation
Europe	High-equity	69	0.1437	0.0443	0.2416
	Low-equity	14			
North America	High-equity	17	0.2353	0.0920	0.5302
	Low-equity	13			
Latin America	High-equity	0			
	Low-equity	2			
Asia	High-equity	10	0.0849	0.0515	0.0961
	Low-equity	11			
Africa	High-equity	0			
	Low-equity	4			
Total		**140**			

The deal size has only been evaluated with reference to mergers and acquisitions. It is the ratio between purchase price and market capitalization of the acquiring firm. Entry mode: high-equity (mergers, acquisitions and establishment of subsidiaries abroad) vs. low-equity (joint ventures and purchase of minority stakes).

enterprises seem to have relied upon joint ventures as the favourite entry mode. This evidence is consistent with the suspicious behaviour of Italian medium-sized firms towards internationalization in the past decades. Consistent with their entrepreneurial orientation, younger firms seem to have a higher preference than older firms for internationalization by means of M&As (Table 11.3). When we move to the classification of events by the field of industry (Table 11.4), a typical attribute of the Italian economy is to be noted: a small number of events is concentrated in high R&D-intensity fields (10 per cent) and most observations are from fields of the '*made in Italy*' industry.

The analysis of the stock price reaction to the announcement of an event involving a firm's international expansion has been carried out in two steps according to the event study methodology (Fama *et al.*, 1969):

1) Estimation of abnormal returns in the period around the event announcement.
2) Analysis of the statistical significance of abnormal returns (i.e., null hypothesis of zero abnormal return is tested).

Table 11.2 Distribution of events by country's level of development and country risk

Country of destination	**Target country level of development**	**Country risk**	**Number of events**
Europe	Advanced	Low	80
		High	0
	Developing	Low	3
		High	0
North America	Advanced	Low	29
		High	0
	Developing	Low	0
		High	1
Latin America	Advanced	Low	0
		High	0
	Developing	Low	0
		High	2
Asia	Advanced	Low	2
		High	0
	Developing	Low	10
		High	6
Africa	Advanced	Low	0
		High	0
	Developing	Low	0
		High	2
Unclassified			5
Total			**140**

Level of development of the target country follows the classification provided by the International Monetary Fund (advanced vs. developing and emerging economies). Country risk is evaluated by using Standard & Poor's rating scores: low risk is associated with investment-grade ratings; high risk is associated with speculative-grade ratings. Unclassified contains countries with no rating.

The first step is performed by employing the market model in order to estimate expected returns as follows:

$$R_{i,t} = \alpha_i + b_i R_{m,t} + \eta_{i,t} \text{ for t } = 1,2,....., \text{ T} \quad (1)$$

Where:

$R_{i,t}$= Return on security i in period t.
$R_{m,t}$= Return on market index in period t.
α_i= Intercept.
μ_i= Disturbance term.
T = Number of periods in the estimation period.

Table 11.3 Distribution of events by period, firm age, entry mode and country of destination

Panel A

		Number of events			
Country of destination	**Entry mode**	**Before 1998**	**After 1998**	**Young**	**Old**
Europe	High-equity	10	59	25	44
	Low-equity	5	9	5	9
North America	High-equity	4	13	7	10
	Low-equity	7	6	3	10
Latin America	High-equity	0	0	0	0
	Low-equity	0	2	0	2
Asia	High-equity	0	10	2	8
	Low-equity	2	9	3	8
Africa	High-equity	0	0	0	0
	Low-equity	3	1	0	4
Total		**31**	**109**	**45**	**95**

Panel B

Country of destination	**Entry mode**	**Before 1998 (%)**	**After 1998 (%)**	**Young (%)**	**Old (%)**
Europe	High-equity	32.26	54.13	55.56	46.32
	Low-equity	16.13	8.26	11.11	9.47
North America	High-equity	12.90	11.93	15.56	10.53
	Low-equity	22.58	5.50	6.67	10.53
Latin America	High-equity	0.00	0.00	0.00	0.00
	Low-equity	0.00	1.83	0.00	2.11
Asia	High-equity	0.00	9.17	4.44	8.42
	Low-equity	6.45	8.26	6.67	8.42
Africa	High-equity	0.00	0.00	0.00	0.00
	Low-equity	9.68	0.92	0.00	4.21
Total		100.00	100.00	100.00	100.00

Entry mode: high-equity (mergers, acquisitions and establishment of subsidiaries abroad) vs. low equity (joint ventures and purchase of minority stakes). Before and After 1998 include events occurring, respectively, before and after the entry into force of the TUF (the Consolidated Italian Law on Financial Intermediation). Young and Old comprise events related to firms with an age, respectively, lower than and greater than or equal to 12 years. Panel A shows the number of events; Panel B shows their percentage incidence.

Next, we estimate abnormal returns by subtracting the expected return from the observed (actual) return as follows:

$$AR_{i,t} = R_{i,t} - R^{*}_{i,t} \qquad (2)$$

Table 11.4 Distribution of events by Pavitt taxonomy and industry R&D intensity

Pavitt taxonomy	**Industry**	**Number of events**	**R&D intensity**
Supplier-dominated	Apparel and other finished products of fabrics	9	**Low (37.15%)**
	Food and kindred products	5	
	Ophthalmic goods	2	
	Textile mill products	4	
	Lumber and wood products	5	
	Total	**25 (17.86%)**	
Scale-intensive	Electronic and other electrical equipment	5	
	Electric lighting and wiring equipment	4	
	Soap, detergents, cleaning preparations, perfumes, cosmetics	1	
	Rubber	3	
	Cement	7	
	Pottery and related products	5	
	Motor vehicles and passenger car bodies	1	
	Glass and glassware	1	
	Total	**27 (19.29%)**	
Specialized suppliers	Electromedical and electrotherapeutic apparatus	3	**Medium (19.29%)**
	General industrial machinery and equipment	18	
	Plastic products	3	
	Electronic components and accessories	3	
	Total	**27 (19.29%)**	
Science-based	Industrial and agricultural chemicals	5	**High (10.00%)**
	Pharmaceutical preparations	4	
	Electronic computers	5	
	Total	**14 (10.00%)**	
Services	Computer programming, software, integrated systems design	33	
	Transportation services	2	**Medium–low (32.86%)**
	Retail stores	1	
	Mailing, reproduction, commercial art and photography	2	
	Communications services	2	
	Hotels and motels	1	
	Electric services	3	
	Operators of building	2	
	Total	**46 (32.86%)**	
Unclassified		1	
	Total	**140 (100%)**	

The first column identifies the Pavitt taxonomy according to Pavitt (1984). He proposed a classification of industrial firms into four groups (supplier-dominated, scale-intensive, specialized suppliers, science-based) depending on the sources of technology, the requirements of the users and the appropriability regime. We consider high R&D-intensity fields to be those included in the science-based category (industrial and agricultural chemicals, pharmaceutical preparations, electronic computers, aircraft and space vehicle building) and, for non-industrial firms (excluded from the Pavitt taxonomy), those operating in the software industry. Industry classification stems from Standard Industrial Classification (SIC) codes.

where:

$AR_{i,t}$ = Abnormal return for security i in period t.
$R_{i,t}$ = Observed return on security i for period t.
$R^*_{i,t}$ = Expected return on security i in period t.

According to the literature on event studies, the length of both estimation period (i.e., period used to estimate parameters of market model) and event period (i.e., period containing the announcement) is left to the researcher; therefore great differences among studies are found (Peterson, 1989; Binder, 1998). Normally, the estimation window ranges from 100 to 300 days for daily studies and from 24 to 60 months for monthly studies. The event window ranges from 21 to 121 days for daily studies and from 25 to 121 months for monthly studies (Peterson, 1989). In this study, we have picked daily returns (see Brown and Warner, 1985, for the properties of daily returns in the case of event studies), a 300-day window for estimation period (–41; –340) and a 31-day window for event period (–15; +15). We have specifically excluded the event period from the window employed to carry out estimations, because parameters in the market model would be biased, since the disturbances are not mean zero (Fama *et al.*, 1969). We have employed the simple market model without any correction to take into account concerns related to infrequent (non-synchronous) trading. Dimson (1979) and Scholes and Williams (1977) proposed methods to correct market model parameter estimations that could be affected by severe biases, especially when daily data and highly illiquid shares are used to make assessments. However, because these alternative techniques seem to convey no clear-cut benefit in an event study (Brown and Warner, 1985; Jain, 1986; Beer, 1997; Bartholdy and Riding, 1994; Kim, 1999; Vazakides, 2006), we have tried to sort out the problem by removing stocks that faced clear and evident illiquidity problems.

We introduce the cumulative abnormal return to accommodate multiple sampling intervals within the event period:

$$CAR_{i,n} = \sum_{t=1}^{n} AR_{i,t} \tag{3}$$

where $CAR_{i,n}$ is the cumulative abnormal return for security i over n periods.

Then, we obtain the cumulative average abnormal return for the portfolio of announcements by averaging each $CAR_{i,n}$ as follows:

$$CAAR_{N,n} = \frac{1}{N}\sum_{i=1}^{N} CAR_{i,n} \tag{4}$$

where $CAAR_{N,n}$ is the cumulative average abnormal return for a portfolio of N securities for a period of length n.

The second step is performed by following the Patell (1976) approach, which takes into account the increase in variance due to event period outside estimation period. Brown and Warner (1980, 1985) show that potential cross-sectional dependence is not a concern in the use of a market model in which the events are from different sectors and randomly selected, thus keeping clustering problems away. Therefore, we use individually standardized abnormal returns as follows:[1]

$$SAR_{i,t} = \frac{AR_{i,t}}{\delta^{*}_{i,t}} \tag{5}$$

where:

$SAR_{i,t}$ = Standardized abnormal return for security i in period t in the event period.
$AR_{i,t}$ = Abnormal return for security i in period t in the event period.

$\delta^{*}_{i,t} = \delta_i \sqrt{1 + \frac{1}{T} + \frac{(R_{m,t} - \overline{R_m})^2}{\sum_{\tau=1}^{T}(R_{m,\tau} - \overline{R_m})^2}}$ = standard error of the forecast for security i in period t in the event period.

where:

$\delta_i = \sqrt{\frac{\sum_{\tau=1}^{T} AR_{i,\tau}^{\;2}}{T-2}}$ = standard error of the estimate for security i over T periods in the estimation period.

T = number of periods in the estimation period.
$AR_{i,t}$ = abnormal return for security i in period t in the estimation period.
$R_{m,t}$ = market return for period t in the event period.

$\overline{R_m}$ = mean return on the market over the estimation period.
$R_{m,t}$ = market return for period τ in the estimation period.

Further, it is possible to sum the standardized abnormal returns to form the standardized cumulative abnormal return. The test statistic is given by:

$$SCAR_{i,n} = \frac{\sum_{t=1}^{n} SAR_{i,t}}{\sqrt{n}} \tag{6}$$

where $SCAR_{i,n}$ is the standardized cumulative abnormal return for security i over n periods (the length of event period). The distribution of $SCAR_{i,n}$ is Student *t* with T-2 degrees of freedom. For a large estimation window (T > 30), the distribution of $SCAR_{i,n}$ is well approximated by the standard normal.

For a sample of securities, the portfolio standardized abnormal return is a normalized sum given as follows:

$$SCAR_{N,n} = \frac{\sum_{i=1}^{N} SCAR_{i,n}}{\sqrt{\sum_{i=1}^{N} \frac{T_i - 2}{T_i - 4}}} \tag{7}$$

where:

$SCAR_{N,n}$ is the standardized cumulative abnormal return for a group of N securities over n periods.
T_i is the number of observations in the estimation period for security i.
The $SCAR_{N,n}$ is assumed to be distributed unit normal for large N.

Mikkelson and Partch (1988) argue that regression residuals will likely be time-series-correlated, being based on the same parameter estimates. Sweeney (1991) and Salinger (1992) show that the bias could be trivial, depending on the relative length of both estimation period and event period. The smaller the latter in proportion to the former, the smaller the bias of the test statistic will be. In our case, the relative proportion of both periods is quite large, therefore making test results close to the correct ones.

Information concerning internationalization announcements and deal prices has been collected from *Il Sole 24 Ore*, Italy's soundest financial newspaper; data related to stock returns have been collected from *Datastream Thomson Financial* database.

11.4 Main results

Abnormal returns

The results of the study (Table 11.5) show that stock prices of Italian medium-sized listed firms have a positive and significant reaction to the announcement of internationalization strategies ($CAAR_{-15,+15}$ = 2.98 per cent, significant at the 1 per cent level), providing support to Hypothesis 1. The outcomes are largely affected by the abnormal returns of both high-equity operations and operations in advanced economies. Based on our results, announcements of international mergers and acquisitions as well as establishment of subsidiaries abroad show a $CAAR_{-15,+15}$ equal to 4.01 per cent, significant at the 1 per cent level. Announcements of operations in advanced economies perform equally well: the $CAAR_{-15,+15}$ for these events is 3.78 per cent, significant at the 1 per cent level.

The above evidence partially supports Hypothesis 3 (we predicted a positive and weaker market reaction to the announcement of high-equity operations than low-equity operations), but it does not seem to provide any confirmation of Hypothesis 2. We attempt to explain the results by relying on two arguments: the first is based on the lack of visibility of low-equity operations on the stock market, poor information about the actors involved, and the size of the deal (Freeman, 1987); the second exploits the results obtained with reference to the relative size of the deal. Consistently with Hypothesis 6, we find (Table 11.5) that only large deals within mergers and acquisitions show significant abnormal returns ($CAAR_{-15,+15}$ = 4.23 per cent, significant at the 5 per cent level). Low-equity operations are more likely to be carried out with a smaller investment than high-equity ones (in our sample, there is a huge and statistically significant difference in the relative size of the deal between high-equity and low-equity operations: the former have an average relative size equal to 16.23 per cent while the latter show nearly a 3 per cent average relative size. Both t-test and Kruskal–Wallis test are shown to be significant at the 1 per cent level). Based on such introductory results, we could argue that the entry mode is important, depending on other factors such as the size of the deal.

Table 11.5 Abnormal returns: whole sample and breakdown by country of destination, entry mode, deal size, R&D intensity, country risk, relative country risk, firm age and enactment of the TUF

Grouping variable	All events	CAAR (−15; +15) 0.0298***	Difference between means
Country of destination	Advanced (111)	0.0378***	(Advanced – Emerging) 0.0384
	Emerging (29)	−0.0006	
Entry mode	High-equity (96)	0.0401***	(High-equity – Low-equity) 0.0327
	Low-equity (44)	0.0074	
Deal size	Small (28)	0.0032	(Small – Medium and Large) −0.0231
	Medium (54)	0.0181	
	Large (28)	0.0423**	
R&D intensity	High (47)	0.0484**	(High – Low) 0.0280
	Low (93)	0.0204**	
Country risk	High (11)	−0.0022	(High – Low) −0.0370
	Low (124)	0.0348***	
Relative country risk	Higher than Italy (30)	−0.0095	(Higher – Lower) −0.0503**
	Lower than or equal to Italy (108)	0.0408***	
Firm age	Old (95)	0.0291**	(Old – Young) −0.0021
	Young (45)	0.0312	
TUF enactment	Before 1998 (31)	0.0021	(Before – After) −0.0356
	After 1998 (109)	0.0377***	

Significance level: * (10%), ** (5%), *** (1%). CAAR: cumulative average abnormal return. In parentheses, the number of events. Country of destination: advanced economies vs. emerging economies according to the IMF classification. Entry mode: high-equity (mergers, acquisitions and establishment of subsidiaries abroad) vs. low-equity (joint ventures and purchase of minority stakes). The deal size has only been evaluated with reference to mergers and acquisitions according to the following classification: small deals (the ratio between purchase price and market capitalization of the acquiring firm is smaller than the lower quartile), medium deals (the ratio between purchase price and market capitalization of the acquiring firm is between the lower and the upper quartile), large deals (the ratio between purchase price and market capitalization of the acquiring firm is larger than the upper quartile). R&D intensity is measured by following the Pavitt (1984) taxonomy. He proposed a classification of industrial firms into four groups (supplier-dominated, scale-intensive, specialized suppliers, science-based) depending on the sources of technology, the requirements of the users and the appropriability regime. We consider high R&D-intensity fields to be those included in the science-based category (industrial and agricultural chemicals, pharmaceutical preparations, electronic computers, aircraft and space vehicle building) and, for non-industrial firms (excluded from the Pavitt taxonomy), those operating in the software industry. Country risk is evaluated by using Standard & Poor's rating scores (low risk is associated with investment-grade ratings; high risk is associated with speculative-grade ratings). Relative country risk is evaluated by comparing the rating of Italy with that of the host countries. Firm age distinguishes old firms (age greater than or equal to 12 years) from young firms (age lower than 12 years). TUF enactment classifies the events depending on their chronological occurrence according to the evolution of information disclosure regulation (before and after the enactment of the TUF).

Moving to the country of destination (Table 11.5), we show that, if the variable is analysed without any interaction with other variables, the results are straightforward: market reaction is positive and significant ($CAAR_{-15,+15}$ = 3.78 per cent, significant at the 1 per cent level) if the country in which the firm internationalizes is advanced. No significant price reaction ($CAAR_{-15,+15}$ = −0.06 per cent) results from announcements of internationalization strategies in emerging countries. At first glance, the result seems to be counter-intuitive: emerging countries offer greater growth opportunities. But, as discussed in Section 3, growth opportunities could be partially or totally cancelled out by the risks stemming from investments in a potentially unstable economic and political scenario. This trade-off is more likely to be large when the firm size is not large and the international experience is still limited. Accordingly, if the market were have a much lower risk perception regarding operations in advanced economies, it would require a lower risk premium, which could lead to an easier price growth. Moreover, international expansion strategies in advanced economies are often accompanied by a more complete disclosure of information, allowing the market to perform a more accurate assessment of the fair transaction value. The above discussion is confirmed by the results of the country risk variable (Hypotheses 9 and 10 are supported). Market reaction is positive and significant ($CAAR_{-15,+15}$ = 3.48 per cent) if the country in which the firm internationalizes has a low risk. No significant price reaction arises from announcements of internationalization strategies in countries with a high risk. We obtain qualitatively similar results by considering the relative measurement of the country risk: the market reaction is positive in foreign operations made in countries with country risk lower than or equal to Italy's ($CAAR_{-15,+15}$ = 4.08 per cent, significant at the 1 per cent level), while it is negative but not statistically significant in countries with country risk higher than Italy's.

In a second stage, we look at interaction of country of destination with entry mode, based on the assumption that, especially for the low-equity entry modes, the country of destination could affect the results in the same way as the relative size of the deal. Table 11.6 shows that only high-equity operations performed in advanced economies result in a positive and significant market reaction ($CAAR_{-15,+15}$ = 4.57 per cent, significant at the 1 per cent level): Hypothesis 4 is confirmed, but not Hypothesis 5.

With reference to the other variables, we analyse the relationship between stock market reaction to announcements of internationalization strategies and industry R&D intensity. Hypothesis 8 is

Table 11.6 Abnormal returns: How combinations of entry mode and country of destination affect the stock price reaction

		Entry mode	
CAAR (−15; +15)		**High-equity (96)**	**Low-equity (44)**
Country of destination	Advanced (111)	0.0457*** (84)	0.0133 (27)
	Emerging (29)	0.0014 (12)	−0.0020 (17)

Significance level: * (10%), ** (5%), *** (1%). In parentheses, the number of events. CAAR: cumulative average abnormal return. Country of destination: advanced economies vs. emerging economies according to the IMF classification. Entry mode: high-equity (mergers, acquisitions and establishment of subsidiaries abroad) vs. low-equity (joint ventures and purchase of minority stakes).

partially confirmed by the results. Despite the fact that the value creation is higher in investments made in high R&D-intensity industries ($CAAR_{-15,+15}$ = 4.84 per cent, significant at the 5 per cent level) than in low R&D-intensity industries ($CAAR_{-15,+15}$ = 2.04 per cent, significant at the 5 per cent level), both abnormal returns are positive and statistically significant. This means that the R&D expenditures are important in explaining the abnormal returns, but with the same intensity found in low R&D-intensity industries.

Hypothesis 7, on the correlation between firm age and market performance, is not supported. The data show a positive and significant abnormal return in foreign operations made by older firms ($CAAR_{-15,+15}$ = 2.91 per cent, significant at the 5 per cent level) and a positive but not statistically significant abnormal return in foreign operations made by younger firms ($CAAR_{-15,+15}$ = 3.12 per cent). Supposing that both older firms and younger firms have the same degree of market knowledge, the results might stem from the possibility that older firms have a better knowledge on how to manage the internationalization process and thus need to overcome fewer obstacles than younger firms. Older firms can rely on experience gained from previous operations in foreign countries: the market seems to value experience to a greater extent than the entrepreneurially oriented behaviour of younger firms. The non-significant result of younger firms is also due to the high volatility of returns, as most of them are related to new economy firms during the internet bubble.

Finally, we analyse the market performance before and after the enactment of the TUF, and, in agreement with Hypothesis 11, we find a positive and significant market reaction ($CAAR_{-15,+15}$ = 3.77 per cent, significant at the 1 per cent level) to announcements of foreign operations made after

1998 and a non-significant market reaction ($CAAR_{-15,+15}$ = 0.21 per cent) to announcements of foreign operations made before 1998. Although the small number of observations related to foreign operations made before 1998 could have affected the results, we think that the evolution of the information disclosure landscape helped the Italian medium-sized firms reduce asymmetric information problems and lack of visibility.

Cross-sectional determinants of abnormal returns: regression analysis

In order to strengthen and further validate the results obtained by the event study approach, we perform a regression analysis in which each grouping variable is coded into an explanatory variable of the standardized cumulative abnormal return. The purpose is to identify key determinants of value creation of internationalization strategies. The model is estimated as follows:

$$SCAR_{i,n} = a + b_1 COUNTRY_i + b_2 RISK\_R_i + b_3 ENTRY_i + b_4 TUF_i + b_5 AGE_i + b_6 R\&D_i + \epsilon_i \quad (8)$$

Where:

$SCAR_{i,n}$ is the standardized cumulative abnormal return for security i over n periods (the length of event period).

COUNTRY is a variable taking value 1 if the country of destination is emerging, 0 if advanced.

RISK_R is a variable taking value 1 if the country of destination is riskier than Italy according to the Standard and Poor's rating scores, 0 otherwise.

ENTRY is a variable taking value 1 if the entry mode is a joint venture or a purchase of minority stakes and value 0 if it is a merger or an acquisition.

TUF is a variable taking value 1 if the announcement is made after entry into force of TUF, 0 otherwise.

AGE is a variable that expresses the firm age at the announcement date.

R&D is a variable taking value 1 if the announcing firm operates in a science-based industry according to Pavitt (1984), 0 otherwise.

ϵ_i is the error term.

Despite its relevance, we exclude from the model the relative size of the deal (SIZE) because the missing observations of this variable would make the sample far too small to perform a regression. The correlation *able 11.7* Correlation matrix

	$SCAR_{i,n}$	ENTRY	COUNTRY	RISK	RISK_R	TUF	R&D	AGE	SIZE
$CAR_{i,n}$		−0.0809	−0.0499	−0.0679	−0.1263	0.1177	−0.0837	0.0314	0.2163
NTRY			0.3121	0.1973	0.1997	−0.1343	−0.1031	0.1236	−0.0764
:OUNTRY				0.6321	0.8472	0.1004	−0.2293	0.0919	−0.1248
ISK					0.5753	0.0049	−0.1367	0.1436	−0.0547
ISK_R						0.1219	−0.2192	0.0454	−0.1435
UF							0.0563	−0.3965	−0.1259
&D								−0.3367	−0.0822
GE									0.1638

% critical value (two-tailed) = 0.1900. <<Eqn28.eps>> is the standardized cumulative abnormal eturn for security *i* over *n* periods. COUNTRY is a variable taking value 1 if the country of estination is emerging, 0 otherwise. RISK is a variable taking value 1 if the country of destination as a speculative grade rating, 0 otherwise. RISK_R is a variable taking value 1 if the country of estination is riskier than Italy according to the Standard & Poor's rating scores, 0 otherwise. ENTRY s a variable taking value 1 if the entry mode is a joint venture or a purchase of minority stakes and alue 0 if it is a merger or an acquisition. TUF is a variable taking value 1 if the announcement is nade after the entry into force of the TUF, 0 otherwise. AGE is a variable that expresses the firm age t the announcement date. R&D is a variable taking value 1 if the announcing firm operates in a cience-based industry according to Pavitt (1984), 0 otherwise.

Table 11.8 Regression analysis

	Model 1 ($SCAR_{i,n}$)			**Model 2 ($SCAR_{i,n}$)**		
Variables	**Coefficient**	**Std. Error**	**t-ratio**	**Coefficient**	**Std. Error**	**t-ratio**
const	−0.1196	0.3218	−0.3718	−0.0646	0.3183	−0.2030
COUNTRY	−0.3640*	0.2084	−1.7472			
ENTRY	−0.1008	0.1873	−0.5385	−0.1273	0.1849	−0.6886
TUF	0.4695**	0.2122	2.2130	0.4552**	0.2195	2.0743
AGE	0.0058	0.0040	1.4330	0.0057	0.0040	1.4270
R&D	0.0584	0.2571	0.2272	0.0321	0.2652	0.1211
RISK_R				−0.4312**	0.1917	−2.2497
R-squared	0.0636			0.0741		
Adj. R-squared	0.0284			0.0387		
N	140			138		

Significance level: * (10%), ** (5%), *** (1%). $SCAR_{i,n}$ is the standardized cumulative abnormal return for security *i* over *n* periods. COUNTRY is a variable taking value 1 if the country of destination is emerging, 0 otherwise. RISK_R is a variable taking value 1 if the country of destination is riskier than Italy according to the Standard & Poor's rating scores, 0 otherwise. ENTRY is a variable taking value 1 if the entry mode is a joint venture or a purchase of minority stakes and value 0 if it is a merger or an acquisition.

TUF is a variable taking value 1 if the announcement is made after the entry into force of the TUF, 0 otherwise. AGE is a variable that expresses the firm age at the announcement date. R&D is a variable taking value 1 if the announcing firm operates in a science-based industry according to Pavitt (1984), 0 otherwise. R-squared and Adj. R-squared express the model goodness-of-fit.

matrix (Table 11.7) shows a high level of correlation between the variables COUNTRY, RISK_R and RISK. In order to avoid multicollinearity problems, COUNTRY and RISK_R are estimated into two independent regression models. RISK (a variable taking value 1 if the country of destination has a speculative grade rating, 0 if it has an investment grade rating) is excluded because of the higher explanatory power of the relative measurement of the risk (RISK_R) and the high correlation with it.

Table 11.8 (Models 1 and 2) provides a confirmation of the event study results: the low risk of the host country, the improvements of information disclosure regulation, and the high level of development of the host country are key determinants of positive abnormal returns in response to announcements of internationalization strategies. The variable AGE has a positive coefficient, statistically significant at the 16 per cent level. The only variable providing results inconsistent with the event study methodology is ENTRY: the negative sign of the coefficients in both models supports M&As as value creation determinants, but the coefficient is not statistically significant, so that we cannot say that the entry mode is an influencing variable.

However, the results of the regression analysis face the drawback of small sample size: 140 observations are not enough to provide strong statistical evidence, but they help support the event study methodology.

11.5 Conclusions

We explore a fruitful area of enquiry by studying market appreciation of medium-sized firms involved in internationalization strategies. The evidence shows that the market seems to be confident in the soundness of strategies carried out by medium-sized enterprises in foreign countries. They are viewed positively by both economists and investors. Besides, several variables are relevant in affecting market reaction. Market reaction is strong and statistically significant to announcements of high-equity entry modes in advanced economies; less involving entry modes seem to receive no market evaluation, no matter what the country of destination. The deal size and the larger sample of high-equity operations in advanced countries can account for the previous result. Industry R&D intensity does not matter: low R&D-intensity industries perform as well as high R&D-intensity fields: this evidence is likely to be a result of the Italian economy's reliance on traditional sectors. As expected, going abroad to countries with low risk is appreciated by investors, who trust in the stability of the host country, which allows firms to seize investment value easily. We show the importance of the evolution of the regulation aimed at enhancing the transparency of strategic operations and their fair valuation. Investors seem to appreciate the internationalization of older firms more because of their accumulated experience in foreign operations.

An illuminating and comprehensive explanation that would merge the key points of the story is provided by Freeman (1987). He suggests that information on large firms is more readily available than that on small firms. The shares of larger companies are generally owned by institutional investors, who have sufficient resources and find it cost-effective to monitor companies' activities, and hence independent analysts' coverage becomes irrelevant. Larger firms can also afford to hire credible public relations managers to remain visible on the market. Therefore, the level of information asymmetry between the managers and outside investors is a decreasing function of firm size. Such an argument is suitable to support our results on the relative size of the deal (small and medium targets do not lead to any market reaction), the entry mode (joint ventures are likely to involve a lower amount of funds and the announcement of their contractual terms is often more opaque than the contractual terms of M&As), the regulation on information disclosure (abnormal returns are shown to be statistically significant only after the entry into force of the TUF), the country of destination and the country risk (target firms in emerging countries are likely to be smaller and riskier than firms in advanced countries and, therefore, asymmetric information problems reach high levels). Finally, our sample is composed of medium-sized firms experiencing a higher intensity of asymmetric information problems, thin trading, and a limited coverage by analysts.

Notes

A revised version of the paper was published in: Morresi, O., Pezzi, A. (2011) '21 years of international M&As and joint ventures by Italian medium-sized listed firms: Value creation or value destruction?', *Research in International Business and Finance*, 25(1), 75–87. Copyright Elsevier.

1. However, for purposes of comparison, we have also employed the Brown and Warner (1980) approach with crude dependence adjustment, obtaining qualitatively similar results.

References

Agarwal, S. and Ramaswami, S. (1992) 'Choice of foreign market entry mode: Impact of ownership, location and internalization factors', *Journal of International Business Studies*, 23(1), 1–27.

Ahern, K. and Weston, F. (2007) 'M&As: The good, the bad, and the ugly', *Journal of Applied Finance*, 17(1), 5–20.

Arrighetti, A. and Ninni, A. (2008) *Dimensioni e Crescita nell'Industria Manifatturiera Italiana. Il Ruolo delle Medie Imprese* (Milano: Franco Angeli).

Asquith, P., Bruner, R. and Mullins, D. (1983) 'The gains to bidding firms from merger', *Journal of Financial Economics*, 11, 121–39.

Autio, E., Sapienza, H. and Almeida, J. (2000) 'Effects of age at entry, knowledge intensity, and imitability on international growth', *Academy of Management Journal*, 43(5), 909–24.

Bartholdy, J. and Riding, A. (1994) 'Thin trading and the estimation of betas: The efficacy of alternative techniques', *The Journal of Financial Research*, 17(2), 241–54.

Bartlett, C. and Ghoshal, S. (1989) *Managing Across Borders: The Transnational Solution* (Boston: Harvard Business School Press).

Bausch, A. and Van Tri, D.L. (2007) 'Internationalization in German companies into Chinese market – An event study of the consequences on financial performance from a RBV perspective', *International Journal of Business Research*, 7, 213–32.

Beamish, P. and Newfield, C. (1984) 'Diversification strategy and multinational enterprise performance', in Ragab, M. and White, R. (eds), *Proceedings of the Administrative Sciences Association of Canada Conference*, 5(6), 3–12.

Becattini, G., Bellandi, M. and De Propris, L. (eds) (2009) *A Handbook of Industrial Districts* (Cheltenham: Edward Elgar Publishing).

Beer, F.M. (1997) 'Estimation of risk on the Brussels stock exchange: Methodological issues and empirical results', *Global Finance Journal*, 8(1), 83–94.

Binder, J. (1998) 'The event study methodology since 1969', *Review of Quantitative Finance and Accounting*, 11, 111–37.

Bloodgood, J., Sapienza, H. and Almeida, J. (1996) 'The internationalization of new high potential US ventures: Antecedents and outcomes', *Entrepreneurship Theory and Practice*, 20(4), 61–76.

Brouthers, K., Brouthers, L.E. and Werner, S. (2003) 'Transaction cost-enhanced entry mode choices and firm performance', *Strategic Management Journal*, 24(12), 1239–48.

Brown, S. and Warner, J. (1980) 'Measuring security price performance', *Journal of Financial Economics*, 8, 205–58.

Brown, S. and Warner, J. (1985) 'Using daily returns: The case of event studies', *Journal of Financial Economics*, 14, 3–31.

Chen, H., Hu, M. and Shieh, J. (1991) 'The wealth effect of international joint ventures: The case of U.S. investment in China', *Financial Management*, 20(4), 31–41.

Collins, M. (1990) 'A market performance comparison of US firms active in domestic, developed and developing countries', *Journal of International Business Studies*, 21(2), 271–87.

Coltorti, F. (2006) 'Il capitalismo di mezzo negli anni della crescita zero', *Economia Italiana*, 3, 665–87.

Covin, J., Slevin, D. and Covin, T. (1990) 'Content and performance of growth-seeking strategies: A comparison of small firms in high- and low technology industries', *Journal of Business Venturing*, 5(6), 391–403.

Cowling, K. and Sugden, R. (1987) *Transnational Monopoly Capitalism* (Brighton: Wheatsheaf).

Demos, A., Filippaios, F. and Papanastassiou, M. (2004) 'An event study analysis of outward foreign direct investment: The case of Greece', *International Journal of the Economics of Business*, 11(3), 329–48.

Depperu, D. (1997) *L'Internazionalizzazione delle Piccole e Medie Imprese* (Milano: Egea).

Dimson, E. (1979) 'Risk measurement when shares are subject to infrequent trading', *Journal of Financial Economics*, 7, 197–226.

Doukas, J. and Travlos, N. (1988) 'The effect of corporate multinationalism on shareholders' wealth: Evidence from international acquisitions', *Journal of Finance*, 43, 1161–75.

Draper, P. and Paudyal, K. (2008) 'Information asymmetry and bidders' gains', *Journal of Business Finance & Accounting*, 35(3–4), 376–405.

Dunning, J. (1979) 'Explaining changing patterns of international production: In defence of the eclectic theory', *Oxford Bulletin of Economics and Statistics*, 41(4), 269–95.

Dunning, J. (1988) 'The eclectic paradigm of international production: A restatement and some possible extensions', *Journal of International Business Studies*, 19, 1–31.

Fama, E., Fisher, L., Jensen, M. and Roll, R. (1969) 'The adjustment of stock prices to new information', *International Economic Review*, 10, 1–21.

Freeman, R. (1987) 'The association between accounting earnings and security returns for large and small firms', *Journal of Accounting and Economics*, 9, 195–228.

Fuller, K., Netter, J. and Stegemoller, M. (2002) 'What do returns to acquiring firms tell us? Evidence from firms that make many acquisitions', *Journal of Finance*, 57, 1763–93.

Gerpott, T. and Jakopin, N. (2007) 'Firm and target country characteristics as factors explaining wealth creation from international expansion moves of mobile network operators', *Telecommunications Policy*, 31, 79–92.

Grant, R. (1987) 'Multinationality and performance among British manufacturing companies', *Journal of International Business Studies*, 18(3), 79–89.

Houston, J. and Ryngaert, M. (1994) 'The overall gains from large bank mergers', *Journal of Banking and Finance*, 18(6), 1155–76.

Hsu, C.C. and Boggs, D. (2003) 'Internationalization and performance: Traditional measures and their decomposition', *Multinational Business Review*, 11(3), 23–49.

ICE (2009) *L'Italia nell'Economia Internazionale*. Rapporto ICE 2008–2009.

Ietto Gillies, G. (2002) 'Hymer, the nation-state and the determinants of multinational corporations' activities', *Contribution to Political Economy*, 21, 43–54.

Ietto Gillies, G. (2005) *Imprese Transnazionali. Concetti, Teorie, Effetti* (Roma: Carocci).

International Monetary Fund (2009)*The World Economic Outlook (WEO) Database, April*.

Ireland, D., Hitt, M. and Sirmon, D. (2003) 'A model of strategic entrepreneurship: The construct and its dimensions', *Journal of Management*, 29(6), 963–89.

Jain, P. (1986) 'Analyses of the distribution of security market model prediction errors for daily returns data', *Journal of Accounting Research*, 24, 76–96.

Janakiramanan, S., Lamba, A. and Seneviratne, C. (2005a) 'A comparison of the shareholder wealth effect of firms announcing domestic and international joint ventures', *Investment Management and Financial Innovation*, 4, 33–49.

Janakiramanan, S., Lamba, A. and Bailey, J. (2005b) 'International joint ventures and political risk', *Journal of Business and Policy Research*, 1(1), 1–19.

Jarrell, G. and Poulsen, A. (1989) 'Stock trading before the announcement of tender offers: Insider trading or market anticipation?', *Journal of Law, Economics and Organization*, 5, 225–48.

Jensen, M. and Ruback, R. (1983) 'The market for corporate control: The scientific evidence', *Journal of Financial Economics*, 11, 5–50.

Johanson, J. and Vahlne, J.E. (1977) 'The internationalization process of the firm. A model of knowledge development and increasing foreign market commitments', *Journal of International Business Studies*, 8, 23–32.

Kim, D. (1999) 'Sensitivity of systematic risk estimates to the return measurement interval under serial correlation', *Review of Quantitative Finance and Accounting*, 12, 49–64.

Kiymaz, H. and Baker, K. (2008) 'Short-term performance, industry effects and motives: Evidence from large M&As', *Quarterly Journal of Finance and Accounting*, 47(2), 17–44.

Kogut, B. (1983) 'Foreign direct investment as a sequential process', in Kindleberger, C. and Audretsch, D. (eds), *The Multinational Corporation in the 1980s* (Cambridge, MA: MIT Press), pp. 35–56.

Kumar, V. and Subramanian, V. (1997) 'A contingency framework for the mode of entry decision', *Journal of World Business*, 32(1), 53–72.

La Porta, R., Lopez-de-Silanes, F., Shleifer, A. and Vishny, R.W. (1997) 'Trust in large organizations', *American Economic Review*, 87, 333–8.

Larimo, J. and Pynnönen, S. (2008) 'Value creation in FDIs: Empirical evidence from foreign acquisitions by Finnish firms', in Larimo, J. (ed.), *Perspectives on Internationalization and International Management* (Vaasa: Proceedings of the University of Vaasa), pp. 317–39.

López-Duarte, C. and García-Canal, E. (2007) 'Stock market reaction to foreign direct investments: Interaction between entry mode and FDI attributes', *Management International Review*, 47(3), 393–422.

Lu, J. and Beamish, P. (2001) 'The internationalization and performance of SMEs', *Strategic Management Journal*, 22, 565–86.

Lu, J. and Beamish, P. (2006) 'SME internationalization and performance: Growth vs. profitability', *Journal of International Entrepreneurship*, 4, 27–48.

Lumpkin, T. and Dess, G. (1996) 'Clarifying the entrepreneurial orientation construct and linking it to performance', *Academy of Management Review*, 21(1), 135–72.

McDougall, P. and Oviatt, B. (1996) 'New venture internationalization, strategic change and performance: A follow-up study', *Journal of Business Venturing*, 11(1), 23–40.

McNamara, G. and Vaaler, P. (2000) 'The influence of competitive positioning and rivalry on emerging market risk assessment', *Journal of International Business Studies*, 31, 337–47.

Mariotti, S. and Mutinelli, M. (2009) 'L'evoluzione delle imprese multinazionali italiane e il ruolo del quarto capitalismo', *Economia e Politica Industriale*, 1, 123–34.

Mediobanca – Unioncamere (2009) *Le Medie Imprese Industriali Italiane, 1997–2006*.

Merchant, H. (2002) 'Shareholder value creation via international joint ventures: Some additional explanations' *Management International Review*, 42(1), 49–69.

Mikkelson, W. and Partch, M. (1988) 'Withdrawn security offerings', *Journal of Financial and Quantitative Analysis*, 23, 119–34.

Morck, R. and Yeung, B. (1991) 'Why investors value multinationality', *Journal of Business*, 64(2), 165–88.

Morck, R. and Yeung, B. (1992) 'Internalization: An event study test', *Journal of International Economics*, 33, 41–56.

Oviatt, B. and McDougall, P. (1994) 'Toward a theory of international new ventures', *Journal of International Business Studies*, 25, 45–64.

Pantzalis, C. (2001) 'Does location matter? An empirical analysis of geographic scope and MNC market valuation', *Journal of International Business Studies*, 32(1), 133–55.

Patell, J. (1976) 'Corporate forecasts of earnings per share and stock price behavior: Empirical tests', *Journal of Accounting Research*, 14, 246–76.

Pavitt, K. (1984) 'Sectoral patterns of technical change: Towards a taxonomy and a theory', *Research Policy*, 13, 343–73.

Peterson, P. (1989) 'Event studies: A review of issues and methodology', *Quarterly Journal of Business and Economics*, 28, 36–66.

Rugman, A. (1981) *Inside the Multinationals: The Economics of Internal Markets* (New York: Columbia University Press).

Rugman, A. (1986) 'European multinationals: An international comparison of size and performance', in Macharzina, K. and Staehle, W. (eds), *European Approaches to International Management* (New York: Walter de Gruyter), pp. 16–22.

Salinger, M. (1992) 'Standard errors in event studies', *Journal of Financial and Quantitative Analysis*, 27, 39–53.

Sapienza, H., Autio, E. and Zahra, S. (2003) 'Effects of internationalization on young firms' prospects for survival and growth', *Academy of Management Proceedings*, G1–G7.

Scholes, M. and Williams, J. (1977) 'Estimating betas from non-synchronous data', *Journal of Financial Economics*, 5, 309–27.

Stopford, J. and Dunning, J. (1983) *The World Directory of Multinational Enterprises, 1982-83. Company Performance and Global Trends* (Detroit: Gale Research Company).

Sweeney, R. (1991) 'Levels of significance in event studies', *Review of Quantitative Finance and Accounting*, 1, 373–82.

Uhlenbruck, K., Rodriguez, P., Doh, J. and Eden, L. (2006) 'The impact of corruption on entry strategy: Evidence from telecommunication projects in emerging economies', *Organization Science*, 17, 402–14.

Ulissi, R. (2000) 'Company law reform in Italy: An overview of current initiatives', in *Company Law Reform in OECD Countries: A Comparative Outlook of Current Trends* (Stockholm, Sweden), 7–8 December, http://www.oecd.org/dataoecd/21/32/1857507.pdf. Accessed on 18 April 2011.

Van Agtmael, A. and Errunza, V. (1982) 'Foreign portfolio investment in emerging securities markets', *Columbia Journal of World Business*, 17(2), 58–63.
Vazakides, A. (2006) 'Testing simple versus Dimson market models: The case of the Athens stock exchange', *International Research Journal of Finance and Economics*, 2, 26–34.
Zucchella, A. and Maccarini, M. (1999) *I Nuovi Percorsi di Internazionalizzazione. Le Strategie delle Piccole e Medie Imprese Italiane* (Milano: Giuffrè Editore).

12 Managers' Capital Structure Decisions – the Pecking Order Puzzle

Ted Lindblom, Gert Sandahl and Stefan Sjögren

12.1 Introduction

What is the rationale behind capital structure decisions in business firms? Theories targeting these decisions depart from more or less reasonable assumptions about market efficiency in terms of the objectives, expectations and information access of different stakeholders, like shareholders, creditors and managers. In this respect the theories alone provide only a partial understanding concerning the choice of a certain capital structure. On the one hand, we have the irrelevance theorem of Modigliani and Miller (1958), stating that value creation is independent of the financial mix. Their separation between value creation and financing constitutes the foundation for modern corporate finance, even though the assumption of perfect capital markets and zero transaction costs is an illusion. On the other hand, introducing a market imperfection in the form of corporate tax makes the funding of assets relevant to the market value of the firm. A clear preference will be given to debt financing to benefit from the tax shield arising from interest expenses. In principle firms should be financed by debt only. However, empirical evidence lends no support to such extreme debt reliance. The debt capacity of a firm is limited (c.f. Donaldson, 1961). The reason is that high debt leverage will increase financial distress risks, which has a negative impact on the market value of the firm. Myers (1977) shows how reduced investment activity within the firm is related to financial distress. Management tends to underinvest in order to avoid a value transfer to debtholders. Hence, promising investment opportunities might be foregone. This duality of debt financing implies that an optimal capital structure exists, which lays the foundation for the *static trade-off theory* (Myers, 1984).

The static trade-off theory rests on the assumption that there are no market imperfections except for corporate tax and financial distress costs. Stakeholders inside and outside the firm have access to identical market information. These conditions are relaxed in alternative theories explaining how and why firms choose between different kinds of capital. For example, the *free cash flow theory* (Jensen, 1986) emphasizes the impact of conflicts of interest between managers and shareholders, whereas the *signalling theory* (Ross, 1977) and the *market timing theory* (Ritter, 1991) focus on transaction costs arising from asymmetric information. None of these theories, however, challenges the fundamental idea of static trade-off and an optimal capital structure. Introducing conflicting interests allows agency costs to be incorporated in an *extended trade-off theory* (cf. Myers, 1984), and consideration of asymmetric information raises moral hazard problems. The search for funding of a firm's assets at the lowest possible cost is, in addition, made explicit in the market timing theory, claiming that low-cost equity capital can be found at certain points in time. Taking this into consideration, the trade-off theory has only one opposing challenger; the *pecking order theory*.

The pecking order theory originates from the early empirical work of Donaldson (1961) and is founded on observations of managerial financial decision-making in practice. Myers (1984) coined the term 'pecking order' when conceptualizing the theory into an asymmetric information setting where managerial incentives are perfectly aligned with the overall objective of maximizing shareholder value for the current owners. This theory does not acknowledge any optimal capital structure within firms. A firm's actual capital structure is seen as the aggregated result of successive financial decisions made by managers. In conditions of asymmetric information between insiders and outsiders, the pecking order theory concludes that the implicit alliance between management and the current shareholders makes it costly for the firm to attract new investors; the lower the priority of a new security, the higher its cost. This creates a rank between different securities, where those with highest priority are ranked before securities with a lower priority. Following this logic, management's first choice is internally generated funds. Thereafter attention is directed to various forms of debt in a ranking order with respect to priority. In this pecking order new equity is regarded as a last resort. It should be noted that, because of asymmetric information, debt is preferred to equity even without corporate taxes.

In this chapter the aim is to test the explanatory power of the pecking order theory on the financial decisions in large Swedish firms. It also explores how these decisions relate to the trade-off theory in its static and extended forms. The results are compared to the findings of Graham and Harvey (2001) and Beattie *et al.* (2006) concerning firms in the US and in the UK. These and other studies on factors determining firms' capital structure (Stonehill *et al.*, 1975; Norton, 1990; Allen, 1991; Shyam-Sunder and Myers, 1999; Chirinko and Singha, 2000; Bancel and Mittoo, 2004; Brounen *et al.*, 2004), contribute important insights for understanding financial decision-making within firms. However, the surveys lend partial support to several theories. In that respect they share the ambiguity of previous research (Myers, 1984; Harris and Raviv, 1991; Rajan and Zingales, 1995; Barclay and Smith, 2005; Beattie *et al.*, 2006). The partial support for different theories suggests that there might be an underlying latent factor that is common to the majority – if not all – of the theories. In this chapter we make special efforts to distinguish this factor. We argue that managers avoid uncertainty and strive for manoeuvrability. This explains the contradictory empirical findings, giving partial support to both pecking order theory and the idea of an optimal capital structure.

The following section presents the survey method and the data. In Section 3 we perform a probit regression, which is compared with findings presented in Lindblom *et al.* (2011). This allows us to explore the managerial rationale behind capital structure decisions in greater depth. Our conclusions are presented in Section 4.

12.2 Research method and data

Our survey targets all non-financial firms with Swedish headquarters listed on the Swedish stock exchange and the remaining non-listed ones belonging to the 500 largest firms in Sweden.[1] In total 393 business firms qualified to be included in the survey. In 2008 a questionnaire was sent to either the Chief Financial Officer (CFO) (342) or, if there was none, the Chief Executive Officer (CEO) (51) of each firm together with a personally signed covering letter explaining the purpose of the survey. All questions had gone through rigorous testing at several research seminars and the final draft of the questionnaire was piloted on both professionals outside academia and research colleagues. This procedure resulted in a questionnaire containing over 100 questions and sub-questions related to capital structure decisions in large

Table 12.1 Distribution of responses with respect to response time, firm size and ownership

		Firm size (turnover)			Ownership		
Firm Characteristic	**Response time**	**Large**	**Medium**	**Small**	**Listed**	**Non-listed**	**Total**
First round	*(April 2008)*	30 (22.9%)	17 (13.0%)	25 (19.1%)	33 (15.9%)	39 (21.10%)	**72** (18.3%)
Second round	*(May 2008)*	17 (13.0%)	9 (6.9%)	10 (7.6%)	20 (9.7%)	16 (8.6%)	**36** (9.2%)
Final round	*(August 2008)*	11 (8.4%)	6 (4.6%)	14 (10.7%)	20 (9.7%)	11 (5.9%)	**31** (7.9%)
Total	Response sample	**58** (44.3%)	**32** (24.4%)	**49** (37.4%)	**73** (35.3%)	**66** (35.5%)	**139** (35.4%)
	Total population	*131*	*131*	*131*	*207*	*186*	*393*

business firms. As shown in Table 12.1, the final response rate was 35.4 per cent, or 139 answered questionnaires, after two reminders.[2] The table also shows the distribution of responses with respect to early or late response time, firm size in terms of turnover, and ownership, in terms of the firm being listed or not.

As the table clearly indicates, the response sample is biased toward larger firms. Not shown in the table, the sample mean and median turnover (in SEK million) are 12,776 and 2,692, respectively, whereas the corresponding values for the total population are 8,634 and 2,275, respectively. However, statistical two-tailed t-tests do not confirm any significant difference (at the five per cent level) between the mean values of the sample's three size groups and the corresponding mean values of the population.[3] Despite the variation in response time of large, medium and small firms, the t-tests do not confirm any significant difference between early and late responders' turnover means.[4] Large firms are over-represented among listed firms, whereas there is no significant difference between the sample and the whole population of non-listed firms.

12.3 Empirical findings

12.3.1 The explanatory power of the pecking order theory

In order to find out whether managers in Swedish non-financial firms make capital structure decisions in accordance with the pecking order theory, the respondents were asked to rank nine listed types of funding sources (where 1 = first priority). As shown in Table 12.2, the managers tend to make financial decisions as predicted by the pecking order theory. The mean value of 1.85 provides almost as strong evidence for such a ranking order as in UK firms (Pinegar and Wilbricht, 1989; Beattie *et al.*, 2006). Almost two out of three (65.6 per cent) respondents mark internally generated funds as their first choice. Considerably fewer rank bank loans (17.9 per cent) as their first choice, but almost every second respondent (44.7 per cent) marks bank loans as their second choice. This implies that long-term loans are preferred before short-term debt. Leasing is ranked higher than equity, which is consistent with leasing being a substitute for debt financing. However, the ranking of equity before convertibles and bonds is inconsistent with the pecking order theory, but could be explained by the fact that these security markets are small in Sweden.

There is no major difference in the rank of funds with respect to firm size or ownership. The preferences are more or less the same, even though large firms seem to rely more heavily than small ones on internally generated funds. Bank loans are found to be equally important for large and small firms. The results confirm earlier findings that small firms, particularly in fast-growing industries, do not have the ability to build up internal funds. Interestingly, the managers in the non-listed firms assign even higher importance to internally generated funds than those in listed firms.

Even though there appears to be strong evidence on managers' preference for funding in line with the pecking order theory, there are answers to other questions in the survey that show confusing signs of deviations from the theory, supporting the opposing trade-off theory in its extended form (see Lindblom *et al.*, 2011). This motivates a further analysis of the observations to search for a possible underlying factor affecting how managers make capital structure decisions. For this a probit regression model is adopted.

The dependent variable

In the model the ranking made by the respondents in Table 12.2 is transformed into a binary response scheme by assigning each single ranking either 0 if strictly following the pecking order theory or 1 otherwise. This variable is used as the dependent variable.

The independent variables

The likelihood or probability of deviating from the pecking order theory is regressed with the answers to questions related to the other

Table 12.2 Swedish firms' adoption of the pecking order theory

Firm Characteristic	Firm size (turnover)		Ownership		Total		% of first choice								
Funding source	**Large**	**Small**	**Listed**	**Non-listed**	**Mean**	**N**	**1**	**2**	**3**	**4**	**5**	**6**	**7**	**8**	**9**
Internally generated funds	1.51**	2.25**	2.00	1.79	1.85	125	**65.6**	9.6	14.4	4.0	1.6	2.4	1.6	0.8	
Bank loans (long term)	2.70	2.65	2.58	2.47	2.53	123	17.9	**44.7**	18.7	6.5	9.8	2.4			
Short term debt	3.50	3.92	3.83	3.47	3.67	97	3.1	25.8	18.6	**26.8**	12.4	6.2	7.2		
Leasing	4.42	3.93	4.39***	3.12***	3.84	98	12.2	13.3	**28.6**	15.3	11.2	6.1	5.1	4.1	4.1
Equity (new issue)	5.53**	4.33**	4.52**	5.57**	4.91	95	8.4	9.5	13.7	**15.8**	9.5	14.7	11.6	9.5	7.4
Trade credit	4.20**	5.47**	5.42**	4.22**	4.98	82	6.1	6.1	14.6	13.4	**20.7**	13.4	7.3	18.3	
Convertible loans (new issue)	6.00	5.34	5.47	6.24	5.72	76	1.3	6.6	6.6	10.5	18.4	14.5	**25.0**	11.8	5.3
Bonds (new issue)	5.19	6.00	5.67	5.87	5.74	85	1.2	10.6	9.4	10.6	7.1	**21.2**	9.4	22.4	8.2
Personnel debt/ tax debt etc	7.04**	8.06**	8.00**	6.64**	7.51	69	2.9	4.3	7.2	14.5	13.0	8.7	**49.3**		

capital structure theories. The answers to selected questions, which are constructed as statements linked to a five-level Likert scale, are transformed into a binary variable. The 'independent' variable is set to 1 if the respondent agrees / strongly agrees with the statement, or else 0. A robustness check using the original 1–5 Likert scale confirms the results. Control is made for firm and industry-specific variables.

Two variables are related to the static trade-off theory. The first one, *Target*, is based on the answers to the questions in the survey concerning whether or not the firm has set a target for its capital structure and how often the capital structure of the firm is reviewed. If a firm sets a target that is frequently reviewed *Target* is set to 1, as this implies that the manager has a notion of an optimal capital structure, which would be inconsistent with the pecking order theory. Hence, the probability that the manager is deviating from a predicted pecking order scheme should be higher. The second variable, *Balance*, is directly linked to the survey statement: *'It is important to balance debt and equity to maximize shareholder value'*. Respondents who agree with this statement should be more likely to deviate from the pecking order theory, since this implies that they have a notion of an optimal capital structure.

Two variables control for whether the respondents are searching for 'windows of opportunity' in line with the market timing theory. The answers on two statements are used as proxies for the attention paid by managers to *Share value* and *Market sentiment*, respectively. The probability of deviating from the pecking order scheme should be higher if the manager gives an affirmative answer to the corresponding statements: *'Increased share price is an important reason for issuing new equity'* and *'When the access to risk capital is good, priority is given to issuance of new equity before debt'*.

Two variables aim at capturing agency costs according to the free cash flow theory. Managers can create financial buffers in order to avoid or postpone issuing new securities for financing real investments. Such buffers may also be motivated by a wish to strengthen the firm's capability to withstand fluctuations on the financial as well as the product markets and, even more, to survive an unanticipated economic shock. On the one hand, the free cash flow theory views this kind of creation of financial flexibility as managerial opportunism leading to increasing agency costs. On the other hand, buffering in the interest of the current owners may very well be in accordance with the pecking order theory. Hence, the propensity to build up financial flexibility with buffers is negatively related to a deviation from the pecking order scheme.

The variables *Liquidity buffer* and *Investment capability* are based on the responses to the two statements: *'The firm has created financial liquidity buffers'* and *'The firm has had to reject profitable investment projects due to lack of financial means.'*

Finally, two variables are controlling for whether deviations from the pecking order theory are explained by the signalling theory. These deviations should be negatively related to the probability of signal avoidance. The variables *Dividends* and *New issues* follow the respondents' answers to the following two statements: *'The firm aims at keeping dividends on a stable level'* and *'Other firms' issuance of new debt and equity provides important information about their strategy.'* According to Myers and Majluf (1984), the shareholders are not willing to sell out profitable investment opportunities by issuing new securities. The shareholders would rather encourage managers to use internally raised funds. However, if a company seeks signalling avoidance, the best strategy would be not to make any major changes at all in dividends or leverage.

The results of the probit regression analysis shown in Table 12.3 are not fully consistent with the expected outcome. The major contradiction is that *Target* is significantly negative! This suggests that managers in firms that have set a certain capital structure target and are more actively making follow-ups are less likely to deviate from a pecking order scheme. That is a paradox, as pecking order adopters ought to be indifferent to the capital structure of the firm. It is also unexpected that managers agreeing with the statement that an increase in the share price is an important reason for issuing new equity tend to be less likely to deviate from a pecking order scheme. However, other results are fully in line with expectations. Managers who disagree with the statement that the firm has had to give up projects with a positive Net Present Value (NPV) due to lack of financial means are definitely less likely to deviate from the pecking order scheme, as are those agreeing with the statement that the firm has created financial liquidity buffers. That the managers in larger firms are more pecking-order-oriented also seems reasonable.

Probit regression model, maximum likelihood. The dependent variable equals 1 if it deviates from a pecking order scheme, otherwise 0. Robust standard errors are within brackets. The table presents the marginal effects calculated after the probit regression. The second model includes nine industry dummies and the following firm-specific control variables; size measured as sales turnover; ownership structure measured using a Gini coefficient, where private and state-owned firms receive a *Gini* = 1; ownership, where 1 = *listed* firm, otherwise 0; and leverage measured as the ratio of equity to total assets.

Table 12.3 A probit regression analysis of deviations from the pecking order theory

VARIABLES	Without Controls	With Controls
Target	−0.2411***	−0.2691***
	(0.090)	(0.103)
Balance	0.0520	0.0663
	(0.098)	(0.118)
Share value	−0.2757**	−0.2934**
	(0.123)	(0.132)
Market sentiment	0.1652	0.0561
	(0.141)	(0.153)
Liquidity buffer	−0.1339	−0.2477**
	(0.092)	(0.110)
Investment capability	0.3535***	0.3989***
	(0.096)	(0.109)
Dividends	−0.0232	0.0157
	(0.092)	(0.114)
New issues	0.0594	0.1134
	(0.102)	(0.109)
Listed		0.0784
		(0.171)
Gini		−0.2087
		(0.355)
Sales		−0.0095***
		(0.003)
Leverage		0.0004
		(0.009)
Industry dummies	no	Yes
Number of obs	139	132
Waldchi 2(8)	23.23	40.14
Prob > chi 2	0.0031	0.0072
Pseudo R2	0.1116	0.2629

The results of the probit regression analysis give rise to further questions. Why do the capital structure decisions of firm managers appear to be inconsistent? How can it be possible for a manager to adopt the notion of an optimal capital structure and still follow the ranking of the pecking order theory? In the following two sections capital structure decisions are explored in more detail.

12.3.2 The rationale of capital structure targets

Managers acknowledging a target for capital structure are generally referred to as trade-off adopters, with the underlying assumption that an optimal financial mix is targeted. Such a target makes no sense in the pecking order theory. As reported by Lindblom *et al.* (2011), most respondents (75.5 per cent) state that the firm has a certain capital structure target. This is almost as high a percentage as observed by Graham and Harvey (2001) (81 per cent). Considering that almost all respondents (93.5 per cent) state that the firm's capital structure is frequently revised lends further support to the trade-off theory. It is, then, puzzling that we (and many others) also find strong empirical evidence for the pecking order theory (cf. Table 12.2). Contrary to, for example, Graham and Harvey (2001), we arrive at the conclusion that managers are pecking-order-oriented, as the apparent anomaly concerning managers' adoption of a capital structure target can be explained.

The questionnaire comprises a number of statements for finding out to what extent managers adhere to the notion of an optimal capital structure (Lindblom *et al.*, 2011). In general their answers do not point to the trade-off theory in either its static form or its extended version. Twice as many respondents disagree than agree with the crucial statement: *'A capital structure with high leverage contributes to increase firm value'* ($\mu = 2.75^{***}$). They give a similar response to the tax statement: *'Tax consequences mean that high leverage is creating value for shareholders'* ($\mu = 2.70^{***}$). A more affirmative response to both these statements should be expected, unless most firms operate at or beyond their optimal capital structure. The latter is actually implied by the fact that a majority of the respondents agree or strongly agree with the statement: *'It is important to balance debt and equity to maximize shareholder value'* ($\mu = 3.83^{***}$). However, this interpretation seems unrealistic, as almost all firms are reported to set and follow up capital structure targets in terms of book values (84.3 per cent) rather than market values (7.4 per cent) only.[5]

The minor use of market-value-based targets[6] strongly implies that managers in general set capital structure targets for other reasons than for optimizing firm value.[7] Considering the non-affirmative response to the leverage and tax statements, the likely explanation for managers' concern about capital structure is that they do not want the firm to enter into financial distress. This also explains their frequent follow-ups of the capital structure (at least once a year in 95 per cent of the firms). These follow-ups do not seem to be made either for changing the target (in a majority of the firms the target is set less frequently than once a year) or for adjusting the capital structure (most respondents agree / strongly agree with the statement that it is too costly to make an adjustment quickly if the solidity is too low or too high). Apparently, targets are a means for controlling the financial robustness and soundness of the firm rather than a means for finding the lowest funding cost. This makes sense, as losses cannot be absorbed by a high market value. A realized loss has to be covered by equity in the balance sheet! Certainly, the balance sheet may be fuelled through issuance of new equity, but for pecking order adopters this is a last resort that is likely to be very costly and uncertain.

The managerial emphasis on the financial stability of the firm implies that direct capital costs are not regarded as a major issue. Clearly, this is not true. Managers' concern about the firm's debt capacity does not exclude the search for low funding costs. It just suggests that this search is likely to be driven, not by the notion of an optimal capital structure, but rather by a notion that the cost of different funding sources varies. Almost three out of four respondents (73 per cent) agree / strongly agree with the statement: *'The firm is systematically searching for opportunities to lower the cost of capital'* ($\mu = 3.9^{***}$). Even though this suggests a search for 'windows of opportunity', answers to other statements related to the market timing theory fail to lend any significant support to financial decision-making in accordance with this theory – rather the opposite (see Lindblom *et al.*, 2011).

12.3.3 Financial flexibility matters in a pecking order setting

Our results from the probit regression show that managers creating flexibility with *liquidity buffers* are less likely to deviate from the pecking order. The same holds for managers stating that they have not rejected profitable projects due to lack of funds, implying *investment capability*. These results support an extended pecking order theory that, besides asymmetric information between outside investors and insiders, also includes a moral hazard dimension. Graham and Harvey (2001) conclude that *'managers' desire for financial flexibility'* is the most important determinant for leverage. This may lead to the interpretation that the free cash flow theory can explain managers' striving for financial flexibility as pure self-interest and that flexibility provides opportunities for discretionary expenditures. The validity of such an interpretation is not tested directly in our survey. However, the survey includes a number of statements that are related to this issue, and the respondents' combined answers offer an in-depth understanding of the rationale for creating financial flexibility. We use the concept of uncertainty avoidance, with an economic content complementing the inherent social norm described by Hofstede (1980). The concept of uncertainty avoidance is frequently used as a culturally based matter influencing the economic interaction between residents in a society (Guiso *et al.*, 2009; Fidrmuc and Jacob, 2010). Chui *et al.* (2002) find that national culture is an important determinant for debt levels; managers in countries with high scores on uncertainty avoidance tend to use less debt, as they put more emphasis on control, financial planning and cash flows. Moreover, they find that 'mastery', interpreted as having an internal locus of control, greater avoidance of debt covenants and bankruptcy avoidance, also results in lower leverage.

Lindblom *et al.* (2011) found that the propensity to prepare for potential investment opportunities is high and that it is important for managers to avoid external monitoring and preserve manoeuvrability. The majority of them (83 per cent) do not acknowledge that the firm has had to reject profitable investment projects due to lack of funding. Moreover, few respondents consider the possibility of reducing dividends in order to avoid rejection of profitable projects. This suggests that managers are confident that they have sufficient financial buffers or debt capacity to pursue any attractive investment opportunity without having to consider whether funds can be raised on the financial market. Hence, for the manager financial stability does not only mean uncertainty avoidance in terms of mitigating exposure to downside risks; it also gives financial flexibility to realize new investment opportunities.

The use of short-term lending also supports the ideas of uncertainty avoidance and managers mastering their situation with sufficient flexibility. There is significant agreement with the statement: *'Short-term credit availability is an important financial buffer'* (μ = 3.44***). These observations confirm the study by Child *et al.* (2005) showing that financial flexibility encourages managers to use short-term debt, and that this may decrease the agency costs associated with underinvestment. This may explain why respondents generally believe that they do not need to create financial flexibility. They already have financial means for investing in all profitable projects. Very seldom is their aim of keeping dividends unchanged thwarted by dividend cuts for the purpose of preserving funds (c.f. Lindblom *et al.*, 2011). It is also evident that most managers do not consider it important to create equity buffers for offsetting macroeconomic fluctuations in interest, currency, stock, product and supplier markets. These variations in the business environment are obviously supposed to be managed by the operating unit concerned or at the central office. Macro fluctuations should not lead to operational losses absorbed by overcapitalization.

Finally, we observe that many managers believe that a high credit rating offers flexibility in terms of debt capacity. The statement *'A good credit rating is vital for keeping financial flexibility'* ($\mu = 3.68^{***}$) confirms that credit rating seems to be such a factor (Lindblom *et al.*, 2011). Kisgen (2006) finds that *'Firms near a credit rating upgrade or downgrade issue less debt relative to equity than firms not near a change in rating.'* We find that firms with a credit rating make significantly more use of several banks. We also find that firm size influences the probability of deviating from a ranking scheme in accordance with the pecking order theory. A plausible explanation (see Faulkender and Petersen, 2006) is that the source of capital, via active or passive lenders, influences the capital structure of the firm. Opaque firms rely on active lenders, while rated firms also have access to the financial markets (passive lenders). Borrowing from active lenders is assumed to be at a higher cost. Accordingly, rated firms have more leverage. These results confirm a pecking order of debt, as the asymmetry of information between the issuing firm and the passive lender is presumed to be higher than that between the firm and the active lender.

12.4 Conclusions

Most empirical studies of financial structure decisions find evidence supporting both the static trade-off theory and the pecking order theory. Our survey also demonstrates decision-making in accordance with both theories in the same firm. An explanation that has been put forward is that under certain conditions a trade-off is prevalent when a manager makes a capital structure decision, and under others a pecking order. Even if this sounds reasonable, the explanation is not fully convincing, as the notion of an optimal capital structure is not relevant in a pecking order setting. We are able to discern a stronger preference for a pecking order in our survey, and that is our motive for running a probit regression wherein the likelihood of deviating from a pecking order ranking of funds is tested against variables used as proxies for alternative capital structure theories. On the one hand, we do not find any relationship between the likelihood of deviating from a pecking order scheme and managers timing the market or avoiding signalling. On the other hand, we find that managers creating buffers are less likely to deviate from such a scheme, indicating that the extended pecking order theory is valid.

The seemingly most puzzling result is that managers who set targets are unlikely to deviate from a pecking order scheme. However, this anomaly is explained by the fact that, in a clear majority of the firms, targets are based on book value rather than market value. This implies that earlier studies using targets as a proxy for the trade-off theory may have arrived at the wrong conclusion. A target that is not based on market value cannot be used for obtaining an optimal capital structure. Our conclusion is that targets play another role. We argue that managers' main concern is uncertainty avoidance and manoeuvrability. Their use of targets, adhering to a pecking order scheme, and their strong striving for financial flexibility fit well with uncertainty avoidance. Most managers have not faced financial constraints preventing profitable projects, indicating that managers do actually succeed in creating flexibility. Managers seek control over the financial situation of the firm and are strongly governed by accounting values.

Notes

1. We have used the VA500 list for 2006. Firm-specific data that are either missing or not included in VA500 have been complemented from various data bases, mainly Affärsdata, Datastream and VPC.
2. The actual number of responses was 149, but 10 questionnaires were not completed due to 'lack of time', because the survey was considered irrelevant to the business of the firm, or due to a general rule not to answer questionnaires. Despite this, the response rate is high for this type of survey. The major survey by Graham and Harvey (2001) received less than 9 per cent and the one by Beattie *et al.* (2006) slightly over 23 per cent. Pinegar and Wilbricht (1989) received a response rate of 35.2 per cent to their more focused survey.
3. The size interval of each sample group is derived from the corresponding population tertian.
4. Tests conducted for significant differences in the answers of early and late responders do not indicate that there should be any time bias.
5. The percentage numbers are based on those 108 respondents who did answer this question. The remaining 8.3 per cent are using a mix of book and market values.
6. A majority of these firms were either real-estate companies or investment firms.
7. Clearly, the book value may be regarded as a reasonable approximation of the market value if the firm has adopted International Financial Reporting Standards (IFRS). However, there is no significant difference between adopters and non-adopters in their choice of target measure. The book value based equity-to-asset ratio (solidity) has a long tradition as a capital structure measure in Sweden.

References

Allen, D.E. (1991) 'The Determinants of Capital Structure of Listed Australian Companies: the Financial Manager's Perspective', *Australian Journal of Management*, 16(2), 103–28.

Bancel, F. and Mittoo, U.R. (2004) 'Cross-Country Determinants of Capital Structure: A Survey of European Firms', *Financial Management*, 33(4), 103–32.

Barclay, M.J. and Smith, C.W. (2005) 'The Capital Structure Puzzle: The Evidence Revisited', *Journal of Applied Corporate Finance*, 17(1), 8–17.

Beattie, V., Goodacre, A. and Thomson, S.J. (2006) 'Corporate Financing Decisions: UK Survey Evidence', *Journal of Business Finance and Accounting*, 33(9/10), 1402–34.

Brounen, D., de Jong, A. and Koedijk, K. (2004) 'Corporate Finance in Europe: Confronting Theory with Practice', *Financial Management*, 33(4), 71–101.

Childs, P.D., Mauer, D.C. and Ott, S.H. (2005) 'Interactions of corporate financing and investment decisions: the effects of agency conflicts', *Journal of Financial Economics*, 76, 667–690.

Chirinko, R.S. and Singha, A.R. (2000) 'Testing Static Tradeoff against Pecking Order Models of Capital Structure: A Critical Comment', *Journal of Financial Economics*, 58, 417–25.

Chui, A.C.W., Lloyd, A.E. and Kwok, C.C.Y. (2002) 'The determination of capital structure: is national culture a missing piece to the puzzle?', *Journal of International Business Studies*, 33, 99–127.

Donaldson, G. (1961) *Corporate Debt Capacity: A Study of Corporate Debt Policy and the Determination of Corporate Debt Capacity* (Boston: Harvard Graduate School of Business Administration).

Faulkender, M., and Petersen, M.A. (2006) 'Does the Source of Capital Affect Capital Structure', *The Review of Financial Studies*, 19(1), 45–79.

Fidrmuc, J.P. and Jacob, M. (2010) 'Culture, agency, and dividends', *Journal of Comparative Economics*, 38, 321–39.

Graham, J.R. and Harvey, C.R. (2001) 'The Theory and Practice of Corporate Finance: Evidence from the Field', *Journal of Financial Economics*, 60(2/3), 187–243.

Guiso, L., Sapienza, P. and Zingales, L. (2009) 'Cultural biases in economic exchange?', *Quarterly Journal of Economics*, 124, 1095–131.

Harris, M. and Raviv, A. (1991) 'The Theory of Capital Structure', *Journal of Finance*, 46(1), 297–355.

Hofstede, G. (1980) *Culture's Consequences: International Differences in Work-related Values* (Beverly Hills, CA: Sage Publications).

Jensen, M.C. (1986) 'Agency Cost of Free Cash Flow, Corporate Finance and Takeovers', *American Economic Review*, 76(2), 323–39.

Kisgen, D.J. (2006) 'Credit Ratings and Capital Structure', *Journal of Finance*, 61(3), June, 1035–1072.

Lindblom, T., Sandahl, G. and Sjögren, S. (2011) 'Capital Structure Choices', *International Journal of Banking, Accounting and Finance*, 3, 4–30.

Modigliani, F.F. and Miller, M.H. (1958) 'The Cost of Capital, Corporation Finance, and the Theory of Investment', *American Economic Review*, 48(3), 433–43.

Myers, S.C. (1977) 'Determinants of Corporate Borrowing', *Journal of Financial Economics*, 5(2), 147–75.

Myers, S.C. (1984) 'The Capital Structure Puzzle', *Journal of Finance*, 39(3), 575–92.

Myers, S.C. (1999) 'Financial architecture', *European Financial Management*, 5(2), 133–44.

Myers, S.C. and Majluf, N.S. (1984) 'Corporate Financing and Investment Decisions when Firms Have Information Investors Do Not Have', *Journal of Financial Economics*, 13(2), 187–221.

Norton, E. (1990) 'Similarities and Differences in Small and Large Corporation Beliefs about Capital Structure Policy', *Small Business Economics*, 2, 229–45.
Pinegar, J.M. and Wilbricht, L. (1989) 'What Managers Think of Capital Structure Theory: A Survey', *Financial Management*, 18(4), 82–91.
Rajan, R.G. and Zingales, L. (1995) 'What Do We Know About Capital Structure Choice? Some Evidence from International Data', *Journal of Finance*, 50(5), 1421–60.
Ritter, J.R. (1991) 'The Long-Run Performance of Initial Public Offerings', *Journal of Finance*, 46(1), 3–27.
Ross, S. (1977) 'The Determination of Financial Structure: The Incentive Signalling Approach', *Bell Journal of Economics*, 8, 23–40.
Shyam-Sunder, L. and Myers, S.C. (1999) 'Testing Static Tradeoff against Pecking Order Models of Capital Structure', *Journal of Financial Economics*, 51, 219–44.
Stonehill, A., Beekhuisen, T., Wright, R., Remmers, L., Toy, N., Pares, A., Shapiro, A., Egan, D. and Bates, T. (1975) 'Financial Goals and Debt Ratio Determinants: A Survey of Practice in Five Countries', *Financial Management*, 4(3), 27–41.

Index